For LOVE & LIBERTY

For Greg + Denise —
Freedom Ferki Catch It!
Best wishes,
Stephen Grimble
October 2011

STEPHEN M. GRIMBLE

Wasteland Press

www.wastelandpress.net
Shelbyville, KY USA

For Love & Liberty
by Stephen M. Grimble

First Printing – September 2011
ISBN: 978-1-60047-613-6

Other books by Stephen M. Grimble:
Setting the Record Straight: Baseball's Greatest Batters
©1998 Stephen M. Grimble
Cedar Tree Books, Ltd.

Printed in the U.S.A.

0   1   2   3   4   5   6   7   8   9   10   11

*To the memory of
my mother and father
with everlasting love and gratitude*

The God, who gave us life, gave us liberty at the same time.
Thomas Jefferson

They who can give up essential liberty to obtain a little temporary
safety deserve neither liberty nor safety.
Benjamin Franklin

I believe there are more instances of the abridgement of the freedom
of the people by gradual and silent encroachments of those in power
than by violent and sudden usurpations.
James Madison

The American Republic will endure until the day Congress discovers
that it can bribe the public with the public's money.
Alexis de Tocqueville

There can be no liberty unless there is economic liberty.
Margaret Thatcher

Those who won our independence believed…liberty to be the secret
of happiness and courage to be the secret of liberty.
Louis Brandeis

The way to love anything is to realize that it may be lost.
G. K. Chesterton

1

Washington, DC
June 2015

The sudden rupture of the abdominal aortic aneurysm led instantly to vascular collapse. Within seconds, Margaret Thurston, the forty-fifth president of the United States, was dead. She had been reading alone in the Yellow Oval Room on the residential second floor of the White House. The moment her breathing ceased, a discreet alarm sounded on the Executive Mansion's ground floor. Not a minute later, two Secret Service agents and the president's personal physician were at her side. The recently widowed president, age sixty-four, was pronounced dead at 11:35 p.m., June 25, 2015.

The news, while shocking and sad, was not a great surprise to the president's physician who had diagnosed the aneurysm six months earlier. At that time, it was determined that Maggie or President Maggie, as she was known affectionately to the American public, probably would not survive surgery due to her other health complications. Besides Maggie and her doctor, only Harley Keenan, her devoted chief of staff, was apprised of the severity of her medical condition. With prescription drugs and a modestly curtailed schedule, the president probably could survive at least twelve months, according to the doctor's prognosis. She lived barely half that much time.

Upon learning of her likely fate, the president's first thought had been to resign immediately, but she could not bring herself to quit. Instead, she decided to continue in office for as long as her health permitted. She was planning in September to announce she would not seek a second term. The more prudent decision would have been to step down, but few people, especially politicians at the pinnacle of power, surrender that power voluntarily. Maggie had been an overachiever all her adult life: graduating first in her class at the Air Force Academy, becoming one of the very few women to pilot a B-52 strategic bomber, and ultimately attaining the rank of lieutenant general. Following retirement from the air force, she entered local politics in Iowa, was elected mayor of Cedar Rapids, her hometown, and later became governor of the Hawkeye state.

After six successful years as Iowa's governor, Maggie captured the Republican nomination for president in 2012. In an upset, she defeated the incumbent president who had been plagued by bad luck, unpopular decisions, and an overwhelming array of intractable problems that defied his administration's efforts to mitigate or contain. The American people don't expect presidents to solve all problems confronting the country, but they do expect to see evidence that tangible progress is being made, particularly on the economy, and to feel confident the future will be brighter than the past.

Self-assurance, optimism, unflappability, competence, and the ability to inspire trust are among the essential attributes of a successful modern president, especially in the era of 24/7 television and never-ending public scrutiny. In recent history, Dwight Eisenhower, John Kennedy, and Ronald Reagan were perceived to possess these attributes, and all were successful, popular presidents. America's four presidents immediately following Reagan were perceived by a majority of the electorate to lack one or more of these essential attributes; with the exception of Bill Clinton, all left office far less popular than when they arrived.

President Thurston had possessed all the essential attributes to be successful, along with a deep reservoir of public goodwill, because she was the first of her gender to hold the office. She also possessed a magnetic personality that appealed broadly to both men and women. She communicated in public and private in a direct manner that was disarming for a politician and engendered trust across the political spectrum. An attractive woman always perfectly coifed and immaculately attired, President Maggie reminded many Americans of that other famous Maggie, the Iron Lady Margaret Thatcher who served as Britain's prime minister during the 1980s and early 1990s.

Despite these assets, during her truncated term of office, President Thurston, like her predecessor, failed to achieve significant improvement in either the economy or the high unemployment rate. Moreover, the nation's annual budget deficits and ever-growing debt burden, if not brought under control, posed a graver threat to the U.S. than terrorism, illegal immigration, or global warming. Thurston faced a fractious Congress, with the House controlled by Democrats, and the Senate narrowly in the Republicans' hands, which produced gridlock and thwarted her efforts to rein in spending or raise taxes.

Beyond the usual obstacles of partisan politics, as with most modern presidents, Thurston's agenda on entering office was overtaken by events that, if not unforeseen, were outside her control. The Israeli government concluded that the interregnum between the November 2012 election and the president-elect's inauguration on January 20, 2013 provided the best and perhaps last window of opportunity to attack Iran's nuclear weapons facilities. There was no doubt among the world's major intelligence agencies that Iran was about to cross the threshold of becoming a nuclear power if it had not already done so. For Israel, this posed a clear and present threat to its continued existence. Israel's well-planned, high-risk military strike was carried out with its typical panache and competence, achieving complete surprise and dealing a crippling blow to Iran's nuclear weapons program, setting it back perhaps a decade.

The predicted aftermath consumed the better part of the first year of the incoming administration's time and energy. The U.S. military had an effective, comprehensive contingency plan, which the new president ordered to be executed. The navy repelled Iranian attempts to close the Strait of Hormuz, the narrow sea passage connecting the Persian Gulf and the Gulf of Oman, through which 40 percent of the world's seaborne oil transited. Both the U.S. Air Force and Navy degraded Iran's command and control and naval assets undermining the regime's ability to project force into the Persian Gulf. U. S. Army Special Forces and Marine units made a series of covert, rapid incursions across Iran's border with Iraq, successfully eliminating the bulk of Iran's military assets poised to be launched into Iraq. While not revealed to the public for diplomatic and security reasons, these units located and killed a number of senior al Qaeda figures who, for several years, had been granted safe haven in a luxurious residential compound outside Teheran. As a result of this fortuitous event, al Qaeda had been greatly diminished, but still remained a terrorist threat.

While this military effort was ultimately successful in containing Iran and maintaining the flow of oil with few disruptions, flare-ups occurred periodically throughout Thurston's administration necessitating continued vigilance. This required the president to devote a large portion of her time in office to international diplomacy and guarding against avenging terrorist attacks at home and abroad. By any objective measure, she was successful, but domestic issues by comparison suffered benign neglect. At the time of her death, President Maggie had resolved to focus the remainder of her term on the economy and working out a bi-partisan, "everybody's ox gets gored" grand bargain to bring the government's enormous deficit and debt burden under control. President Margaret Thurston probably would not be remembered by history as a great president, but as the nation's first woman president, she was a historic figure who managed the war on terror with competence and significant accomplishments.

Unlike her three immediate predecessors, Maggie was not a viscerally polarizing president. Her sincere efforts to reach across party lines, at least on some issues, achieved modest results, and for this she received bipartisan kudos. Despite these efforts, however, American politics remained bitterly partisan with fealty to one's party too often seeming to trump the larger interests of the country. Indeed, over the previous quarter century, politics at the national level had become angry and dysfunctional. The endless feud between the Republicans and Democrats, both the professional politicians and rank-and-file citizens, had degenerated to the point that trust and the capacity to compromise were virtually nonexistent. Problems festered while each party hurled epithets and blame at the other for failure to take action. Consequently, urgent, complex fiscal and budgetary challenges went unaddressed, threatening an irreversible decline and perhaps collapse of America's economy.

The American people recognized that President Thurston had endeavored to bridge the partisan divide, albeit with only a modicum of success, but for her effort, she deservedly would be held in esteem and affection by her countrymen. Although impossible to foretell or imagine at the time, President Thurston's death would make possible a chain of events over the ensuing three years that would shake the American Republic to its foundation.

2

Shortly before midnight on June 25, the deceased president's chief of staff, Harley Keenan, called the vice president at his residence in the old Naval Observatory that had served as the official residence of vice presidents since the 1970s. Bradley Ignatius "Biff" Fubarsky fumbled for the ringing phone. Without any greeting, Keenan said, "Mr. Vice President, I am profoundly sorry to inform you that President Thurston suddenly passed away of natural causes less than a half hour ago."

Fubarsky, still half asleep, could only manage to mumble, "What did you say?"

Keenan repeated his shocking news and added, "Mr. President, it is imperative that you be formally sworn in as soon as possible. Is there any particular judge you would like to have on hand for this?"

The fog of slumber lifted, and Fubarsky suddenly felt like the loneliest, most hapless guy in the universe. Harry Truman's reaction when told that President Franklin Delano Roosevelt had died was that it felt as if the "sun, the moon and the stars had fallen upon him." Biff blurted out the name of Jim Baxter, a Supreme Court Justice whom

Fubarsky had shepherded through his Senate confirmation process ten years earlier. Keenan replied, "Yes, sir, I'll call Justice Baxter and have him at your residence by 4:00 a.m., if that is agreeable to you."

The new, somewhat dazed president responded, "Harley, was it sudden? Did Maggie suffer?"

"She went out like a light, according to the doctor. Apparently, it was an aneurysm. The problem was diagnosed and determined to be inoperable about six months ago."

Fubarsky reflected on this information. Until recently, like many vice presidents before him, Biff had been an outsider within the administration. He was relegated to making junkets to second-rate countries, attending occasional funerals of friendly and not-so-friendly heads of state, making college commencement addresses, and standing in for the president at sundry ribbon-cutting ceremonies. He now understood why five months ago, Maggie abruptly had brought him into her inner circle and had him briefed on all the most sensitive issues facing her administration. She must have anticipated that she might not be long for this world and wanted him to be up-to-speed and prepared to take over, when and if necessary.

Biff was grateful for this and momentarily thought of the stark contrast between how Maggie had dealt with him and FDR's irresponsible treatment of his VP, Harry Truman. FDR knew his health was rapidly failing. He should not have run for an unprecedented fourth term in 1944. Yet, he never brought Truman into his confidence. When FDR died less than three months into his fourth term, Truman had not been briefed about the Manhattan Project to develop the atomic bomb.

"I'm happy to know she did not suffer, Harley. I'll miss her and so will the country; she was a marvelous lady and a fine president. I assume you have informed her sons."

"Yes, we have, Mr. President," replied Keenan.

Biff was not yet accustomed to being addressed this way. "Harley, call a meeting of the cabinet, the White House staff, and my staff following the 7:00 intel briefing. I'll address the nation at 9:00, followed by a brief press conference. Also, I want to call Maggie's sons first thing in the morning. Anything else I need to do?"

"No, Mr. President," replied Keenan. "We have already notified the protocol office to execute the plan for a State funeral. The last president to die in office was JFK over fifty years ago, but these plans are periodically reviewed and kept current."

"Very well, I'll see you in the morning at the daily intel briefing." Fubarsky hung up the phone.

Because of Biff's incessant snoring, his wife Dolly slept in an adjacent bedroom. He went to her, waking her gently and telling her she was the first lady of the United States. After recovering from the shock, she looked at Biff and said, "I'm so sorry for you, honey, but I'll be at your side as always."

Biff leaned over and held her close, whispering, "Thank you, Dolly. I couldn't possibly take on this job without you." He was not a particularly romantic man, but Biff was grateful to have Dolly for his wife. She understood him like no one else, and always knew when and how to rein in his oversized ego and propensity for pomposity. Truman once remarked, "If you want a friend in Washington, get a dog." Biff had something far better than a pet dog; he had his devoted spouse.

Biff returned to his bed and lay staring at the ceiling. He was like the proverbial dog that finally caught the car he had been chasing every day, and suddenly realized he didn't know what to do with it. For at least a quarter century, since a few years after arriving in the Senate, Biff had thought he had the right stuff to be president one day. Of course, virtually all senators think they are presidential timber, and in fact, of the previous eighteen presidents, himself included, he was the seventh to have served in the Senate.

Biff Fubarsky was the poster boy for how important luck is in life. Were he an introspective man, he would have marveled at how fate had allowed him to ascend to the presidency. One thing Biff was not, however, was introspective. Not infrequently, he was boorish, pompous, and a verbal bully. While intelligent in a savvy, street smart way, he fancied himself an intellectual and never failed to overestimate his mental capacity. The good news about this trait was that true intellectuals did not intimidate him, and he was only too willing to surround himself with such people and take credit for their good and sometimes bad ideas. A big bear of a man, undistinguished in appearance except for the obvious peroxided hair plugs that sparsely adorned his scalp, Biff was personable, had a firm handshake, looked a man in the eye, and was untainted by corruption. Well, except for the alleged cheating in law school and the question as to how, on a U.S. Senator's salary and little outside income, he could afford the home he and Dolly had purchased in Providence, Rhode Island, some twenty years ago. But those were nothing compared to the corruption of many other public officials.

Biff was a professional politician, which meant he was often cynical and hypocritical. Without a trace of shame or embarrassment, he rationalized and vigorously defended his position on any given issue, unless and until it became politically expedient to flip flop. His priorities during his thirty-four-year career as a senator from Rhode Island were getting reelected, exercising all the perks of office, supporting his party, and pursuing good public policy, in that order. In all his years serving in the Senate, Biff never had a major piece of legislation with his name attached to it. He was, to paraphrase Winston Churchill, an immodest man with much to be modest about.

The unlikely forty-sixth president of the U.S., Bradley Ignatius Fubarsky, was born to modest circumstances in Woonsocket, RI, in 1948. He was named after a five-star general of World War II fame and a Catholic saint. His initials were the source of his lifelong nickname. At an early age, Biff's family moved to Providence, RI. Following high school, Biff entered the University of Rhode Island, and upon graduation was accepted into a second-tier law school commensurate with his mediocre grades. Biff took a leisurely five years to earn his baccalaureate and three more years to obtain his law degree. It was the late 1960s and early 1970s, during which the Vietnam War was at its peak. Biff's primary objective was avoiding the draft by lingering as long as possible in college to maintain his draft-deferral status. By the time he completed law school, the U.S.' involvement in the war was rapidly winding down, and the draft was no longer a threat.

Following law school, Biff hung out his shingle in Providence and eked out a living as an ambulance chaser. In 1976, he surprised almost everyone by standing for election as a Republican and unseating a Democratic incumbent in Rhode Island's legislature. This led to his big break two years later, when no other Republican stepped forward to run against a popular three-term Democratic senator and former Rhode Island governor. The senator had wanted to retire, but the Carter White House prevailed upon him to stand for what was believed to be an easy reelection. Young Biff, who had not yet turned thirty, out-hustled his opponent who did not take him seriously. Biff's sister, Victoria, managed his campaign brilliantly and deserved most of the credit for her brother's upset victory by a scant two thousand votes. Learning from his opponent's indifference toward his campaign, Biff resolved never to take any election for granted. He made the Senate his sinecure, and in five subsequent elections, he retained his seat, never winning less than 55 percent of the vote.

In 2012, after more than a third of a century in the Senate, Biff was one of its most senior members. He had run for the Republican nomination for president on three occasions and never won more than ten thousand votes, always bowing out by the New Hampshire primary, if not sooner. He still had the presidential itch, but by now had recognized his personal ambition was unlikely to be realized. Then, in a fortuitous twist of fate, Maggie Thurston captured the 2012 nomination and needed a running mate.

Seeking an unconventional individual from outside politics, Thurston first chose Reb McCoy, distinguished CEO of Magnolia Petroleum & Chemical Co. in Dallas, Texas. Thurston had met McCoy on several occasions over the years and was favorably impressed. Having a deserved reputation for integrity and being an outstanding business executive, he was the type of person Thurston thought was needed in public life. Although McCoy felt honored and humbled by Thurston's offer to be her running mate, he had never found active involvement in politics appealing. Fortunately, at the time, he was involved in restructuring Magnolia and committed to leading that effort to a successful conclusion, giving him a gracious and legitimate reason to decline Thurston's offer. Moreover, from his knowledge of history, McCoy subscribed to the philosophy of John Nance Garner, FDR's first vice president, who famously remarked, "The vice presidency isn't worth a pitcher of warm piss."

Failing to win her first choice, Thurston considered and rejected several other potential candidates before settling on Senator Fubarsky. There were downsides to Biff such as his frequent verbal gaffes, undisciplined verbosity, and pompousness. Some quipped that he suffered from "chronic diarrhea of the mouth and constipation of the brain." Others unkindly suggested Biff stood for "big, ignorant, fat f**ker." Then there were those unfortunate incidents several years before in Mexico and Russia while leading congressional junkets to those countries. After two days in Mexico City gorging on chips and salsa, chile rellenos, and refried beans, washed down with several margaritas, Biff's stomach started to rebel. On the morning of the third day following a breakfast meeting with Mexican dignitaries, Biff arose from his chair and let rip a window-rattling fart. He then turned to his aide and said, "Think I drew mud on that one. Where the hell is the men's room?"

As it happened, a reporter with a camcorder was there to bear witness to Biff's distress. Within hours, the episode was reported by several Internet blogs. The New York tabloids had a field day. One humbling headline read: FART(SKY), DUMP(SKY) BY FUBARSKY: MONTEZUMA GETS HIS REVENGE ON U.S. SENATOR.

The episode in Russia occurred about a year later at a formal reception Biff attended in Moscow with the Russian foreign minister and his wife, a bosomy woman attired that evening in a low-cut gown. As the evening drew to a close, the minister's wife approached the senator to say goodnight. She tripped on the carpet, and as she lunged toward the startled Biff, he instinctively reached out to break her fall. Biff's eyes were wide as saucers, his upper dentures came loose, and his hands inevitably grabbed hold of the woman's enormous boobs. It all lasted only a couple of seconds, but long enough to be caught on camera. The ever-cruel Internet blogs and the newspapers soon spread the photo around the globe with unflattering captions. One headline read, BIFF GETS FUBAR(SKY). Every military vet knew that FUBAR was slang for F**ked Up Beyond All Recognition. Fortunately for Biff, he had a thick skin and could laugh at himself. After each incident, he merely kept a low profile until the uproar and late night TV jokes at his expense subsided.

Thurston and her staff were well aware of Biff's contretemps, but they also knew that the public's attention span had a short half-life, and that the media circus long since had moved on to countless other sensational stories in its endless, inane, and futile quest to escape ennui. On balance, Biff could be an asset to the ticket. He was a seasoned Washington hand and was not a polarizing figure. He was affable and an energetic campaigner. By giving him scripted speeches and limiting press access, the risk of embarrassing verbal flatulence would be minimal. As a moderate Republican from Rhode Island, Biff brought balance to the ticket and might tip a couple northeastern states into the Republican column in the general election. Indeed, this came to pass and, in what turned out to be a close election, was the margin of victory for the Thurston–Fubarsky ticket.

Now, two-and-a-half years later, Maggie was dead, and Biff was president of the United States. As he lay awake in bed contemplating his future, he could not suppress his lifelong political instincts. The 2016 presidential election was sixteen months away, and Biff wanted to win a term in his own right. He was more comfortable thinking about getting elected, which he had spent most of his adult life doing, than reflecting on the enormous responsibilities and challenges that had suddenly been thrust upon him.

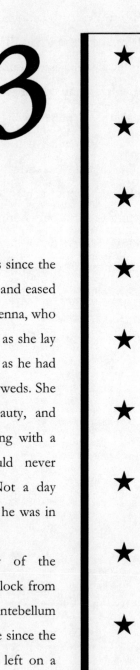

3

Austin, Texas
June 2015

As was his habit, Reb McCoy, governor of Texas since the start of the year, awoke at 5:00 a.m. on June 26, and eased his way out of bed so as not disturb his wife Marlenna, who appeared as always both beautiful and vulnerable as she lay gently sleeping. He was as crazy about her today as he had been nearly forty years ago when they were newlyweds. She was blessed with an uncommon, timeless beauty, and possessed an irresistible, captivating charm, along with a sharp mind. Why she chose him he would never understand, but he would be ever grateful. Not a day passed that he did not tell her at least once that he was in love with her.

McCoy went downstairs to the library of the Governor's Mansion, which was situated a city block from the Texas State Capitol in Austin. A columned, antebellum mansion, it had served as the Executive residence since the 1850s. McCoy reached for the morning papers left on a reading table by the valet and simultaneously flipped on the Fox News Channel. He did a double take. Maggie Thurston dead? He had first met her about ten years before, and since then they had become close acquaintances, although they had had little contact since her election to the presidency. Maggie had not resented Reb's spurning of her offer to be vice president, and he briefly reflected that had he not done so, his life this June morning would be forever changed. He was grateful he had said no in 2012, and now was profoundly saddened at her passing. Maggie Thurston had brought class, dignity, honor, and sorely needed executive experience to the presidency.

While she had experienced both success and setbacks as president, she never resorted to blaming her predecessor for any of the problems she faced. Blaming others was typical of most politicians, but Maggie, like McCoy, found such tactics to be pusillanimous, counterproductive, and a waste of time. No self-respecting military officer or business executive would engage in such behavior. If you accept or are elected to an executive position, it is your implicit duty and responsibility to shoulder whatever problems come with the office and set out with all due celerity to improve the situation. The past can't be changed, but the future can be if one has a vision and a plan for executing it.

For a president, who is the only elected official in America who represents all its citizens, to whine about the problems left by his or her predecessor seemed politically short-sighted in McCoy's opinion. After all, a significant minority of the electorate probably still supported the previous president, so criticizing one's predecessor after having won the election wouldn't generate much goodwill from those voters and would appear petty. Unfortunately, with America's seemingly endless election campaigns and around-the-clock media coverage, the most telegenic candidate and best campaigner generally wins, and the country has to hope the winner is able to switch out of campaign mode and govern responsibly. One can only wonder, McCoy mused, if Abraham Lincoln could have been elected or even earned his party's nomination had television been around in the mid-nineteenth century.

Maggie's death was a profound personal loss for McCoy and a great loss for the country. Perhaps her finest moment was standing up for Israel after its attack on Iran's nuclear facilities. The knee-jerk reaction of most other countries around the world was to heap calumny upon the Jewish state. In reality, most of those countries, including those in Western Europe and the moderate Arab regimes in the Middle East, were privately ecstatic that Israel had taken action. They all feared the consequences of Iran's possessing nuclear weapons. In the aftermath of the attack, it was confirmed that Iran had already produced a nuclear device, and was close to developing the technology to mate a nuclear warhead with a sophisticated medium-range ballistic missile. The world may have averted a conflagration narrowly, but the ingrained hatred of Israel and Jews in general was too deep for most governments to dare say publicly anything other than to condemn Israel.

The crawl across the TV screen informed McCoy that President Fubarsky would address the nation and hold a brief press conference at 8:00 a.m. Central Time. He decided to awaken Marlenna to tell her of the president's death. Though not friends, Marlenna and Maggie shared a genuine fondness for each other. Maggie had lobbied Marlenna to try to get Reb to reconsider being her running mate. Out of respect for Maggie, Marlenna made a half-hearted effort to influence her husband to change his mind. She was unsuccessful but not disappointed, because she knew Reb would not be happy in the role of vice president.

Marlenna was as shocked as Reb on hearing the news. President Fubarsky made some brief but appropriate prepared remarks, praising his predecessor and pledging to follow her example to the best of his ability. He then invited questions from the assembled White House press corps. The first reporter Fubarsky called on began by saying, "Thank you, Madam President."

There were some titters and groans, but the new president handled the faux pas with aplomb. "I know you are all accustomed, as am I, to hearing the president addressed as Madam President. Tragically, President Thurston is now gone, and it will take some time for that reality to sink in."

The press conference was subdued and respectful, as even the jaded press corps was shaken by the president's unexpected death. The only incongruous note was Fubarsky's response to a question as to whether he had an agenda for the country. "I will endeavor to follow the course set by President Thurston, particularly with respect to international affairs and national defense. Domestically, the country faces numerous challenges that merit attention. Regarding those issues, I intend to pursue a policy of accelerated gradualism."

The press people looked bewildered by this remark and several reporters tried to pose a follow-up question, but Harley Keenan, not wanting the president to make any further extemporaneous remarks on this topic, immediately shouted, "Thank you, Mr. President," abruptly ending the press conference.

Marlenna turned to Reb and said, "Well, I don't know much about Fubarsky, but he seemed to handle himself in a dignified, confident manner."

Reb nodded in agreement, but then added, "Except for that vacuous comment at the end about pursuing a policy of 'accelerated gradualism.' What the heck is that? Sounds like nonsense to me, like 'hope and change we can believe in.' Why not adopt a policy of graduated acceleration instead? Keenan was smart to end the press conference right away. With the primary focus being on Maggie's passing, hopefully the press and the Democrats, and especially Biff, will forget about it."

"Oh, Reb, give the guy a break. He must be in a state of shock like the rest of us."

"Maybe you're right, baby, but politics is savage, especially at the presidential level. Cynics in the press and political opponents are constantly trying to find reasons to fault and ridicule. Biff better get ready for prime time in a hurry, for both his and the country's sake. The next election is just sixteen months away. Biff's honeymoon will be shorter than most."

"Shorter than ours?" Marlenna teased, alluding to the fact that two days after their wedding, Reb had to depart on a two-week business trip to Brazil. He didn't take his bride, because he would be working long hours and didn't want to leave her alone in a hotel, especially in a foreign country.

"Yeah, but I've been happily making it up to you ever since," as he hugged her and kissed her good morning.

4

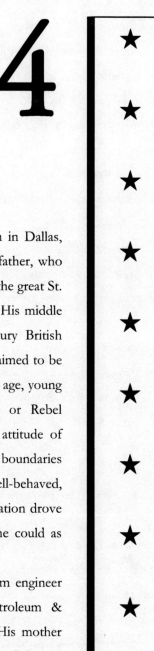

A Reluctant Hero's Life Story

Rogers Edmund Burke McCoy had been born in Dallas, Texas, in 1950. His first name came from his father, who was named by his father after Rogers Hornsby, the great St. Louis Cardinals second baseman of the 1920s. His middle names were in honor of the eighteenth-century British political philosopher and statesman who was claimed to be an ancestor on his mother's side. From an early age, young McCoy naturally acquired the moniker Reb or Rebel because of his initials, as well as his general attitude of flouting or at least questioning rules and boundaries established by his parents. He was in truth a well-behaved, happy boy, but his natural curiosity and imagination drove him to question most everything. His nickname could as easily and aptly been "Why" McCoy.

Reb's father was a brilliant young petroleum engineer and rising executive with the Magnolia Petroleum & Chemical Company, headquartered in Dallas. His mother had been an elementary school teacher before Reb was born. Reb's mother in particular was a beautiful, upbeat person of deep faith. She was blessed with a spontaneous, natural gift for inspiring affection, trust, laughter, and goodwill in virtually any person, including committed curmudgeons, who came within the field of her charismatic aura, be it a relative, friend, or stranger. Reb's father was more reserved and intellectual, but he possessed a rapier wit and adored his family. As their only child, Reb was the center of his parents' attention, but he was not a spoiled child. His parents imparted to him a strong set of values, especially personal integrity and a love for reading. At a precocious age, Reb was reading Mark Twain, Daniel Defoe, Robert Louis Stevenson, and Jack London.

This idyllic family was abruptly shattered shortly after Reb's eleventh birthday, when the Magnolia corporate aircraft in which his parents were traveling with several other company executives and their spouses was lost without a trace over the Java Sea. They were on the third leg of a business trip to acquire rights to explore for oil in the Indonesian archipelago. Suddenly, Reb was an orphan; his world imploded on him. He was devastated with inconsolable grief that left him nearly catatonic.

At the time of his parents' deaths, Reb had been staying with his widowed maternal grandmother at Hillcrest, his grandparents' ten-acre family farm in Springfield, Ohio. His grandmother Myrl, who had lost her husband a few years before and was now struggling to cope with her own unbearable grief over the loss of her daughter and son-in-law, immediately decided that Reb would live with her. Taking after his late grandfather, Reb affectionately addressed his grandmother as Myrlie. Not only was she a published writer and poet, as well as an accomplished pianist, but Myrlie was a formidable woman who possessed great wisdom and common sense.

She subscribed to two daily newspapers and used articles in them to illustrate for Reb how mankind too often committed one or more of the seven deadly sins. Myrlie particularly made sure Reb understood the sin of pride, which she thought to be the deadliest of all. "Pride is an almost universal affliction, especially among men of power," she lectured Reb. "Genuine humility is the mark of a truly great and decent man. Consider the example of Abraham Lincoln; one can possess ambition without pride. Take pride in what you do, but beware of self-pride."

Myrlie also educated Reb about his namesake Edmund Burke, who was related to Myrlie on her father's side and of whom she was most proud. Burke's writings took up a couple bookshelves in Myrlie's study. His quotations rolled off her tongue from memory, and many were framed and hanging on the walls of Hillcrest. She also informed Reb that one famous quote attributed to Burke – "All that is necessary for the triumph of evil is that good men do nothing." – he never wrote or said, but no doubt would have agreed with the sentiment. By osmosis, Reb began to drink in the wisdom of his great ancestor, and he memorized a number of Burke's quotations, much to Myrlie's delight. Two of his favorites were:

"Never despair; but if you do, work on in despair."

"No one could make a greater mistake than he who did nothing because he could do only a little."

Myrlie never revealed her favorite Burke quote. "He was a fount of ideas and common sense, and to select one as a favorite could not do Mr. Burke justice," she would say. While she never said as much to Reb, Myrlie was thrilled that he took an interest in his namesake Burke, because she shuddered whenever she thought that her grandson's first and other given name was after a baseball player! Happily, Reb, not Rogers, was the name by which her grandson was known to all.

About a year before he passed away, Grandfather McCoy told Reb all about the great Rogers Hornsby. Reb was then almost ten years old and had become fascinated with baseball. Grandfather McCoy, who lived and worked in St. Louis all his adult life, had seen the great Rajah play many games.

According to grandfather, Hornsby was the greatest hitter who ever lived. Reb, who had begun reading books on baseball history, wondered how he could be better than Babe Ruth or Ty Cobb.

The old man conceded that "Ruth was baseball's greatest player. He revolutionized the way the game was played, and perhaps saved the sport following the 1919 Black Sox scandal with his colossal and prolific ability to hit home runs, but Hornsby was the greatest hitter, even better than Cobb, and I can prove it."

"But, Grandfather," Reb protested, "Cobb had the highest all-time career batting average and won twelve batting championships to Hornsby's seven batting titles."

"All true, my son, but what makes Hornsby the best hitter ever is that he holds the greatest hitting record of all time, and baseball never acknowledges much less celebrates it. Only eight hitters since 1900 have hit .400 in a season, the last being Ted Williams in 1941. Now, from 1921 through 1925, Hornsby hit over .400 three times and came close the other two seasons. Over those five consecutive seasons, his batting average was .402. No other hitter ever accomplished that. Cobb came closest, averaging .400 over four straight seasons beginning in 1910.

"Some player both lucky and great, as Joe DiMaggio certainly was, may someday challenge and perhaps surpass his fifty-six-game hitting streak in 1941, which baseball rightly celebrates. It is also conceivable," Reb's grandfather added presciently, "that Ruth's home run records will be surpassed in the future. And some day, another player will come along and hit .400 over the course of a season. No one, however, will ever come close to hitting .400 over a half decade. And Hornsby hit with power during his five-year run, leading the league in hitting and slugging each year, and winning the Triple Crown twice, something only Ted Williams also managed to do. That means he twice led the league in homers, runs batted in, and batting average in the same season. This is why Rogers Hornsby was the greatest hitter who ever lived, and why I proudly named your father after him, and he passed that name on to you."

Young Reb reflected on his grandfather's soliloquy. "I see why Hornsby was the best hitter, but by having his name, do you or Dad expect me to do what he did?"

"Of course not, son," grandfather chuckled, "I don't even expect or particularly want you to play professional baseball. Only a handful of boys have the talent and drive to make the major leagues, and far fewer than that will be star players like Rogers Hornsby was in his day. By the time you graduate from college, I hope you will discover a worthwhile pursuit that you love and have an aptitude for, and then dedicate yourself to being the best you can be. Strive for excellence like Rogers Hornsby did, and you will be a credit to yourself and your name."

Myrlie would never be caught discussing the subject of baseball, although she believed it to be a wonderful game for young boys to play during summer. What Myrlie provided Reb was desperately needed tenderness and affection plus high expectations. The love, attention, and patience Reb received from this remarkable woman, in time, pulled him out of the emotional abyss.

She encouraged and answered all Reb's questions about his mother and father, knowing this not only would help him deal with his grief, but hers as well. Photographs of his parents were displayed in virtually all the rooms of the old farmhouse, and she passed on to him countless anecdotes about their lives and love for him. Myrlie was determined to instill in her grandson a fond, vivid, and indelible memory of his parents that would remain with him for the rest of his life.

Within a year of losing his parents, he had recovered his equilibrium and could laugh again. With Myrlie's persistent encouragement, he resumed his avid reading and learned to ride Heartland, a dapple-gray gelding stabled at Hillcrest. When reflecting on his youth years later, Reb would smile to himself that a young Texas boy had to go to Ohio to become a horseman. In summer, he helped his grandmother grow her raspberries and rhubarb, and harvest the peach orchard. He and his school chums also had plenty of time to play the sport that had captured his heart: baseball.

Upon completing the eighth grade, Myrlie decided it would be in Reb's best interest to go to a private boarding school for boys rather than continue his upbringing under the tutelage of an elderly, widowed woman. The insurance and legal settlement from his parents' deaths plus the nest egg his father had saved left Reb with a substantial trust. As his guardian, Myrlie utilized the trust's income to pay only for Reb's clothing, but now these funds would also be used to cover tuition, plus room and board at Washington Military Academy and College (WMAC) in Pennsylvania.

Situated on two-hundred-fifty acres of rolling hills along the Philadelphia Main Line, WMAC was founded in 1928 by then-Major Throckmorton G. Brubaker III who had served in the army during World War I. After leaving the army in the 1920s, he persuaded several wealthy benefactors to bankroll his dream of establishing a private military academy for grades nine through twelve, plus a two-year junior college. Brubaker's concept was to mold boys into men using the discipline and organization of a military structure that emphasized academic excellence. In selling WMAC to a prospective cadet's parents, he often said, "Send me your underachieving boy, and I will return to you a well-educated, well-rounded young gentleman." The school motto, "Courage, Honor, Conquer," was the ideal that Brubaker hoped to instill in the cadets who graduated from WMAC, and thereafter became proud lifelong members of the Long Grey Line.

By 1964, the year Reb matriculated, WMAC had long since become a lovely campus of colonial-style brick buildings, named for Revolutionary War heroes or deep-pocket donors, a parade ground, and athletic fields. Over the years, the school developed many revered traditions, one of which was a requirement that every new cadet, or plebe, complete successfully a noncredit course on the Founding Fathers, the American Revolution, and the Constitution. Brubaker believed, as did the Founders, that a well-informed citizenry was essential to sustaining a democratic republic. He also resolved that no cadet, who passed through WMAC's main gate, would depart without knowing a good deal about George Washington, in whose honor WMAC was named.

WMAC was a formative experience that left an indelible imprint on young Reb. At first, like almost every other cadet in his plebe year, he was homesick and had difficulty dealing with the regimentation of reveille at 5:30 a.m., taps and lights out at 10:00 p.m., three-hour study hall in barracks five nights a week, drill, inspections, and parades. Attendance at WMAC's nondenominational Protestant chapel, which could hold comfortably two thousand worshipers and featured beautiful stained glass windows reflecting glorious events of the American Revolution, was mandatory on Sundays and Tuesday evenings for vespers. The entire corps of cadets, one thousand strong, formed up on the main area in their dress gray wool uniforms with stiff collars, black striped trousers, and military hats to march off to chapel, where families and girlfriends of cadets joined them in worship. Following Sunday's chapel service, there was a parade led by WMAC's magnificent marching band. The corps also formed up to march to second and third mess daily, and one afternoon a week the corps practiced military drill. Demerits and tours were given for any rule infractions. One tour meant one hour of marching in full uniform and rifle during a cadet's free time. A cadet caught lying, cheating, or stealing was sent before the honor council, comprised of cadet captains. If a cadet was found guilty of an honor code violation, punishment could range from twenty-five tours to dismissal.

Academic achievement, physical fitness, proper etiquette, and military bearing were all emphasized. Any cadet who fell short in any of these areas was required to take appropriate remedial instruction or training. Each cadet was also expected to be involved in one or more clubs or activities such as choir, ballroom dancing, debating, and military history. The corps of cadets was run by the cadet NCOs and officers with close supervision of faculty and tactical officers. Virtually all professional personnel wore the uniform of the U.S. Army whether or not they had ever actually served. Many of the tactical staff in particular had had distinguished military careers either in the U.S. or British military.

Reb quickly overcame his longing for home and became a standout plebe. He was among the first to earn his cap shield, which entailed memorizing and reciting the contents of the Cadet Manual. He also excelled in all his freshman courses, especially mathematics, English literature, and history. One particular event during his plebe year, which was mortifying at the time but thereafter a fond, enduring memory was the visit in November 1964 of former President Dwight Eisenhower, affectionately known as Ike.

He was one of only nine U.S. Army and Navy officers to attain five-star rank as a General of the Army or Admiral of the Navy. This rank was created by Congress during World War II. A five-star officer never formally retired from active duty. In Ike's case, he surrendered his rank when he assumed the presidency in 1953, but reclaimed it when he left the White House in 1961. Brubaker had been recalled to service as a colonel in World War II and assigned to Eisenhower's staff at Supreme Headquarters Allied Expeditionary Force in England. As Supreme Commander SHAEF, Ike led the allied effort in 1944 to liberate Western Europe from Nazi domination. Brubaker and Ike developed a friendship during this period, and by the end of the war, the colonel had risen to the rank of lieutenant general.

Over the years since the war, Ike had been supportive of Brubaker and admired all he had accomplished with WMAC. After departing the presidency, Brubaker had assiduously pursued Ike to make a visit to WMAC. A date in November 1964 was chosen, because WMAC planned to dedicate in Eisenhower's honor the new officers' mess and reception hall erected at the east end of the parade ground.

To welcome Gen. Eisenhower, the corps of cadets was lined up by company on either side of Continental Way, the broad drive that began at the main gate and wound its way through the center of the campus to the main area where the marching band was formed up with their instruments. The cadet companies were arrayed alphabetically with A Company first on down through G Company to which Reb was assigned to the 1st platoon. On that raw, windy November day, the cadets were in full dress uniform, including overcoats, dress belts, white gloves, shakos, and rifles. The latter were World War I vintage M1903 Springfield bolt-action, military drill rifles that the corps of cadets carried on parade. Cadet officers and senior NCOs carried sabers or swords.

The reviewing party was led by the instantly recognizable General of the Army, in mufti and sporting a dark cashmere top coat, gray scarf, and natty fedora. WMAC Superintendent Lt. Gen. Brubaker was to his left, straining to keep up with the brisk pace of the seventy-four-year-old general. They were followed closely by commandant of cadets, Brigadier General Andrew Maddendorf, with his ever-present monocle and swagger stick, and the cadet first captain. As Gen. Eisenhower approached each company, the cadet company commander called his company to attention and present arms. Despite excitement and nervousness among the corps at the visit of such a distinguished guest, everything was going without a hitch. As the reviewing party approached G Company, Reb's company commander called the company to attention and present arms. As Reb lifted his rifle, he brought its sight a bit too high and close, hitting his shako brim. Simultaneously, a gust of wind blew his now unsteady shako to the ground in the path of Gen. Eisenhower. Reb swallowed hard and felt his sphincter reflexively tighten, but managed to remain steady at attention, eyes front, as he had been drilled to do. His mind ran amok thinking about what dire punishment awaited him. He would probably be marching tours through Christmas break.

Reb's peripheral vision caught a glimpse of Gen. Eisenhower's attention being distracted by the wayward shako rolling at his feet. The great man came to a halt and stooped to retrieve the shako. He stood before Reb with that kindly, expressive face Ike always displayed in newspaper photos. Fourteen-year-old Reb was petrified, not of Ike, but of what Brubaker or even worse, Maddendorf, would do to him. Known behind his back to all cadets as "Mad Andy," some cadets unkindly speculated whether the never smiling commandant had fought on the Nazi side in WW II because of his German surname and stern, no-nonsense approach to cadet discipline. Gen. Eisenhower flashed a warm smile and replaced the shako on Reb's head, saying "Windy day today, isn't it, son?"

Reb blurted back, "Yes, sir. Thank you, sir."

Ike asked Reb where he was from, and Reb replied, "Texas, sir. Dallas."

"Were you born there?" Ike asked.

"Yes, sir, General."

"What's your name, son?" the general inquired.

"Cadet Reb McCoy, sir."

"Well, then, Mr. McCoy, we have something in common. We're both Texans." Ike was born in Dennison, Texas, although few knew that fact, as he had grown up in Abilene, Kansas.

The reviewing party proceeded to the main area, where the band played ruffles and flourishes. This was followed by a 21-gun salute from the parade ground cannons and the national anthem. The rest of Gen. Eisenhower's

WMAC visit went as planned, and the superintendent expressed his pleasure by extending leave on the upcoming Saturday and Sunday by two hours until 11:00 p.m. and 9:00 p.m., respectively.

Reb received a lot of ribbing from other cadets for his faux pas, but the severe disciplinary action he feared never came to pass. That night, his hard-ass platoon sergeant ordered him to sleep in his narrow upper bunk bed with his rifle, bolt open and sight cover off, which could do irreparable harm to one's young manhood if he was a restless sleeper. Before taps and lights out the next night, however, Reb's company commander mercifully told him to stow his rifle. By then, one cadet had loudly teased Reb that he was the only guy he knew who had more experience sleeping with a rifle than with girls. It was a funny line and quite true. This fact of Reb's young life would not change until the summer before his senior year at WMAC, when Lola Lovett, a sexy, worldly wise girl a grade ahead of him in Springfield High, gave him a couple nights to remember while her parents were away. This milestone event Reb found to be infinitely more pleasurable than sleeping with his rifle.

A couple days after Gen. Eisenhower's campus visit, Reb's company commander informed him that the cadet first captain directed him not to discipline Reb in any way at Gen. Eisenhower's request. Apparently, the old general recalled how plebes were hazed in his day as a cadet at West Point, and he didn't want anything similar to befall Reb.

From this memorable, albeit trivial, event, Reb learned a lesson on leadership that stayed with him the rest of his life. He realized that truly significant, great men retain their humanity, humility, and empathy no matter how high they may rise. They also are able to relate easily and sincerely with people at all levels of the social spectrum. The world-famous general and former president of the United States took the time to stop and share a kind word and a smile with a fourteen-year-old boy who he knew was embarrassed and mortified about what was an insignificant, unintentional contretemps. In that moment, the general had made Reb a fan of his forever. Reb resolved that if ever he attained a position of leadership, he would always endeavor to treat those who reported to him as well as or better than those who outranked him. His beloved late mother and his grandmother Myrlie had taught him the Golden Rule, and he understood it, but the brief encounter with the general made it part of his character. The old verities are timeless, even if they are periodically denounced or forgotten.

Reb's time at WMAC had a salutary effect on his character development. He possessed a natural charisma attributable to his good nature, academic excellence, and athletic ability. By the time he was a third classman, or sophomore, he was a starting pitcher on the academy baseball team and a second-string wide receiver on the football team. As a second classman, he was appointed cadet first sergeant, G Company, and won the Patrick Henry debating medal, among numerous other awards. By then, he had matured into a tall, blue-eyed, fine-looking young man who exhibited outstanding military bearing and a quiet yet strong masculinity that made him a natural leader and attractive to the opposite sex.

Invited to return early for his first class year to help train the new plebes, Reb expected to be made a cadet officer, perhaps commander of   G Company, when the school year commenced. A few days before the cadet officers' "make list" was announced, Reb was summoned to the superintendent's grand office in Lafayette Hall, which featured a splendid view of the campus, and a dramatic painting of Gen. Washington praying at Valley Forge, while genuflecting in the snow, with his great bay stallion standing at his side. Gen. Brubaker stunned Reb by offering him the position of cadet first captain and regimental commander.

The only downside to being regimental commander was that any time Gen. Mad Andy, the commandant of cadets, who seemed never to sleep or take a day off, was disappointed with anything about the corps of cadets, he chewed out Reb. And Mad Andy, a man of impossibly high standards and bereft of humor, was frequently disappointed. Reb perceived Mad Andy as a martinet, but at least he was consistent and predictable. Dealing with a mercurial personality is more challenging than one that is constant, even if it is difficult. By now Reb had recognized that the commandant had devoted nearly forty years, his entire professional life, to WMAC. It was understandable that all he cared about was the continued success and excellence of his beloved corps of cadets. Consequently, he learned not to take the commandant's sharp tongue personally, realizing he was just letting Reb know one should never be self-satisfied but constantly strive for improvement.

Early in the school year, the commandant called the first captain on the carpet to excoriate him for the unmilitary appearance of the corps while on parade. He was also displeased with recent barracks inspections. Reb had to admit to himself that the performance of several companies left much to be desired. Sternly tapping his swagger stick on his desk for emphasis, the commandant went on to say that the situation was unacceptable, and if Reb didn't take charge of the situation promptly, he would do so himself. Reb replied, "Yes, sir," saluted, and departed the commandant's office.

That evening, Reb summoned all cadet captains to attend a meeting immediately after study hall in the Honor Council room. When everyone had gathered, Reb began the meeting. "The commandant is disappointed with the military bearing and discipline displayed at the last three parades. I agree with him. Each of us has worked hard during our years here to earn appointments as cadet captains. Now is not the time to slack off and coast through the school year to graduation.

"I suspect we all agree that the military drill, parades, and inspections are a bit Mickey Mouse, a game that is not that important. Well, we each have played that game successfully in order to become senior cadet officers. By freely accepting the leadership positions entrusted to us, we have assumed a responsibility to the corps that we cannot shirk. Each of us must prove every day that we deserve the shiny brass pips we are privileged to wear on our epaulets. For the sake of our reputations and more importantly next year's officers who will succeed us after we graduate, we need to work together in a spirit of 'one for all and all for one,' and bring leadership and discipline to our commands. You can count on my support, and I trust you will reciprocate.

"By the way," Reb continued, "I don't believe in mass or group punishment because of a few slackers or goof-offs in your respective companies. But I will hold each of you and your company officers accountable for substandard performance of the cadets you lead. We must instill pride in the corps to want to 'play the game' and be the best that they can be. I believe we can have fun and be sharp militarily at the same time.

"One last thing," Reb wrapped up. "I won't tolerate hazing. If I learn of any NCO or officer forcing a cadet to sleep with his rifle or tying someone to a chair and sitting him under a cold shower, I'll have him busted to private. Just because most of us were hazed as plebes doesn't make it right for us to behave in the same way now that we have the power to do so. Push-ups, tours, and denial of leave are all acceptable punishments if justified by the infraction, but hazing is not discipline or leadership. It's cruelty. Are there any questions or comments?"

Several cadet captains replied that they were on board and thanked Reb for his candor and support. Several others conceded that their companies were not performing acceptably, but they were going to meet promptly with their officers and NCOs to convey Reb's message and turn the situation around. From that moment forward, the corps of cadets showed steady and sustained improvement in all respects for the remainder of the school year. It was by far the longest speech Reb made to his cadet officers that year. In time, he understood this meeting to have been a turning point. He had established that he was the regimental commander, and thereafter commanded the respect of his cadet captains. Reb recalled that the first captain during his third class year was ineffectual and relegated to being a mere figurehead. The commandant lost confidence in him and dealt directly with the battalion and company commanders. Reb was not about to suffer the same fate if he could help it. His confidence as a leader blossomed. Another life lesson learned: Be active, not passive; be decisive, not diffident.

While nothing could top the honor of being the cadet first captain, Reb's final year at WMAC exposed him to a history course that had a profound impact on how he thought about that subject. Because he enjoyed his previous history courses and received top grades in all of them, Lieutenant Colonel Kelly Kernel invited him, along with nine other cadets, to take her select class on Alternative History. Col. Kernel was in her mid-thirties, quite attractive and had great legs. With her ash blonde hair, stunning blue eyes, flawless complexion, and high cheekbones, Reb surmised she must be of Swedish or perhaps Dutch ancestry. Many cadets, Reb included, had carnal fantasies about Col. Kernel, but alas she was happily married and unattainable.

Although Reb thought her alliterative rank and name were evocative of a madcap character from Joseph Heller's 1961 book, *Catch-22*, Col. Kernel was nobody's fool. Indeed, she was very bright and the only woman on the faculty, having come to WMAC after five years in the army, where she had been a captain, and earning a doctorate in history from Princeton. By Reb's senior year in 1968, Col. Kernel had been at WMAC for six years. Because of her gender and the different perspective she brought to teaching history, cadets who were fortunate to be selected for her class called the course "Herstory."

Col. Kernel began the first day of her class by declaring, "Gentlemen, you will find no answers in this course, only questions. My objective is to be provocative by challenging you to view history from different, often contradictory, perspectives. It is said that the winners write history. The goal of history is or should be to seek truth, yet most history is written from a particular point of view. There is always another side to every story. By learning from and about the past, we can understand the present and perhaps shape the future. Two final thoughts: History fundamentally is biography and geography, and history is rarely if ever inevitable."

Reb found this to be the best course he took at WMAC, because it appealed to his naturally inquisitive nature and penchant for questioning conventional wisdom. He also learned that few issues a free society grapples with are either black or white; rather, they are usually complex, which is to say they are different shades of gray. Often, particularly in politics, one has to decide on the least bad course of action instead of pursuing the ideal solution. Finally, democracy, he learned, necessitates compromise, but there is rarely ever a sound reason to compromise fundamental principles.

Col. Kernel challenged her students to "beware of 'presentism' in judging historical figures. "By this, I mean we should not apply modern standards and mores to people who lived in, say, the fourteenth or eighteenth century. Doing so does them an injustice and warps our perspective of past events."

She also reminded her class, "Most history concentrates on political and military figures. This is fine, but we must not overlook the enormous accomplishments and contributions of scientists, artists, and businessmen, among others. Galileo, Isaac Newton, Albert Einstein, Thomas Edison, and Henry Ford, to name just a few, had a far greater impact on mankind and how society evolved than most politicians or military figures you can name. Artists, composers, and writers such as Dante, Leonardo da Vinci, Michelangelo, Mozart, and Shakespeare had enormous and lasting influence on the world."

Among the eye-opening insights Reb learned in Col. Kernel's class was that the Soviet Union, for all practical purposes, had turned the tide against Germany before the United States had engaged its military against the Nazis. The Soviets had received materiel aid from the U.S. and Britain, which helped their war effort, but was not a deciding factor. By the time the U.S. had landed troops in North Africa in November 1942, the Soviets were on the verge of encircling and defeating the German 6th Army at Stalingrad, following a titanic struggle. Eight months later, in July 1943, while the British and the Americans invaded Sicily, the Russians defeated the Germans in the greatest tank battle in history at Kursk, which most western histories of the war barely mention. With few exceptions, the Germans were in retreat thereafter on their Eastern Front.

This is not to diminish the efforts of America and the British Empire in Italy in 1943, and later on D-Day in June 1944. Had the allies not been successful under Eisenhower's command in liberating France and marching on to Germany, the war would have been prolonged at much greater cost in lives and treasure, and the Soviets might have achieved hegemony over all of Europe instead of only Eastern Europe.

Reb also learned that the victory over Germany was not inevitable. Hitler's hubris led him to make a number of terrible strategic and tactical decisions that resulted in his destruction, not the least of which was his colossal unforced error in declaring war on the U.S. following the Japanese attack on Pearl Harbor. In recounting the Allies' victory, most historians ignored or downplayed the Nazi blunders. Moreover, few Western historians commented on the war's staggering cost to the Soviets. Stalin ruthlessly sacrificed an estimated twenty-seven million of his people, military and civilian, to prevail over Germany, but in the end, he triumphed.

A large amount of class time was devoted to the American Civil War. Would there have been a war had South Carolina not fired on Fort Sumter,

April 12, 1861? That was, after all, Lincoln's casus belli. Had either side known beforehand the staggering number of casualties it would suffer during the four-year conflict, would the war have been averted? If Britain or France had recognized the Confederacy as a sovereign nation, would that have stayed Lincoln's hand?

Reb reaffirmed his belief that Lincoln was a truly great man. He was almost certainly the only political figure of the time, who might have been a plausible candidate for president, to have carried out the war to its bitter end in order to save the Union. All other prominent politicians of the era almost certainly would have negotiated a peaceful separation of north and south. Purging the country of slavery, America's original sin, might have justified the war, but to Reb's surprise that was not Lincoln's initial objective. He was willing to accept continuation of slavery in states where it was still legal, if the southern states rejoined the Union.

Most intriguing to Reb was that Lincoln perhaps was wrong on the fundamental issue of whether secession was legal. Lincoln made a logical and persuasive case against the legality of secession, and most all subsequent history written on the Civil War accepts without criticism that he was correct in his position. The Constitution drafted in 1787, however, does not discuss secession or establishment of a Union in perpetuity. The Pledge of Allegiance mentions "one nation, indivisible," but that is not a legal document; it was written in 1892 to be recited by children in public schools. Many of the Constitution's Framers considered secession to be appropriate in extreme cases, and that the people in each of the sovereign states had the ultimate say on remaining in the newly formed Union.

The entire matter of the Civil War and secession generated spirited debate among Reb and his fellow classmates. In the end, as Col. Kernel had promised at the start of the course, she provided no definitive answers, only provocative questions. "Herstory" was the most intellectually stimulating academic survey Reb had ever experienced, and it made him an ardent student of history the rest of his life.

Just prior to Christmas break, Gen. Brubaker received word that former cadet Jack Wayne had been killed in Vietnam. Brubaker held a memorial chapel service in Wayne's honor, which was very emotional for many cadets who had known Jack, including Reb. Jack had been Reb's company commander his plebe year. He was someone everyone looked up to and admired. Mature beyond his years and a natural leader, Jack was a suave, polished young man, liked by all and emulated by many.

Reb had followed the Vietnam War and other current events by reading the newspapers daily in the WMAC library. While he knew about the protests against the war, which escalated after North Vietnam's 1968 Tet offensive, he instinctively supported America's commitment to keep South Vietnam free of communist subjugation. Youthful testosterone, fueled by the patriotism in which WMAC's culture was steeped, was a contributing factor, but Wayne's death was the tipping point that convinced Reb it was his duty to enter the army as soon as he turned eighteen, shortly after graduation. The war probably would start winding down after the 1968 presidential election no matter who won, because it was rapidly losing the country's support. Indeed, the war's gathering unpopularity compelled President Lyndon Johnson not to stand for reelection. Vietnam was his generation's war, and if Reb didn't enlist in the military soon, it would pass him by.

At the start of his first class year in 1967, Reb planned to enter college following graduation from WMAC. He applied for early admission to Rice, Princeton, and Stanford. His grade point average, SAT scores, and extracurricular activities virtually guaranteed he would be accepted to all three schools. In fact, that came to pass, but by then Reb had made up his mind to enter the army, even though an undergraduate college deferment from the draft was a legitimate and respectable reason to postpone military service.

While on Christmas break, Reb told Myrlie of his decision. She was devastated, but did not let on to Reb. After extensive discussion, she reluctantly concluded that her only grandson could not be dissuaded from his decision. Besides, her husband had served in WW I, and Reb's father just barely had been old enough to serve in the Pacific during the last year of WW II. How could she pressure her only grandson to postpone serving his country until after college? Reb was a mature, responsible young man. In any event, once he turned eighteen in July 1968, she could do nothing to stop him from enlisting. Myrlie gave Reb her blessing, but not without profound heartache and apprehension.

As the end of the school year approached, Cadet First Captain Reb McCoy was pleased with how the corps of cadets had developed jaunty pride in its military bearing, especially on parade. In May, Mad Andy took Reb aside one day. "Mr. McCoy, the corps of cadets this year is the best we've had in at least five years. You and your officers should be gratified. You have come a long way from where you and the corps were last October."

Reb was nearly speechless, never having heard the commandant give him or anyone else a compliment, but he managed to say, "Thank you, sir. I'll pass on your kind words to the cadet captains. Praise from you is especially appreciated."

Mother's Day weekend was always emotional for all cadets, but this year it was particularly meaningful to Reb. Traditionally, the regimental commander's mother reviewed the Sunday parade following chapel. Reb invited Myrlie to take the reviewing stand, and after the public address announcer recognized all the mothers and grandmothers in attendance, Reb stepped up to the reviewing stand and kissed Myrlie on the cheek. She beamed with pride, and Gen. Brubaker leaned over to whisper, "Ma'am, you have a mighty fine grandson." That day the corps of cadets looked particularly sharp on parade.

Reb just missed being class valedictorian, but he had no regrets as his four years at WMAC drew to a close at the end of May. He expressed his appreciation to his fellow cadet officers for making their corps of cadets a memorable one, and they gave him a rousing standing ovation that brought tears to his eyes. After making his individual farewells and best wishes to all his friends and the WMAC staff, he strode up to the superintendent and commandant and said, "General Brubaker, General Maddendorf, thank you both for your unwavering support and confidence by asking me to lead the corps this past year. It has been a distinct honor and privilege that I will never forget."

Gen. Brubaker replied, "Reb, you have done yourself and your alma mater proud. No doubt you will be successful in all your future endeavors. Godspeed."

Gen. Maddendorf added, formal to the end, "Mr. McCoy, next year's regimental commander will have a hard act to follow."

Reb smiled and responded, "Thank you, sir," saluted, and departed with Myrlie for Springfield.

5

Prior to enlisting in the army, Reb had six weeks at home in Springfield, where he worked out, helped with farm chores, and caught up on his pleasure reading. He also had a few rolls in the hay, literally, with the lovely Lola Lovett.

Having completed her freshman year at Wittenberg University, Lola was working part time the summer of 1968 in a Springfield drugstore. She was a free-spirited, happy, uninhibited young woman who had embraced with boundless enthusiasm the sexual revolution that was sweeping the country in the 1960s. Lola was flirty and sexy, but she was not promiscuous, as she dated only one guy at a time. Of course, she never dated any one guy longer than a few months, although she might loop back to a previous beau from time to time. It seems Lola bored easily, but Reb held her undivided attention during his brief summer in Springfield.

Myrlie could not help liking the pretty, blonde, green-eyed Lola, despite her bold, sensual manner and too tight apparel. Any red-blooded young man would be attracted to Lola, and that's what concerned Myrlie. One evening, Myrlie sat Reb down for a little chat. "Reb, I am sure you

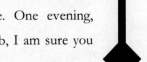

have learned the facts of life by now. I want you to know that I don't approve of sex outside marriage, but I also realize time has passed me by, and that today's young people don't pay much attention to what folks my age have to say. Lola is a looker and a charmer, and I can tell you are smitten with her. I like her spirit and obvious intelligence. Why you are attracted to her is no mystery, but please be careful and don't end up doing anything you both will regret. This is all I have to say on the subject."

Reb felt sheepish and embarrassed, yet he adored his Myrlie's moxie for telling him forthrightly what she believed was in his best interest. After a few moments, Reb said, "Myrlie, please don't worry. I won't let anything happen that would hurt Lola or me, or embarrass you."

It was easy for Reb to speak with such confidence, because Lola never went anywhere without several condoms in her purse, and she was expert in using them whenever the need arose, as it were. On several occasions that summer, while Myrlie was in town for the afternoon or out for the evening with her bridge club, he and Lola would fool around in the barn hayloft with Heartland standing sentinel below. No telling what Heartland thought of their high jinks; the discreet old horse never revealed his thoughts to Reb on their quotidian rides together.

While Reb more than liked Lola, he did not love her, which both surprised and in some way disappointed him. He always had assumed that he would fall in love with the first girl with whom he had sex. Conveniently, Lola was not in love with him either, so no hearts would be broken when the time came for Reb to depart for military service. Lola lived for the moment, and when she was not with the guy she "loved," she "loved" the guy she was with.

Besides enjoying each other's bodies, Lola and Reb spent much of their time together talking about their hopes and dreams for the future. Lola was bright and ambitious, with no plans to be merely an obedient, stay-at home-wife looking after the children. Reb was sure she would be successful at whatever she did and would have fun doing it. When it came time for Reb to leave Springfield for the army, Lola told him, "If you come back with all your parts still working, look me up, preppy."

"I'll be sure to do that, Lola. In fact, if I get sent to war, I'll write you from time to time."

"I'd like that, and I'll send you a perfumed letter sealed with a lipstick kiss in return."

With that, she gave him a passionate kiss and sped away from Hillcrest in her convertible, her blonde tresses flowing and the Beatles's latest hit "Hey Jude" blaring from the car radio. As she reached the end of the driveway and gave him a last wave, Reb smiled and said sotto voce, "There goes a chick that is both cool and hot."

The year 1968 was marked by tragedy, turmoil, and rising anger over the Vietnam War, especially on college campuses across the country. At times, TV nightly news seemed to be reporting on a nation unraveling in real time. Following the murder of Martin Luther King, Jr. in April, Bobby Kennedy was murdered in June moments after winning the California Democratic primary. Less than five years earlier, his older brother, President Kennedy, had been assassinated in Reb's hometown, Dallas. The country was in shock.

In August, Reb enlisted for three years in the U.S. Army. With his WMAC experience, he easily sailed through boot camp and was assigned to the 101st Airborne Division (Airmobile) based at Fort Campbell, Kentucky. The "Screaming Eagles" had an illustrious past, particularly in World War II, where units of the 101st were dropped behind enemy lines the night before D-Day, June 6, 1944. Later, the 101st was involved in the ill-fated Market Garden operation immortalized in Cornelius Ryan's book, *A Bridge Too Far*, and the Battle of the Bulge, where Hitler made a last desperate counterattack on his crumbling western front. Following several more months of rigorous air assault combat training, Reb received orders for Vietnam in February 1969, a month after Richard Nixon was inaugurated president.

By the time Reb arrived in 'Nam, the number of American military personnel had peaked at five-hundred-forty thousand, and over thirty thousand Americans had been killed in action. By the time America's active military involvement finally ended in 1974, over fifty-eight thousand U.S. military personnel had lost their lives in a protracted war that bitterly divided the country and was never in America's vital national interest. To sacrifice so many lives in such a misguided venture was one of America's greatest follies and tragedies.

The 101st Airborne Division was assigned to I Corps, the northernmost of the four military districts of the Republic of South Vietnam. I Corps bordered North Vietnam to the north, Laos to the west, and the South China Sea to the east. Some eighty thousand North Vietnamese Army (NVA) regulars and Viet Cong (VC) operated in the region. The rugged jungle of the mountains along the Laos border was difficult terrain, but it provided a favored route and staging area for the NVA to move supplies and troops south. East of the mountains lay rice paddies and hundreds of small hamlets and villages, as well as the large cities of Hue and Danang.

In May 1969, General Creighton Abrams, commander, Military Assistance Command in Vietnam (MACV), launched Operation Apache Snow. The purpose of the campaign was to destroy the NVA bases critical to the enemy's logistical network in the remote A Shau Valley. Achieving this objective required seizing control of Ap Bia, a mountain that dominated the northern valley just a mile from the Laos border. Officially named Hill 937, because it towered 937 meters, or three thousand feet, above sea level, Ap Bia was a daunting challenge for an attacking force. The NVA and VC had built an extensive hidden network of tunnels, fire bases, and booby traps. The mountain was wilderness covered by double and triple canopy jungle, bamboo thickets, and razor-sharp, waist-high elephant grass. The NVA had a significant home-field advantage.

The 9th Marine Regiment and elements of the 101st Airborne Division were tasked to carry out Operation Apache Snow. Reb's unit was part of the 3rd Battalion, 187th Infantry, which had been ordered to undertake a reconnaissance in force of Hill 937. The 187th was airlifted by helicopter to the staging area and began to search out and destroy enemy troops and supply bases. Reb had been on numerous patrols since arriving in country and had been involved in a few firefights, but neither he nor his fellow army grunts had faced a battle as difficult as Hill 937 would turn out to be.

The NVA and VC were not going to give up Ap Bia without a protracted fight. Casualties mounted quickly, and soon the GIs informally renamed Hill 937 Hamburger Hill, because those who fought there felt like they had been through a meat grinder. The inhospitable terrain and tenacious, organized resistance of the enemy took a fearful toll. Maneuver was restricted because of the narrow trails and dense jungle. By the fifth day, the 187th had come within two-hundred-fifty feet of Hill 937's summit, and most units were engaged in close-order, hand-to-hand combat.

Reb had shot at and hit many enemy soldiers in various firefights before this operation, but he had fired from a distance and was not absolutely certain whether any round he fired had killed another man. On Hill 937, however, Reb came face to face on several occasions with enemy soldiers determined to kill him, but either they missed him, or he fired first. In the midst of battle, he had no time to think about it, but after the operation was over, he was overcome with a profound sense of guilt and loss of innocence that tormented him for many months. He knew he was in a kill-or-be-killed situation, with no other option available, but intentionally killing a human being, even in war, even in defense of your self or your fellow soldiers, his soul told him was a mortal sin. Reb would leave a part of himself on

Hamburger Hill. He also learned he was not fit to be a priest, nor meant to be a warrior. The latter insight was a blessing, because he could not live with himself had he turned into a professional soldier who took pleasure in killing. In time, Reb locked these thoughts away in his subconscious memory and resolved never to reveal them to another person.

As night fell on the fifth day, half of Reb's platoon had been cut down, but there was more brutal combat to come. The after-action report would show that the 187th suffered appalling losses. Of the unit's four-hundred-fifty soldiers, over 60 percent were killed or wounded including two of four company commanders and eight of twelve platoon leaders. Many of those killed were lost, because choppers could not land for two days to evacuate the wounded.

In this maelstrom, Reb became a reluctant hero. Courage is overcoming fear, and Reb was scared shitless. His platoon leader and sergeant had been killed, leaving him, a corporal, in charge of what remained of his platoon and remnants of a couple other units. Most of the unwounded men were as scared as Reb and hunkered down, awaiting orders. During the night, Reb ordered a hundred-yard pullback from their position in order to bring the wounded out of the direct line of fire. One of the wounded was Duane Darby, a black PFC with whom Reb had become close. Darby was a tough soldier, but he had lost a lot of blood from a severe leg wound that left him virtually immobile.

Reb figured that if he was to get his troops including the wounded off the mountain, he had to overwhelm the NVA regulars who still held control of the summit. Reb called battalion headquarters, explained his situation, and requested an Air Force AC 47 Spooky to be sent up the next night to level the mountaintop. HQ at first thought Reb was nuts and couldn't believe a corporal was the highest rank in charge. Reb said he probably could hold on through the next day, but if they were to take the summit and have any chance of being extricated, they had to wipe out the NVA. HQ said they would get back to him, as if Reb had all the time in the world.

During the next day, Reb took six soldiers on a recon mission to see how the NVA were deployed. He figured they would be resting during daylight. The enemy obviously didn't know how dire his situation was, or they already would have finished off his company. The recon force stumbled onto a nest of NVA regulars, surprised them, and killed at least ten. Reb ordered his unit to retreat while he provided covering fire. Some shrapnel caught him in his right arm while reloading his M16, but he managed to toss a grenade with his uninjured arm, killing three enemy soldiers. To distract the enemy from his retreating men, he quickly reloaded, stood up, and began raking the enemy with his weapon at point blank range. They beat a retreat back up the mountain.

By the time Reb returned with his recon force to the rest of his unit, dusk was approaching. Battalion HQ called on the last operating field phone. A gruff major came on the line and asked Reb, "Corporal, what's your current situation?"

Reb filled him in and again requested a Spooky that night. The major barked, "We'll have one on station at 2100 hours. Give me your exact position, so we don't take any friendly fire casualties."

Reb provided his coordinates and said, "Major, thanks for your help. Many of our wounded can't hold out much longer, but if we can take Hill 937 tonight and get choppers in here tomorrow, I think we can make it."

"What's your name, son?"

"Corporal McCoy, sir."

"You are a helluva soldier, corporal. I look forward to meeting you soon. Hang in there."

"Yes, sir."

Spooky was a modified C 47, a twin-engine propeller aircraft, which had been a dependable workhorse transporting troops and cargo during World War II. In Vietnam, it was converted into an AC 47 and outfitted with three 7.62mm six-barrel mini guns mounted in two side windows and the cargo hatch on the aircraft's port side. The guns were remote controlled by the pilot, who no doubt was far younger than his plane.

Spooky provided close air support to ground troops with suppressing fire. Usually operating at night to minimize its vulnerability to enemy ground fire, the aircraft could loiter over the target area for a couple hours, flying at 120 knots at an altitude of three thousand feet in a counter-clockwise circular pattern. Each of its guns fired a withering six thousand rounds per minute, with every fifth round a tracer. The sight was fearsome, and the results were more so. A target area the size of a football field could be leveled, the entire jungle cover obliterated, along with anyone or anything beneath it, within minutes. For good reason, the North Vietnamese regulars and VC feared this weapon system like no other. Many of the enemy thought Spooky was a monster fire dragon, because the mini guns' tracer rounds illuminated the night sky over the battlefield, exposing the enemy to ground fire.

Army grunts generally disdained the air force because of the relative comfort they enjoyed at their bases, which offered real beds, hot meals, and hot showers. But the grunts all welcomed the arrival of Spooky, or Puff the Magic Dragon, when one appeared to help ground troops out of a tough spot. Ironically, Spooky was the oldest technology used in the war, dating back to the 1930s. And while the mini gun was state-of-the-art, even it was based on the Gatling gun, which first was introduced a century before, during the Civil War.

Spooky arrived as scheduled above Hill 937, where it stayed for two hours and achieved just what Reb had hoped. There were a few anxious moments when Spooky's enfilade came perilously close to Reb's position, but there were no friendly fire casualties. The enemy fled the battlefield, were cut down by Spooky, or felled by ground fire from the men in Reb's unit still able to fight. The next morning, the 187th possessed Hill 937. The number of enemy casualties suggested that the force the 187th faced was much larger than originally thought. Choppers arrived at dawn to bring fresh reinforcements and to evacuate the dead and wounded. Reb was one of the last to depart.

There were so many wounded soldiers from Hamburger Hill that the nearest army field hospitals could not handle all the cases. Some soldiers, including Reb and his buddy Duane Darby, were evacuated to 3rd Field Hospital in Saigon. Darby's injuries required extensive surgery and convalescence. In time, he made a full recovery from all his wounds, except he was left with a gimpy leg for life, but at least he didn't lose it.

Reb's upper arm wound was worse than he had thought. The docs at 3rd Field were able to extract all the shrapnel, but struggled to eliminate a tenacious infection that for several days left him fevered and gravely ill. This prolonged his hospital stay by nearly a month, but he finally recovered fully and was patched up as good as new, save for a permanent beauty mark.

Once he had come down off the adrenalin high from prolonged, intense combat, Reb started to appreciate the environment at 3rd Field. He had a comfortable bed, excellent food, hot showers as often as he wanted, and air conditioning. When grunts referred to "the world," most were talking about the United States. Compared to his living conditions during his first four months in country, 3rd Field for him was "the world."

He also read daily *Stars & Stripes*, the armed forces' newspaper, and was able to catch up on events back home and around the globe. Reb was not returned to his unit until late July. By that time, he had celebrated his nineteenth birthday, and Apollo 11 had landed men on the moon and returned them safely to Earth, fulfilling President Kennedy's bold challenge laid out less than a decade earlier. Reb was never more proud of his country.

During Reb's convalescence in Saigon, the 3rd Battalion's executive officer visited the wounded men at 3rd Field Hospital. The ExO congratulated Reb on his splendid performance on Hill 937 and told him that he had been awarded a battlefield promotion to sergeant and would be receiving a Purple Heart. He also said that Reb would be recommended for a medal for gallantry. Reb was surprised by the promotion, but grateful for the recognition. He did not tell the ExO, but Reb was still wrestling with his personal demons that had begun to gnaw at him as soon as the operation was over. He wasn't a pacifist, but the taking of another human being's life, no matter the justification for doing so, haunted him.

As the ExO was about to leave, he asked Reb if there was anything he needed. Reb replied, "No, sir, but I would like to speak to the pilot of that Spooky you sent up to Hill 937, so I can thank him for giving our guys a chance to get back alive."

"Sergeant, I'll call 7th Air Force when I get back to battalion HQ and ask them to have the pilot get in touch with you."

A couple days later, Reb was told to report to 3rd Field's admin office where he was put on the phone with the Spooky pilot. Reb expressed his everlasting gratitude for literally saving the lives of his troops. The young pilot mentioned that it was part of his job; he was glad to be of help and happy he had not accidentally shot any of the good guys. He cut the conversation short, because he had to rush over to the flight line for a mission. Reb had hoped to chat a bit longer, but figured the pilot was on his way to help out some other grunts in a jam. At least Reb had had the opportunity to thank him by phone, and was surprised when the pilot told him no other officer or noncom had ever made the effort to contact a Spooky pilot after an operation.

Several weeks before returning to I Corps and the 101st, Reb was cleared to spend time in Saigon, but he had to return to 3rd Field by 10:00 each night. Reb toured the bars, not to drink, but to meet Vietnamese women. While he thought them quite pretty and sexy, it did not escape his notice that most of the bar girls had had breast implants to cater to the American GIs' fascination with big boobs. Through hands-on experience, Reb discovered that these early breast implants were extremely hard, nothing like Lola's firm and lovely natural breasts. But other than this observation, Reb was attracted to Vietnamese women. He wondered what might become the fate of the girls, especially those who got pregnant cavorting with GIs, when the time came for America to withdraw its forces from South Vietnam. Would they and their half-American bastard children be ostracized or punished? He shuddered at the thought of what might befall them if the North one day succeeded in taking over the South.

Before rejoining his unit, Reb said good-bye to Darby, who was returning stateside to complete his recovery. He, like Reb, was a native Texan, from a rough neighborhood in Houston. Their respective life experiences could not have been more different, but during their six months serving side by side in Vietnam, they forged a close and lasting friendship. Before they parted, Darby said, "Hey, man, it's been an honor serving with you in this God-forsaken hell hole. I owe you my life for what you did on Hamburger Hill. For that, I will always be in your debt. I never thought I'd owe anything to some honky, but you're okay for a white guy. If there's any justice in this war, you should get a big-time medal for what you did."

"Duane, you don't owe me a thing. I reacted instinctively to a bad situation and got lucky. I dodged a few bullets and got nicked by one. You weren't so lucky. Thankfully, you are going to make a full recovery. I promise to look you up when I get back home."

"Don't worry, my man. I'm sticking close to you from here on out. You were born under a lucky star and are going to go places in life. If I hang around you, maybe some of that luck will rub off on me."

Reb ended the farewell saying, "I'm proud to have you as my friend, Duane."

When Reb returned to his unit, he learned that barely two weeks after seizing control of Hamburger Hill, the 101st had abandoned it. What was the point of all the bloodshed for that wretched piece of real estate if it had no strategic purpose? Reb later found out that the high casualty numbers from the battle had filtered back to Washington, and key senators were loudly critical. Reb did not second-guess the politicians so much as wonder how the military command could order Operation Apache Snow and not realize they were pursuing a meaningless objective to be paid for with much blood and many lives. At this point, he became disillusioned with the war and started counting the days till the end of his one-year tour in Vietnam.

In September, Reb spent his one week R&R in Hong Kong. After returning to combat, most of the action he saw was patrolling hamlets and villages in I Corps. His unit was engaged in several fire fights. His first priority was to keep his men as safe as possible while still carrying out the assigned mission. During one engagement in early November, Reb disobeyed a direct order by his platoon leader, a second lieutenant who had been in country only two months. The lieutenant had orders that the villages they were searching that day were abandoned, and that any persons found should be assumed to be VC. In this particular village, however, there were some twenty-five women, children including a few infants, and elderly people. Reb's jaw dropped when the lieutenant ordered him to have them shot. Reb moved close to the lieutenant, so the other troops could not hear him.

"Lieutenant, these people obviously are not VC. Even if any of them are sympathetic to the enemy, they pose no threat to us."

"Sergeant," the lieutenant replied angrily, "our orders say that any personnel we find in this village are presumed to be VC."

"Sir," Reb protested, "battalion intelligence obviously is not accurate in this case. Recommend we call HQ and explain the situation. We can interrogate several of these folks and be on our way."

"Look, Sergeant, I have my orders, and you have yours. Shoot these people now!"

"Sir, I cannot carry out your order. Please reconsider."

"McCoy, you are hereby relieved of duty. I will report you for insubordination and defying a direct order while on combat patrol."

Reb knew this could mean his court-martial and perhaps dishonorable discharge. He also saw that the troops were noticing the intense discussion going on between him and the lieutenant. He looked the lieutenant in the eye and said, "Sir, these people are South Vietnamese. We are here to protect them and help them fight off the NVA and VC. How can you kill defenseless people in cold blood? I know you have orders, but you also have discretion to ignore those orders based on conditions in the field."

"McCoy, stand aside and cease interfering with my command."

"To kill them, Lieutenant, you'll have to order the men to shoot me first."

The lieutenant knew McCoy had the trust and confidence of his fire team and that they would never shoot him. If nobody obeyed his order, he would have a mutiny. He decided to take several of the village elders back to base for interrogation and leave the rest of the villagers alone. He would also bring McCoy up on charges.

Two days after returning to base, Reb was ordered to appear at battalion HQ and answer the charges as part of a preliminary inquiry that could lead to his court-martial. Reb explained his side of the story, and was ordered to remain at battalion HQ until he received further orders. A couple of days later, while passing his time perusing *Stars & Stripes*, he saw the breaking story on the My Lai massacre that apparently had been covered up or ignored by the army for nearly two years. In January 1968, a platoon under command of a Lieutenant William Calley had murdered at least 347 and perhaps as many as 500 women, children, babies, and old people in the village of My Lai. Except for being on a much larger scale, this was precisely what Reb's platoon leader would have done but for Reb's refusal.

Shortly thereafter, Reb was notified that the charges against him had been dropped. He was ordered to return to his unit. When he got back, he learned that his platoon leader, who had filed charges against him, had been reassigned. Reb never saw him again.

The remainder of Reb's tour in Vietnam was relatively uneventful, except for an unexpected award ceremony he was ordered to attend at MACV headquarters in Saigon in January, a few weeks before he returned stateside. At the appointed time, Reb arrived at MACV and was escorted into the commander's conference room. He found himself in the company of three officers and a senior enlisted man, along with several aides scurrying around to prepare the room for the arrival of Gen. Creighton Abrams, MACV Commander.

At 10:00 a.m. sharp, Gen. Abrams strode into the conference room with three staff officers in tow. Like Reb and the others in attendance, the MACV commander was dressed in olive drab jungle fatigues. Four black stars, his rank insignia, were sewn onto both of his jacket lapels. The name ABRAMS appeared above his right breast pocket. Reb noticed that unlike his uniform, the general's was immaculately cleaned and pressed. After appropriate introductions and pleasantries, the general began the ceremony. Reb and four others were to be awarded the Distinguished Service Cross, or DSC, the second-highest medal for gallantry after the Congressional Medal of Honor. Reb was dumbfounded. He had been told he was to be written up for a medal after the Hamburger Hill operation, but never thought that it would be the DSC.

The DSC may be awarded to a member of the U.S. Army for extraordinary heroism and risk of life while engaged in actual combat against an armed enemy force. During the entire Vietnam War, a thousand DSCs were awarded, 40 percent posthumously. Gen. Abrams required that he meet all living DSC recipients and personally pin the medal on their uniforms. Later Reb would learn that Abrams himself had won two DSCs in World War II in the space of four months!

As Reb was the junior-ranking DSC recipient that day, his citation was read last. As far as he could recall, his citation accurately recited the facts of his several days on Hill 937, although he thought some of the descriptive adjectives were exaggerated. Reb was amazed at the details mentioned in his award citation and wondered how the information had been gathered and verified.

Finally, the general congratulated Reb and pinned on his medal. It was a bittersweet moment. He was extremely proud to receive such a high honor, but he could not help recalling the terrible price paid in casualties, including many guys in his platoon, to capture Hill 937. He wished he had had the guts to ask the general why he ordered Operation Apache Snow, only to abandon Hill 937 a few weeks after so much blood was shed to secure it.

In February 1970, Reb's long, eventful year in Vietnam came to an end, and he departed for home. His war experience had taught him a great deal. For one thing, he no longer looked upon war as glamorous. In fact, he believed that killing another man, even in a justifiable war, diminished one's humanity. Reb also learned that he possessed the fortitude and physical courage to lead men in combat while being exposed to great personal peril, and the moral courage to stand up to a superior officer and refuse to carry out a dishonorable order. Finally, Reb appreciated how much luck, or more likely divine Providence, had determined his fate. On multiple occasions, a soldier by his side was killed in action, yet Reb escaped unscathed or with relatively minor wounds. Sgt. McCoy returned home a highly decorated soldier, having been awarded the DSC, a Bronze Star, and two Purple Hearts. Best of all, he returned home physically and psychologically sound.

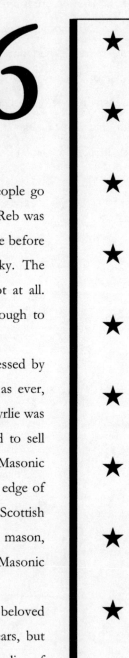

6

Although Springfield, Ohio, is not where most people go on vacation in winter, or summer for that matter, Reb was happy to be there enjoying some well-deserved leave before he reported for duty at Fort Campbell, Kentucky. The bitter cold and occasional snow bothered him not at all. The joy of being back home in America was enough to keep him warm.

Hillcrest looked the same, but Reb was distressed by Myrlie's frail appearance. Her mind was as sharp as ever, but she looked older than her seventy-five years. Myrlie was cognizant of her physical decline and had decided to sell Hillcrest come spring and move to the Springfield Masonic Home, an extended-care retirement facility on the edge of town. Reb's grandfather had been a 33rd degree Scottish Rite Master Freemason, so, as the widow of a mason, Myrlie was eligible to take up residence in the Masonic Home.

Reb at first protested Myrlie's giving up her beloved Hillcrest, where she had lived for nearly forty years, but soon conceded that her decision was correct. Myrlie, of course, was thrilled to have her grandson home and healthy. She decided immediately that Reb needed more meat on his six-foot-two frame and proceeded to bake all his favorite pastries and prepare three farm-style meals a day. Reb basked in her attention, but knew he could not eat her cooking for long, or he soon would make Jackie Gleason look anorexic by comparison.

Unfortunately, Lola was not around. Myrlie informed him that she had transferred from Wittenberg University in Springfield to Case Western Reserve University in Cleveland, where she was studying engineering. Reb thought about driving to Cleveland to see Lola, but decided he should spend all of his three-week leave with Myrlie. Who knew how many more times he would see her? Not only was she his entire family, but he loved her dearly and was grateful for all she had done for him, especially since the loss of his parents.

Reb was saddened to learn that Myrlie had put down Heartland six months earlier, because he had developed laminitis, an incurable inflammation of the hoof. She had avoided writing Reb about it, not wanting to upset him. Heartland had been a good horse and companion, as well as witness to Reb's memorable summer of '68 frolicking with Lola.

The three-week leave in Springfield went by quickly, and Reb headed for Fort Campbell. He was assigned as a trainer for the 101st Airborne Division's air mobile school. Peacetime military service did not appeal to Reb, although it left him ample time to begin catching up on all the reading he could not do in Vietnam. The troop drawdown in Vietnam was underway, and the army suddenly had more soldiers than it needed. Reb submitted a request for early discharge from active duty so that he could start college. Reb's enlistment was due to expire in August 1971, but because of his outstanding service record, he was able to accelerate that by a year, allowing him to begin college in September 1970.

In anticipation of an early discharge, Reb began the college application process almost as soon as he arrived at Fort Campbell. His first choice was Rice University in Houston. He wanted a first-rate school in Texas, and one that had a high ratio of graduate-to-undergraduate students, so he could mingle with students his age. Rice met these criteria, and he met theirs. Reb majored in chemical engineering, with lots of elective history courses. Wanting to close the gap with his peer age group, Reb attended summer session and was able to graduate in three years, in June 1973.

The Rice curriculum was rigorous, but Reb was comfortable in academia and earned a high grade-point average. Still, he found time for a social life. During his second year, Reb met a single mother at a popular dance club near campus. Her name was April Honeysuckle, and she was the first woman since Lola to become his steady girlfriend. April was tall, blonde, attractive, and affectionate, and had a great body. She grew up on a farm in Nebraska, came to Houston to escape the ennui of the rural plains, married, and was divorced shortly after her little girl was born. Lacking only fifteen credit hours to earn her degree in biology, April was working as a legal secretary and taking evening classes three nights a week.

April always dressed and behaved in public like a girl who had gone to the best finishing school, but just beneath the surface was a smoldering woman who enjoyed, needed, and talked about sex more than the average guy with a supercharged libido. She was fun to be with, and she could find a sexual connotation in almost any innocent remark. When Reb asked her if Honeysuckle was her married or maiden name, April laughed and replied, "While nobody can accuse me of being a maiden, Honeysuckle is the name I was born with, and I'm trying to live up to it."

On their first dinner date, Reb was regaling April with his hackneyed jokes. He sensed that she had heard most of them before, but that didn't keep her from laughing at them more than they deserved. After a cocktail or two, Reb felt uninhibited enough to steer the conversation in a more intimate direction. "Did you know there are two kinds of women, April?"

Before he could answer his own question, assuming she would say no, she shot back in a deadpan, matter-of-fact manner, "Swallowers and spitters," as if everyone knew the answer to that question.

Reb's jaw half dropped and he broke up in laughter. The answer he had planned to give was "girls who either do or do not have sex on a first date."

After a pause, April added with a flirty smile, "When I was a little tomboy and trying to be like the boys playing sandlot baseball, my mother sternly admonished me never to spit, because it was impolite and unladylike. Not wanting to disappoint mother, since then, I have never disobeyed her."

Later during their main course, April mentioned that shortly after her two-year-old daughter was born, she had to undergo a partial hysterectomy. Reb told her he was sorry to hear this, but hoped she had fully recovered. April replied, "Oh, yes, I'm fine. The bad news is I can't have any more children. But the good news is I don't have to worry about getting pregnant. Makes my social life less complicated." Reb almost choked on his wine.

Before dessert arrived, Reb inquired about April's childhood, and she announced, "I'm from Nebraska, where they say the corn grows tall and the farm girls have big knockers."

Reb pondered a moment and replied, "Never having been to Nebraska, I don't know about the corn, but, assuming you are a typical Nebraska lass, I'm convinced the farm girls there have big knockers."

As they were getting ready to leave the restaurant, Reb remarked about an attractive woman who passed their booth as to whether her blonde hair was natural or bleached. April leaned over and whispered in his ear, "I bet she's bleached, but one thing is sure: I'm a natural blonde, honey, and when you take me home, I'll be happy to prove it."

Reb wasn't sure he would be able to stand up to leave. When they got to her place, she proceeded to give him a night to remember. Not even Lola had been as enthusiastic and uninhibited about sex as April was. She enjoyed everything. Within a couple weeks, Reb was sleeping at her place the four nights a week she did not have evening classes. April was obviously interested early on in a permanent arrangement, but Reb was not, and in any case, he was not in love with her.

If he couldn't feel love for a girl like April, Reb began to wonder if he ever would fall in love. Had the loss of his parents closed off his heart for fear of having it broken again? Here was a woman who satisfied his every physical need and loved to cook for him too. One night in the throes of passion, she grabbed Reb's face in her hands and said in all sincerity, "I want you to know, Reb, you can have me anytime, anywhere, and any way."

Reb tried to make light of her comment saying, "Yeah, sure. But how often will you tell me, 'Not tonight, honey, I have a headache'?"

"Never, because I've found that the best way to cure and prevent headaches is to have lots of sex. Now, get back here; I feel a headache coming on."

Afterward, Reb said, "April, is there anything you think of more than sex?"

"Not when you're around. Is there anything you think about more than sex?"

"Not since I met you. At this rate, you're going to kill me, but I'll die smiling."

April looked at him with a grin. "You better not complain unless you aren't completely satisfied. Did you know there are more synonyms for the words penis, vagina, and breast than any other words in the English language? I figure that proves that sex, or at least penises, vaginas, and breasts must be what most healthy people think about most of the time."

Whether or not April's insight was accurate, Reb had no doubt that April knew everyone of those synonyms, because she enjoyed talking lewdly while having sex. Where a nice, wholesome Nebraska girl learned all that April knew about sex, Reb could not imagine.

Despite the fun they had together, as time passed, Reb gradually came to see that while April was all loving and available, she also was a controlling, possessive, and passively domineering personality. She gave completely and willingly of herself, but in return she expected to know where Reb was at all times, whom he was with, and how she could reach him by phone a couple times a day. Reb was feeling smothered. As much as he genuinely liked April, loved having sex with her, and enjoyed her pampering, he couldn't deal with answering her every beck and call.

Finally, after a year of being together and a month before he graduated from Rice, April saw him innocently chatting and laughing with a female student from one of his engineering courses. Later, she confronted him and went into an ugly, jealous tirade. At that moment, Reb knew he had to break off the relationship. Besides, to go on any longer was unfair to April, because she wanted him to marry her, and that wasn't going to happen.

Although tempted to get a job and begin his career immediately after commencement, Reb decided that he would be better off getting an MBA degree first. He intended to make his home in Texas, preferably in Dallas, so he chose to enroll at Southern Methodist University, which also distanced him from the temptation to patch things up with April. Attending SMU turned out to be the most important and fortunate decision of his life, because there he would finally meet the love of his life, future wife, and lifelong companion.

In the fall of his first year at SMU, Reb caught a glimpse of Marlenna Milano in the library one evening, apparently with a girlfriend. At that time, Reb did not know her name, but her style, self-assuredness, and beauty took his breath away. She obviously had emerged from the deep end of the gene pool. As Myrlie would say, Marlenna was a looker. Her figure was stunning, but it was her laugh and expressive eyes that compelled him to stare at her from a distance of perhaps twenty feet with his mouth partially opened. Luckily for Reb, she was unaware of his ogling presence, or she might have assumed him to be a masher and never have agreed to go out with him. Reb also observed that virtually every guy, who noticed and walked by her, even if he was with another girl, allowed his eyes an extra moment to linger approvingly. Yet, Marlenna never appeared to be aware of this attention. This was a woman out of Reb's league, but he had to find out who she was and try to get a date.

Amateur detective work and a couple of lucky breaks provided the information that Reb needed to locate Marlenna and ask her out on a date. Twenty years old, she was an SMU junior and liberal arts major. Best of all, she did not have a steady boyfriend. Apparently, her forbidding Italian father scared most suitors off, but that would not deter Reb. Daddy was a prominent Dallas restaurateur. Milano's had been for years one of the city's best steak and Italian eateries, a favorite watering hole for business moguls and politicians.

When they finally met, Marlenna turned out to be as captivating, warm, and friendly as she was drop-dead gorgeous. She also was strong-willed, intelligent, and loved to laugh. Reb was about to fall in love for the first and only time in his life. On their second date, they went dancing, one of Marlenna's favorite activities. Reb was grateful that he had taken a ballroom dancing class at WMAC. That experience helped him to learn quickly the new dance steps that Marlenna liked. By their third date, Reb was ready to get married, but knew he was moving too fast for Marlenna.

While it didn't occur to him at the time, Marlenna's Italian ancestry and great genes would prolong her beauty well into her seventies, as with Sophia

In time, perhaps in desperation, they sought comfort and solace in a higher power and recaptured their Christian faith. They also began attending meetings of The Compassionate Friends in Dallas, and found that they were not alone in having lost a child. Being able to talk to others who had experienced similar tragedy helped them to deal with their bereavement. From that time onward, they supported this organization with their time and charitable contributions.

Reb and Marlenna survived their grief from hour to hour, then day by day. As the days and weeks passed, their intense heartache slowly softened. Within several months, Reb recovered his emotional equilibrium. He willed himself to be strong for Marlenna. Many nights he held her in his arms as she cried herself to sleep. Nearly a year would pass before she fully regained her naturally sunny disposition and spontaneous, enchanting laugh that Reb so loved to hear.

Gradually they came to accept the undeniable truth that life is not only for the living, but also a wondrous gift that must be celebrated and put to useful purpose. Pain and suffering are inescapable aspects of life to be borne with faith, hope, and courage. Kyle would live on in Reb's and Marlenna's hearts as a cherished memory of life's beauty and wonder. Their mourning would end, but never would a day pass that Reb and Marlenna did not think of their little boy and feel profound gratitude for the tremendous love and happiness he had brought to them during his too brief life.

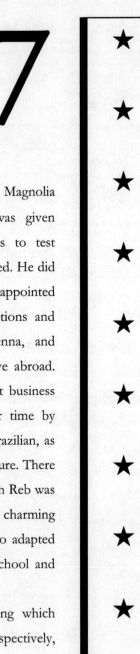

7

Early in his career, Reb was identified by Magnolia management as having high potential. He was given challenging assignments and rapid promotions to test whether his high potential designation was justified. He did well in every job he was given. In 1990, Reb was appointed president of Magnolia's South American operations and transferred to São Paulo, Brazil. He, Marlenna, and Ravenna were excited by the opportunity to live abroad. Reb's position required long hours and frequent business trips, but the independent Marlenna filled her time by becoming fluent in Portuguese, making many Brazilian, as well as American, friends, and embracing the culture. There were many business-related social events, at which Reb was happy and proud to have Marlenna by his side, charming everyone she met. Ravenna, now a teenager, also adapted easily to her new environment, doing well in school and making many new friends.

After five successful years in Brazil, during which Magnolia's South American sales and profits, respectively, doubled and tripled, Reb was reassigned to Magnolia's Dallas headquarters and promoted to vice president of the company's global chemicals business. Three years later, he was named head of Magnolia's global petroleum operations. With this appointment, it became clear that Reb was the odds-on favorite to replace Magnolia's CEO when he retired in 2002.

By this time, Reb and Marlenna were wealthy, but they eschewed conspicuous consumption, except for Marlenna's wardrobe and their lovely home. They now lived in a recently renovated, large stone house built in 1940 that featured a slate roof and casement windows and was situated on two beautifully landscaped acres in Highland Park, one of the most prestigious residential communities in Dallas. Affluence had not changed either of them. Reb and Marlenna remained down-to-earth people who never put on airs or considered themselves superior to those less fortunate or affluent.

At age fifty-two, Reb McCoy was appointed chairman and CEO of Magnolia Petroleum & Chemical Company. His climb to the top had been meteoric, but virtually all his colleagues agreed that he was an excellent choice. Reb recognized luck had much to do with his career success. Other Magnolia executives were as smart as or smarter than Reb, but few worked harder than he did. What differentiated Reb from his colleagues was his conviction that the only constant in life is change. Values, principles, self-evident truths, and the laws of physics are constant, but virtually all else is compelled to change. He believed there is no lasting status quo, no matter how successful or dominant an individual or company might be. People and organizations must continuously change, adapt, and grow, or they will inevitably stagnate, atrophy, and die. He was committed to change not for the sake of change, but for continuous improvement and greater excellence.

The natural instinct of most people is to defend the status quo, reject change, and embrace new ideas only if forced to do so. Reb observed that often there was an inverse correlation between how high an individual rose in an organization and his or her receptivity to change. Many successful people develop inflated egos and become increasingly smug and arrogant the higher they ascend the corporate ladder. Those at the highest levels tend instinctively to believe that they are infallible in their business judgment. Their vision of the future is a continuation of the past, only better.

The management of a large, hierarchical organization with a long history of success typically is resistant to change, because its deeply embedded culture tends to reject people who don't conform. Therefore, change agents often are discouraged or purged. Similar to coronary artery disease, the decline of a large corporation usually occurs gradually and unnoticed over a long period of time. Management insiders often ignore the trend, deny it, or rationalize it as temporary until it is too late to reverse the decline. Reb understood this psychology. To overcome it, he approached his superiors with ideas for change by subtly crediting them for the ideas. This stroked their egos and won the imprimatur of the organization to adopt a proposed change. Reb was more interested in obtaining results than receiving credit, but as his career progressed, he came to be viewed as a proactive change agent who was a team player.

In the decade Reb was CEO of Magnolia, he succeeded in transforming the company from a lackluster performer into a highly profitable and competitive enterprise. The petroleum operations were the first to be reorganized. Reb sold off the downstream refining business, because it was a capital-intensive, cyclical business with volatile profitability. He decided that Magnolia should concentrate on its upstream petroleum exploration and production business. It too required enormous amounts of capital investment, but investment returns were consistently high, despite the volatile price of crude oil in the global market.

Next, Reb addressed his attention to Magnolia's chemical operations. Its profitability was hurt by a number of old-line commodity businesses that required lots of capital, but generated mediocre profits. He divested these units to focus on the specialty and proprietary product lines in which Magnolia enjoyed pricing power and a strong competitive position. The funds realized from selling off assets and businesses were used to retire debt, invest in core business units, and make strategic acquisitions.

In addition to redefining the company's strategic vision, Reb put his stamp on Magnolia's culture. He stressed integrity, safety, excellence, and performance as the four essential attributes, by which all employees would be measured. He also preached that every task, every dollar spent must be to serve, in order of priority, customers, community, colleagues, and shareholders, and that all four stakeholders had to be satisfied for the business to be successful. For Reb, these values were not said for show, they were the essence of what he demanded of himself and expected of everyone else in the company's employ, particularly management.

The compensation system he instituted was built around these values. All Magnolia employees with five or more years of service were eligible for profit-sharing, provided threshold earnings targets established at the start of each year and disseminated to all employees were exceeded. This made eligible employees partners in the company's success. In addition, employees at relatively junior levels were eligible for annual performance bonuses paid out in stock and cash. Senior executives also could be granted stock options that would vest only if Magnolia's performance over three- and five-year periods exceeded established benchmarks.

Reb understood, however, that money alone did not motivate people for very long. What most people want is a challenging job, a reasonable degree of autonomy to do their job within the company's values framework, and recognition. The profit-sharing plan was a tangible way to recognize employees at all levels of the organization as partners and true colleagues.

A controversial policy that Reb had established as CEO was to close the company's political action committee that made contributions to political candidates, and to end all lobbying by Magnolia of either state or federal legislators and agencies for special tax breaks or other benefits for the company. He believed that the incessant growth in crony capitalism going back fifty years was a threat to the free enterprise system, and he didn't want Magnolia to participate in it. The indirect exchange of money for political favors, the special deals and "free lunches" for certain favored companies, and the manipulation of regulatory agencies to favor one firm at the expense of a competitor or the public was cynical and corrupt, even if technically legal.

Of course, the more government enacted laws and regulations affecting the private sector, the more inevitable it became for the private sector, especially large companies with great wealth and influence, to try to gain advantage or limit constraints on their business activities. President Eisenhower, Reb's old hero from his days as a plebe at WMAC, wisely warned the nation in his 1961 farewell address about the military-industrial complex. The problem today was far more pervasive and menacing. The United States now faced, Reb believed, an incestuous political/regulatory-big business complex, or crony capitalism, that was undermining individual free enterprise and liberty.

Eight years after becoming CEO, Magnolia's sales had doubled to over $25 billion; net earnings had nearly quadrupled to $4 billion, and the company's stock price had more than doubled. Reb successfully navigated the company through the financial market meltdown and recession that ensued from the implosion of the housing bubble in 2008. Despite this stellar performance, as Reb and his senior management team looked to the future, they concluded that over the long term, Magnolia probably could not compete successfully against its far bigger rivals, especially in an uncertain economic environment. Both the chemical and petroleum industries for some time had been consolidating to achieve economies of scale and amass the capital necessary to compete in the global marketplace. Moreover, Wall Street could not decide whether Magnolia was a petroleum concern or a chemical company; consequently, its stock generally traded at a lower premium than its peers in either industry, making it a likely acquisition target.

In the face of this reality, the board of directors decided in late 2011, Magnolia's centennial year, to find a merger partner or a buyer for the company. In 2012, after evaluating prospective partners and buyers, Magnolia's board voted to sell the petroleum business to Conoco, a major oil concern, and to sell the chemicals business to the DuPont Company, a large chemical manufacturer. In addition, the Magnolia Building, the company's twenty-nine-story corporate headquarters in Dallas since 1922, along with its iconic corporate logo atop the building—the neon Flying Red Horse Pegasus—would be sold to a private hospitality management company and converted into a boutique hotel. The total per-share value in stock and cash of the combined transactions was 30 percent higher than the price of Magnolia's stock the day before the deals were announced. Over 85 percent of Magnolia's nearly twenty-five thousand employees would have equivalent jobs and benefits with Conoco or DuPont. Those whose jobs were eliminated would receive generous severance packages and job-placement assistance.

When the deals closed in June 2012, Magnolia Petroleum & Chemical Company, founded in 1911, passed out of existence and into history. While it was a bittersweet end to an era, Reb understood that Magnolia's fate was a part of the natural, never-ending process of "creative destruction" inherent in free-enterprise capitalism. At age sixty-two, Reb McCoy was out of a job, but the value he received for his Magnolia stock and stock options exceeded $200 million. As CEO, Reb reaped the highest payout, but many other employees received million-dollar-plus payouts, and those relatively junior level employees, who had held onto their profit-sharing stock over the years, realized six-figure payouts.

Because of his reputation, Reb received, unsolicited, several CEO offers from marquee companies. While flattered by the offers, he declined them all, because he felt that ten years as CEO of a large enterprise was enough. Such a job, at least the way he approached it, typically meant seventy-hour workweeks, plus extensive travel and frequent business-related entertaining. He still had the energy, but he no longer possessed the "fire in the belly" drive common to almost every successful CEO. Moreover, piling up more money was no incentive, because he had amassed more than he and Marlenna could ever spend.

Finally, neither he nor Marlenna was willing to leave Dallas at this point in their lives. Ravenna, now thirty-five years old, was a physician in Dallas, married to Jeff Hamilton, a Dallas architect rising in prominence. Both Marlenna and Reb were very fond of Jeff; a better son-in-law they could not imagine. Ravenna and Jeff were the parents of precocious two-year-old fraternal twins, Kyle and Deanna, whom Marlenna and Reb spoiled and adored. Marlenna was ecstatic when Ravenna and Jeff named their son after her late brother, and with Deanna extended the family's naming tradition to the fifth generation.

Within a fortnight of closing the Magnolia deal, Reb instructed his financial advisor to donate $100 million to the Marcoy Foundation that he and Marlenna had established with a gift of $15 million several years earlier. Both he and Marlenna were grateful for all their blessings and shared a strong commitment to philanthropy. Over the remainder of their lives, they planned to make additional seven-figure annual gifts to their foundation.

The timing of the Magnolia asset sale was fortuitous, because it came a couple months before another sharp drop in the stock market in the fall of 2012, which was attributed to Washington's inability to rein in the federal government's trillion-dollar-a-year deficits. Neither Reb nor his financial advisor had a premonition about the coming market meltdown, but his and Marlenna's personal wealth after the large gift to Marcoy Foundation was about $120 million and too heavily concentrated in Conoco and DuPont stock, plus other equities. The bulk of their wealth was reinvested in various high-quality tax-exempt and taxable bonds, with the remainder in a diversified stock portfolio. Their medium-term objective was to preserve principal, minimize taxes, and generate substantial annual income. When the stock market plunged, the market value of their investments fared far better than that of the average investor.

In August 2012, Reb and Marlenna embarked on an extended stay in Europe. They decided to sail over on the Cunard Line's *Queen Mary*. The first two months would be spent at a rented villa near Siena, Italy, after which they would tour the continent until Christmas, when they would fly home to celebrate the holidays with Ravenna, Jeff, and the twins.

Reb and Marlenna turned the Atlantic crossing and their entire sojourn in Europe into a honeymoon. He still adored Marlenna at fifty-eight, as much as he had when they were first married. Her preternatural beauty, quick wit, charming laugh, and allure were ever captivating. As desirable as Marlenna was dressed, she was even more so undressed. And the combination of her natural body scent with her favorite perfume, Obsession, only heightened his desire for her. They both were amused and grateful that they still eagerly enjoyed making love on a regular basis.

One evening, after they had settled into their leased Italian villa enjoying a postprandial lemoncello and the sunset, Marlenna asked Reb what he planned to do once they returned to Dallas. It was a good question. He had already declined an offer to run for vice president of the United States, and several corporate opportunities. "I'm not sure, pretty. Guess there isn't much point sitting around counting our money. Earlier today, I looked at our investment statement. Compound interest is an incredible wealth multiplier. Did you know that when asked to name man's greatest invention, Einstein reputedly replied the concept of compound interest?"

"No, Reb, I did not know that," Marlenna replied dryly, suggesting she was unimpressed. "But then poor old Einstein didn't live long enough to see the invention of Viagra and Astroglide. If he had, I bet he would have said they topped compound interest. What do you think?"

Reb laughed. "I think you're right, as usual, pretty."

Marlenna returned to her original question, "What do you want to do with your time? I don't think managing the foundation will keep you fully occupied."

"You're right. Ding Bell called me after he learned I had turned down Maggie Thurston's offer to be her running mate. He is urging me to take an active role on the Madison Committee that he wants to organize when I get back to Dallas. I just may do that, because I see America will soon reach a tipping point when the idea of liberty, safeguarded by a government of limited powers, will have been lost forever. It may already be too late."

D. Ewing "Ding" Bell was the senior U.S. senator from Texas and a good friend of Reb's for many years. Ding liked to say that he was a quarter Comanche Indian, a quarter cowboy, and half grizzly bear. A burly, savvy man with an incandescent personality and booming laugh, he was a legendary figure in Texas. Born and raised on a west Texas cattle ranch where a large oilfield was discovered when he was still a boy, Ding was wealthy, even by Texas standards. At age fifty, he accepted a dare and ran against an incumbent U.S. senator as a conservative Republican and won. Now in his mid-sixties, he was in his third term. Marlenna knew Ding and liked both him and his politics.

"What can this Madison Committee do to have any effect on the direction of the country? And couldn't you have had a more immediate and greater impact on the country's direction as vice president?" Marlenna asked.

"To your second question, no, I don't think so, because the vice president has no independent authority and must support the president without reservation. By definition, he is a Washington insider, part of the establishment. Only political outsiders, insurgents like the tea party, for example, can have any hope of bringing about real change. I doubt that change will ever emanate from the Washington fraternity of elected politicians."

"Well, back to my first question, how can the Madison Committee bring about needed change?"

"I'm not sure, but it may have some potential to shake people out of their apathy and help them appreciate what may soon be lost if we don't change direction. Then again, it might have no more lasting impact than skipping a flat stone across a placid pond. Our generation is primarily responsible for the increasing disregard for the Constitution and the fiscal catastrophe we face. For the sake of Kyle and Deanna and future generations, I feel that I at least have to try to do something instead of just bitch about it.

"You know, pretty, as I reflect on the precarious state of our country, I have come to realize that in order to protect and preserve the legacy of freedom bequeathed to America by our Founding Fathers, each subsequent generation of Americans is called to honor liberty by securing its blessings to posterity. So far every generation has answered the call. What will be the epitaph for our generation?"

Silently, Marlenna reached out for Reb's hand, and together they marveled at the brilliant crimson sky as the setting sun dipped below the horizon. She had a mild, inexplicable sense of foreboding that their lives soon would be changed forever.

8

Shortly before Reb and Marlenna departed on their European vacation, Sen. Ding Bell had invited Reb to become a charter member of the Madison Committee. Named in honor of the Father of the Constitution and fourth president of the United States, James Madison, the committee was formed to discuss ideas for restoring the concept of a federal government exercising limited powers, as enumerated in the Constitution that Madison played the most prominent role in drafting.

Over the past seventy-five years, the federal government, irrespective of which political party held the majority, had steadily expanded its power beyond what was contemplated in the Constitution and its subsequent amendments. Today, the federal government is virtually omnipotent and has no effective check on its power. Even public opinion strongly opposed to a particular government action or policy often is disregarded. Gradually, many powers and rights that once inhered in the states and the people have been usurped or denied by the federal government.

The cumulative effect of this ever-expanding power has been to make the individual citizen increasingly dependent on the federal government at the cost of individual liberty. It is axiomatic that the more power, control, and influence the government has over the individual, the less power, control, and influence the individual has over him or herself. Moreover, the unfunded financial obligations of the federal government have grown exponentially, thereby saddling future generations of Americans with the enormous costs of entitlement programs and benefits enjoyed by the current generation. Because of these legal but actuarially unsound government-imposed Ponzi schemes, America's young and unborn will face diminished liberty and prospects for pursuing happiness, two unalienable rights, by which all people are endowed by their Creator.

Sen. Bell and Reb arranged to meet for lunch at Milano's in a private booth usually reserved for Mrs. McCoy. Marlenna had taken over management of the restaurant after her father died some years before. In 2005, she sold the business, including the real estate. The new owner wanted to continue using the Milano's name, which was highly regarded by discriminating Dallas diners. In exchange, Marlenna received a minority ownership interest in the new restaurant, a commitment by management to maintain the high standards and quality that had been associated for many years with her father's eatery, and a specific booth now occupied by Reb and Ding.

As was his custom, Ding ordered a single malt scotch on the rocks, and Reb had his usual Arnold Palmer, half iced tea and half lemonade, on the rocks in a short glass. After downing his drink in two gulps, Ding turned to business. "Reb, we both are concerned with the direction the country is headed, and in particular, the ceaseless erosion of the Constitution. Both parties have contributed to the problem, although as a Republican, from my biased perspective, the Democrats have more to answer for, but there is plenty of blame to go all around."

Pausing to order another drink, Ding went on, "Over my fifteen years in the Senate, the partisanship on both sides of the aisle has gotten out of hand. We no longer deliberate up there. We mostly yell and shout and impugn each other's motives. And it's even worse in the House. Too many people in both parties have greater loyalty to their respective party's interests than to the national interest. And the Constitution generally is ignored, except to excoriate with hypocritical piety the other side when it suits one's purposes."

Reb interjected, "My sense is that we have abandoned the notion of being a government of laws. Instead, we have descended into being a government of arrogant men and women who believe they are an elite, enlightened ruling class. Anything that can command a majority vote becomes law, whether or not it is constitutional. Also, unelected judges have too often expanded their legitimate role of interpreting the law to legislating from the bench. This has gone on for so long, how can it be changed?"

"To be honest, Reb, it may too late to change without a revolution, and I don't see that happening. Maybe we need a third party."

"Ding, you know the history of third parties. Ross Perot in 1992, George Wallace in 1968, Strom Thurmond in 1948, and former president Teddy Roosevelt in 1912 all ran serious campaigns for president on third party tickets, but none came close to winning. What's the point of a third party if it simply results in tilting the election to one or the other major parties?"

"Look, you may be right. But neither the Republicans nor the Democrats will experience an epiphany that reveals to them the virtues of limited government under the Constitution without some powerful outside catalyst. Now, what I have in mind is recruiting several eminent citizens from outside politics who are well informed, successful, and imaginative. These luminaries would establish what I propose be called the Madison Committee. They would meet regularly to discuss the problem of an ever-encroaching federal government, and to consider bold ideas for reining it in. If a proper constitutional balance is ever to be restored, I believe the states will have to lead the effort. What better state to lead such a restoration than Texas? And I can think of no better citizen to chair the Madison Committee initiative than you."

"Your idea is noble, Ding, and I am flattered that you see me as leading the committee. But with all due respect, only a fool or an egomaniac would seriously think such an endeavor would have any real effect on the government. There are too many entrenched interests that benefit from the status quo. Hell hath no fury like an elected official or a crony capitalist whose political self-interest or place at the public trough is threatened."

"If we don't try, Reb, despite the odds against us, it's certain nothing will force the federal government to alter its course. We'll continue to drift along from crisis to crisis. Each crisis will provide an excuse to expand further government intrusion into the private sector. At some point, Americans will be living under a soft tyranny. Respectable, accomplished citizens like you can't sit back and do nothing. What are we going to bequeath to future Americans?"

Reb sighed and said, "Okay, Ding, I'll cogitate on this while I'm in Europe. Marlenna and I will return home for the holidays. Let's plan on getting together early in January."

"Good. In the meantime, I suggest we both think about who else we might invite to be members of the Madison Committee. I think we ought to keep it to a manageable group of six or at most eight people."

"One final thought, Ding. I understand why we should exclude politicians as committee members, because most have little credibility anymore and would undermine whatever we do. One exception to this rule, however, is that you must be involved at least as an ex officio member. I respect your judgment, and you can educate us about the politics of whatever we decide to do. We also will need someone inside the belly of the beast in Washington who can represent the Madison Committee's views."

"Agreed," replied Ding, "Have a safe and pleasant vacation in the Old World, Reb, and give my warmest regards to your beautiful wife."

"Thanks, Ding. You probably could sell shit to a sewage plant, which explains why you are a successful politician. Not sure what I am getting myself into, but my instinct tells me I am about to embark on a quixotic fool's errand."

With that, Ding stood up and announced he had to rush off to catch a plane back to Washington, DC, leaving Reb alone to pick up the check, as usual.

9

During his trip to Europe with Marlenna, Reb devoted considerable time to thinking about the Madison Committee project. He took with him a pocket copy of the Constitution and the Declaration of Independence, which he read and reread several times, something he had not done in many years.

In his notebook computer bag, Reb stuffed a paperback edition of *The Federalist*, a series of eighty-five essays written by three of the country's Founding Fathers, Madison, Alexander Hamilton, and John Jay, to promote adoption of the Constitution, which was drafted in Philadelphia during the summer of 1787. These commentaries were written and published in the popular press during the year following the Constitutional Convention, and are invaluable to understanding the ideas and thinking of the Framers as they drafted the Constitution.

Even though written by a "bunch of dead white guys," the two-hundred-twenty-five-year-old Constitution was still as relevant in the twenty-first century as it was when it was drafted in the eighteenth century. Reb marveled at the genius of the men who created a democratic republic predicated on the ideals of self-government and individual liberty. At the time, the countries of Europe were governed by hereditary monarchs or military strongmen. The idea of common citizens governing themselves through elected representatives with fixed terms of office was astounding.

The Constitution created a federal government divided into three coequal and interdependent branches: legislative, executive, and judicial. The legislative and executive branches were each granted specific powers, but generally could not exercise those powers without the consent of the other. This separation of powers was intended to guard against an inordinate and dangerous concentration of power in one branch, in particular the executive, or president. The Constitution vested legislative power in a bicameral Congress, consisting of a House of Representatives whose members were apportioned by population and elected to two-year terms of office, and a Senate comprised of two members from each state elected to six-year terms of office.

By giving each state equal representation in the Senate, regardless of size, smaller states could not be dominated and rendered irrelevant by larger states. This fine balance established the new government as a federation of equal, sovereign states that had delegated limited and specific powers to the federal government, but all other rights and powers were retained by the states or their respective citizens. This concept was reinforced with adoption of the Ninth and Tenth Amendments as part of the Bill of Rights.

All legislation must be passed by majority vote of both the House and Senate before being forwarded to the president for approval, after which it becomes law. If the president disapproves the legislation via the veto power, it is returned to Congress, which can override the veto with a two-thirds majority vote in both the House and the Senate. Any law challenged in federal court, the judicial branch, ultimately may be appealed to the Supreme

Court, which may decide to uphold the law, or overturn it, provided a majority of the nine justices determine some or all of it is unconstitutional.

The Constitution was far from perfect. Slavery, America's original sin, was a fact of life in the eighteenth century, and would not be abolished until ratification of the Thirteenth Amendment in 1865, following the Civil War. It was not until 1920, with adoption of the Nineteenth Amendment, that women were guaranteed the right to vote, although many states had granted women suffrage long before then.

To have the Constitution adopted, which required ratification by nine of the thirteen original states, assurances had to be given that it would be amended with a Bill of Rights. Accordingly, during the first Congress in 1789, Madison proposed twelve amendments, ten of which were adopted in 1791. Collectively known as the Bill of Rights, these ten amendments guaranteed, among other things, freedom of religion, speech and the press, and the rights to bear arms, due process of law, and a speedy trial by impartial jury.

The Ninth and Tenth Bill of Rights Amendments, Reb thought, were the most important to securing individual liberty, because they explicitly established the limits of the federal government's power. In his layman's opinion, however, over the past half century, these amendments too often were overlooked or ignored by the courts, as judges rarely struck down the federal government's relentless expansion of its powers. Reb committed the Ninth and Tenth Amendments to memory:

> • "The enumeration in the Constitution of certain rights shall not be construed to deny or disparage others retained by the people."

> • "The powers not delegated to the United States by the Constitution, nor prohibited by it to the States, are reserved to the States respectively, or to the people."

Obviously, the Framers of the Constitution intended the federal government to have limited, enumerated powers, rather than broad, unlimited powers. Reb noted with interest how Madison addressed this subject in *Federalist No. 45* in which he wrote:

> "The powers delegated by the proposed Constitution to the federal government are few and defined. Those, which are to remain in the State governments, are numerous and indefinite. The former will be exercised principally on external objects, as war, peace, negotiation, and foreign commerce.... The powers reserved to the several States will extend to all objects, which, in the ordinary course of affairs, concern the lives, liberties, and properties of the people, and the internal order, improvement, and prosperity of the State."

Given the federal government's ever-increasing scope and power, Reb wondered whether today any individual rights and freedoms would be respected by the federal government without the Bill of Rights standing as a bulwark against tyranny. The Framers understood the inexorable tendency of government for aggrandizement at the expense of individual liberty. Therefore, they took great care to design adequate safeguards in the Constitution to restrain and control this tendency. But if the men and women entrusted by the people to govern them disregard these safeguards, government will be unconstrained and liberty inevitably diminished. In a speech during the 1788 Virginia Convention to consider ratification of the Constitution, Madison offered this prophetic admonition:

> "I believe there are more instances of the abridgment of the freedom of the people by gradual and silent encroachments of those in power than by violent and sudden usurpations."

A few days before Reb and Marlenna departed Italy for the rest of their European tour, Marlenna remarked, "Honey, you seem so pensive. What's on your mind?"

They were enjoying a warm autumn afternoon on the terrace of their rented villa overlooking the rolling Tuscan landscape, much of it covered in a blanket of bright red poppies. No wonder so many artists are moved to paint such scenes. Marlenna was in her bikini, looking tan and delicious as always, with one leg pulled up and the other stretched out on the chaise lounge. For all her charms, Reb found her long, shapely legs particularly appealing. He loved just to look at her and be grateful she shared her life with him. Normally he would be holding her hand or gently caressing her leg when they were sunning in the privacy of their terrace, but this afternoon his mind was far away.

"Oh, sorry, pretty, lost in thought."

"About what?" she asked.

"Oh, you know I've been reading and thinking about the Constitution of late." He held up his pocket edition of the document and went on, "Marlenna, did you ever consider what a miracle it is that an eighteenth-century document written by hand on parchment, which fills only forty-two printed pages in this little booklet, could still be the fundamental law governing the United States in the twenty-first century?"

"No, I guess, like most every American, I take the Constitution for granted. Years ago, I remember reading *Miracle at Philadelphia,* Catherine Drinker Bowen's wonderful book about the Constitutional Convention. I recall being so impressed by the brilliance of the men who wrote the Constitution and the intellectual quality of their debates. We could use some brilliant men and women in politics today, but I would settle for serious, intelligent debate of the major issues the country faces."

"The Framers were brilliant men," Reb agreed, "but as true as that is, they could not possibly have foreseen how wealthy and diverse the country would become, much less the unimaginable technological advances we take for granted. And yet, the Constitution they drafted in the summer of 1787 was flexible enough to accommodate all the changes in American society since then. Excluding the Bill of Rights, which really ought to be considered as part of the original Constitution, it has been amended only seventeen times, and one of those amendments repealed an earlier amendment that unwisely imposed prohibition on the country."

"Yes," replied Marlenna, who was well informed and enjoyed cool-headed conversation and debate, "but it seems to me that modern politicians and judges have stretched it far beyond what it says or what was intended. So, we have had de facto amendments. Certainly the men who created our government never envisioned that it would consume 25 percent of the country's economy as it has the last couple years. That can be called many things, but not limited government."

"I agree. In recent decades, the Constitution's remarkable flexibility has evolved into elasticity, and in several important ways it has been stretched close to the breaking point. Still, think of its durability and adaptability. In 1787, the country's population was just under four million, including seven hundred thousand slaves. Nearly 95 percent of the people lived in rural areas. Today, the U.S. population tops 300 million and is a melting pot of races and ethnicities. Only 19 percent reside in rural areas; the rest are urban dwellers like us. By the end of the 1860s, slavery had been abolished; a country of thirteen original states on the eastern seaboard extended from the Atlantic to the Pacific, connected by a transcontinental railroad; and Alaska had been acquired from Russia. By the 1920s, electricity, automobiles, the telephone, and radio were widespread, the airplane had been invented, and the U.S. was the world's preeminent power following the end of World War I in 1918.

"In the century since," Reb continued, "the country endured the Great Depression, prevailed in World War II, won the Cold War, and for better or worse, instituted the New Deal and the Great Society. Over that same period, we have witnessed phenomenal technological breakthroughs such as the splitting of the atom, air conditioning, television, the container ship, computers, cell phones, the Internet, and the landing of men on the moon.

Even more incredible than these achievements may be all the miracle drugs and medical breakthroughs that have increased both quality and length of life. Most of these developments have occurred in our lifetimes, and many were inconceivable when I was born in 1950. And yet our eighteenth-century Constitution, sometimes battered and tattered, has provided the basis by which we have governed our affairs for well over two hundred years."

"That's all true and generally wonderful," Marlenna remarked, "but what about the future? Will the Constitution survive another hundred years? Or will it become just a historical document in a glass case that politicians pay pious lip service to, but then go out and do whatever they wish? I read somewhere once that the Soviet Union's Constitution was even better than ours in terms of the rights guaranteed to its citizens, but in practice was not worth the paper it was written on. I don't worry that we'll ever have a hard tyranny like Stalin imposed on his people, but we could be gradually headed toward a soft tyranny."

"Gosh, Marlenna, I don't think things are that bad, at least not yet, but I certainly agree the country faces enormous problems, especially the crushing debt and unfunded liabilities, that must be addressed, or America will sooner or later face financial collapse. If that happens, future generations will have much bleaker prospects and fewer opportunities than we have had. Our generation will deserve to be remembered as America's worst if that comes to pass."

"But do the politicians have the courage and the will to make hard choices?" Marlenna continued. "Is there any way to restore the bipartisanship that my father said existed from the end of World War II until the mid-1960s? I remember him telling me that the Democrats and Republicans of that era worked together on foreign policy. I think the saying was, 'Politics stops at the water's edge.' And on major domestic issues such as civil rights and Medicare, landmark legislation was passed with broad support of both parties. If today's politicians can't declare a truce and agree to work together in good faith for the good of the country, I don't see any hope for solving the debt and spending crisis."

"No question," Reb responded, "that politics today is dysfunctional and has been for years. I suppose it started with Vietnam and grew worse during Watergate. Also, over the past twenty years, the parties have become increasingly polarized. In the 1950s, both political parties were dominated by moderates; the Democrats were left of center, the Republicans right of center. Over the last twenty years or so, both parties have essentially purged moderates from their ranks. Consequently, the Democrats in general, and especially their leaders, are now far to the left, and the Republicans are equally far to the right. There is little desire or incentive to reach compromise, so both sides amuse themselves hurling verbal hand grenades at each other and blaming all the country's problems on their 'good friends on the other side of the aisle.' But as bleak as this is, we can't just give up; otherwise, we are lost. Ding Bell seems to believe that the Madison Committee may be helpful. I'm not as optimistic as he is, but I feel I can't turn down his request to become personally involved. I don't believe in tilting at windmills, and if no tangible progress is evident after six months or so, I'll declare victory and withdraw."

They both reached for their cold sodas and took a few moments to marvel silently at the beautiful view extending to the horizon. After awhile, Reb mused, "How could it be that during the Renaissance, one city here in Italy—Florence—in the span of thirty years produced three of the greatest artists in history: Botticelli, Leonardo da Vinci, and Michelangelo? Now, consider the late eighteenth century in America. Most of our Founding Fathers also were born in a span of thirty years between 1725 and 1755. The genius of Adams, Jefferson, Madison, Hamilton, Washington, and their esteemed colleagues all came together in Philadelphia either to declare independence in 1776 or to draft the Constitution in 1787. How can two such concentrations of genius—one artistic, the other political—occur without divine Providence?"

After a few minutes reflecting on Reb's rhetorical question, Marlenna commented, "The genius of the Renaissance masters and America's Founders cannot be denied. But I imagine the works of the Renaissance masters, which came two hundred to two-hundred-fifty years before America's independence, will be enjoyed by art lovers long after the artistry of the Founding Fathers turns to dust."

"Not a comforting thought, my dear, but I expect what you foresee will one day come true. I hope somehow the nation can get its act together in time to postpone your prophecy indefinitely."

10

Dallas, Texas
March 2013

The Madison Committee held its first luncheon meeting in the library off the main dining room of the Rosewood Mansion on Turtle Creek. Originally the estate of a 1920s-era Dallas cotton baron, it had been converted in 1980 into a luxury boutique hotel. The location, a few miles northwest of the city center, was chosen for its privacy and convenience to Dallas Love Field, a commercial airport just a ten-minute drive from the hotel. The date of the meeting was Saturday, March 16, 2013, the two hundred sixty-second anniversary of James Madison's birth.

In addition to Reb and Sen. Bell, others in attendance were Judge Wyatt Solomon, retired federal appellate court judge from Austin; Abigail Abbeville, distinguished professor of finance at the SMU Cox School of Business and former board member of the Dallas Federal Reserve Bank; Benjamin Pippin, an acclaimed historian of nineteenth-century America who lived in Baton Rouge, Louisiana; and Duane Darby, Reb's old friend dating back

to their time together in Vietnam and now a senior partner at the prominent Houston law firm, Bunker, Hill & Shiloh.

Reb had known for years all the people he and Ding had invited to join the Madison Committee, but, except for Darby, he had known Judge Solomon the longest. Solomon, sixty-seven years old, was a fourth-generation Texan whose great-grandfather had served under Sam Houston at the Battle of San Jacinto in 1836. There, the Texas Army, barely six weeks after the Alamo had been overrun and every defender killed, defeated the Mexican Army to gain independence and establish the Republic of Texas. Judge Wyatt was a tall, distinguished gentleman with piercing blue eyes, long white hair combed straight back from a high forehead, and a full gray mustache. He carried himself with the moral rectitude one would expect of a judge, but he had a warm and courtly personality. After graduating from the University of Texas School of Law, Judge Wyatt went into private practice in Austin. His career was interrupted by military service, which included a year in Vietnam as an army staff officer. President Reagan appointed Judge Wyatt to the federal bench in 1987, and he was elevated by President George H. W. Bush to the appellate court in 1991, where he served until retiring in 2011. He was considered by liberals to be a conservative jurist, because he interpreted the law as written and made no attempt to legislate from the bench.

Everyone at the Madison Committee's first meeting had been briefed by Reb and Ding that its purpose was to identify and agree on the most egregious breaches of the Constitution by the federal government, and to debate how the government's expanding hegemony at the expense of states' rights and individual liberty might be reversed. After everyone got settled and Reb dispensed with the preliminaries, Judge Wyatt said, "With only two months since being inaugurated, shouldn't we give President Thurston and her new administration time to set a new course for the country?"

"Wyatt, the issues we here are concerned with transcend parties and administrations," responded Reb. "I am sure President Thurston will be an improvement over the past two administrations, especially in terms of curbing runaway spending and rebuilding business confidence so the economy can begin growing again."

For the past five years, the U.S. economy had been mired in recession or at best anemic growth. The unemployment rate fluctuated between 9 and 10 percent, more than double its average level over the quarter century prior to the 2008 housing bubble burst that triggered the recession. Enormous amounts of so-called economic stimulus spending by the government had made little lasting effect. Moreover, a significant tax increase in 2012, which at the margin makes sense during a robust period of economic expansion but not during a downturn, further retarded the economic recovery, and therefore did not generate the tax revenue anticipated. Consequently, the federal budget deficits worsened. Because economic growth was tepid and credit tight, several "too big to fail" businesses were taken over by the federal government during the 2012 election year to keep them from going under. This was in addition to the banks, insurance firms, and auto companies the government had taken control and partial ownership of in 2008 and 2009 to stave off economic collapse.

Reb continued, "President Thurston has her hands full with the fallout from the Israeli attack on Iran's missile and nuclear facilities just before she took office. It appears that the U.S. will soon be in direct conflict with Iran to keep the oil lanes through the Strait of Hormuz open and to prevent an attack on the Saudi oilfields. Trying to deal with this and keeping the economy afloat will consume her administration's time for the foreseeable future. The matters we will deal with won't be a first-order priority for the president, although I believe they have to be addressed over the next few years if we ever hope to restore the federal government to its proper place in our constitutional system."

Ding Bell chimed in. "Wyatt, your point is well taken, but even if the new administration had the time and inclination to rein in the overreaching government, it has to contend with a Democratic Congress. Now normally I advocate divided government, because it tends to restrain the natural impetus to spend and expand. Even if a Republican government controlled both houses of Congress and the White House, I doubt there would be a substantive change. The nature of elected politicians of both parties, especially those who view politics as a career, which most of them do, is to give out more goodies to constituents and make them ever more dependent on government to solve their problems. Anyone who even proposes slowing the growth of a favorite program, much less actually reducing it, is shouted down by the opposition and the press as an evil, cruel misanthrope. The idea of self-reliance being an integral aspect of individual liberty began to fade away with FDR's New Deal in the 1930s. Today we are a nanny state on steroids, and we are broke."

"Picking up on your last point, Senator," interjected Abigail Abbeville, known as Abby to her friends, and Professor Abby to her students, "the U.S. debt currently is $17 trillion and has been growing at an annual rate of more than $1 trillion since 2009 because of the government's chronic budget deficit. By the way, to run an annual deficit of $1 trillion is hard work. It means the government is spending each day $2.75 billion more than it collects in taxes. Every hour, spending exceeds revenue by $114 million. Think about that. As you all know, the cumulative deficits are financed by selling government bonds. Over 50 percent of our debt is held by foreign countries. At some point, those creditors will demand a higher interest rate to purchase or roll over maturing treasury notes. At current rates of about 3 percent, the annual interest on the outstanding debt is $500 billion. If rates rise to 5 percent, the annual interest will jump to $850 billion.

"People have difficulty grasping a billion of anything. A trillion is a thousand times a billion and next to impossible to conceptualize. If you could print and spend a hundred-dollar bill every second without stopping, 24/7, year in and year out, it would take just under four months to spend a billion dollars, and *three hundred seventeen years* to spend a trillion dollars. If we set aside a $100 a second to retire the current U.S. debt, it would take nearly *five thousand four hundred years* just to pay off the principal, and we would still owe the interest."

Abby paused a moment to let what she had said sink in. Born near Beaumont, Texas, into a wealthy family whose fortune was based on oil, she had been in academia her entire adult life, obtaining a PhD at the University of Chicago in both finance and economics. Now, at fifty, married and the mother of two adult children, Abby was an attractive, stylish woman who wore oversized glasses that flattered her soft features and expressive eyes. A third-generation Texan, her grandfather had witnessed Spindletop, the oil well in southeast Texas that gave birth to the word gusher, when it blew in 1901. That one well instantly increased oil production in the U.S. by 50 percent and in the world by 20 percent. Many subsequent oil discoveries across Texas and in other states would make the U.S. the biggest oil producer in the world until after World War II. Spindletop enabled the nascent automobile industry to take off, because gasoline, the safest, most convenient, and efficient way to propel a motor car, suddenly became cheap and plentiful. The gusher also ushered in the petrochemical industry and the cornucopia of products, "better things for better living through chemistry," that followed from that.

Reb always believed that January 10, the date in 1901 that oil was struck at Spindletop, should be a day of national celebration, because from that moment the American century began. All through the twentieth century, and probably the twenty-first century as well, oil was and would continue to be the basis for America's superpower status and unmatched standard of living. Oil is the lifeblood of modern society. It directly or indirectly affects virtually every aspect of the world economy and day-to-day human life. A century after Spindletop, the U.S. is no longer self-sufficient in oil. Today, nearly 70 percent of the oil consumed in the U.S. is imported, much of it from unstable or unfriendly countries. This is a significant reason for the country's chronic trade deficit, which drives the nation's indebtedness ever higher.

"But the current debt is only the tip of the iceberg," Abby continued. "The unfunded future obligations for the entitlement programs, Social Security and Medicare, are estimated by the trustees of those programs to be as high as $100 trillion. Some actuaries say the figure is much lower, but no one believes it is less than $50 trillion. That is a crushing financial burden. The country simply can't honor those obligations. Anything that can't go on forever won't. The programs have to be placed on an actuarially sound footing based on demographic reality by reducing benefits, increasing age eligibility limits, and raising taxes. The longer we wait, the more painful the adjustment. People have been sounding the alarm about this for years, but there has not been the political will or courage to address it. If we don't, however, the global financial markets at some point in the near future, I believe, will conclude the U.S. isn't going to get its fiscal house in order. At that point, confidence in the dollar will collapse, interest rates will soar, inflation will skyrocket, and the economy will go into freefall."

"Goodness, Abby, what's the bad news?" Wyatt sardonically remarked. "I feel like finding a tall building and jumping out a window. If what you foresee comes to pass, the country likely would collapse, civil society would breakdown, and some strongman probably would emerge to seize control of the government to impose order. The Constitution would be a dead letter."

Benjamin Pippin, known to all as Pip, spoke for the first time. "As bleak a picture as Abby paints, I have to agree with her. When the first Social Security benefits were paid out in 1940, the average lifespan for American men was sixty-two years, and for women it was sixty-seven years. A lot of people didn't live long enough to collect benefits. At that time, there were sixteen workers for each retiree. Today, the average lifespan for men and women has increased to seventy-six and eighty years, respectively. In addition, there are now only about three workers per retiree, and that number is declining. The combination of retirees living longer and the lower ratio of workers to retirees will bankrupt the program within twenty-five years. Logic would suggest raising retirement age eligibility and curtailing benefits. Instead, we've left retirement age virtually unchanged, and benefits over the years have been made more generous. Medicare was already a financial disaster when an unfunded prescription drug benefit was added about ten years ago, by Republicans, I might add. This new benefit increased the unfunded liability for Medicare by $15 trillion."

Pip settled back in his chair. He was a strikingly handsome man of forty-five. Suave and debonair, he reminded folks old enough to remember of Cary Grant. As a young marine platoon leader in Desert Storm, the first Gulf war that liberated Kuwait from Iraq in 1992, Pip had his right arm blown off at the shoulder. As he could not be fitted for a prosthesis, the empty right sleeves of his immaculately tailored suit jackets and monogrammed shirts were sewn to the sides of those garments. Pip never acknowledged his disability, and was almost entirely independent having learned to do such things as knot a four-in-hand tie, comb his hair, and tie his shoes with one hand. A terrific athlete before his injury, he learned to play one-handed golf and had an eighteen handicap off the ladies' tees.

Following his discharge from the marines, Pip obtained a PhD in history at LSU. After several years teaching history at his alma mater, he turned to writing history full time and became quite successful. His books, aimed at the general public, typically focused on American figures and events during the antebellum period and the Gilded Age of the latter nineteenth century. He also wrote a popular college textbook covering American history up to the Spanish American War. He had a deserved reputation for being a historian who tried to let history speak for itself, and not color it with modern ideas, ideology, and value judgments that might be currently in vogue. This is what impressed Ding and Reb, and why they asked Pip to join the Madison Committee.

Judge Wyatt took a sip of iced tea and said, "Everything I have heard from Abby and Pip I have no reason to doubt, but the entitlement programs have been with us many years, have been ruled to be constitutional, and are part of our social fabric. These programs are theoretically financed with specific taxes on income, and the Sixteenth Amendment authorized Congress to collect income taxes. The fact that the taxes collected are insufficient to pay the promised benefits is not, per se, unconstitutional. If we are looking for government encroachments on the rights of states or individuals, why are we focused on Social Security and Medicare?"

Reb replied, "Wyatt, you are absolutely right, but did the Framers and the Constitution they crafted intend for any generation of Americans to go on an out-of-control borrowing spree to pay themselves overly generous benefits, and then pass the bill off to Americans too young to vote or not yet born, thereby diminishing their liberty and opportunities to pursue happiness? If the Constitution was intended to last in perpetuity, does not each generation have a fiduciary responsibility to all future generations? Even if not explicitly stated, implicit in the Constitution is a solemn duty to protect the rights and liberties of those who come after us. In fact, the Preamble states, among other things, that the Constitution for the United States of America was ordained and established to 'secure the Blessings of Liberty to ourselves and our Posterity.' Interestingly, the word 'ourselves' was written in lower-case, while 'Posterity' was capitalized. This presumably was intentional and suggests to me that the Framers believed future generations were more important than themselves, and that their first duty was to ensure the blessings of liberty to posterity."

"You make an eloquent and compelling argument, Reb," responded Wyatt.

"I'll tell you one thing," Ding interjected, "whenever any elected politician I know thinks of posterity, he or she is thinking about getting reelected. That's about as far into the future as their horizon extends. Very few are concerned about future generations of Americans. After all, they can't vote. That may sound cynical, but it's true."

Duane Darby, who had been silent but absorbing every word, now joined the discussion. "The Constitution is a masterful document, because it reflects the Framers' astute insight into human nature, especially the lust many men have for power, by designing a government with many built-in checks and balances to prevent undue concentration of power in the hands of a few. They could not envision or anticipate, however, all the clever schemes future politicians would devise to circumvent their intentions. That the government would run up enormous deficits, debts, and unfunded obligations surely was unimaginable to them. Had they contemplated this, perhaps they would have included a balanced budget requirement in the Constitution or the Bill of Rights to ensure against the intergenerational theft going on now.

"By the way, the accounting rules for publicly owned companies require them to disclose the present value of future liabilities for pension and healthcare benefits. If any company kept its books the way the government does, reporting only current year actual cash revenue and expenses and ignoring obligations in future years, its top management would be hauled off to prison."

Following military service, Duane went to college on the G.I. Bill, eventually earning his law degree from the University of Houston. Reared by a single mother in a Houston ghetto, Duane, unlike many other boys in his neighborhood, managed to escape a life of drugs, gangs, and despair primarily because of his mother's strong values and high expectations. She was determined that her son would have an opportunity for a better life. Duane did not disappoint her. From law school, he took a position with Bunker, Hill & Shiloh, one of Houston's most prestigious corporate law firms. He rose steadily to senior partner and became a wealthy man. After two failures, his third attempt at marriage was successful and still going strong after twenty years.

Duane never forgot or turned his back on his humble beginnings. Through his charitable foundation, he established three weekend retreats in predominantly black neighborhoods of Houston that offered a safe haven off the streets for boys aged eight to eighteen. Supervised by trained adult counselors, the weekend retreats provided structured activities aimed at instilling strong moral values, a desire for education, and self-reliance. Over the years, many young boys, who otherwise might have been trapped in the ghetto ethos, matured into fine young men, went on to college, and led respectable, productive lives. Duane let others take credit for the success of this program, but he took justifiable pride in its accomplishments.

Prompted by Duane's comments, Ding said, "Many of you might recall that back in the mid-1990s, there was serious discussion about a balanced budget amendment, but it didn't get off the ground no doubt, because it would circumscribe Congress's addiction to irresponsible spending. It is an excellent idea, however, and perhaps essential if the country is ever to deal seriously with its debt and deficits. A constitutional amendment initiated by

Congress requires a two-thirds majority vote in both houses. I don't see that happening, and even if it did, three-fourths of the states would have to approve it as well before the amendment would be ratified."

"Well, Article V of the Constitution provides that two-thirds of the state legislatures may petition Congress to call a convention to propose amendments," replied Judge Wyatt. "If ratified by three-fourths of the states, they would be adopted as the law of the land. Of course, the states have never petitioned Congress to call a constitutional convention. All twenty-seven of the Constitution's amendments have been initiated in Congress and then sent to each of the states for ratification."

"Because the states have never made a serious effort to meet in convention since 1787, Wyatt, do you think there is any practical chance of this happening?" Pip asked. "Many people fear a new constitutional convention might attempt to alter radically or replace the Constitution."

"You may be right, Pip. But it seems to me after two hundred twenty-six years, it's time for the states to assemble in convention and consider some long overdue changes to the constitutional order. At least, such a convention would demonstrate to the politicians in Washington that the states have an important and powerful role in the federal system. As far as worries about a rogue convention that might scrap the Constitution and start over with a blank sheet of parchment, it would require 75 percent of the states, thirty-eight out of fifty, to ratify anything approved in convention. A rogue convention does not concern me. What concerns me more than amending the Constitution is the fact that the one we have is so often ignored or disregarded by Congress, the president, and the courts."

"Give me a couple examples, Wyatt," asked Abby.

"Well, how about securing the borders and processing immigrants in an orderly manner? If a country fails to fulfill that fundamental obligation, it forfeits its sovereignty." Wyatt pulled from his jacket's breast pocket a well-worn booklet copy of the Constitution and flipped through its pages before continuing. "Article I, Section 8, states that Congress shall have the power to provide for the common defense, and to establish a uniform rule of naturalization. Congress has passed laws to carry out this duty, but recent presidents of both parties have not seen fit to execute those laws faithfully. As we all know, the illegal immigration issue is fraught with politics, and both parties jockey for advantage to avoid alienating primarily Hispanic voters. In the meantime, we are losing control of our borders. A couple of years back, Arizona stood up and decided to control its porous border with Mexico in the face of federal negligence. Instead of the feds being shamed into doing their duty, they decided to sue Arizona on the basis that it lacked jurisdiction. The entire situation is a disgrace. In effect, the federal government said to Arizona, and every other state, you can't secure your borders, because that's a federal responsibility, but we aren't going to fulfill that responsibility. What a bizarre Catch-22 that is."

"You are absolutely right, Wyatt," replied Ding. "The issues of illegal immigration and defending our borders have become intractable problems, and further evidence of the dysfunctional state into which politics has descended. We have some 15 million illegal immigrants in this country, and the number increases by a half million per year. We all favor immigration; that's how our ancestors got here and how this country was built. But immigration has to be done in an orderly, controlled manner. There is also the clear and present danger to the country of terrorists entering the country via our unsecured borders."

Wyatt was just getting wound up. "Another breach of the Constitution, in my considered judgment, is the various unfunded mandates imposed on the states by Congress. The states complain, but almost always end up caving in to the feds. One of the worst recent breaches of individual liberty is the mandate that all citizens purchase healthcare insurance. This was included in the two-thousand-page healthcare reform legislation of 2010, which I am sure not one senator or congressman read in its entirety before or after voting on it. Never before has the federal government required a citizen to purchase a product or service, and nowhere is such a power delegated to the federal government by the Constitution. It's true that in order to own a motor vehicle, one must purchase automobile insurance, but this is an inapt analogy for two reasons. First, nobody forces a person to buy a car, but if one chooses to do so, proof of liability insurance is required to register and operate it, as is a valid driver's license. Second, this is a requirement imposed by individual states and is in accord with the Tenth Amendment."

"I suppose," Pip said, "that Congress rationalized this unprecedented encroachment on individual liberty by claiming it falls under the so-called 'commerce clause.' That clause, which also appears in Article I, Section 8, has already been stretched by Congress and the courts to justify almost anything. The clause as written empowers Congress 'to regulate commerce…among the several states.' The original intent was to ensure that states did not impose tariffs on other states. Over the past one-hundred-twenty years, however, it has been used to justify the regulation of virtually all interstate commerce. If the Supreme Court upholds the mandatory purchase of health insurance by all citizens, it will establish yet another precedent that can be used in the future to justify any manner of mandates or restrictions on individual behavior."

"Another abuse of the Constitution," Pip continued, "is bypassing the explicit power of Congress to declare war, established in Article I, Section 8. The last declared war was World War II. Since then we have fought wars in Korea, Vietnam, Iraq, Afghanistan, and against al Qaeda for years in each case, yet Congress never formally declared the nation to be at war. Oh, Congress passes a supporting resolution and appropriates the necessary funds, but to send the military into combat for years at a time without declaring war seems to me to be a violation of the Constitution, and cedes more power to the president and commander-in-chief than the Framers contemplated.

"I also have a problem with wiretaps of citizens' phone calls without a court warrant. This is justified as an important tool to avert future terrorist attacks, but it also violates the Fourth Amendment right 'against unreasonable searches and seizures,' without a court-ordered warrant based on probable cause. Finally, I think so-called 'signing statements' are not within the president's authority. When legislation is sent to the president, and he signs it into law, he can't issue a separate statement listing the portions of the law he disagrees with and will not enforce. The president can either approve or veto legislation in its entirety. He cannot pick and choose which parts of legislation he signs into law that he will execute."

"For what it's worth," offered Duane, "I believe crony capitalism is a gross distortion of the Constitution and the notion of equal treatment under the law. It also gives traditional capitalism and free enterprise a bad name. As government increases its regulatory oversight of business activity, businesses inevitably will lobby to have laws and regulations written to favor their interests, or to be detrimental to their competition. Politicians routinely take campaign contributions from companies wanting to shape legislation. There may be no formal quid pro quo, but corporations don't throw money around unless they expect to earn a return on their 'investment.' And frequently we see 'regulatory capture,' whereby regulated entities arrange for insiders to be appointed as regulators. Before long, the regulations are being manipulated by the regulated. It is an incestuous relationship between big companies and big government, and the public interest too often suffers for it.

"An example of what I believe to be government overreach," offered Abby, "is the 2005 Supreme Court case, *Kelo v. City of New London*, that ruled in favor of the town of New London, Connecticut, by expanding government's eminent domain power to permit the taking of a person's private property—an individual's home in that case—so that another private entity could convert the property to 'a more productive use.' Prior to this case, the government's right of eminent domain, as set forth in the Fifth Amendment, extended only to taking private property, with just compensation, for public use such as a highway or government facility. With the Court's *Kelo* decision, the term 'public use' was expanded to mean a higher private purpose that would generate more jobs and tax revenue. In my view, this is a clear example of unelected judges throwing out two hundred years of precedent and legislating from the bench."

"Another egregious example," Abby continued, "is the arbitrary and peremptory disregard of longstanding bankruptcy law when Chrysler's secured bondholders in 2009 were demonized and browbeaten by the president and his aides into surrendering their legal rights to company assets that collateralized their bonds. Instead, Chrysler's unsecured obligation to its union employee pension fund was given preference by awarding the union a 55 percent ownership interest in the restructured company. This violated the secured creditors' rights, but because most of the secured bonds were held by large financial institutions that feared government sanctions, they were bullied into accepting the government's restructuring plan. Many of the bonds were owned by state employee pension funds and mutual funds, which were owned in turn by small investors. Yet the government tried to paint all the bondholders as evil plutocrats. Even plutocrats have rights. The Fifth Amendment guarantees that no person shall be deprived of property 'without due process of law.' That guarantee didn't apply in this case."

"This has been a stimulating discussion," opined Ding. "It is clear to all of us that the federal government is and has been overstepping its bounds with impunity for a long time at the expense of the Constitution, states rights, and individual liberty. This is why Reb and I formed the Madison Committee and invited you to be founding members. The challenge is how to take effective action to remedy these breaches of the Constitution and preserve it for future generations."

Wyatt interrupted, "I am honored to have been asked to serve on this committee with such distinguished people, patriots all. As a recovering federal judge, I agree with most everything I have heard this afternoon. But speaking for myself, and with all due respect, I fail to see how six citizens, none of whom except you, Ding, is an elected official, can have any significant impact in restoring a proper constitutional balance. Many public officials have decried the same things we have been discussing here today, but it gets drowned out in the cacophony, and the circus moves on. The federal government is like Godzilla. The people are powerless before it and can hope only that it will be benevolent and avoid disaster. I don't think any of us wants to waste each other's time discussing these important questions if we are impotent to influence events. I don't mean to be pessimistic, only realistic."

"Wyatt, I thank you for your candor," Reb began, "which is one of the reasons each of you was asked to join the Madison Committee. I have no intention of wasting my time or yours. If, after three or four meetings, we are unable to define a credible action plan, I will be the first to recommend dissolving our committee. Because the stakes are so high, however, and no one else, to my knowledge, is addressing these issues in a thoughtful, deliberate, comprehensive, and non-partisan manner, I think we owe it to ourselves, our children, and their children to make the effort. We are a small group, but collectively we possess a great deal of intelligence, wisdom, and talent. I am impressed with the quality of our discussion today. We are not focused on policy matters such as whether taxes should go up or go down, or Democrat versus Republican, or left versus right. We are centered on the Constitution, which should not be distorted or marginalized in order to further any political agenda or ideology. We know elected politicians, regardless of political party, are going to push the Constitution's limits as long as they can get away with it, and will never propose amendments that would weaken their power. By default, it is left to us to make this effort."

Abby asked, "Where do you propose we go from here, Reb?"

"Well, assuming we all remain committed to this effort, we are scheduled to meet again in two weeks here at the Rosewood. Before then, I'll provide everyone a proposed agenda for subsequent meetings. Is this path forward agreeable to everyone?"

All nodded or expressed their agreement, at which point Reb said, "Thank you all for your active participation in this project. The first meeting of the Madison Committee stands adjourned."

11

Several days after the Madison Committee met, Ding Bell telephoned Reb. "How do you feel about our first meeting?"

"To tell you the truth, Ding, I think the challenge before us is next to impossible. The country has been on the path to a virtually omnipotent federal government for so long, it is entrenched in the minds of the political parties and the public. Since the 1930s, the public has been conditioned like Pavlov's dog to believe that the federal government will solve all problems. In the process, generations of politicians have persuaded the people to surrender some self-reliance, freedom of choice, and individual liberty in exchange for becoming increasingly dependent on the government to provide comfort and security at all stages of life. But liberty and dependence are mutually exclusive, and, if history is a guide, once individual liberty is ceded to government it is permanently lost. Has individual security supplanted individual liberty as a higher order American value?"

"God, I hope not," Ding responded. "My favorite Founding Father, Benjamin Franklin, once said, 'They that can give up liberty to obtain a little temporary safety deserve neither liberty nor safety.'"

"Yeah," Reb replied, "and in response to a citizen who asked him after the Constitutional Convention what he and his fellow delegates had given the people, old Ben reputedly said, 'a Republic if you can keep it.' Perhaps the idea of a federal republic that vests only limited and enumerated powers in the federal government while leaving all other powers and rights with the sovereign states and the people is obsolete or no longer workable. We may be too big, too diverse, too complex a society for the people to exercise liberty the way the Founders envisioned. Perhaps the inexorable tide of history made the long march from a federal republic to an all-powerful national government inevitable. If so, then we are just a couple of old dinosaurs that should be on display in a museum of natural history."

"You don't believe that anymore than I do, Reb. Look, things are bad and getting steadily worse. Each action, large or small, that the federal government has taken over the past eighty years or so that expanded its powers beyond the intended boundaries of the Constitution, I am sure the politicians at the time could rationalize as being for the greater good of society. And no doubt many of those actions were popular with the voters. The problem is not with any particular action, but with the cumulative deleterious effect all those actions have had on individual liberty. It has taken nearly a century for the mighty river of the federal government to overflow its constitutional levees. As you point out, this problem has become the accepted norm for many citizens and politicians. It can't be corrected overnight, but I think we both have a pretty good idea what has to change to swing the pendulum of power back from government to the individual."

"Ding, I have no doubt the Madison Committee can produce a laundry list of things that have to change, but how will our small group carry that into action? Our merry band of six concerned citizens has grit, but, compared to the establishment and the government at whose altar it worships, we are at a greater disadvantage than David was against Goliath."

"All true, Reb, but you're forgetting that David defeated Goliath."

"Yeah, with a lucky shot. Anyway, I like to enter a fight with something more than luck on my side."

"Well, that's about all the Founding Fathers had going for them when they decided to secede from the mother country, Great Britain, then the most powerful nation on earth. But things turned out pretty well for them."

"It was a close-run thing, Ding. Washington lost most of his battles, but he was shrewd and lucky enough not to lose his army. Still, without the French as our allies and their navy off the Virginia coast at the Battle of Yorktown, the colonists might not have prevailed."

"And they most certainly would not have prevailed had they not had the fortitude and perseverance to try."

"I can't disagree with that, Ding. My ancestor Edmund Burke wrote, 'The greatest security of the people, against the encroachments and usurpations of their superiors, is to keep the Spirit of Liberty constantly awake.' We need to reawaken the Spirit of Liberty in the breast of every citizen."

"I like the sound of that," replied Ding. "Now, what is your agenda for the next Madison Committee meeting?"

"I am going to ask Judge Wyatt and Pip Pippin, respectively, to provide the committee a legal and historical overview of how the federal government evolved from one of limited powers into the colossus we have today. At our following meeting, we'll endeavor to reach consensus on the constitutional amendments the Madison Committee would propose to ameliorate the deficiencies we discussed at our first meeting. Assuming we reach consensus on the amendments we would adopt, had we the power to do so, we'll devote subsequent meetings to designing an effective strategy for getting this before the American people and shaking them out of their lethargy."

"Sounds like a good approach, Reb. I look forward to what should be an intellectually stimulating exchange of ideas at our next meeting."

12

"The Constitution is a political document that established a republic whereby the original thirteen sovereign states delegated to the new federal government limited and enumerated powers." The second meeting of the Madison Committee was underway with all members in attendance and Judge Wyatt presiding.

"All powers not delegated to the federal government were retained by the states or the people. The Constitution was the product of intense debate and careful compromise among the Framers who were brilliant, pragmatic men. The language, virtually every word, in the final document was carefully chosen. The Framers meant the Constitution to mean what it said. In the individual state ratifying conventions, there was vigorous debate over the meaning of various phrases and grave concern over rights of states and citizens being adequately protected against usurpation or encroachment by the new government. To allay concerns that the new government would have inordinate power, Madison, Hamilton, and Jay authored *The Federalist* commentaries to explain and clarify the Constitution. Still, in order to win ratification by several key states, including

Massachusetts, Virginia, and New York, a promise was made to consider promptly a Bill of Rights as soon as the new government was formed.

"Under Madison's leadership," Wyatt continued, "the 1st United States Congress in 1789 considered twelve amendments to the Constitution, eleven of which were submitted to the states for ratification. By December 1791, ten of these amendments, known ever after as the Bill of Rights, had been ratified and adopted. The Bill of Rights was based on the Virginia Declaration of Rights written in 1776 by George Mason, a Founding Father deserving greater recognition than history has seen fit to give him.""

Pausing to drink some water, Wyatt resumed, "From the beginning, there were some politicians like Hamilton who believed in a strong federal government and in particular a strong executive. This viewpoint at that time was in the minority. Most politicians like Madison and Jefferson adamantly believed in a government of limited powers. They were strict constructionists in that they did not take an expansive view of the Constitution. The federal government had specific powers delegated to it, and trying to divine implicit powers beyond those enumerated was unconstitutional. Today, adherents to the strict constructionist position are often called 'originalists,' because they don't try to read anything into the Constitution that is not written. They also look to documents such as *The Federalist* commentaries to gain insight and context into what the Framers meant when they wrote phrases subject to interpretation.

"Over the past century, there has developed a theory of a 'living, breathing' or 'evolving' Constitution that can meet the needs of a constantly changing society. No doubt the world today is light years away from the eighteenth century, and for the Constitution to be relevant in modern times, it has had to adapt to meet today's challenges and needs. After all, since 1789, America has been transformed from a primitive agrarian society into a predominantly urban industrial economy, which has evolved into the Internet age. Also, the country's population has grown nearly a hundredfold since its founding. Perhaps I am not doing the theory justice, but this enormous societal change is the basic rationale for a 'living, breathing' Constitution. There are also many politicians and academicians who believe government can and should solve most of society's perceived ills and injustices if only a cadre of enlightened, self-anointed elitists who believe they know what is best for the rest of us could access power and implement their utopian agenda. To achieve this grand objective legally requires embracing the 'living, breathing' Constitution theory.

"Now, I am an 'originalist,'" averred Wyatt, "I believe the brilliance of the Constitution written in the eighteenth century is its inherent flexibility to accommodate societal and technological change without having to depart significantly from its original wording and meaning. The fundamental principles of liberty and limited government are constant. To the extent the Constitution ever needs to be updated, however, the Framers had the foresight to provide in Article V two methods, by which it can be amended. Adopting amendments is difficult and time-consuming, requiring 75 percent of the states to agree to do so, but that is as it should be, in my opinion. If amendments could be adopted with a narrow majority, we would suffer frivolous changes to our fundamental law based on the passions of the moment or the seductive oratory of a demagogue."

Clearing his throat, Wyatt continued, "The idea of a 'living, breathing' Constitution has been taught at many of the best law schools for years and is embraced by many lawyers, jurists, and politicians. In my view, this theory is spurious and dangerous, because the law has to be clear and definite, especially the supreme law of the land. If it can be contrived to mean whatever a judge, a court, or a majority of Congress wants it to mean, at any moment in time, then we are no longer governed by law, we are governed by the whims of men. And because men and women who hold power rarely if ever seek to limit their power, a 'living, breathing' Constitution leads to ever bigger, more powerful central government and less individual liberty. It is especially odious when unelected judges decide they have the power to legislate from the bench. A judge's proper role is to interpret and apply the law in a fair, objective manner, and to determine that the law is constitutional. Making law is beyond a judge's authority, no matter how brilliant he or she may be. An activist judge who wishes to legislate should resign from the court and run for Congress. The concept of a 'living, breathing' Constitution is not a respectable legal theory. It is a political theory embraced by those desiring to enact an agenda that requires the expansion of government beyond its constitutional authority."

"But, Wyatt," interjected Pip, "wasn't the Supreme Court's unanimous 1954 decision in *Brown v. Board of Education*, which desegregated public schools, an example of an activist court legislating from the bench and overturning a terrible injustice?"

"That's an excellent question, Pip. The short answer is no. *Brown* belatedly overturned an 1896 Supreme Court decision, *Plessy v. Ferguson*, which was an unconstitutional ruling that stood as the law of the land for nearly sixty years. The *Plessy* case institutionalized segregation by ruling that separate but equal facilities for blacks and whites were legal. In *Brown*, the Court ruled that segregated facilities were inherently unequal and in violation of the Fourteenth Amendment, which says that no state shall 'deny to any person within its jurisdiction the equal protection of the laws.' Prohibiting access by a particular group of citizens to public facilities available to all other citizens is a denial of equal protection of the laws. The *Plessy* Court incorrectly applied the law and the *Brown* Court corrected that mistake. In effect, the *Plessy* Court embraced the 'living, breathing' Constitution theory, whereas the *Brown* Court followed the Fourteenth Amendment's original intent."

"What about the Louisiana Purchase, Wyatt?" asked Duane. "As an originalist, what is your view of that transaction?"

In 1803, Thomas Jefferson, by then president of the U.S., negotiated the purchase of the Louisiana Territory from France for $15 million. The lands acquired doubled the size of the United States, extending from the Mississippi River to the Rockies, the Canadian border to the Gulf of Mexico, and ultimately encompassing fourteen states. It must have been the largest peaceful accession of territory by one country from another in recorded history. The Louisiana Purchase virtually assured the United States would be a major world power.

"Duane, the exception proves the rule," replied Wyatt. "Because Jefferson was a strict constructionist, he was concerned that the Constitution did not provide government the authority to make such an acquisition. Article IV, Section 3, provides that new states may be admitted by Congress to the Union, but there is no reference to acquiring territory. Jefferson, however, was more concerned with New Orleans and the Mississippi River being under France's control. As long as any foreign power controlled such a strategic position, America's freedom of commerce and national security would be in jeopardy, and sooner or later war likely would ensue. These arguments trumped questions of constitutionality. For the sake of America's posterity and manifest destiny, President Jefferson made the correct decision, and the Senate, after heated debate, ratified the treaty with France formalizing the purchase. While one can argue the Louisiana Purchase was technically unconstitutional, it did not disturb the constitutional rights of states or citizens, so it was at most a benign violation that has had an everlasting benefit to the nation. I believe it is more prudent and respectful of liberty and limited government to approach the Constitution as an originalist, yet be open to departing from that position in exceptional circumstances, rather than to view the document as 'living, breathing,' which encourages one to contrive it to mean whatever is convenient or expedient in order to obtain a desired outcome."

"Although no more than an amusing mental exercise," interjected Pip, "but consider what might have happened if Jefferson had not purchased the Louisiana Territory, or Napoleon had not offered to sell it. In 1815, Napoleon escaped from his first exile on Elba, an island in the Mediterranean near Tuscany. Instead of making his way to Paris and rallying his army to meet his fate at Waterloo, what if he had sailed with elements of his Imperial Guard to New Orleans and established the empire of New France on the Louisiana Territory? Implausible you may argue, but not impossible. One can only imagine how that would have changed American and world history. Most of us take history for granted, but it is never inevitable, and the story of man hinges upon all manner of implausible events, both remembered and forgotten, as well as decisions both great and seemingly trivial. One can never know the road not taken, but clearly Jefferson made a wise choice when presented with a serendipitous opportunity."

Following Pip's digression, Reb invited Wyatt to comment on the language in the Constitution that has been subject to contentious interpretation over the years. "The Bill of Rights," Wyatt began, "has been an ongoing source of legal contention. The courts have wrestled with defining the boundaries of citizens' individual rights, but, by and large, I think they have come to appropriate determinations. I should think few American citizens feel insecure in their freedom to speak, worship, or bear arms. Many efforts have been made to curtail or eliminate the right to own guns, but all have been unsuccessful. The media certainly exercise their freedom of the press guaranty, although often irresponsibly in my judgment."

"What about rights that are overlooked or ignored?" asked Reb. "Specifically, I have in mind the Ninth and Tenth Amendments. If those amendments were consistently honored by the courts, we would have today a smaller, less intrusive federal government."

"Well, there is no doubt," Wyatt replied, "that those amendments essentially have lain dormant for many years, because the direction of the federal government over the past century has been to justify its expansion. To do that means disregarding those parts of the Constitution that limit federal power while finding other parts that can be interpreted or stretched to justify broader powers. There are four primary clauses that believers in a 'living, breathing' Constitution rely on to attribute powers to the federal government that go far beyond those enumerated in the Constitution. They are the commerce clause, the necessary and proper clause, the general welfare clause, and the supremacy clause. I'll briefly address each." Before going any further in his remarks, Wyatt distributed booklet copies like his own of the Constitution and the Declaration of Independence.

"We discussed the commerce clause at our first meeting in connection with the requirement under the 2010 healthcare reform law that all citizens are required to purchase health insurance or be subject to fines and penalties. You'll recall that this clause appears in Article I, Section 8, which grants Congress the power 'to regulate commerce...among the several states....' Probably no other clause in the Constitution has been more frequently cited to justify government involvement in Americans' daily lives. Originally, this clause was interpreted narrowly to prohibit trade or tariff barriers among the states. *The Federalist* discusses the commerce clause only in terms of trade or exchange. Numerous Supreme Court decisions over many years have given a much broader interpretation to the commerce clause.

"The most famous or infamous, depending on your viewpoint, expansion of commerce clause authority is the 1942 Supreme Court case *Wickard v. Filburn* in which the Court ruled that Roscoe Filburn, an Ohio chicken farmer, could not produce wheat in excess of the quantity allotted to his farm by the government, even though he was going to consume all of it on his farm and not sell any to third parties. The theory was that by harvesting more than his allotment, Roscoe would not buy the 'excess' amount he needed on the open market thereby depressing the price of wheat. Obviously, Roscoe alone would not affect the price of wheat, but if a large number of farmers exceeded their allotments, the market price for wheat would drop. The Agricultural Adjustment Act passed in 1938 was aimed at stabilizing the price of wheat, which fluctuated dramatically in international markets during the Depression. As a consequence of the Court's ruling, Filburn had to destroy the excess wheat or pay a fine, but, more importantly, the federal government could now regulate intrastate commerce that might impact interstate commerce, thereby expanding the commerce clause power to cover virtually all gainful activity."

Duane frowned at this and said, "So much for the old adage that 'a man's home is his castle.' I always thought that that was one of the most basic rights enjoyed by all men and women. The ruling also seems to violate an individual's right to private property."

"I agree with you, Duane," said Ding. "The Court effectively ruled that the commerce clause power trumped the Ninth and Tenth Amendments."

"You both sum it up very well," replied Wyatt, "The Court's general tendency, especially since the New Deal era, has been to disregard or give lesser weight to the ringing clarity of the Ninth and Tenth Amendments when those amendments conflict with other more ambiguous or recondite clauses of the Constitution that can be interpreted in a way that expands government's scope and reach."

"Lest you think," Wyatt continued, "that I disapprove of any broader interpretation of the commerce clause than that held by the Framers, I believe the Food and Drug Administration, or FDA, established in 1938, represents a prudent and justifiable application of the commerce clause by the federal government. The Framers lived in a world where there were no pharmaceuticals, and most people grew their own food or bought fresh local produce in their hometowns. In the America of today, and for the better part of a century, most people have bought the food they eat, and much of it is processed in plants across the country or around the world. Moreover, most people consume an increasing number of prescription or over-the-counter drugs and cosmetics that are produced far and wide. To protect the safety of the people with respect to food and drugs sold interstate and internationally, and to enforce uniform standards, the federal government is the only government entity that can discharge this responsibility. If each of the fifty states was left to set its own regulations and standards, there would be chaos, interstate commerce would be crippled, and economic growth stifled. The Congress has been delegated the power 'to regulate Commerce with foreign Nations, and among the several States.' I believe the FDA's mission is consistent with this power. While this is conjecture, I also believe the Framers would consider the FDA in today's world an appropriate activity of the federal government. The FDA is an example of the Constitution's flexibility to accommodate change in society without violating the principle of limited government.

"I'll turn now to the necessary and proper clause, which appears in the last enumerated power granted to Congress in Article I, Section 8. It reads in part,

> To make all Laws which shall be necessary and proper for carrying into Execution the foregoing Powers, and all other Powers vested by this Constitution in the Government of the United States.

"At the time of the state ratifying conventions, a great concern was expressed over the meaning and intent of this clause. According to Madison, the intent was to grant Congress the power to enact the necessary and proper legislation specific to carrying out the *foregoing* enumerated powers delegated in Article I, Section 8, to the federal government. Thomas Jefferson argued that if the government interpreted 'necessary and proper' to mean 'convenient,' then the government would effectively have unlimited power, the opposite of what was intended and affirmed by the Framers. Then in 1819, the Supreme Court in *McCulloch v. Maryland* held that under the 'necessary and proper' clause, Congress could establish a national bank, although it had no express power to do so, in furtherance of its express power to collect taxes and pay debts. This decision established the doctrine of implied powers available to Congress under the 'necessary and proper' clause that were useful or 'convenient' in pursuance of its enumerated powers. In effect, this decision rejected the view of Madison and Jefferson and granted more expansive powers to the federal government."

Continuing his tutorial, Wyatt turned to the general welfare clause. "The first enumerated power under Article I, Section 8, grants Congress the power to collect taxes, 'to pay the Debts and provide for the common Defense and general Welfare of the United States.' There also is the phrase 'promote the general Welfare' in the Preamble, but the Preamble is a statement of objectives and not a grant of government authority. Madison asserted the general welfare clause was limited to spending related to the enumerated powers. Following ratification of the Constitution, Hamilton, who favored strong central government, argued for a broad interpretation of this clause, claiming that the power to spend on the general welfare of the nation was itself an enumerated power granted to Congress. For the first hundred fifty years of the republic, the Supreme Court applied a relatively narrow interpretation to the general welfare clause. In 1936, however, the Court ruled in *Butler v. United States* that the general welfare clause was an enumerated power independent of other such powers; therefore, Congress could spend public money for national public purposes. This expansion of the general welfare clause's meaning granted Congress the power to appropriate funds for virtually any expenditure related to a national purpose, such as Social Security, Medicare, and so forth.

"Finally, we come to the supremacy clause, which appears in the second paragraph of Article VI." Wyatt still had his audience's undivided attention. "The pertinent language reads as follows:

> This Constitution, and the Laws of the United States which shall be made in Pursuance thereof; and all Treaties made, or which shall be made, under the Authority of the United States, shall be the supreme Law of the Land; and Judges in every State shall be bound thereby, any Thing in the Constitution or Laws of any State to the Contrary notwithstanding."

Wyatt paused to let everyone read the language before continuing, "This appears pretty straightforward. The Constitution and the laws enacted by the federal government are the highest law in the country, and judges at all levels of government must adhere to the Constitution and federal laws, even if they contradict a state's constitution or laws. The bone of contention relates to the proviso that the federal laws shall be made in *pursuance* of the Constitution. If the federal government enacts laws beyond its constitutional authority, are such laws subject to the supremacy clause? In the landmark *Marbury v. Madison* case of 1803, the Supreme Court asserted its power of judicial review, whereby it would be the final authority whether or not a law is constitutional. There is no appeal beyond the Supreme Court except through a constitutional amendment. Given the Court's expansive interpretations of the commerce, necessary and proper, and general welfare clauses, especially over the past century, the federal government has effectively overturned the Constitution. The principle of a limited government possessing specific powers has been supplanted by a government of vast powers, essentially limited only by the imaginations of Congress, the president, and the Supreme Court."

After Wyatt concluded his remarks, Reb said, "Thank you, Wyatt, for a fascinating historical summary taking us from the Constitution and government the Framers established and intended for America to the Constitution we live under today. As I reflect on what you have told us, it seems to me there is virtually no limit or effective check on the federal government's power. The separation of powers and the checks and balances built into the Constitution serve only to control the relative power among the three government branches. The Congress, the Executive, and the Supreme Court do not appear too concerned with circumscribing the power and scope of the federal government, probably because they are the federal government."

"From what I've heard today," Abby remarked, "the federal government is the ultimate and sole arbiter of how far and wide its powers will reach. The states have acquiesced in ceding many of their powers to the federal government. In fact, I would argue we no longer have a federal government. We now have a dominant, monolithic, national government and the states have been reduced to vassalage."

"You've identified the fundamental problem, Abby," responded Reb, "I used to blame the politicians of either party or the courts for the encroachments of the federal government. But that is like blaming a wild animal for obeying its instinct. Elected federal officials and judges instinctively will find ways to spend more money, expand government power, and justify their actions under the general welfare or commerce or some other clause of the Constitution. The Framers were aware of this natural instinct or lust for power and tried to mitigate it in various ways. But a determined congressional majority with a cavalier disregard for the Constitution; an indifferent or assertive president; and a Supreme Court predisposed to being expansive in its application of the Constitution can do virtually anything they decide to do. Moreover, if the so-called 'independent' press abandons its paramount responsibility to criticize, challenge, and speak truth to power, and instead becomes a supine, obsequious cheerleader for government, the ability of citizens to obtain objective information will be diminished."

Pip piped up. "One of the fundamental problems is the careerism in Congress. In the nineteenth century, on average, there was a 45 percent turnover in Congress every election cycle. Few people viewed elective office as a professional career. It was more of a civic duty. Over the past fifty or sixty years, the average turnover in an election year has been about 10 percent. More and more congressmen and senators view public service as a great career. With seniority comes power. The average committee chairman in the House has twenty-seven years of service. Unlike the nineteenth century, today's congresspersons have large paid staffs at their beck and call, and even more staffers if they chair a subcommittee or committee, plus oodles of perks and benefits. Their arrogance is such that they exempt themselves from a number of the laws they impose on common citizens, and too many of them think they are above the laws that do apply to them.

"Basically, we have four-hundred-thirty-five satraps in the House and one hundred barons in the Senate. Most have secure seats, affording them a lifetime sinecure. If power tends to corrupt, we have a lot of potential for corruption in today's Congress. Lobbyists acquire influence on behalf of their clients by throwing gobs of money at incumbent politicians to finance their reelection campaigns. As a result, the 'special interests' and crony capitalists feed at the trough of government, too often at the expense of the average citizen. In my perception, the average congressman of the nineteenth century was a public servant, whereas today's congressperson typically is a public master. Until this situation changes, and I don't see how it will, there is no hope of reining in the federal government short of its financial collapse, which I fear is coming. God help us."

Reb directed a request to Pip, "We've heard from Wyatt about the key court cases that have resulted in the federal government's virtually unchallenged dominance. Please share with us from a historical perspective some of the key trends and events that contributed to this outcome."

"Well, for the first one hundred forty years of the Republic, with the major exception of the Civil War and Reconstruction period from 1861 till 1877, the federal government essentially held to a narrow interpretation of its constitutional powers. The almost dictatorial power Lincoln exercised during the Civil War, and the occupation of the defeated Confederate states by his immediate successors during Reconstruction, fortunately were not lasting precedents. But after the Civil War, the federal government was firmly established as the dominant governmental authority in the U.S, and the states' relative power and influence were permanently diminished. In the early twentieth century, Theodore Roosevelt and Woodrow Wilson, two very different personalities, but both assertive Chief Magistrates, established the presidency as the dominant center of government power and influence. From Lincoln's time until the first Roosevelt came into office, Congress generally was the more dominant branch of government, as the Framers intended, but after TR and Wilson, Congress typically operated in the shadow of the executive branch, which increasingly set the policy agenda."

After a couple sips of coffee, Pip continued. "Of course, the watershed events that permanently and radically expanded the federal government's power and elevated the presidency to near imperial dimensions were the Great Depression, World War II, and the Cold War. Franklin Roosevelt, Theodore's cousin, became president in 1933 at the depths of the Depression and remained in office until his death in 1945, by which time victory in World War II was at hand. FDR gets the credit or blame for creating the Leviathan State and transforming the presidency from Chief Magistrate into Chief Potentate. The economic emergency in the 1930s was so great that extraordinary measures were demanded by the public to address it. This led to massive, unprecedented, and in many cases permanent, government intervention in the economy. From that time forward, the public looked to the president, and to a lesser extent Congress, to initiate government action to keep the economy growing or lift it out of recession, and few of FDR's successors discouraged the public from attributing this power and responsibility to the president."

"How did Congress's role change in relation to the executive branch during this period, Pip?" asked Ding.

"Ever since Wilson's time, the Congress ceded, or some might say abdicated, much of its power to the executive branch. Much of this was due to the growth and complexity of government. Congress is designed to pontificate, debate, criticize, legislate, and provide oversight of the executive branch, but not to administer programs it authorizes. Over the past century, government departments and regulatory agencies with sweeping powers, too numerous to recite, have been established and placed under the president's direction. It is only natural that power increasingly has gravitated into the hands of the executive branch. The size of the White House staff also has grown exponentially to oversee all the cabinet departments, agencies, and huge bureaucracies that report to the president and comprise our modern government.

"Immediately following World War II," Pip went on, "the U.S. quickly demobilized as in all previous wars, but within a couple years the Cold War with the Soviet Union took center stage. This led to the build-up of a huge and permanent military establishment that we have to this day, which further contributed to the trend of centralizing power in the federal government, especially the presidency. To sum up, the combination of extensive involvement in the domestic economy through multitudinous regulations and even the takeover of distressed enterprises deemed too big to fail; the entitlement and social safety net programs; plus the enormous military establishment, explains the steady, uninterrupted growth in the power of the federal government over the past one hundred years and the eclipse of state governments as major players in our constitutional system."

"Thank you, Pip, for your insights," remarked Reb. "Between what we have heard from you and Wyatt, I'm sure we all have a better grasp of how the federal government has grown far beyond the limited, specific powers delegated to it by the states through the Constitution into, as Abby pointed out earlier, a national, almost monolithic, government of virtually unlimited powers."

Duane, who had been impatiently tapping a spoon on the cloth-covered table, interrupted. "But what can we do as a practical matter to change this fact? The omnipresent, omnipotent government genie is out of the bottle. Probably every power the feds have claimed as theirs has been challenged in court, and the Supreme Court generally has ruled in favor of expanding government. That means everything government does is constitutional and the supreme law of the land. Whether or not we agree with it is moot. We certainly can't put the genie back in the bottle, and I don't see how we or anyone can prevent the trend of the past century from continuing for another century."

"As a matter of law, I concur that rolling back the expanded powers the federal government has claimed for itself is unlikely to happen," proffered Wyatt. "The legal principle known as stare decisis holds that prior decisions made by superior courts, and no court is superior to the Supreme Court, are binding precedents that must be obeyed by inferior courts. In addition, under stare decisis, the Court should not overturn a prior decision that has become settled law without a compelling reason to do so. The *Brown* school desegregation decision I discussed earlier is an example of the court overturning the settled law established in the *Plessy* case, because the *Brown* court held the earlier precedent to be so unjust and unconstitutional that it set stare decisis aside. But it is rare for the court to do this."

"Okay," responded Reb, "we can't change the past, but perhaps we can find a way to rein in future encroachments by the federal government. For awhile I thought the Framers, for all their genius, had written a Constitution that lacked adequate restraints on a federal government that would constantly push to expand its sphere of power and influence. But I was wrong. If the Framers were here today, I believe they would be astounded to see that the states have abdicated their sovereignty and the rights available to them under the Constitution to check the federal government. The states have amendment power under Article V, which they have never used. They also can challenge federal overreach in court by asserting that the explicit wording of the Tenth Amendment trumps claims of implicit federal powers that usurp rights retained by the states or the people. Within each of the states resides the ultimate tribune of liberty, the consent of the people. The states have allowed themselves to be marginalized, yet they are the antidote to runaway federal government. States must reassert and reclaim their sovereign rights. The Framers expected the states to be the bulwark against federal encroachment, and that was the role they played at the beginning of the Republic."

Ding spoke up, "Reb, I like your argument and the passion with which you articulate it, but in 1789 there were only thirteen states. How could anyone herd together the fifty states we now have and get them to take a united stand against the government?"

"I don't know, Ding," replied Reb, "but it is not quite as daunting as you suggest. To convene a constitutional convention requires two-thirds or thirty-four states to send delegates. Adoption of any amendments proposed in convention would require ratification by three-fourths or thirty-eight states. There has not been a convention since 1787; after two hundred twenty-five years, however, it is not too soon to convene another. The fact it has never been done does not mean it is impossible. I believe we may be reaching a tipping point that could catalyze enough states to take action. Staggering debts and budget deficits, insecure borders, unfunded mandates, the requirement that citizens purchase health insurance, and now taxpayers in financially responsible states bailing out those states that have been profligate spenders for years are among the issues that have antagonized many states and voters. If only fifteen or twenty states called for a constitutional convention that would probably get the federal government's attention and perhaps some sensible policy changes."

Wyatt raised his hand and said, "Reb, you are right that under Article V, approval of two-thirds of the state legislatures is required to apply for a constitutional convention to propose amendments, but it is Congress that actually has the power to call a convention. Because this has never been done before, there are no precedents or established protocols. If two-thirds of the states ever did apply for a convention, I can imagine Congress would drag its feet or find technical fault with each state's application. I also expect that the hue and cry from thirty-four or more states, and their congressional delegations, might pressure Congress into calling a convention, but as I read Article V, the states could not directly call a constitutional convention.

"Incidentally, the fact that Article V provides for amendments to emanate from the states is because of George Mason who was instrumental in getting the Bill of Rights ratified. As Article V was originally drafted, only Congress had the power to propose amendments, but Mason feared the federal government could become oppressive. To protect against this, he argued successfully that the states should be able to petition Congress to call a convention to propose amendments. If thirty-four state legislatures were ever to do this, I believe it would have a salutary effect on the balance of power between the federal government and the states."

"Thank you for that clarification, Wyatt," responded Reb. "Once our committee has crafted specific proposals, we will have to identify two or three respected governors, ideally from both parties, who will champion the cause with their colleagues in the National Governors Association. From all we've heard today, I trust we agree that the federal government will never voluntarily curb its appetite for power and control without outside intervention. The states are the only constitutional power that can intervene, provided they muster the will to do so."

"I can put out some discreet feelers," suggested Ding, "with folks I know in several states that might be amenable to enlisting in our cause and see if there are one or two governors who might be willing to become ex officio members of the Madison Committee."

"Any other thoughts?" asked Reb of the group. Hearing none, he went on, "This has been a long but productive session. I propose we adjourn until our next meeting in two weeks. At that time, I would like to come up with several proposed amendments to the Constitution that, if adopted, might restore the balance of power among the people, the states, and the federal government. If we can reach agreement, we will turn to the nub of the matter, which is how to advance our agenda."

13

On April Fools' Day, 2013, Vice President Biff Fubarsky was in Texas on a political fence-mending visit, and to encourage the state Republican Party to begin lining up a slate of competitive candidates for the midterm elections in 2014. He was particularly concerned that a strong candidate for governor be nominated by the party. The current Republican governor would be retiring after fourteen years in office. Even though Texas normally was a reliable Republican state, after one-party control of the governorship for twenty years, voters might be in the mood for a change. Looking ahead to the 2016 presidential election, which was never far from the vice president's mind, keeping Texas in the Republican column was critical, because California and New York were almost certain to remain Democratic strongholds, and Florida was rated no better than a tossup. Without Texas and Florida, it would be virtually impossible to stitch together enough electoral votes to win President Thurston and Biff's reelection.

The vice president had arranged to meet with Sen. Ding Bell and Jake Fillmore, entrepreneur and chairman of the Texas Republican Party. Biff and Ding had a close relationship from their years serving together in the Senate, but Ding had no illusions about Biff's modest capabilities. Biff did not know Jake well, but his initial impression was not favorable. Jake was a tall, husky fellow who tended to be sarcastic and blunt. He viewed Biff as an amiable chap, but a self-important buffoon.

The morning meeting was held in Jake's fortieth floor business office conference room with a grand view of downtown Dallas. The vice president and Ding entered together and were greeted by Jake. "Hello, Ding, great to see you as always. Thank you for coming to Texas, Mr. Vice President. A couple of nights ago, I saw a TV news story that reported favorably on your appearance at the funeral of a foreign head of state."

Jake thought to himself that Biff was perfectly suited to represent the U.S. at the funerals of third world thug dictators in places like Crotchistan or Berserkistan. He also thought to himself how glad he was that his longtime friend Reb McCoy had declined to be considered a potential running mate for President Thurston. The vice presidency would have been a waste of Reb's talents.

After coffee was served, Biff asked Jake, "Based on current conditions, what's your assessment of Republican prospects in Texas next year, and can you hold the governorship?"

"Well, because Texas has always been a business friendly state, our economy has been doing better than the rest of the country, but over the past six months, growth has slowed. What we need out of Washington are targeted income tax cuts aimed at corporations and small businesses. If that happened, I'm confident growth would pick up between now and the 2014 election, and Republicans would be in great shape. If we can get a topflight candidate to run for governor, I think we have a good chance of holding that office. I also believe we will hold our own on the down ticket offices, because we have already recruited several impressive candidates. Money should not be a problem; I expect we will be able to outspend the Democrats by nearly a two-to-one margin. Things would be easier, however, if the administration implemented tangible policies in support of economic growth. What are the chances of getting a tax cut, Biff?"

Biff did not appreciate Jake addressing him informally. He expected everyone, other than longtime colleagues like Ding, to address him as Mr. Vice President. A man of his status deserved respect. Jake, an expert at taking the measure of a man, sensed Biff's vanity, but, except for his initial greeting, he refused to pander to this empty suit's ego.

Masking his irritation at this impertinence, Biff replied to Jake's question. "The Democrats will block any tax bill unless we agree to additional spending on their pet programs. The administration proposed pairing spending cuts with tax cuts for business to avoid increasing the deficit, but we can't reach agreement on which programs to cut. I would say we are at an impasse. Do you agree, Ding?"

"Yes, I do. Nothing will happen on tax cuts in this Congress. The bitter partisanship we've witnessed since 2006 has gotten worse. Rarely will either party reach across the aisle and make a sincere effort to forge a compromise, so we have gridlock."

Turning to Jake, Biff asked, "Who is the leading candidate for governor on the Republican ticket? Also, do the Democrats have a strong candidate to oppose us?"

"Of the three Republicans who have announced publicly they intend to run, Joe Harlow, representative from the 20th Congressional District, which includes San Antonio, is the frontrunner. He is a fine guy and a savvy politician, but I don't know how well he will play across the state. The Democrats have at least two strong candidates, either of whom is competitive against Harlow." Ding nodded his head in agreement with Jake's analysis.

"Who is your ideal candidate, and what would it take to persuade him or her to run?"

Ding blurted out, "Reb McCoy, if he would do it."

Jake immediately concurred, "Reb would be an outstanding candidate. A native Texan, he is a decorated Vietnam veteran, successful businessman, has an excellent reputation for integrity, and he is articulate and brilliant. Reb and his wife Marlenna are major philanthropists in Dallas where they are well known, and he has excellent contacts across the state. Also, I have seen him interviewed several times on television, and he is comfortable with that medium."

Jake and Reb met in Brazil in 1990, when both of them were living and working there. Their friendship continued after they returned to Texas. They typically got together socially once a month.

Biff was unenthusiastic about McCoy running for governor, because he was a potential rival. If elected governor of Texas, he immediately would be considered a potential candidate for national office. Biff knew McCoy would never accept the vice presidency, so there was no chance President Thurston would dump Biff to run with Reb for reelection in 2016. Biff's lifelong obsession was to be president, and he finally would have his chance to capture the prize in 2020. If possible, he wanted to clear the field of any strong competitors for his party's nomination. But 2020 was a long way off, an eternity in politics. In any case, to his knowledge, McCoy had never indicated any interest in running for governor, much less for president, so he might be fretting over nothing. Biff interrupted his train-of-thought to ask Jake, "Do you think a non-politician who has never run for elective office would have a realistic chance of being elected governor of Texas?"

"With all due respect, the professional politicians have screwed up the country big time. I believe the voters are desperate for a non-politician with the credentials of a Reb McCoy to stand for office. Of one thing I am certain, he would not engage in doubletalk, backstabbing, or dissembling, all of which are endemic to politicians."

Biff silently reflected on Jake's last comment. He attributed his long and successful career in politics to the fact that he possessed these traits in abundance.

"I second that, Jake," said Ding, "a guy like Reb is the real McCoy, no pun intended, although that might be a great campaign slogan. I've known Reb almost as long as Jake. He is a straight shooter, no bullshit about him, and he is a leader. I am certain there are no skeletons in his closet. What I don't know is whether he could be induced to run for governor. If he was amenable to entering politics, he definitely would not do so unless his wife Marlenna fully supported the idea. I've been working with him on a project lately and have thought about sounding him out on running for governor next year. Also, maybe we should try to enlist Marlenna in our cause."

"Assuming we are able to recruit Reb," said Jake, "I am confident he can win the general election, because he will score well with independent voters. But first he has to win the nomination, and that might be the steeper hill to climb. As a newcomer, he will have no base of party support, unlike Joe Harlow and the other Republican candidates, all of whom are seasoned politicians. If we can convince him to toss his hat into the ring in the next month or two, however, I believe he can mount a successful primary campaign. Reb's a competitive guy who will be committed to winning if he decides to run. Of course, as chairman of the Texas Republican Party, I won't be able to endorse his candidacy, but I can share privately and off the record with other key party leaders my objective assessment as to which candidate has the best chance of winning the general election. And winning is what politics is all about. Ding, I suggest you approach Reb, and at the appropriate time, I'll try to persuade Marlenna to keep an open mind about her husband plunging into politics."

"Sounds like a good plan of action," responded Ding. "I may have an opportunity to broach the subject with Reb in about two weeks." That was when the Madison Committee's next meeting was scheduled.

Despite his selfish misgivings, Biff recognized McCoy would be a great candidate for governor of Texas. "Ding, Jake, I suggest you start courting Mr. McCoy as soon as possible. The election is only a year and a half away. If he agrees to run, it will take time and money to build a top-flight campaign organization. The fact he is not a politician is both his strength and his weakness. This is a tough business as you both know, especially for a political neophyte. He'll have to be a quick study and surrounded by an experienced staff to keep him from making rookie mistakes. Good luck, and please keep me posted."

While Biff had no way of knowing it at the time, his intuitive fear of McCoy as a potential future political rival was well founded, but all that would play out in the future.

14

The Second Bill of Rights

Abigail Abbeville finished reading the proposed constitutional amendments drafted by Reb McCoy and presented to his colleagues at the third meeting of the Madison Committee. The empty plates, used to serve the typically delicious lunch prepared by the Rosewood Mansion chef, had been cleared away, and the doors to the library closed for privacy. Abby looked up over her large glasses and said, "Reb, why is there no balanced budget amendment? We discussed at length our concerns about the ever-increasing, seemingly out-of-control federal budget deficits at our first meeting. The government's debt and unfunded future liabilities imperil the country's future prosperity."

Reb put down his Diet Coke, cleared his throat, and said, "Abby, I had intended to include such an amendment for the reasons you just mentioned, but after doing some research, I concluded that a balanced budget amendment would be extremely difficult to enforce in practice, or if strictly enforced, might preclude the government from taking timely action to address unforeseen events. Also, our objective, I believe, is not to restrict the government from exercising its legitimate powers, but to restrain it from further expanding its powers beyond the Constitution's limits."

"Reb, please expand on your thinking," Duane Darby remarked. "I also share Abby's concern. The idea of a balanced budget amendment has been kicking around for years. I believe thirty-two state legislatures have petitioned Congress for such an amendment, just two states shy of the number needed to call a constitutional convention. This would be the most familiar and probably least controversial amendment we could propose, yet you have excluded it."

"Well, let me elaborate on my reasoning, Duane, by sharing a few arguments I found persuasive that have been raised by thoughtful people who are skeptical about a balanced budget amendment. Assume that Congress, in defiance of such an amendment, authorized appropriations that exceeded that fiscal year's projected revenues. If the president did not veto the excessive spending, but decided to honor the balanced budget mandate, that would require the president to decide which spending to impound or cut. The spending authority, however, resides with Congress, so this would contravene the Constitution's separation of powers. If the courts intervened, they would be engaged in decisions outside their competence. Or the courts might elect to stand above the dispute on the basis that it is for the legislative and executive branches to work out their differences. Moreover, do we want to amend the Constitution in a way that ultimately both the Congress and the president may disregard, and the courts may decline to adjudicate? In such a lamentable situation, we would have the Constitution being explicitly flaunted by those sworn to uphold it, which would undermine respect for the law of the land."

"On what basis would Congress and the executive branch brazenly defy an amendment to the Constitution?" asked Abby.

"Political expediency or political pressure from voters," replied Reb. "To balance the budget will require hard choices as to what expenditures to cut, and how high and on whom to raise taxes. In principle, most everybody is for a balanced budget as long as their ox is not gored. Most of the proposed balance budget amendments I've seen provide for a waiver if the country is at war, or a three-fifths majority vote in both the House and Senate specifies by how much expenditures may exceed revenues in that fiscal year. The odds of getting a supermajority vote in both houses to approve a waiver of the amendment are daunting, and, even if achieved, would likely require a lot of time and political compromises. In the meantime, the government would be helpless to take necessary action to address an urgent problem. To avert such a circumstance, the president might unilaterally suspend the amendment in order to meet the emergency. That is not how we want a constitutional government to operate. These are some of the potential but real unintended and undesirable consequences of adopting a balanced budget amendment."

Duane interrupted Reb. "How will the government ever get on a track of fiscal responsibility without some formal restraint? No matter how much the deficit grows, the clowns in Washington are ever ready to spend more. I'm not yet convinced a balanced budget amendment is not a good idea whose time is long overdue."

In reply, Reb said, "the government needs flexibility to address unforeseen crises promptly without having to obtain a supermajority vote in Congress to act, or compelling a president to suspend an amendment of the Constitution. At the time the fiscal year budget is put together, no one can predict a Hurricane Katrina or a deepwater oil well blowout followed by a massive spill, and rare is the economist who has accurately predicted a recession before it was already underway. In these examples, quick government action and spending are necessary to alleviate human suffering caused by a natural disaster, to contain environmental damage, or to keep a business downturn and accompanying job layoffs from turning into something far worse. In addition, events occur abroad where the United States is the only country with the resources and logistical capability to deliver humanitarian relief expeditiously. That is part of our obligation as the world's sole superpower. In such situations, we can't spend a lot of time deliberating whether or not we will waive the balanced budget requirement."

"How about the states, Reb?" asked Abby. "Most state constitutions mandate balanced budgets. Why shouldn't the federal government be subject to the same discipline?"

"That's quite true, Abby. In order to balance their annual budgets, however, many states resort to gimmicks that fool no one, like ignoring enormous unfunded pension liabilities. Such actions merely postpone the day of hard reckoning. Other states, like Texas, manage their fiscal affairs in a responsible fashion. But remember the federal government has the power to print money, unlike the states, and in the event of disaster, the feds come to the aid of an afflicted state. Setting aside whether the efforts were bungled, Louisiana and other Gulf states did not have the resources to cope with either Hurricane Katrina or the BP oil well blow-out, but the federal government was there to provide vast support."

Reb paused to sip his Diet Coke and continued. "Two final points. As I alluded earlier, the Framers did not explicitly or implicitly require the government's budget be balanced, and this was not an oversight. I am certain they anticipated the nation's fiscal affairs would be conducted with prudence and restraint. No doubt they would be horrified at the deficits and debts we have today and would consider our generation to be profligate beyond comprehension. But they anticipated there would be times, specifically during war, when the government would run a deficit. They also provided in the Constitution for Congress to borrow money, which government does to fund a deficit. To my second point, which will smack of heresy, I believe the federal government can operate at a deficit of 2 or 3 percent of GDP per year without being fiscally irresponsible. The typical annual growth rate of the U.S. economy would support a deficit of this magnitude, provided the government's total debt did not grow to an excessive amount. By the way, except for a brief time during Andrew Jackson's presidency in the 1830s, the U.S. government has always had public debt."

Judging from Abby's and Duane's facial expressions, Reb could tell they weren't entirely convinced. To move the discussion along, he said, "If I may, let me suggest we review the amendments I've drafted, with input from each of you since we last met, which I believe address the structural spending issue without putting the government into a fiscal strait jacket, or forcing elected officials to ignore a balanced budget mandate. If most of you still are not persuaded, we can include a balanced budget amendment. Mind you, a few days ago, I was convinced a balanced budget amendment was necessary, but after learning what I have just shared with you, I have concluded that the adverse consequences of such an amendment outweigh its reputed virtues."

Everyone turned their attention to the draft amendments, which Reb referred to as the Second Bill of Rights. The amendments were numbered in sequence beginning with XXVIII, because that would be the number of the next ratified amendment. Reb reminded the group he was not a lawyer, so the wording probably would need work. The proposed amendments were as follows:

Amendment XXVIII
Within three years following ratification of this amendment and thereafter, the total gross public debt of the United States, defined as the sum of debt held by the public, plus intergovernmental debt held by United States government agencies, plus debt of government sponsored enterprises guaranteed by the United States, shall not exceed one hundred percent of the gross domestic product of the United States, except as hereinafter provided. This limit may be increased to a specific percentage above one hundred percent by a three-fifths roll call vote of the whole number

of each House of Congress; or by a majority vote of each House of Congress in the event of war declared by Congress. Any increase in the gross public debt limit above one hundred percent shall expire coincident with the term of Congress authorizing such increase, and must be reauthorized by the successor Congress if it is to be continued. Congress shall act in good faith to reduce the gross public debt limit to no more than one hundred percent with all due celerity. Setting the gross public debt limit at any level below one hundred percent of gross domestic product shall be authorized by a majority vote of each House of Congress.

Amendment XXIX

Within three years following ratification of this amendment, all legislated rights to annuity or insurance entitlements granted by Congress to citizens on the basis of specific eligibility criteria that guarantee a current or future pecuniary benefit shall be actuarially sound and financially solvent, such that the present value of projected entitlement tax revenue shall not be less than the present value of projected entitlement expenditures, for no fewer than twenty-five years, as determined by an annual independent assessment. If the annuity and insurance entitlements granted by Congress thereafter fail to meet the annual actuarial and financial solvency standard, Congress shall adjust the benefits, tax rates, or eligibility criteria to ensure the entitlements meet the standard within no more than two years, so that future generations shall not be unduly burdened by the profligacy of earlier generations.

Amendment XXX

No member of Congress shall be eligible to serve in office longer than twelve years in either or both houses. Members of Congress at the time this amendment is ratified may be elected to serve another term irrespective of their total years of service, but the twelve year term limit shall apply thereafter.

Congress shall not exempt former, current, or future members from any laws and any such exemptions in effect prior to adoption of this amendment shall be null and void thereafter.

Following adoption of this amendment, no person shall be eligible to be a Representative who shall not have attained to the age of thirty five years; nor be eligible to be a Senator who shall not have attained to the age of forty years; nor be eligible to the Office of President, or the Office of Vice President who shall not have attained to the age of forty five years. Persons serving in any of the foregoing offices at the time this amendment is ratified shall be exempt from these minimum age eligibility requirements.

Amendment XXXI

Engagement of the United States military in hostilities against a foreign enemy shall not extend beyond thirty days without a resolution of approval by Congress, nor extend beyond ninety days without a declaration of war by Congress.

Amendment XXXII

The United States is delegated the power, duty, and primary responsibility to take necessary and proper measures to secure, protect, and defend its sovereign international borders. Any State by adopted resolution of its legislature and governor that asserts its international border is inadequately secured, protected, or defended may seek redress from the United States. Within sixty days, unless extended by mutual consent, the aggrieved State and the United States shall endeavor in good faith to negotiate a mutually satisfactory remedy. If agreement cannot be reached, the aggrieved State may unilaterally take necessary and proper measures to secure its international border, provided that in doing so it shall not violate the sovereign international border of a foreign country.

Amendment XXXIII

The Judicial power of the United States vested in the Supreme Court and various inferior Courts is limited to interpretation of the Constitution and the laws of the United States enacted in pursuance thereof, and to judicial review of the constitutionality of laws enacted by Congress, and by the States if such laws relate to powers delegated to the United States by the Constitution. The Judicial power shall not extend to changing or creating law, which power is vested solely in Congress. If the Courts deem a clause, section, article, or amendment of the Constitution to be ambiguous, open to different reasonable interpretations, or in conflict with another part of the Constitution, the Courts shall look to prior precedents and case law to inform opinions rendered. Due deference and consideration shall be accorded Amendments IX and X whenever either of those amendments appears in conflict with another clause, section, article, or amendment of the Constitution.

Amendment XXXIV
Commencing with the twenty fifth anniversary year of this amendment's adoption and every quarter century thereafter, a Constitutional Convention shall be convened during the third calendar quarter at a time and place designated by the Congress. Constitutional Conventions shall meet in public session, be attended by no fewer than three and no more than five delegates from each State, and be presided over by the Chief Justice of the United States. Each State shall have one vote in Convention, and delegates shall be chosen by each State from among its citizens in a manner it deems appropriate, provided that no more than one delegate from each State shall hold elective office during the time a Convention is in session.

The primary objects of Constitutional Conventions are to reaffirm the Constitution as drafted in the year one thousand seven hundred eighty seven and subsequently amended; to educate and remind the people that free government and the blessings of liberty can be preserved only through an informed citizenry and eternal vigilance; and to propose amendments as may be deemed necessary and proper by a majority of the States, such amendments, if any, to be referred to the several States for ratification in accordance with Article V of the Constitution.

◦———◦

After everyone had read the proposed constitutional amendments, Ding Bell spoke. "These are quite impressive, and it's obvious a good deal of thought has gone into each amendment. I suggest we discuss each one to see where we may have agreement or reservations. Then we can turn to considering other amendments anyone may wish to offer."

"Reb," began Abby, "I didn't grasp it on my first reading, but I now see that the proposed 28th and 29th amendments get at the balanced budget question in a novel way. Effectively capping the gross national debt and mandating that entitlement programs theoretically be solvent for at least a quarter century addresses the country's structural fiscal imbalance and places us on a path to fiscal responsibility. I'm not sure a debt to GDP ratio of 100 percent is too high or too low, and I'd be more comfortable requiring the entitlements to be solvent for half a century."

"You may be right, Abby," responded Reb, "the benchmarks perhaps should be adjusted after more thorough analysis by experts, such as yourself. I do know that the Congressional Budget Office estimates the public-plus-intergovernmental debt to be around $19 trillion by the end of this fiscal year 2013, which is 100 percent of forecast GDP. Over two-thirds of that debt is held by the public, including foreign countries and persons. By 2020, the CBO forecasts the public debt alone will equal 100 percent of GDP, because of projected budget deficits the government will incur over the next seven years. As defined today, gross federal debt does not include government guaranteed debt of the federal home mortgage loan entities, Fannie Mae and Freddie Mac, which totals $5 trillion. This guaranteed debt would be included in total gross debt as defined in the proposed 28th amendment. That would drive this year's gross debt to GDP ratio up to 130 percent, and perhaps over 150 percent by 2020. Under the proposed 28th amendment, Congress would either have to reduce the ratio to 100 percent, or obtain a supermajority vote in both houses to keep it above that level. Perhaps the language should be modified to allow Congress five instead of three years to reduce the debt in an orderly manner after the amendment is adopted. Regarding the solvency of entitlements and whether twenty-five years is adequate, that is a minimum standard. Congress could choose to modify the programs to ensure they are solvent for a longer period."

Duane spoke next. "Reb, after considering your remarks about the drawbacks of a balanced budget amendment, I agree that the proposed 28th and 29th amendments would be a more effective way to force fiscal discipline on Congress. By limiting total U.S. debt to a percentage of GDP instead of a specific dollar amount, politicians in both parties will be incentivated to pursue pro-growth economic policies. As the economy grows, so will government's capacity to issue debt, if necessary, and simultaneously, increased tax revenue will flow into the U.S. Treasury. Also, requiring a supermajority vote in both houses of Congress to increase the gross debt above 100 percent of GDP should engender confidence in the international financial markets that there will be an effective upper-limit constraint on U.S. government spending and borrowing.

"By the way, did you consider an amendment to abolish the Federal Reserve Bank and replacing it with a hard currency backed by gold as the country had until the 1930s?"

"That's a question beyond my competence, Duane. Perhaps Abby can answer you."

"There are many advantages and disadvantages to having the currency linked to a gold standard," replied Abby. "It's a complicated topic, but on balance I believe a gold standard is not sufficiently flexible to manage monetary policy, and therefore could exacerbate recessions and inhibit long-term economic growth. Many, but by no means all, economists blame the gold standard for worsening and prolonging the Great Depression of the 1930s. It was only after the U.S. abandoned the gold standard in 1933 that the economy began to recover.

"Following the 1944 Bretton Woods conference in New Hampshire, the U.S. returned to a partial gold standard, whereby foreign currency transactions could be settled in dollars or gold at a fixed exchange rate. In 1971, President Nixon abandoned this convertibility agreement by closing the international gold window. Since then, the dollar's value has been determined via floating exchange rates. As a practical matter, there isn't enough gold to return to a gold standard. As I recall, the total quantity of gold extracted in all of history is around six billion troy ounces. At today's price of $1,700 per ounce, the value of the world's gold is approximately $10 trillion. That is about equal to the money supply in circulation in the U.S. today. The U.S. government's official gold reserves total around 260 million ounces and are worth about $450 billion, less than 5 percent of our money in circulation. For a gold standard to be credible, the government should have gold reserves equal to about 40 percent of the money supply."

"What about the Federal Reserve System, Abby?" asked Duane.

"There are many who condemn the Federal Reserve System. Some believe it was a conspiracy cooked up by Wall Street and politicians to benefit fat cat bankers. But it has been with us now for a century, and to replace it with some other central banking system would be destabilizing and doubtless have its own unforeseen flaws. At least the Fed is independent, which insulates it to a great extent from short-term political pressure and manipulation. It has made mistakes and bad judgments over the years, but it also has been effective at holding down inflation the past thirty-five years, and facilitating economic growth. No central bank, however wise its monetary policy, can compensate for irresponsible government fiscal policies. That's why I would focus on that problem, which the proposed 28th and 29th amendments do."

Reb thanked Abby for her insights and said, "I think we should not focus on limiting or narrowing the enumerated constitutional powers of Congress, even if some of the legislation it enacts, agencies it creates, or policies it embraces pursuant to exercising those powers you and I may consider misguided. My goal is to try to erect a stronger constitutional fence that will prevent the federal government, even if its intent is benign, from extending its authority into areas beyond the specific powers granted to it."

"I'd like to turn to the proposed 30th amendment, which places a twelve-year term limit on Representatives and Senators," bellowed Ding, a twinkle in his eye. "You're going to force me to find honest work, Reb. Are you willing to deny the good and wise voters of Texas the freedom to reelect me till I die? Seriously, this is the most important of the proposed amendments in my opinion. We need to air out Congress, let the sun shine in, get rid of the dead wood, and have a regular influx of new blood. It would be invigorating and a great disinfectant."

"I heartily agree," said Pip Pippin. "With the exception of George Washington, and possibly Abraham Lincoln and Gen. U.S. Grant, there are no indispensable individuals in American history. We need to end the careerism, which, I believe, has been a major contributing factor to the unbridled growth of government. I also applaud prohibiting Congress from exempting itself from laws imposed on the rest of us. Senators and congressmen have exempted themselves from many laws, including affirmative action, minimum wage, equal employment opportunity, and civil rights. The hypocrisy and cynicism of the people's elected representatives placing themselves above any law they pass is outrageous."

Judge Wyatt Solomon joined in saying, "I concur with Ding and Pip. I also believe that raising the minimum age requirement is a good idea. There aren't that many people in Congress under age forty, but raising the age of eligibility by ten years for elective federal offices implies that people should accomplish something in life before arriving in Washington. Not to pick on Vice President Fubarsky, but he was an ambulance chaser for five years after he got out of law school, was elected to a low level local office, and then lightning struck at age thirty when he was elected to the Senate, a seat he held for over thirty years before being selected as the president's running mate. He is one of many similar examples I could cite. The people are better served by representatives who are experienced, seasoned, and successful, ideally in the private sector, before they get to Washington, and who know their time in Congress is finite. Such people, I believe, are more apt to put the country's interest ahead of their personal or party interest. Of course, Ding, you are an example of the type public servant we need, but, for God's sake, not for more than a dozen years."

"Hey, Reb," asked Ding, "how come you didn't put in a mandatory retirement age for judges like Wyatt here?"

Reb laughed and said, "I don't want to be accused of discrimination against the elderly."

"One thing is certain," opined Wyatt, "imposing term limits on Congress could be initiated only by the states, because Congress will never propose such an amendment for obvious reasons. No amendments have ever been initiated by the states. And none of the seventeen amendments since the Bill of Rights, all of which were initiated by Congress, has curtailed the power of the federal government. No surprise there."

"One of the criticisms of term limits I've heard," commented Duane, "is that forcing a popular congressperson to retire denies the voters the freedom to elect the candidates they want to represent them. After all, Fubarsky was reelected five times by large majorities, so Rhode Island voters must have liked him. Another criticism is that the government is so big and complex, a cadre of officials with twenty years of service or more is essential to preserve institutional memory and the wisdom that comes with seniority."

"Well, speaking as someone who has served in the sausage factory called Congress," responded Ding, "your point about restricting voters' freedom is bogus, because, as Pip said earlier, there are no indispensable people, and public service ought to be viewed as a temporary duty and honor, not as a career in elective office. The only freedom being denied is that of a particular senator or representative to stay in office forever. You rarely hear anyone complain about presidents being limited to two terms in office, which has applied to every president since Harry Truman. As to your second point, one of the primary reasons government is so big and complex is because the barons and baronesses in Congress, many of whom have been there a quarter century or longer, spend most of their time dreaming up ways to expand government and to raise campaign funds even if they have a safe seat. And take it from me, among my Senate colleagues, wisdom is in short supply, but everyone is shrewd enough to protect their turf. As far as institutional memory is concerned, that's what history books and the permanent staff employed by Congress can provide."

"As I already mentioned, I agree with twelve-year term limits for Congress," said Pip, "as well as raising the age eligibility requirements. As a historian, however, I note that Theodore Roosevelt was forty-two and John Kennedy was forty-three when they became president. History generally holds both men in high regard, but had this proposed 30th amendment been in effect back in their day, neither could have been president."

Duane immediately replied, "Yes, but they could have waited a few years until they reached age forty-five, and then run for president or vice president. I think the fact that only two of the country's forty-five presidents thus far were under age forty-five on entering office suggests that the proposed age limit is reasonable. "

Reb then asked Pip to discuss the proposed 31st amendment, which he and Duane had recommended.

"Thanks, Reb. Congress has not declared war since World War II, yet over the past sixty years, America's armed forces have been sent into combat on numerous occasions, now mostly forgotten. I bet most Americans would be surprised to learn that the total number of Americans killed during undeclared wars since 1950 exceeds one-hundred-eighteen thousand; wounded total two-hundred-eighty-five thousand. The major conflicts, of course, were Korea, Vietnam, Iraq, and Afghanistan. From my perspective, if the nation is going to ask its young men and women to fight on foreign battlefields where many will be killed or wounded, and they are expected to kill enemy combatants, Congress has a moral and constitutional obligation to declare war. A resolution supporting a military mission and appropriating funds is not sufficient, especially for a prolonged military campaign. A formal declaration of war is an unequivocal commitment by the United States government to a hazardous endeavor that is vital to the national interest. We should not ask our troops to risk and perhaps give their lives for anything less."

For a moment, the room was silent. Everyone's attention focused on Pip whose empty right sleeve was a constant reminder of what going to war had cost him.

Duane spoke first. "Vietnam was Reb's and my war. I have to wonder how that long conflict, which tore the country apart, saw fifty-eight thousand soldiers die, and ended up with Congress shamefully abandoning its pledge to support South Vietnam after the U.S. military departed in 1973, would have been affected had this proposed 31st amendment been in effect in 1965. Either Vietnam would have been a declared war in which case it presumably would have had broad public support and the government's commitment to win, or it would have been over in ninety days. As it was, the war was shaped more by domestic politics than by military judgment. That's the worst way to fight a war. It was a surreal experience for a Vietnam vet to return home and be spat upon or have epithets hurled at him if he wore his uniform in public. Most of those guys didn't volunteer to go to war; they were drafted and had no choice unless daddy was rich and connected. This amendment is long overdue. I suspect that when the Framers gave Congress the power to declare war, they hoped it would not have to be exercised, but expected it would be in the event of a major and extended conflict." Everyone nodded in agreement.

"Thank you, Duane," remarked Reb. "I second your and Pip's eloquent remarks. The next proposed amendment, the 32nd, relates to border security. That such an amendment is needed should shock any citizen. The most fundamental reason for government to exist is to secure, protect, and defend the country's sovereign borders. Unfortunately for years, both Democratic and Republican administrations have not effectively secured or controlled the U.S.' borders, in particular with Mexico. Consequently, about sixteen million illegal immigrants reside within the United States. I believe we all favor legal immigration on a controlled, orderly basis. We are a nation that welcomes immigrants from all over the world. They are the tapestry of America's history. No serious country, however, can maintain its sovereignty without securing its international frontiers.

"Apart from illegal immigrants, Mexico's drug wars are threatening border cities like El Paso and Laredo, and a few early stage terrorist plots aimed at the U.S. have been uncovered that were being planned in Mexico. Securing our two-thousand-mile border with Mexico is a challenge, but it can and must be done. Because the federal government has been derelict in this regard, this amendment explicitly states border security is a primary duty of the United States, but if it fails to perform that duty, the states can petition the government to remedy the situation and failing that, the states may take unilateral steps to control their international borders. If adopted, this amendment would end the spectacle of the government suing a state for protecting its borders, as happened several years ago with Arizona."

"I support this amendment," commented Abby, "although I am disappointed it is needed. The irony is farcical. Here we have a federal government constantly seeking to expand its power beyond its constitutional mandate, while failing to exercise its inherent power and obligation to defend the country's borders. But why is the amendment silent on how to deal with the illegal immigrants residing in the U.S.?"

Before Reb could respond, Ding spoke up, "Abby, the handling of illegal immigrants is an issue, I believe, best solved through politics, elections, and the passage of time. Any politician who has advocated, as I and others have, a pragmatic, fair, and humane solution that includes an earned pathway to citizenship for illegal immigrants is castigated for favoring amnesty. Other folks argue irrationally that we should round up and deport all the illegal immigrants. We are talking about five percent of the country's population! The raw emotions and heated rhetoric triggered by this issue are such that I doubt an amendment addressing illegal immigration could be written that would win ratification. If we effectively secure our borders, however, which the proposed 32nd amendment would do, the illegal immigrant problem would solve itself in a couple generations."

"Abby, are you satisfied with Ding's answer to your question?" Abby nodded, and Reb turned to Wyatt. "Judge, would you please comment on the proposed 33rd amendment, which you drafted?"

"Sure, Reb. The intent is to impose boundaries on and clarify the powers of the federal courts. Courts are to interpret the law, never make law. This amendment also would enshrine in the Constitution the Supreme Court's power to declare laws unconstitutional, which it has asserted since the *Marbury v. Madison* case in 1803. Finally, the forgotten Ninth and Tenth Amendments, the key safeguards of the numerous and indefinite rights of individuals and states that are not to be encroached upon by the federal government, are restored to prominence by being specifically emphasized. If adopted, one would hope that judges in the future would follow both the letter and the spirit of this amendment in adjudicating cases brought before them."

"Okay," said Reb, "we now come to the 34th amendment, which may be the most controversial. As we all know, there has not been a constitutional convention since 1787. I believe that is one key reason we have drifted so far from the Founding Fathers' original idea of a limited federal government possessing specific, enumerated powers into today's leviathan national government. Had constitutional conventions been held from time to time since the Constitution was ratified, the states would have had greater leverage to curb federal overreach. Just the threat of amendments to rein in the feds might modify behavior, and if three-fourths of the states agreed, the Constitution could in fact be amended. Also, a constitutional convention would be an opportunity to reintroduce Americans to the history and ideas behind our system of self-governance, and reinforce the imperative of maintaining the proper balance among the individual, the states, and the federal government that is the foundation of the republic and our liberties."

"This is an excellent idea," said Ding, "but holding a convention only every quarter century years seems too infrequent to me."

"Hell, Ding, we haven't had a constitutional convention in over two-hundred-twenty-five years, and now you think every twenty-five years is not frequent enough," Reb joked. "Actually, at first I thought a convention should be held every fifty years, but then I decided each generation deserves the opportunity to experience a constitutional convention and to reaffirm its commitment to limited government and individual liberty. Of course, the only chance this amendment has of ever being considered for adoption would be if two-thirds of the states petition Congress to call a convention, because you can bet your last dollar Congress will never initiate this amendment or any of the others we have discussed today."

Wyatt turned to Reb and said, "I applaud this idea, but some fear a constitutional convention might spin out of control and come up with off-the-wall amendments and perhaps throw out the original Constitution and start over."

"In my opinion, Wyatt, that is not a serious concern. Even if a majority of the states attending a convention did run amok, say eighteen out of thirty-four, it would still be necessary for three-fourths of all the states, at least thirty-eight, to ratify any amendments. I have faith there always will be at least thirteen sober and responsible states that can be counted on to vote against and therefore block ratification of absurd amendments."

Abby spoke next, "Reb, these are all excellent amendments, and I sense all of us support them. But, in looking over my notes from our first meeting, a number of constitutional concerns were raised then, which have not been addressed. These include requiring citizens to purchase health insurance, imposing unfunded mandates on states, presidential signing statements, questioning the legality of executive orders, wiretapping international phone calls by U.S. citizens without a court ordered warrant, cutting special deals for favored crony capitalists, disregarding secured creditors' rights in bankruptcy, and taking over distressed companies."

"Abby, I'll try to address each of those, and I welcome opinions from anyone else. The Madison Committee's objectives have been, first, to curb the federal government's bloated budget deficits and crushing debt load, which are the biggest immediate threats to the country's future; second, to rein in the government's appetite for encroaching on powers not delegated to it; and third, to level the political order of battle by tilting the balance of power back toward the states and the people. We should limit the number of proposed amendments to those essential to achieving these three objectives. Also, having fewer amendments makes it easier for us and the public to keep them in mind. If we come up with a plethora of amendments, it will be too easy for opponents to pick them off one by one, and it might be easier to characterize what we are doing as being driven by a political agenda.

"We also should be careful," Reb continued, "not to amend the Constitution in a misguided attempt to resolve policy or political disputes. Such matters, I believe, are better sorted out in the normal course of politics, elections, and governance, even if you or I may disagree with a particular outcome. One of you suggested," Reb did not mention it was Duane, "an amendment requiring a supermajority vote by Congress to increase income taxes, which would effectively block Congress from ever raising taxes again. Now, I generally oppose higher marginal tax rates, because I believe experience demonstrates such action is counterproductive. Higher taxes inhibit economic growth and job creation, and do not raise that much marginal tax revenue, because the rich find legal ways to shelter their income. Many brilliant economists argue passionately on both sides of the tax issue. This just proves to me that economics is not an empirical science, nor is it even a social science; it's more akin to political science. The bottom line, in my view, is that federal tax policy is a political issue to be decided by voters and politicians, not by constitutional amendment. Moreover, as a practical matter, any politically viable solution to the deficit problem will require both spending cuts and tax increases.

"I am not so naïve as to think that people, who disagree with what we are proposing, will probably label this effort as a conservative or right wing conspiracy. I suspect most of us are conservative or right of center, but that's not the point. I want to make this about the Constitution, federalism, and individual liberty. People of goodwill on the left and the right of the political spectrum should be able to find common ground on these issues. Granted, liberals generally support expanding federal power, because that makes it easier to implement their utopian agenda. But that is a two-edged sword when conservatives are in charge, because they also have tried to enlarge government power to fit their agenda."

Ding interrupted. "The amendments we have reviewed today appropriately do not set government policy. They establish boundaries that we all believe will minimize future encroachments by the federal government on the rights of states and the people, but leave ample latitude for the government to act. The amendments setting a maximum total debt to GDP ratio and making entitlements solvent are essential, because the elected politicians have demonstrated they are unable or incompetent to deal with these issues, which will bankrupt the country if not resolved soon. The term limits amendment gets at a core reason so much power has shifted to Washington over many years. To send the military into combat is the most solemn decision taken by government. If we are going to engage in hostilities for more than ninety days, it is reasonable to require Congress to exercise its war declaration power for all the reasons Pip and Duane gave us. The amendment for securing the country's sovereign borders unfortunately is necessary to give states the power to control their international borders if the federal government fails to do so. Regarding the judiciary amendment, those who believe in a living or evolving Constitution will oppose it, but most reasonable people would agree that judges should not make law, else why have legislators, and we want the Ninth and Tenth Amendments resurrected. This is certainly consistent with the Founders' idea of limited government. Finally, holding a constitutional convention every twenty-five years is a brilliant idea to empower the states and the people and keep the feds honest. The amendments we have proposed do not encroach on the federal government's powers in an inappropriate way, but they do reaffirm the powers and rights reserved to the states and the people."

"Abby, I want to get back to the items you raised," said Reb, "and go over each one. The requirement that all citizens purchase health insurance, which all of us believe is unconstitutional, is working its way through the judicial system. However it turns out, I don't think an amendment should be crafted to address this specific issue. It seems to me that a fair reading of the Ninth and Tenth Amendments clearly indicates how the courts should rule, although they may decide the commerce clause or general welfare clause takes precedence. Regarding unfunded mandates, again, I think an amendment narrowly aimed at this problem should not be written into the

Constitution. The states should band together and just say no to unfunded mandates. Presidential signing statements and executive orders are separation of power issues. If Congress feels the executive is usurping its constitutional powers, Congress should assert its authority. The same applies to wiretapping without court-issued warrants; either the courts or Congress could direct the president to cease doing this.

"That brings us to your next item, Abby," Reb continued, "crony capitalism. As a recovering businessman, I defer to no one in my contempt for the special deals, subsidies, and tax breaks, as well as regulatory favors, which too many industries and big companies cajole out of government with lobbying and targeted campaign donations. This is legal corruption and distorts the free market. Because government is so gigantic and involved in most every aspect of the economy, and huge, global companies have enormous political influence, I don't see how a firewall can be erected between them. As much as I would like to see an amendment separating business from government, just like religion, this is utterly impractical. Business and government have to interact with each other, and because government is always going to regulate and tax business, executives will rightly lobby government to protect their interests. Anybody have another perspective?"

Wyatt sat up and said, "Unfortunately, I think you are correct, Reb. Modern business and modern government are inextricably linked in a symbiotic relationship. I don't see how to unravel it. Just as Abby remarked earlier about the Federal Reserve System, if you change or abolish it, what will take its place, and will that result in a new set of problems, which might be worse than what we have now? Perhaps an amendment outlawing political contributions by companies and unions, either directly or through political action committees, would remove the appearance and possibly the fact of politicians favoring special interests. Permit political contributions only by individual persons. If the term limits amendment ever is ratified, much of this problem should be mitigated if you believe non-career congresspersons will be less susceptible to granting favors to business interests."

"Now if I may," Wyatt continued, his voice rising, "I would like to address the bankruptcy issue. As we discussed at an earlier meeting, the government's arbitrary negation of the rights of secured creditors in the 2009 Chrysler bankruptcy proceeding was inexcusable. Even worse, the courts upheld this action, although they lamely said it did not constitute a precedent. That may be small comfort for other secured creditors. This is 'living, breathing' law, where the unequivocal terms of a legally binding contract entered into voluntarily and in good faith by a borrower and lenders are set aside by a third party—the federal government—for some higher social good. But how does one amend the Constitution to deal with this? Article I, Section 8, already grants to Congress the power to establish 'uniform Laws on the subject of Bankruptcies throughout the United States.' If the president, who is sworn to 'preserve, protect and defend the Constitution of the United States,' willfully disregards the bankruptcy laws, or any other laws, passed by Congress, and neither Congress nor the courts countermand the president's action, writing a constitutional amendment saying the president shall uphold the bankruptcy laws, as he has already sworn to do, will be of no effect. The Constitution is nothing more than quaint eighteenth-century legal prose written on parchment if the persons sworn to uphold it in all three branches of the government don't take their duty seriously."

"Thank you, Wyatt," remarked Reb. "Your analysis, as usual, is persuasive. Let's move on to the last item on Abby's list—government takeover of distressed businesses."

Duane jumped in first. "Nothing in the Constitution grants the power to the government to assume control of a privately held or publicly traded company in the private sector. An exception is the banking industry, which is heavily regulated for good reason, because the collapse of one or more large institutions could cascade into an economic meltdown, which might have occurred in 2008, had the Federal Reserve and the Treasury Department not stepped in quickly to restore confidence. Money and credit provided through the banking system are as essential to a functioning economy, as the flow of blood is to a living human being. But what is the legal justification for taking over General Motors or Chrysler? If government can do that, what can prevent it from taking over any other large company or industry in the future it deems too big to fail?"

"I share your concerns, Duane," muttered Ding, "but had GM and Chrysler been allowed to collapse, the economic damage would have been calamitous and affected countless communities across America. Not only would employees of GM and Chrysler have lost their jobs, but auto dealerships would have closed and parts suppliers would have gone under, which likely would have dragged Ford into bankruptcy. Then there are all the indirect jobs in restaurants, hardware stores, and many other mom-and-pop shops that depend on auto industry workers to patronize their businesses. Frankly, had I been in either Bush or Obama's shoes in 2008 and 2009, I would have held my nose and bailed out GM and Chrysler. Yet, I concede there is no constitutional authority for government to take over private sector companies and pour taxpayer dollars into them. In this case, however, I would have invoked the general welfare clause to justify such action."

Wyatt asked, "Why couldn't GM and Chrysler have been reorganized under the bankruptcy laws without being backstopped by the government? They would have continued doing business as before while bankruptcy court sorted out how much creditors would be paid. This process happens all the time and most companies emerge from bankruptcy in a healthy financial condition or its business is acquired by another company."

"Wyatt, in principle, I agree with you," responded Reb. "The process of 'creative destruction' is necessary for the free enterprise system to flourish and capital to be efficiently allocated to the most competitive and profitable firms. The automobile business, however, is not the same as a detergent maker, restaurant chain, airline, book store, or most any other business. Consumers will continue without reservation to patronize a business or buy a consumable product or a service from a firm that is in bankruptcy. But a bankrupt car company probably would see sales plummet, because customers would be concerned whether the warranty would be honored and the dealer would be there to service the vehicle. A car is the largest or second largest purchase the average person ever makes. Confidence that the manufacturer will honor its warranty and the dealer network will be around as long as you own your new car is an important consideration in the buying decision. As Ding already related, the failure of GM and Chrysler would have had a huge ripple effect on the economy. Consequently, the government probably had no choice but to step in to keep their sales from collapsing and to avoid widespread economic calamity."

Duane jumped into the conversation. "I'm not familiar with Chrysler's background, but GM's problems didn't pop up unexpectedly because of the 2008 burst housing bubble and subsequent recession, events beyond its control or ability to predict. These events only accelerated GM's inevitable fate. The genesis of its problems goes back thirty or forty years. Several generations of incompetent management; an ossified, inbred corporate culture; and a shortsighted union conspired to bring down the once largest and most profitable company in the world. In a way, GM is a cautionary tale for the U.S. government if it doesn't slash its budget deficits soon, but I'm not sanguine the politicians grasp this insight. If GM and Chrysler were too big to fail, would it not have been better for the feds to step in five, ten, or twenty years ago to broker necessary changes in management and to curtail union demands, perhaps averting the near collapse and government takeover in 2009?"

"Duane, expecting government to be clairvoyant," replied Reb, "or to know when to intervene in the management of a major corporation or industry is not only beyond its competence, but borders on empowering government to nationalize a major corporation or industry whenever it sees fit to do so. That certainly is at odds with the principles of limited government, individual liberty, private property rights, and free enterprise. I struggled to craft an amendment to address this issue. One thought was to require prior approval of Congress to take over a private sector company, provided that within two years said firm would have to be sold to the public, or its assets liquidated, unless Congress authorized a one-time extension of no more than two additional years. I oppose such an amendment, however, because one party in control of the presidency and both houses of Congress potentially could abuse this power to impose its political agenda on the private sector. Such an eventuality could fatally compromise the free enterprise system. That is too much to risk."

"One way to deal with this problem," suggested Wyatt, "might be to determine which companies are too big to fail, based on legislatively established criteria related to size, financial health, and economic impact in the event of bankruptcy. A company so designated could be preemptively required to break up into smaller independent entities before the government felt compelled to take it over. Administered by an independent agency, such as the Federal Reserve, a 'Business Too Big to Fail' law would be similar to longstanding antitrust law, which provides government the remedy of forcing the break up of business cartels and monopolies that might harm competition or restrain trade. But I agree with Reb, a constitutional amendment is not a good idea."

Checking his watch and realizing the meeting was running late, Reb began to wrap up. "Folks, this has been a terrific discussion. If adopted, our proposed amendments would represent the most fundamental redirection of the federal government in over a century. Taken together these seven amendments truly are a Second Bill of Rights that would reaffirm the founding principles of limited government, states rights, individual liberty, and financial solvency, which have been eclipsed too long by the federal government's relentless march toward centralizing ever more power and spending in Washington."

"Now, at our next meeting," continued Reb, "we need to develop a realistic strategy for moving our ideas forward. Whatever that strategy might be, it will have to be aimed at getting the states on board, because we have all said that members of both parties in Congress would correctly see our proposals as threats to their power and prerogatives and dismiss them out of hand. This is a tall order for five citizens and one U.S. senator."

At this point, Wyatt spoke, "We may be on a fool's errand, but if not us, who? And if not now, when? I have led a charmed life, and more than my fair share of America's blessings have fallen upon my shoulders like pixie dust. But I fear for the future of America and the generations that come after us. Therefore, I am committed to this endeavor until such time as we achieve our goal, or we all conclude the effort is futile."

"We need to jolt the system," said Ding. "We must change the perception in most Americans' minds that there is no alternative to the status quo of virtually unchecked federal power. We have to persuade citizens at the grassroots level that the nanny state's intrusion into every nook and cranny of daily life is not inevitable or irreversible, and most important, it is inimical to individual liberty and personal responsibility. President Gerald Ford once said, 'A government big enough to give you everything you need is big enough to take everything you have.'"

Reb said, "President Ford's wise and pithy insight is a good place to conclude our meeting. See you all in two weeks."

As everyone stood to depart, Ding pulled Reb aside and said, "If you've got a few minutes, I'd like to chat with you. I don't know about you, but I'm stiff from sitting too long. Why don't we go for a walk?"

"Okay," replied Reb. "Let me put my papers in the car, and we'll take a stroll down Turtle Creek Boulevard."

15

Reb and Ding exited the Rosewood's lobby and headed down the hill turning left on Turtle Creek Boulevard, a lovely, shaded residential street of high-end homes and condominiums. They walked in silence for several minutes. When they reached Lee Park, a nine-acre urban oasis carpeted in lush green grass and dappled with American red oak trees and banks of azaleas, Ding suggested they trudge up the hill to the monument.

In 1936, President Franklin Roosevelt attended the dedication of Lee Park. During his Dallas visit, he stayed at the Rosewood Mansion, which was a private home at that time. Lee Park was named in honor of General Robert E. Lee, the heroic and gallant Confederate commander during the Civil War. Three score and eleven years after the Civil War ended, FDR's presence at the dedication was a magnanimous gesture to the man who embodied the honor and chivalry of the Confederacy, and symbolically acknowledged that the history of Texas and the South during the Civil War was part of the reunited nation's common history.

At the center of the park stands a wonderful, larger-than-life bronze equestrian statue of Gen. Lee astride his famous horse, Traveller, posed with left front hoof raised. To Lee's right and slightly behind him is a statue of a young rebel soldier riding a smaller horse and representing all the men of Lee's army. Reb admired the statue and the man it honored, but thought it unusual that the sculptor posed Lee holding his hat in his right hand. As Reb recalled, the other equestrian statues of Gen. Lee he had seen at Charlottesville, Richmond, and Gettysburg, all portrayed him without a hat. To the best of Reb's recollection, he had never seen another equestrian military statue where the general honored did not have his hat on his head. He wondered why Lee's sculptors chose to depict him sans hat, although it certainly drew one's attention to the general's handsome visage, which Reb thought reflected the character of the man.

Reb and Ding took a moment to admire the statue that had stood there over seventy-five years, and then continued ascending the hill to Arlington Hall, a two-thirds-scale replica of Lee's Virginia home outside Washington, which was confiscated by the Union during the Civil War and later became the site of Arlington National Cemetery. On this chilly, overcast April afternoon, there were no other visitors in the park. Ding turned to Reb and said, "I am gratified with what the Madison Committee has achieved in just three meetings. I did not know how things would unfold when we formed the committee, but so far it has exceeded my expectations. Where do you think we should go from here, Reb?"

"It's never a good attitude at the outset of an endeavor to doubt the odds of success. I must confess, however, the idea that the Madison Committee will launch a movement that results in a constitutional convention and the adoption of amendments even remotely resembling what our committee has drafted is almost laughable. Nothing ventured, nothing gained, I suppose. However, I do have a few ideas that I've kicked around with Pip and Wyatt."

"Good, please share them with me."

"We need to reach the legislators and the governors in all fifty states. By the way, there are precisely seven thousand three hundred eighty-two state legislators, so we will have an extensive mailing list. I think we should prepare a pamphlet that essentially lays out much of what we have discussed at our committee meetings. We should refer to the Founders' intentions and the understanding, by which the sovereign states ratified the Constitution, cite relevant passages from *The Federalist* commentaries, summarize how unchecked government encroaches on individual liberty, and finally set forth our proposed amendments with supporting commentary."

"Who do you have in mind to write this pamphlet?" asked Ding.

"Pip our historian and Wyatt our jurist are well suited to take the lead in drafting this document, and then the full committee can review and comment on it. A working title might be: *The Second Bill of Rights: Reaffirming the Constitution and Securing the Blessings of Liberty to Posterity.* My thought is to maintain our anonymity by signing the pamphlet Publius, just as Madison, Hamilton, and Jay signed *The Federalist* commentaries, or Concerned Citizens of the Madison Committee. At some point our names could become public, but ideally not until there is broad support or at least interest in most states. By then, many people will want to be associated with this effort and claim credit for it, which is fine with me. Once the pamphlet is printed, we will see that every state legislator and governor receives a copy. To build momentum, we should identify the key legislators in those states we believe might be most receptive to embracing our proposals, and arrange follow up contacts, preferably in person."

"Great idea, Reb. What else have you got in mind?"

"We should identify at least one highly regarded liberal and one similarly esteemed conservative nationally syndicated columnist, send both of them the pamphlet, and encourage them to write several, hopefully supportive columns on this effort. I assume you could take the lead on this. We also should identify key commentators and opinion makers in every state and get the pamphlet into their hands."

"I know just the columnists to approach when the time is ripe," said Ding. "It also will be crucial to recruit a governor well respected by his peers to be the point person for building support among as many governors as possible. Strong support and leadership among the governors is necessary to get this on the legislative agenda in their respective states."

"I agree, Ding, but do you have anyone in mind? The Texas governor is retiring after his term is up next year. We need a governor who will be in office at least two, preferably four more years to see this through. Can you recruit to our cause another governor?"

"Funny you should ask, Reb. Recently, Jake Fillmore and I met with the vice president during his Dallas visit to discuss the current state of Texas politics and the Republicans' prospects in 2014. After considering the putative candidates for the Republican gubernatorial nomination, the three of us concluded the field is mediocre. We all agreed the ideal candidate would be someone of great stature who is new to politics and is a prominent, accomplished, highly respected Texan. When the vice president asked who Jake and I thought filled this bill, we both said without hesitation Reb McCoy."

Reb laughed derisively and waited for Ding to tell him he was pulling his leg. As Ding showed no sign he was joking, Reb said, "You have got to be kidding or out of your freaking mind."

"I'm deadly serious, Reb."

"Ding, I never have had the slightest inclination to run for elective office. Moreover, at sixty-two, it is a bit late to get started. In any event, I do not have the temperament to be a politician. The idea is absolutely bonkers."

"Reb, you are the ideal person for the times. People are fed up with professional politicians. They are yearning for a citizen of maturity and substance who is a leader and will talk straight to them. If the Madison Committee is to achieve its objectives, we will need a governor from a major state who can earn quickly the trust and respect of his fellow governors to move our agenda forward. The vice president, Jake, and I have no doubt that you are exactly the right man at the right place and time. Neither of them knows anything about the Madison Committee, but for me that is the compelling reason you should give this serious consideration. I would not have suggested this to you otherwise."

"Ding, this idea is bizarre. I could not be more shocked if you had said Jerry Jones wants to make me his first-round draft pick to play middle linebacker for the Dallas Cowboys. I need time to think about this and weigh the pros and cons. Right now, I can think only of the cons. I've never thought about who and what are required to put together a winning campaign organization. I suppose it's not unlike organizing to achieve a business objective, except I would be the product being marketed. You have to plan, organize, amass resources, and establish a strategy to deploy them over a finite time frame. If you do all that better than the competition, you win the election."

"Jake and I can help you assemble top-flight people to organize the campaign. Don't let that be a worry. He and I have been to a few rodeos, and we will provide you the benefit of our experience, as well as our full support. You would have to win the party's nomination first, and then the general election. If you accept this challenge, Reb, you will have to decide within the next couple months, because the primary is only a year away, and the election is about a year and a half from now."

"Look, we are getting ahead of ourselves, Ding. I need to give this careful thought and consideration. I will not consider running under any circumstances unless Marlenna is fully supportive."

"I fully understand, Reb. I am grateful that you will at least entertain the possibility. Both Jake and I figured Marlenna would have to be on board before you would make a final decision, so I took the liberty of asking Jake to call Marlenna this afternoon during the Madison Committee meeting to discuss the idea with her and ask her to keep an open mind about it. Of course, I haven't heard from Jake on how the call went, but Marlenna won't be surprised when you bring this subject up tonight. I hope you'll forgive our contacting Marlenna without your knowledge."

"Oh, that's okay. Marlenna and I have known Jake for many years. He is a good and trusted friend. Better that she hear of this ludicrous idea first from someone other than me. That way our conversation about this won't come as a total shock to her."

Both men turned to walk back down the hill toward Turtle Creek and the Rosewood Mansion where their cars were parked. As they approached the Lee monument, Reb paused a moment and said, "Did you know that before the War Between the States," Reb never used the term Civil War, because the South did not rebel nor did it attempt to overthrow the United States government; it seceded or withdrew from the Union, "Lee, then a colonel, was posted by the U.S. Army in Texas as second-in-command of the Second Cavalry Regiment, whose mission was to protect settlers against attacks by the Apaches and your Comanche ancestors?"

"I did not know that."

"When Texas became the seventh state to secede from the United States in February 1861, the Second Cavalry surrendered to the local civilian authority, but Lee remained loyal to the Union and returned to Washington. On April 12, 1861, South Carolina fired on the federal Fort Sumter in

Charleston Harbor. Lincoln issued a proclamation three days later calling on the states to raise a seventy-five-thousand-man army. By that act, Virginia voted to secede on April 17, followed by North Carolina, Tennessee, and Arkansas over the ensuing seven weeks. On April 18, Lee was offered promotion to major general and command of a Union army. He instead resigned his commission, and on April 21 he became commander of Virginia's armed forces, later designated the Army of Northern Virginia. Lee had little sympathy for slavery, but once Virginia decided to join the Confederacy, he placed his loyalty to Virginia and states' rights ahead of the United States and the Constitution he had served so honorably all his life to that point."

"At that time in our history," remarked Ding, "many people placed allegiance to state above country. In fact, before the Civil War, or War Between the States as you refer to it, 'United States' was accompanied by a plural verb in common usage. Only after the war did 'United States' become a singular noun. If your perspective is that each state is sovereign and a member of a confederation, your paramount loyalty will be to your state. Conversely, if you perceive the state as being part of an indivisible nation, your highest loyalty will be to country. I have no doubt that Lee loved his country, but when Virginia seceded, he was forced to decide whether his paramount loyalty lay with his country or his state. He could not bring himself to lead an army against his fellow Virginians."

"He had a third option, Ding. He could have resigned his U.S. Army commission and sat out the war as a civilian."

"I don't believe that was a viable option for a distinguished career military officer like Lee," replied Ding. "He would have been branded a coward and a traitor by both sides."

"History has been kind to Lee," continued Reb. "I believe it was Orwell who said, 'History is written by the winners.' In the case of the War Between the States, however, southern historians made sure their point-of-view was kept alive and impossible to disregard. As a result, the historical reputations of Confederate military figures have received favorable treatment even in histories written by northern sympathizers. The South also managed to spin defeat into the romance of 'The Lost Cause,' and Lee became in history the heroic, tragic leader who fought valiantly against hopeless odds. History has treated Lee and his colleagues far better than the losers in other internecine conflicts. Personally, I think he deserves to be highly regarded. In the end, he was vanquished, but his stand was principled, and he was a great commander who won many battles despite being greatly outnumbered."

Ding added, "Whether or not you think Robert E. Lee was right or wrong, a hero or a traitor, when called at a critical moment in history to choose his destiny, he did not stand passively aside, nor did he temporize. Instead, he acted decisively by pledging his life, his fortune, and his honor to what he believed was a worthy cause. As a romantic myself, I have never forgotten Teddy Roosevelt's inspiring words: 'It is not the critic who counts.... The credit belongs to the man in the arena ...who strives valiantly...who spends himself for a worthy cause; who at best knows...the triumph of high achievement, and who at worst, if he fails, at least fails while daring greatly.' We both understand that America is at a turning point in her history. At the risk of being melodramatic, Reb, I hope you will bear Lee and TR's examples in mind as you decide whether you will be one of the men in the arena."

"I have loved history since I was in high school, Ding. I've always been fascinated with what might have been, and understood that history is never inevitable. I also know that history, like time, awaits no man. The unchangeable past is prologue to an unknown, uncertain future, and the individual men and women who seize the moment will determine the future, which will become tomorrow's history. I'll give serious consideration to your suggestion that I run for governor and make a decision within two weeks."

"That's all I can ask of you, Reb. Whatever it is, I'm sure you will make the right decision."

Lost in reflection, the two men walked in silence back to the Rosewood.

16

Marlenna was in the kitchen when Reb arrived home. After all their years together, her beauty still took his breath away. She was barefoot, tan, and wearing short shorts and a tank top. Their eyes met, and they smiled at each other. He gave her an emphatic hug and kissed her, lingering a moment over her inviting lower lip. "How was your day, pretty? Smells good in here. What are you making for dinner?"

She ignored his question and said, "Guess who I saw today?"

"I dunno. Tell me who you saw today."

"Jake Fillmore. He called me right after you left this morning, saying he needed to talk to me as soon as possible, preferably in person. I told him he could meet me at Milano's for lunch. He wouldn't tell me over the phone what he wanted to talk about, but I assumed he and Carmela might be having trouble."

Jake was in his third marriage and Carmela was his second Brazilian wife. She was sultry and thirty years younger than Jake. Marlenna figured this age discrepancy and Jake's prior track record as a husband did not auger well for a stable relationship. Reb and Marlenna met Jake

175

and his first wife Roxanne in 1990 in São Paulo, Brazil. The two couples quickly became good friends. Jake had been living and working in São Paulo for seven years before the McCoys arrived. Fillmore was the great, great grandson of the less-than-great thirteenth president of the United States, Millard Fillmore, whose chief claim to fame was having installed the first bathtub in the White House. Alas, even that modest accomplishment was apocryphal, having been based on a satirical story by H. L. Mencken written over sixty years after Fillmore's presidency, which gullible historians treated as fact.

Jake's father left the family homestead in Buffalo, New York, after World War I to strike out on his own. He wended his way to Waco, Texas, where he landed a job with the iconic soft drink firm, Dr Pepper, and settled down. He remained single until his mid-forties, when he met and married a Waco girl. A few years later, in 1948, Jake was born. While partying his way through Baylor University on a golf scholarship, Jake met Roxanne Deville at The Wick Dipper, a topless bar outside Waco. There she performed as a pole dancer under the name "Foxy Roxy," clad only in a G-string and CFM pumps. A truly nice Baptist girl with a great body, Roxanne was earning money to put herself through college. After graduating from college, Jake and Roxanne were married. By now, she had quit The Wick Dipper and worked as a paralegal for a Waco law firm, while Jake entered graduate school and tried his hand at professional golf. Unfortunately Jake's golf game was erratic. If only the two best of four rounds counted toward winning a tournament, Jake would have been a star on the PGA tour. Ever a realist, Jake quit wasting time on golf, finished up grad school, and took a job with a major insurance brokerage firm. In the early 1980s, he was transferred to Brazil.

By the time Reb was transferred to Brazil to run Magnolia's South America business, Jake was a prominent expatriate businessman in São Paulo. He had long ago left his employer and set up his own brokerage business, which flourished. A gregarious guy, who spoke Portuguese fluently, Jake established close relationships with many key Brazilian businessmen and politicians. One of his Brazilian connections offered Jake a partnership position in a private investment banking firm, which soon would acquire Antartica, Brazil's largest brewery, in a leveraged buyout. Jake was on his way to making his first fortune.

When Reb and Marlenna met the Fillmores, they were living in an exclusive gated community of private homes in Morumbi, a suburb of São Paulo. Surrounded by a ten-foot wall, their six-thousand-square-foot home with outdoor pool and cabana was a great place for parties, and Jake and Roxanne loved to party. After a couple drinks, Jake enjoyed regaling new friends with the story of how he met his wife "Foxy Roxy" at The Wick Dipper in Waco. Roxanne never seemed to be the least bit embarrassed about her past, although she herself rarely raised the subject.

Two years after Reb and Marlenna arrived in Brazil, Jake began an affair with his secretary. When Roxanne found out, she returned to Waco with their two children, retained a take-no-prisoners divorce lawyer, and sued Jake for divorce. Their wealth, rumored to be upwards of $10 million, was invested in joint accounts in the U.S. She got most of it; the lawyer got a chunk; Jake was left with the crumbs.

After a second marriage to the secretary fell apart, Jake had to sell the house in Morumbi to pay her settlement. By this time, there was a misunderstanding between Jake and the Brazilian authorities over unpaid taxes. To resolve this matter, he was forced to sell out his partnership interest in the investment banking firm. He took the small nest egg he had left and his new bride, Carmela, back to Texas, where he settled in Dallas. Jake never looked back. He opened an all-you-can-eat, Brazilian-style steakhouse called Rodesio Brasileiro, offering quality cuts of Brazilian and Argentine beef served in a trendy ambience featuring Brazilian music. The restaurant was modeled after one popular in São Paulo. Before long, Jake had attracted investors, opened similar restaurants in five other Texas cities, and was planning to franchise Rodesio Brasileiro in major cities around the country.

Jake was again a multimillionaire. Never bitter over his first divorce, which he readily acknowledged was his fault, he used to joke that he had lost his first fortune to wine, women, and song. When asked once what lessons he learned from that experience and how he was able to earn his second fortune, Jake quipped, "I gave up singing."

In the late 1990s, Jake became actively involved with the Texas Republican Party. He had no interest in being a candidate, figuring his checkered past made him unelectable, but he wanted to be a behind-the-scenes mover and shaker. Affable, extroverted, street smart, wealthy, a scratch golfer, and able to hold his liquor, Jake was a natural at schmoozing, raising money, and devising winning election strategies. In 2010, Jake agreed to serve as chairman of the Texas Republican Party, which would be fortuitous for Reb if he decided to run for governor in 2014.

Belatedly, Reb responded, "So, what was on Jake's mind?"

"You...utter insanity. He wants you to run for governor! Have you ever heard anything so ridiculous? And he wants me to support you in this. You're a wonderful husband, and I love you dearly. I thought I knew you, but never have you expressed any desire to run for political office. Only a year ago, you turned down the opportunity to run for vice president. If you spurned that offer, why would you want to be governor? How long has this been on your mind?"

"Marlenna, you actually heard about this crazy scheme before I did. After the Madison Committee met this afternoon, Ding Bell asked me to join him for a walk and some fresh air. It was then that he suggested I run for governor. My initial reaction was similar to yours, but after thinking about it,

I believe it deserves serious consideration. There is no way, however, that I will ever run for any political office without you at my side and fully supportive."

"Oh, Reb, why would you want to get involved in politics? It is nothing more than deceit, corruption, and hypocrisy. I can't think of a dirtier, sleazier profession. I've seen lots of politicians over the years at Daddy's restaurant, and, believe me, most of them I would not want to associate with."

"I agree, it is not a pretty business, but not everyone is a bad apple. Ding and Jake are straight shooters."

"Well, why doesn't one of them run for governor?"

"Marlenna, I would not give the idea a second thought were it not for the work of the Madison Committee. I suspect that sly old fox, Ding, had this in mind when he recruited me to chair the committee. I've kept you up-to-date on the committee's deliberations. At today's meeting, which I'll fill you in on later, we made excellent progress. Now, we have to implement a strategy for moving our ideas forward. Ding is right; we need a governor of a major state, fully conversant with the committee's agenda, who can try to proselytize other governors to the cause. You and I both understand the country is at a critical juncture in its history. The federal government's power is virtually unchecked, and each new crisis is an excuse to justify further expanding its power. Out-of-control government debt and deficits threaten to capsize the financial markets, swamp the economy, and steal liberty, opportunity, and prosperity from future generations.

"I think the Madison Committee's proposals, if adopted, could help to restore balance and sanity to America's constitutional system. Believe me, I don't see myself as a man on a white horse. No doubt there are far better qualified people to lead this effort, but I'm involved and feel an obligation to join with others as an active participant instead of remaining a passive spectator, even if the odds of success are slim."

"When do you have to let Ding know your decision?"

"Two weeks," responded Reb.

"Are you prepared for the inevitable scurrilous personal attacks impugning your integrity? If your opponent can't debate and win on the issues, he or she will try to destroy your reputation and character. People predisposed to vote against you, as well as a lot of those on the fence, will believe anything negative said about you, whether or not it's true."

"That is one of the uglier aspects of politics, but if all the good guys allow themselves to be scared off by that, only the bad guys would run for office. If I were to run, it would not be for a personal ego trip. In my mind, this is about something far more important than any individual; it's about trying to catalyze positive change in the country's direction. As far as attacks on me, I trust that you and Ravenna can separate fact from fiction. The worry I have is that some organization or group, probably not directly affiliated with my opponent, would cast aspersions on you or Ravenna. That is way below the belt, but in recent years politics has at times descended into that gutter. I would respond to such attacks if they occurred, but I could not prevent them. I'm also concerned about security for you, Ravenna, Kyle, Deanna, and Jeff, but that can be worked out."

"At the appropriate time," said Marlenna, "we'll have to talk it over with Ravenna and Jeff to hear their concerns. If I know our daughter, she will enthusiastically support you. I am the one with reservations. If you decide to go forward with this, Reb, you have to promise me that you will never knowingly dissemble or engage in doubletalk, telling one voting group one thing and then telling another group the exact opposite, or respond to personal attacks in kind. I know no man with higher integrity than you, but politics and the lust for power have a way of compromising a good person's integrity. People become consumed with winning, especially when the loser goes home to ignominious obscurity. Losing is tolerable in sports, because there is always another game or season. In politics, winning is the only thing and everything. Winning is life; losing is death. It is war, but without bullets or hand grenades. In such a contest, it isn't difficult to rationalize that the end justifies most any means. I couldn't bear to see that happen to you."

"Whatever the decision is, baby, it will be our decision. It will be unanimous. If we do decide to jump together into the cauldron, you will be my conscience. I am not an indispensable man, nor am I my country's savior. And I am unwilling to do anything for any reason that would compromise my integrity in your eyes or mine. The two indispensable things in my life are my personal integrity and you, Marlenna."

17

Within a few days of their discussion, and, after talking it over with Ravenna and Jeff, Marlenna gave Reb her enthusiastic blessing to run for governor. She had weighed the pros and cons, and concluded that Reb's reasons for running trumped her misgivings about her husband getting involved in politics. She would be by his side and do whatever she could to support his candidacy if that was what he decided to do. Reb was grateful for his wife's endorsement but not surprised. She had supported him without reservation throughout his business career and was a major reason for his success.

Before making an irrevocable decision to run, Reb wanted to talk with Jake Fillmore. They arranged to meet at the Marcoy Foundation, which was headquartered near the Dallas Arts District. Jake ambled into Reb's office. They exchanged an *abraço*, the Portuguese word for embrace that all friends and close acquaintances in Brazil give each other upon meeting or departing. Jake plopped his six-foot-five, two-hundred-sixty-pound frame into a groaning chair and said in his laconic style, "How you doing, stud?"

Reb began the serious discussion. "Jake, we've known each other a long time. I'm leaning toward running, but before making a final decision, I want to hear your thoughts on how to maximize the chances for success."

"Reb, your strengths are obvious, so I'll not recount them here. We've been good friends for over twenty years, and I know your character is impeccable. But I have to ask, do you have any skeletons in your closet that would embarrass you, your family, or your supporters if revealed during the campaign? If so, what are they, and would it be better for you to disclose preemptively any youthful indiscretions early in the process before the press or an opponent discovers them? Do you have any potentially disqualifying health issues? Did you ever smoke dope, cheat on a college exam, get arrested for DWI, or anything else? Did you ever evade taxes, get a girl pregnant, mess around with jail bait, make a sex tape, or cheat on your wife? I'd bet my life you've never cheated on Marlenna. No man lucky enough to have her for his wife would ever look at another woman."

"Guess I've lived a too sheltered life, Jake, because I've never done any of those things. And you're certainly right about Marlenna. I'm still as crazy about her as the day we were married. I don't deserve her, and am grateful every day she shares her life with me. For a man my age, I am blessed with good health, and Marlenna is my motivation for staying physically fit."

"Those are the answers I expected. In my case, if I answered truthfully, I've done all those things at one time or another in my life, except make a sex tape, and that's only because I forgot to put film in the camera. Anything else you can imagine that could be brought up and twisted into something ugly?"

"When I was in Vietnam, I was charged with a court-martial offense—disobeying a direct order of my superior officer—but after an investigation, the charges were dropped, because the order was stupid, illegal, and certainly immoral. I don't know if there is any reference to this in my army personnel records, but if it ever came out, I would have no problem addressing it. Speaking of military service, I refuse to tout that as a reason someone should vote for me. Too many politicians like to wrap themselves in that flag when, for most, it has no relevance to their qualifications for office. It's different for someone like President Thurston who was a high-ranking career military officer. In my case, I was a grunt who served less than three years over forty years ago. I couldn't ask someone to vote for me based on that."

"Well, I think your military service speaks to your character and patriotism," shot back Jake. "If the story I've heard is true, you volunteered for service, instead of taking your chances on the draft. Guys like me, Fubarsky, Clinton, and Cheney worked every angle in the book to avoid the draft and Vietnam. A lot of voters value highly a candidate who served his country in the military, Reb, so I wouldn't dismiss that part of your résumé out of hand. I've also heard that you are a highly decorated veteran. Humility is good up to a point, but a successful politician has to sell himself. It's not a business for shrinking violets. You have to educate voters about your virtues and convince them you are better than your opponent. Also, you can't let your opponent define you, because obviously he or she will paint a negative or distorted picture. Finally, you will have to convey passion and conviction, as well as likeability, in order to win, because you are generally unknown to voters."

"How much money will we have to raise to be competitive, Jake?"

"I'd say at least $20 million for the primary, and if you win the nomination, probably another $50 million for the general election, perhaps more depending on how well financed your opponent is. As the new kid on the block, you will have to spend more on TV ads than a better known figure."

"The price of poker is pretty steep. How does one go about raising those amounts of money? By the way, just between us, Marlenna and I will ante up $5 million, plus a loan to the campaign of another $5 million."

"That's great, because you will be able to hit the ground running from the moment you announce your candidacy. I can recommend the best rainmaker in the business to head up your fundraising effort. She is ethical and up-to-speed on all the arcane campaign finance laws. You have many deep-pocket friends and extensive contacts in the business and philanthropic communities, especially in Dallas, whom you can tap for money. The Internet is the modern way to raise lots of money quickly in small individual donations. We have to turn you into a phenomenon, Reb, a new political superstar. You look good on TV, and the times I've seen you do interviews, you came across as attractive, relaxed, sincere, and very intelligent. You need to get plenty of face time on TV in both live appearances and campaign ads. You also will have to campaign across the state, hitting all twenty-eight major media markets. If she is willing to get in front of the public, one of the best assets you have is Marlenna. She is eye candy with charm and brains. That's an unbeatable trifecta. Both men and women are attracted to her; she is charismatic and many will think, at least subliminally, if you are good enough to be her husband, you are probably good enough to hold high office. In a close election, Marlenna could be the difference between winning and losing."

"Marlenna certainly enjoys engaging with people and has an intuitive ability to make them feel comfortable and special. As you know, for the past few years, she has been the chairperson for the annual Dallas Arts District fundraising gala. She knows how to work a room and deliver a witty yet moving impromptu speech. That's a gift. And she always manages to get the richest misers and curmudgeons in town to open their wallets wide for worthy causes. I'm sure she will be happy to do whatever she can for the campaign, but I don't want to overexpose her or push her to exhaustion. She and I will jointly agree what role she will play. Actually, between the two of us, she would be the better candidate."

After taking a sip of water, Reb changed the subject, "Who do you suggest I hire to be my campaign manager?"

"I can line up someone who has run many successful campaigns. He learned the business working for Karl Rove. He knows Texas inside and out, and I'm certain he would be elated to work for you. You also need to get a top-flight spokesperson who can keep the media beast happy, and a pollster who tells you the truth and not what you want to hear. I can give you a few names for those jobs also."

"One thing, Jake, I refuse to run a negative campaign, engage in dirty tricks, or tolerate personal attacks against my opponents. If you tell me such tactics are necessary to win, I won't run. I promised both Marlenna and myself.... "

"Don't worry. That kind of stuff is for bad or desperate candidates. I would strongly advise against it in any event. You are a fresh face above all the nastiness in politics, a private citizen with new ideas willing to serve if elected. That is a major part of your appeal. Now, this is not patty cake. You have to hit hard on the issues, compare and contrast your positions with those of your opponent, and defend yourself when attacked. But there is no reason for you to allow yourself or surrogates to be dragged into a mud fight."

"Another thing, Jake, I will retain total control over my message and the positions I take during the campaign. I won't allow the state or national party to dictate my agenda. Will that be a problem for you or anyone else?"

"Not at all, Reb. You will lay out your program during the primary and if you win the gubernatorial nomination, it will be because Texas Republicans are sold on your ideas. The national party will have no say or control over you, but remember they can provide financial and organizational support during the general election campaign, which could be very important, so you don't want to alienate them."

"Can I count on your support, Jake?"

"Reb, as state party chairman I can't publicly favor one candidate over another during the primary. Joe Harlow, congressman from San Antonio, I expect, will be your strongest competition for the nomination. I believe you can defeat him, but it won't be a cakewalk. He's an experienced politician, although not well known outside his district. He is effective out on the stump speaking to a live audience, but, in my opinion, is unimpressive on television. I want you to win, because you are in my mind far superior to Harlow, and you can win the general election handily. But for the sake of party unity, officially I'll be neutral. I will, however, be pleased to give you behind-the-scenes advice and support, as I am doing now."

"Well, nothing you've told me today has scared me off, so my decision to run is final. The next thing I need to do is tell Ding my decision. Once the key campaign staff positions are filled and we can meet to develop a preliminary strategy, I'll formally announce my candidacy with as much media fanfare as we can muster. Do you have any other words of wisdom for me, Jake?"

"Your work ethic and long experience as an outstanding CEO of a major corporation will serve you well as you embark on this adventure, Reb. A political campaign in a state the size of Texas, especially for someone who is relatively unknown, will demand virtually all your waking hours from now until the election in November 2014, assuming you win the primary next April. The best candidate with the most money can lose, if he is not a good executive who can build a strong, nimble, professional organization and lay out a solid strategy for winning."

"Thank you for your candid advice and encouragement, Jake. They are greatly appreciated. You may rest assured that having decided to run, I am committed to win."

After Jake departed, Reb telephoned Ding Bell on his direct line. Checking his caller ID, Ding answered on the first ring and said, "How are you, my friend? Are you calling with news I want to hear?"

Reb responded saying, "Jake Fillmore just left my office. Nothing he said made me change my mind, so for better or worse, I have decided to run for governor of Texas."

"That's wonderful news. The campaign will demand a tremendous amount of your time and effort, but, win or lose, this will be one of the most gratifying experiences of your life, Reb. As ugly, messy, and dysfunctional as democracy can be, at its best politics is a noble calling. I am confident you will win, and, believe me, convincing a majority of the electorate to place their trust in you will be an exhilarating and humbling experience. I believe you are the right man at the right place and in the nick of time."

"I appreciate your vote of confidence, Ding, but let's not get carried away. By the way, I want you to know that your clever manipulation of me has not gone unnoticed. You owe me big time."

Ding chortled loudly and said, "Yeah, you're one of the biggest fish I've ever caught, and I'm proud to have done so. I always try to look out for the best interests of the Lone Star State and the United States. Have you thought about when you will announce and when to tell the Madison Committee?"

"Jake is putting me in touch with people he recommends for my senior campaign staff. Once I've organized the senior team and we map out a game plan, I'll announce my candidacy. I'm tentatively thinking that will be in late June or early July. I'll inform the Madison Committee in strict confidence at our next meeting. What do you think?"

"That will have you in the race for the nomination nine or ten months before the primary. There probably won't be another candidate who is a non-politician, and certainly not one with your business résumé. Those who support one of the four or five political pros in the race, I figure will see you as their second choice. But there are a lot of undecided voters and others looking for a fresh face who will gravitate toward you. By the time you present yourself to the voters, I'm betting many of those who start out backing a traditional politician will switch their allegiance to you. Mark my words, Reb. I'm attuned to the Texas Republican voter. Regarding the Madison Committee, I agree you should inform them, but they should be sworn to secrecy. How will the committee fit into your campaign?"

"We'll discuss that at our next meeting. Wyatt and Pip have already made good progress drafting the pamphlet you and I discussed after the last meeting. I want to develop a plan for completing that project and getting it into the hands of governors and state legislators across the country, as well as to a couple key opinion makers. As to the election campaign, I will request their support in any way they can help, but, most importantly, I want the committee to offer ideas on how I can lay the groundwork during the campaign for setting forth our ideas for restoring constitutional balance and a federal government of limited powers. If I am elected, one of my major initiatives will be to persuade the Texas Legislature and my fellow governors to embrace our amendments. Getting thirty-four state legislatures to petition Congress to call a constitutional convention is still the longest of long shots, but we have to try. Of course, my campaign also will devote substantial time to addressing key issues of particular concern to the citizens of Texas."

"This is why I lobbied you to run for governor, Reb. How long do you think the Madison Committee should be kept out of the public eye?"

"I don't know, Ding, but I hope we can control the timing of when we go public, rather than being scooped by an enterprising reporter before we're ready. Ideally, after we get the pamphlet published and distributed, we'll remain incognito long enough to create an aura of mystery about the Madison Committee. We need to build interest, curiosity, and debate. By late fall, I'll start speaking regularly on the committee's work, and just before then we can reveal its members to the public. This is an agenda item for our next meeting."

"Okay, Reb, I'll look forward to seeing you at the next Madison Committee meeting. I'm sure everyone will be surprised and pleased to learn that you will be running for governor. Please give Marlenna my love. I know that without her support, you would not be doing this. Did Jake tell you our recommended slogan for your campaign?"

"No, he didn't."

"Settle for nothing less than the best. Vote for the Real McCoy."

"The first part sounds a bit corny, Ding, but I like the sound of 'Vote for the Real McCoy.'"

18

The Lone Star State

If indeed size matters, Texas is a place of stupendous consequence. The second largest of the fifty states, it is equal in size to the five largest of the original thirteen states—Virginia, Georgia, North Carolina, New York, and Pennsylvania. England and France would fit within Texas's borders with room to spare. The privately owned King Ranch in Texas is bigger than Rhode Island.

The driving distance from the northwest corner of the Texas Panhandle to Brownsville on the Gulf of Mexico is over nine hundred miles. The distance between El Paso on the southwest border near New Mexico to Texarkana on the northeast border with Arkansas is over eight hundred miles. For perspective, El Paso is closer to Los Angeles than to Texarkana, which is closer to Chicago than to El Paso. The Rio Grande River flows for nearly one thousand two hundred fifty miles between Texas and Mexico. Texas also has a three-hundred-seventy-mile coastline along the Gulf of Mexico.

With over twenty-five million people, Texas is the second most populous state. Over the past decade, its population has increased 19 percent, more than double the percentage increase in the country's total population during the same period. The state's demographic breakdown is 4 percent Asian, 12 percent Black, 37 percent Hispanic, and 47 percent non-Hispanic Caucasian. Texas boasts six of the twenty-five largest U.S. cities, and it has twenty-eight cities with populations in excess of a hundred thousand.

The history of Texas, which derives from an Indian word meaning friends, is a rollicking tale replete with heroes, scoundrels, larger-than-life figures, and assorted implausible characters. Independence and rugged individualism were common traits of early Texans, and that continues to this day. Nicknamed the Lone Star State, Texas is the only state to have been a sovereign and independent republic before becoming a state. California briefly declared itself a republic in 1846 during the Mexican-American War, but it did not form a government, and lasted less than four weeks before being annexed by the United States.

Since the seventeenth century, six national flags have flown over Texas. France briefly laid claim to territory that became Texas during the 1680s. Fearing French encroachment on New Spain, which later would become Mexico, Spain displaced the French in 1690 and ruled until Mexico gained its independence in 1821. Because it was sparsely populated, the government of Mexico encouraged Americans to immigrate to Texas. By 1835, over thirty thousand American and European immigrants had settled in Texas, far outnumbering the Mexicans living there. The Mexican government under President and Gen. Antonio Lopez de Santa Anna wanted to impose dictatorial control over Texas, while the American settlers, or Texians, chafed for greater independence.

The Texas Revolution began in October 1835, and on March 2, 1836, the Texians declared their independence from Mexico and established the Republic of Texas. This occurred in the midst of the Battle of the Alamo near

San Antonio, where during a thirteen-day siege virtually all the two hundred to two hundred fifty defenders, including Jim Bowie and Davy Crockett, were killed by Santa Anna's superior force of two thousand four hundred soldiers. The Texians put up a valiant fight, however, killing an estimated four hundred to six hundred of Santa Anna's troops. "Remember the Alamo" has been the proud rallying cry of Texans ever since, no doubt the most celebrated lost battle in history. A few weeks after the Alamo fell, Santa Anna ordered three hundred forty-two Texians taken prisoner near Goliad south of Victoria to be executed. The Goliad Massacre was carried out on Palm Sunday 1836. Only twenty-eight Texian prisoners managed to escape.

Santa Anna now wanted to finish off the main Texan Army, which was led by Gen. Sam Houston. The decisive battle of the revolution was fought at San Jacinto near today's city of La Porte, Texas. Santa Anna, with a force of about one thousand four hundred, believed he had Houston and his army of nine hundred men surrounded. After resting his troops, Santa Anna planned to attack the Texians on April 22, 1836. Instead, Houston launched a surprise attack on April 21 while the Mexicans were enjoying their afternoon siesta, many with their wives or lady friends who had accompanied them in the field. Santa Anna's fatal blunder was to fail to post sentries, thus he had no warning. In terms of consequence relative to cost and duration, the Battle of San Jacinto is one of the greatest military victories in history. It took less than twenty minutes to defeat Santa Anna's army, although the pursuit and killing of fleeing Mexicans went on for another hour. The Texians were short on mercy after the Alamo and Goliad. Mexican losses were over six hundred men killed, two hundred wounded and over seven hundred captured, including Santa Anna himself. Texian forces suffered only nine killed and thirty wounded, one of the latter being Gen. Houston who, while leading his infantry into battle, was shot in the ankle and had one, perhaps two horses shot from under him.

Texas had won its independence and would remain a sovereign nation until 1845 when it agreed to be annexed by the United States as the twenty-eighth state. It is the only state to join the Union by means of a treaty. Boundary disputes with Mexico persisted and finally triggered the Mexican-American War in 1846, which resulted in the United States fulfilling its "Manifest Destiny" by acquiring a vast territory that encompasses the states of California, Nevada, Arizona, New Mexico, Utah, and parts of Oklahoma, Kansas, Colorado and, Wyoming.

Houston is the single greatest figure in Texas history. He arrived in Texas at age thirty-nine from Tennessee, where he had been governor, and a protégé and supporter of President Andrew Jackson. After the successful revolution, he was elected the first and third president of the Republic of Texas. Strongly favoring annexation by the United States, Houston clashed politically with a faction of fellow Texans, formerly Texians, who wanted to remain an independent nation and to extend the republic's territory west to California and the Pacific Ocean. The pro-annexation forces ultimately prevailed. A major cotton producer, Texas entered the Union as a slave state. All the former republic's public lands were awarded to the new state, which is why the federal government owns little land in Texas, unlike most other western and southwestern states acquired during the Mexican-American War. The joint congressional resolution authorizing annexation also provided that Texas could organize itself into five states including Texas, a provision it has never attempted to exercise.

Although not a matter of controversy at the time, in securing its independence from Mexico, Texas claimed its seaward boundary extended three leagues or nine nautical miles into the Gulf of Mexico. The U.S. government generally recognizes seaward boundaries of only one league or three nautical miles for states situated on a littoral. As a sovereign nation entering into a treaty of annexation, the United States agreed to recognize

Texas's boundaries and claims to all public lands. By the 1940s, large reservoirs of offshore oil in the Gulf of Mexico had been discovered. More than a century after annexation, the U.S. government in the 1950s challenged Texas's seaward boundary in court in an effort to reduce it to three nautical miles. Ultimately, the Supreme Court upheld Texas, which ensured the state, not the federal government, would reap enormous lease and royalty payments when offshore oilfields were developed later in the twentieth century.

When Texas entered the Union, it was much larger than it is today. Its northern boundary extended to the Arkansas River, which encompassed the Oklahoma panhandle, southwestern Kansas, and southeastern Colorado. The western boundary reached the Rio Grande, which included over half of New Mexico, and a narrow panhandle extended north through Colorado into Wyoming. In exchange for the assumption of $10 million in debt, Texas ceded all territory beyond its current boundaries to the United States in 1850.

On February 1, 1861, Texas seceded from the United States and joined the Confederate States of America, the sixth flag to fly over the Lone Star State. Although the vote to secede was overwhelming, Gov. Sam Houston, opposed to secession, resigned his office, and retired to Huntsville where he died in 1863, shortly after the Battle of Gettysburg. Houston is the only person to be governor of two states, Tennessee and Texas, and the only American to be president of a country other than the United States. His everlasting claim to fame and admiration, however, is leading his Texian Army to victory in the Texas Revolution against Mexico.

During the War Between the States, Texas was primarily a "supply state" to the Confederacy until the fall of Vicksburg in July 1863, which won the Union control of the Mississippi River. There were few military engagements in Texas during the war, but the Texas Brigade, comprised of the 1st, 4th and 5th Texas Infantry Regiments and the 3rd Arkansas Infantry Regiment, was assigned to Gen. Robert E. Lee's Army of Northern Virginia, and fought in thirty-eight major battles. The 1st Texas lost over 80 percent of its two hundred twenty-six men during the Battle of Antietam near Sharpsburg, Maryland, on September 17, 1862. This was the highest single action loss of any unit on either side during the war. The most sanguinary day of combat in American history, Antietam claimed over three thousand six hundred Union and Confederate soldiers killed in action.

Lee's favorite troops were the Texas Brigade, which he referred to as "My Texans." They generally were the shock troops first to advance in battle, and served as the rearguard during retreats. Although it had a distinguished record in many battles, the Brigade's most famous engagement was the taking of Devil's Den on the second day at Gettysburg, despite being heavily outnumbered and suffering horrific casualties. Of the nearly five thousand four hundred men who enlisted in the Texas Brigade, only six hundred were on hand when Lee surrendered his army to Gen. Ulysses S. Grant at Appomattox Court House, Virginia, on April 9, 1865, effectively ending the War Between the States. On March 30, 1870, Texas was restored to the Union.

At the end of the war, Armour and Company established a large meat processing and packing plant in Chicago, which drove up the demand for cattle. In Texas, the cattle industry grew rapidly to meet the demand, and cowboys drove their herds north along the Chisholm Trail to Abilene, Kansas, the nearest railhead. The cowboy culture of rugged individualism, honesty, and chivalry, which traced its origins to the Mexican vaqueros, reinforced the image of Texans as being strong, self-reliant frontiersmen. By the 1890s, the era of great cattle drives was over, as the open range gradually had been fenced in to prevent overgrazing; the railroads had extended into Texas and further west; and meat-packing plants were located closer to the herds. But the cowboy tradition lived on, and ranching remains today a significant part of the Texas economy.

Between the end of the war and 1900, cattle, cotton, and lumber were the major pillars of the Texas economy. In 1901, with the discovery of oil at Spindletop near Beaumont in southeast Texas, the Oil Boom or Gusher Age commenced. This transformed the Texas economy and "gushered" in the American century that saw the United States become the wealthiest, most powerful country in the world based on plentiful, cheap oil. Soon oil reserves were discovered all across Texas, attracting speculators and wildcatters, and making some men fabulously rich. The oil industry attracted related major industries such as oil refining and petrochemicals, which were concentrated around the city of Houston, named for the hero of San Jacinto. Cities all across Texas experienced tremendous growth. By World War II, half the population of the once rural state lived in urban areas. With the discovery of oil in East Texas in 1930, Dallas became the financial center for both the Texas and Oklahoma oil industry.

During World War II, the U.S. military established a number of bases in Texas that remain to this day. After the war, Texas's service economy expanded rapidly, but the oil and chemical industries continued to be a major part of the state economy. At the start of the twenty-first century, Texas provided 22 percent of total U.S. oil production, second only to Alaska's 38 percent. A key indicator of Texas's economic clout is that fifty-seven Fortune 500 companies are headquartered in the state, the same number as are in California. Of these fifty-seven companies, twenty-four are based in Houston, and another twenty-four are based in the Dallas-Fort Worth metropolitan area. Texans have always embraced with enthusiasm President Calvin Coolidge's famous maxim: "The chief business of the American people is business."

As a young boy before his parents died, Reb recalled visiting fascinating places all around the state and listening to stories his father told him. He learned that two native sons of Texas, both Americans of German ancestry, rose to five-star rank in the military and led America to victory in World War II. Chester W. Nimitz, born in Fredericksburg in the Hill Country, commanded America's Pacific air, land, and sea forces that defeated Japan. Dwight D. Eisenhower, born in Denison on the Red River, commanded the allied forces that liberated Western Europe from Germany, and went on to become president during the 1950s.

Texas also produced the most decorated American soldier of WW II, Audie Murphy, who was awarded the Medal of Honor and virtually every other medal for valor while fighting in Sicily, Italy, and France. Born in Kingston, northeast of Dallas, Murphy was one of twelve children born to poor sharecroppers. His sister altered his birth certificate to make it appear he was a year older than his actual age of seventeen, so he could enlist in the army six months after Pearl Harbor. Following his heroic exploits and return home, the handsome Murphy was featured on the cover of *Life* magazine in July 1945. This led to Hollywood, and a movie career in which he starred in over forty movies, mostly westerns.

Reb also loved the tales his father would tell him about the legendary Texas Rangers, the oldest statewide law enforcement agency in the United States, which dated its origins to before the Texas Revolution. As a boy, Reb dreamed of being a Texas Ranger and wearing the distinctive round badge with a star cut out in the center. He learned later the badges are made from Mexican five peso silver coins. Over its history, the Rangers fought Indians to protect Texian settlers and tracked down, and often killed in gunfights, all manner of desperados including Bonnie and Clyde. Today, the Texas Ranger Division is an elite force whose duties include conducting criminal investigations, apprehending felons and members of organized crime, suppressing criminal activities in areas where local authorities are unable to cope, and providing protection to the governor and other dignitaries as necessary.

Both in his travels with his parents as a lad and during his adult life, what struck Reb about his native state was the enormous size of so many monuments and structures. The state capital, Austin, boasts having the largest state capitol building in the nation, second in size only to the U.S. Capitol. Built in the 1880s of limestone and pink granite, its dome rises to three hundred eight feet, which is seven feet taller than the U.S. Capitol. Atop the state capitol dome is the Goddess of Liberty statue, wielding a sword in her right hand and holding aloft in her left a gilded Lone Star that represents Texas. In lieu of cash, the state government paid the building contractors with three million acres of land in the Texas Panhandle.

More recently, in 2009, in homage to the prominence, importance, and profitability of Texas football, the NFL's Dallas Cowboys opened Cowboys Stadium, the largest domed stadium in the world. Located in Arlington, midway between Dallas and Fort Worth, this gridiron temple cost $1.3 billion, $325 million provided by the good taxpayers of Arlington, with the balance privately financed primarily by Cowboys owner, Jerry Jones. The stadium is suspended by two arches that rise to a height of three hundred feet creating the world's largest column-free interior space. With a maximum capacity of one hundred ten thousand, the stadium features a retractable roof and the largest high-definition video screens in the world.

Reb felt that even more indicative than Cowboys Stadium of how crazed Texans are over football, is Allen, a town just north of Dallas, which issued bonds financed by raising property taxes to construct a $60 million football stadium for its high school. The project was completed in 2012, and with a seating capacity of eighteen thousand is only the fifth largest high school stadium in the state. It seemed to Reb that there must be higher spending priorities for public funds, but this reflected the competitive, bigger is better personality of many Texans.

Of the many memorial monuments and statues erected across Texas, Reb always believed one in particular was emblematic of the Lone Star State. In 1936, the centennial year of the Battle of San Jacinto, construction began on a monument to commemorate the last engagement of the revolution that secured independence for the Republic of Texas. Completed in 1939, it is an octagonal, tapered obelisk soaring five hundred sixty-seven feet in the sky, including the thirty-two-foot, two-hundred-twenty-ton Lone Star at its apex. Made of reinforced concrete and faced with Texas limestone, an elevator takes visitors to the observation level over five hundred feet above ground for a spectacular view. Reb always smiled to himself when he recalled that the monument, the tallest memorial column in the world, is twelve feet taller than the Washington Monument. Texas defers to no one, not even the Father of our country, when it comes to phallic memorials. Yes, size certainly does matter in Texas.

Reb McCoy knew well and loved the history of his native state. He was particularly fond of the period from the Texas Revolution through the War Between the States, because that era established the indelible personality characteristics of the state and its people, which largely have been handed down from one generation to the next as if genetically transmitted. A swaggering, bragging, go for broke, don't tread on me independence that combines profound pride and love for Texas, with loyalty to country is the stereotypical description Reb would apply to his fellow Texans. He perceived no other state having such a singular identity and hold on its citizens. There are distinct cultural differences among the various geographic regions of the U.S., but no particular state within a region, is all that different from another state in the same region. Exceptions are California and Florida, and the non-contiguous states Alaska and Hawaii, which are all unique, but none penetrates the soul of its citizens, especially its native sons and daughters, the way Texas does.

Reb could not articulate why this was so, although he sensed it may be partially due to Texas, unlike any other state, having once been a sovereign republic. He recalled years ago reading the book *Travels with Charley* in which John Steinbeck wrote, "Texas is a state of mind. Texas is an obsession. Above all, Texas is a nation in every sense of the word." Reb thought that succinctly captured as best words could the essence of Texas.

19

Running for Governor
2014 Election

In retrospect, total immersion and being constantly in motion is how Reb described the experience of running for statewide elective office, especially in a state the size of Texas. From his formal announcement to run for governor in July 2013, until his election sixteen months later on November 4, 2014, he was on the road six days a week. Marlenna was with him almost all the time, and she quickly proved to be a natural campaigner.

When Reb informed the Madison Committee of his decision to run, everyone was surprised but elated. The committee immediately realized that if Reb won the election, the odds that its efforts might bear fruit would improve from virtually none to at least slim. In June, the pamphlet, *The Second Bill of Rights: Reaffirming the Constitution and Securing the Blessings of Liberty to Posterity*, was completed and approved unanimously by the committee. An initial printing of ten thousand copies was ordered for August. Copies were sent to all governors and state legislators. Ding contacted key legislators in fifteen states, including Texas, lobbying them to give the pamphlet serious consideration and to schedule hearings on the proposed Second Bill of Rights by their respective legislatures.

In September 2013, at Ding's urging, Walter Rothmann, a nationally syndicated columnist and frequent television commentator, wrote the first column on the still anonymous Madison Committee and its proposed Second Bill of Rights. Philosophically conservative and possessed of a towering intellect, Rothmann was one of the most influential opinion makers in the country, respected across the political spectrum. Rothmann found the proposed amendments to have "a refreshing merit that no doubt would have found favor with the Framers," but he thought there was only the slimmest chance of ever getting thirty-four states to petition Congress to call a constitutional convention. He also opined, however, that "curtailing federal power will never be achieved unless the states force the issue, because the three branches of the federal government are institutionally and intellectually incapable of doing so. The natural instinct of virtually all men and women who crave and hold the power to govern the rest of us is to preserve, consolidate, and expand that power, never to diminish it." The Madison Committee was not disheartened by Rothmann's column and was pleased its ideas were finally in public circulation.

In October, Ding persuaded Donald Utopeville, the esteemed doyen of liberal journalists and as widely read as Rothmann, to make the Second Bill of Rights a subject of his weekly column. Surprisingly, Utopeville was more favorable toward the seven proposed amendments than was Rothmann. Convinced that benevolent big government was the only viable solution to society's problems, Utopeville also believed wholeheartedly in democracy and the rights of the common man. In Reb's humble opinion, Utopeville failed to acknowledge or grasp the inherent contradiction in his simultaneously held convictions, but the self-important columnist probably would contend that intellectual consistency was the hobgoblin of small minds. He was that rare liberal, however, who had become disenchanted with "the haphazard, undisciplined, and unfocused way the federal government assumed ever-increasing power and financial burdens without any serious regard to the efficacy or cost of its regulations and social programs." Like conservatives, he recognized that the ongoing deficits and increasing debt were unsustainable. Utopeville concluded his column writing that "the citizens behind the Madison Committee will have to reveal themselves to the public and debate their ideas openly if they are to be taken seriously."

This was a fair comment and when the committee met in November—it was now meeting monthly instead of very fortnight—Reb recommended they go public. The time was ripe, because in December, Reb would begin campaigning for the Second Bill of Rights and reveal his plans, if elected, to work with his fellow governors to advance this project. While most of the subsequent press attention and questions were directed to him, and to a lesser extent Sen. Bell, other committee members also received press inquiries about the Madison Committee's activities. Not everyone relished the idea of dealing with the press, but all members agreed that this was necessary to keep the Second Bill of Rights a subject of public discussion and debate.

In the meantime, Reb's primary campaign for the Texas Republican Party's gubernatorial nomination had been staffed and organized, and was executing the plan he and his team had devised. The campaign director was forty-five-year-old Terry Cassidy, inevitably nicknamed Hopalong or Hoppy, who had been involved in election campaigns since graduating from college. His résumé included directing eight campaigns for various offices, winning seven. Reb and Hoppy quickly developed a warm relationship based on mutual trust and respect. Despite having a neophyte for a client, Hoppy soon realized Reb had a natural instinct for politics, was unflappable, congenial, tireless, and scary smart.

The campaign brain trust divided the state into seven sectors: Piney Woods, Gulf Coast, South Texas, Hill Country, West Texas, Panhandle, and North Texas. During the primary campaign, the candidate spent three consecutive weeks in each sector and then revisited each sector for two additional weeks. This itinerary would be repeated for the general election campaign if Reb won the nomination. A large bus, emblazoned on both sides with the slogan, FOR GOVERNOR, VOTE FOR THE REAL MCCOY, and a leased private jet conveyed Reb, Marlenna, and a few staff, security, and advance personnel around the state to campaign events.

Several campaign personnel were assigned to the largest cities in each sector, with most of the staff based in the Dallas campaign headquarters scheduling events, raising money, polling, mailing literature to likely voters, arranging media interviews, issuing press releases, researching opponents, developing daily speech themes, crafting television campaign ads, updating the candidate's website, and performing countless other tasks. Getting Reb face time with as many voters and local media people as possible was the foremost objective. Even in the Internet age, retail politics was still the best way for a candidate, especially a newcomer, to connect with voters and convey his message, but this was an enormous, time-consuming, and expensive challenge in a state as big as Texas.

The schedule would be arduous. To ensure rest and downtime, the candidate, his spouse, and the personnel accompanying them were flown home for Sundays, and every other week, Saturdays as well. After Reb announced his candidacy at the Battle of San Jacinto Memorial near Houston, the campaign traveled to West Texas where the first stop was Pecos and the world's first and largest outdoor rodeo. The West of Pecos Rodeo had been held annually since 1883, and was celebrating its 131st anniversary in July 2013.

Reb never owned a Stetson hat, but when out in the sun, he wore an Australian bush hat, flat-crowned and broad-brimmed, similar to the type worn by Crocodile Dundee. Reb did not typically affect the cowboy look, although he was fond of western shirts with mother of pearl snap buttons and cowboy boots because of their comfort and practicality. This was his attire when he appeared at the West of Pecos Rodeo, where he doffed his hat, waved to the crowd, and introduced the bronco-riding event. The public address announcer, figuring Reb to be a city slicker, mischievously cajoled him into showing the crowd how he handled a horse. This caught Reb off guard, but with the crowd cheering him on he could hardly duck the challenge. After all, he was running for governor of Texas and was a native son, so he must know something about horses. If he didn't, no doubt he would be jeered as a horse's ass. His fledgling candidacy had met an unscripted make-or-break moment. Without hesitation, Reb agreed to ride a saddled horse around the rodeo ring, but not a bronco.

Reb had not ridden in over twenty years, since he and Marlenna had been weekend guests at the cattle ranch of Magnolia's most important Argentine customer. Suddenly he was profoundly grateful for having spent much of his youth on Myrlie's farm in Ohio riding his horse Heartland, figuring that like riding a bicycle, you never forgot how. Marlenna was nervous and fearful her husband might make a fool of himself, or worse fall and be hurt. She need not have worried, because Reb easily mounted his steed, a beautiful chestnut quarter horse, and sat tall in the saddle as though he did it everyday. The horse was broken but highly spirited, so he had an anxious moment until his firm, steady grip on the reins let the horse know he was in charge. He cantered three turns around the rodeo ring and finished with a flourish by having the horse rear up on its hind legs the way the Lone Ranger always did with Silver at the beginning of that old western TV program. As the crowd roared its approval of Reb's horsemanship and being a good sport, he tipped his hat and beamed his winning smile. After he dismounted, Marlenna laughed with relief and gave him a hug and a kiss.

This was an auspicious start to the campaign. Television crews were there to record the event, and one comely TV news reporter did an impromptu interview, which was picked up by all the media markets across the state. The spontaneous, free news coverage that revealed the candidate's charm and grace was priceless. Hoppy phoned Reb that evening after watching the news coverage and told him, "Hey, boss, this is a splendid launch to the campaign. The only thing wrong is that I can't take credit for orchestrating it. Keep this up, and you'll win in a landslide. After today, you've won the cowboy and good old boy vote, and you'll probably get a ten-point boost in the overnight polling."

"Thanks, Hoppy. I got lucky, but I've always said it's better to be lucky than good."

Overhearing this exchange, Marlenna sidled over to her husband, playfully nibbled his ear lobe as was her wont, and said, "Hey, cowboy, I'll bet almost all the women who saw you on that horse will cast their vote for you. Just make sure that's all they cast at you."

As Reb later reflected on the campaign, he was especially fond of the West of the Pecos Rodeo event, because there he established a positive image of himself with voters that was televised across the state on the evening news, and set the tone that carried through the subsequent campaign. An obvious truism is that you can make a first impression only once, so make one you want to be remembered. Reb did just that at the West of the Pecos Rodeo.

The rest of the campaign swing through west Texas was uneventful compared to the West of Pecos Rodeo, but the crowds were enthusiastic and, relative to the size of the towns, grew larger by the day. Stops were made in Midland and Odessa in the oil rich Permian Basin, which Reb knew well from his years with Magnolia, and in smaller towns like Marfa and Presidio in the Big Bend Country where the Rio Grande River makes a right angle turn north by northeast, before making a great arcing turn back south. The last stop in west Texas was El Paso, the state's sixth largest city, where Reb's prepared remarks focused on the urgency of securing the border. Across the river from El Paso was Juarez, Mexico, which, for all practical purposes, was a battleground between warring drug cartels. No functioning civil authority had existed for several years. So far, the drug wars had not openly spilled over into El Paso, but most residents feared it was only a matter of time before the violence crossed the border. Securing the border became a major campaign theme for all the candidates running for governor.

Reb proposed that Texas should enact a law similar to the one Arizona passed three years before, which had caused a firestorm of controversy. If the federal government abdicated its fundamental duty to protect the border with Mexico, a border state like Texas had to fill the breach. As a better option, Reb also advocated adoption of the proposed 32nd amendment of the Madison Committee's Second Bill of Rights.

Throughout the campaign, Reb constantly refined his message in both speeches and television spots. Early on, he focused on introducing himself and emphasizing the issues of border security, ensuring Texas had a business friendly environment, and strengthening education of the poor and disadvantaged. The latter issue was especially near and dear to Reb and Marlenna's heart. In Dallas, through their Marcoy Foundation, they had copied Duane Darby's initiative in Houston of providing weekend safe houses for inner-city boys. Reb and Marlenna also set up similar houses for girls and a program for single mothers. Reb's idea, which he relentlessly reiterated throughout the campaign, was to enlist large businesses to provide funds and expertise to establish weekend safe houses in the poor neighborhoods of all the state's major cities. He also encouraged companies to adopt inner-city schools.

The incentive he proposed for participating companies was a reduction in the state sales tax by an amount equal to half what was invested in schools and weekend safe houses. Reb's pitch to the large employers of Texas was that every poor child was a potential future customer or employee, if he or she could be steered away from gangs, drugs, and a life of crime on the mean city streets and placed on a track for academic success. He argued that companies who agreed to participate would be making an investment in their future similar to research and development. Much of research and development expense was a sunk cost with little or no return, but R&D was critical to discovering new products and improving manufacturing processes essential to remaining competitive in the future. Reb knew most of the CEOs of the large firms based in Texas and was confident he could gain the support of many. This was a unique idea that became increasingly popular the more Reb discussed it and as he successfully recruited a number of CEOs over the course of the campaign to endorse the concept publicly.

From west Texas, the campaign caravan rolled on into the Texas Hill Country and numerous stops such as the aptly named hamlet of Utopia, Kerrville, a popular retirement community, and Austin, the state capital and fourth largest city. Austin also was home to the University of Texas and its fifty thousand students. Even in this Democratic stronghold, Reb and Marlenna drew large, enthusiastic crowds. The next sector on the campaign itinerary was the Gulf Coast, which stretches nearly three hundred seventy miles in a graceful arc from Brownsville on the Mexico border through Corpus Christi and on to Port Arthur on the Louisiana border. Several days were spent campaigning in Houston, the state's biggest city with a population of over two million people. Then it was on to Marlenna's favorite getaway for a long winter weekend—the coastal island-city of Galveston, which, in its nineteenth-century heyday, was the largest and most affluent city in Texas and second wealthiest in the U.S. In September 1900, Galveston suffered the worst natural disaster in U.S. history when a hurricane struck full force, killing between six thousand and eight thousand of its forty-two thousand residents, leaving fifteen thousand homeless and destitute. The gritty, resilient survivors rebuilt Galveston, using dredged sand to raise the city's elevation seventeen feet and erecting a seventeen-foot-high, ten-mile-long seawall.

By now, Reb was relaxed and confident on the stump. He incorporated humor in his speeches and when the venue was appropriate, he would answer unscreened questions from the audience. Marlenna usually was his warm-up, and she always brought the crowds to a fever pitch. Soon, without a cue, crowds began chanting "Marlenna, Marlenna, Marlenna" and stomping their feet in anticipation of her appearance. When she did appear on stage, the people would erupt in cheers and whistles that sometimes exceeded the greeting Reb received. He was not in the least bit jealous of his wife's popularity. He adored her and knew that she was his best asset. Depending on the number and nature of daily campaign events, Marlenna often changed her clothes three, even four times a day. Frequently, as Reb took the stage following Marlenna's introduction, he jokingly told crowds that the campaign "had to add a second bus just to carry Marlenna's wardrobe, but clearly it is worth it." The crowds roared their approval every time, as Marlenna flashed them her beautiful smile.

In south Texas, campaign events were held in more than a dozen cities and towns including San Antonio, home of the Alamo and the state's second largest city, Laredo, on the Mexican border, and Langtry, home of the colorful and legendary Judge Roy Bean, self-appointed law west of the Pecos in the late nineteenth century. The local lore is that Bean named the town for his favorite actress, Lillie Langtry. After a weekend off, the campaign resumed its Texas tour to introduce Reb McCoy to voters in east Texas, known as the Piney Woods because of its millions of acres of forests, which support the state's lumber industry. The next sector on the campaign schedule was north Texas, home to The Big D, or Dallas, which proudly claims to have the most restaurants per capita in the U.S., and Fort Worth, also known as Cowtown.

From north Texas, the campaign ended its first complete swing through the state in the vast, often desolate Texas Panhandle. Stops were made in places made famous in the Old West like Abilene, Sweetwater, Lubbock, and Amarillo. In a field twelve miles west of Amarillo along Route 66, now I-40, there is a jarring, some might say strange, work of outdoor public art called the Cadillac Ranch. In the 1970s, a wealthy, eccentric Texas character provided the land and financing for three young artists calling themselves Antfarm to bury partially, nose-down, ten Cadillacs, the oldest a 1949 fastback coupe, the newest a 1963 sedan De Ville. The cars were arranged like tombstones in a single row, and all were positioned, for some unknown reason, at the same angle as the Great Pyramid of Giza in Egypt. By being displayed nose-down, the artists captured the evolution of tail-fins, a design feature first introduced by Cadillac that became prominent on mid-twentieth century American cars.

Now, forty years since the Cadillac Ranch was created, Reb saw in the garishly spray-painted sculpture, a depressing metaphor not only for General Motors, but also possibly for America. GM billed Cadillac as "The Standard of the World" and, at the time these now half-buried, permanently immobile cars were built, GM was the corporate standard of capitalism in the world, the largest and most profitable enterprise on earth. One GM executive of the 1950s was quoted without a trace of irony as saying, "What's good for General Motors is good for America." In 2009, thirty-five years after Cadillac Ranch was created, GM had sunk so low it was forced into bankruptcy and a government takeover. Like the phoenix, the once mighty GM has arisen from the ashes of bankruptcy, and once again appears to be prospering.

Reb pondered the reasons for the once seemingly impregnable GM having been driven, like the cars at Cadillac Ranch, nose first into the ground. Was it pride and hubris, or greed and selfishness of succeeding generations of GM management? No doubt all these failings contributed to GM's downfall, but such failings are endemic among people who rise to great power or prominence. No, Reb thought the critical failings of GM's management, as well as America's political leaders, were willful myopia, procrastination, and an infinite capacity for rationalization. In GM's case, for years before its near death experience, the long-term downward trend was staring management in the face, but they refused to see it. Each year of declining financial performance was rationalized as being an unfortunate exception caused by factors outside management's control or ability to predict.

Reb viewed America as the world standard for freedom, wealth, and opportunity, but its financial foundation was crumbling. Just as GM's day of reckoning finally arrived many years after its decline commenced, so would the United States one day be forced to confront its long-running profligacy. Unfortunately there is no government or other earthly power that can or will come to America's financial rescue if the federal government does not take urgent and effective measures to restore the nation to financial solvency. If the government persists in its willful myopia, one day the gods of finance will exact retributive justice, and if they don't, the bondsman surely will. When that occurs, Reb mused, generations of Americans unborn would curse his generation for shackling them in servitude to a crushing debt burden. The Cadillac Ranch offered Reb an eerie and sobering reminder why the Madison Committee's work was vitally important, and why he had entered the "bizarro" world of elective politics.

Following a long, relaxing weekend, Reb, Marlenna, and their traveling campaign staff began a second trek across the state. The cost of the campaign was tracking the budget, but everything depended on a sustained inflow of cash. From the outset, money to finance the campaign flowed in steadily. The campaign finance manager, Natalie Goldwin, had the Midas touch. There were few female fundraisers in politics, but Natalie was among the very best in the business. Reb and Marlenna were reserved for fundraisers attended by deep-pocket donors, but Natalie raised over 60 percent of total campaign contributions via direct mail and the Internet in amounts generally under $250. By the end of the campaign, there was more than enough cash on hand to repay Reb the $5 million he had loaned his campaign when he began his run for governor.

By January 2014, having campaigned extensively in all seven sectors of the state, Reb had begun to emphasize what he viewed were the biggest threats to both Texas and the country: the federal government's expansion beyond its constitutional boundaries, trillion-dollar annual budget deficits, and the staggering unfunded entitlement liabilities that would bankrupt the nation and deny future generations of Americans the blessings and opportunities enjoyed by the current profligate generation.

Invited to address the Texas tea party convention held in Houston in early February, Reb delivered a rousing speech in which he argued that focusing only on replacing the Washington political insiders was unlikely to result in the desired reform of government. The tea party had tremendous success getting its reform candidates elected to congress in 2010, but since then not much had changed, because there were still enough entrenched old guard politicians with the seniority, power, and guile to block many of the necessary initiatives for reducing the size and power of the federal government.

Reb explained the purpose of the reform effort. "The people of each sovereign state through their elected governors and state legislators have to reclaim the powers wrongly usurped by the federal government and to demand restoration of the country's financial solvency. It is futile and hopeless to believe the federal government can or will reform itself in a fundamental and lasting way. There is, however, no reason to despair. In their wisdom, the Framers of the Constitution provided the people and the states the antidote to an overreaching, out-of-control federal government in Article V of the Constitution, which sets forth how amendments may be adopted. It won't be easy, but the solution is to persuade at least thirty-four state legislatures to petition Congress to call a constitutional convention for the purpose of adopting a Second Bill of Rights." Reb went on to summarize the Madison Committee's proposed amendments and pledged, if elected, to work with the Texas State Legislature and his fellow governors to move this agenda forward. Reb received a standing ovation at the end of his speech and the enthusiastic endorsement of the tea party as its choice for governor.

By early 2014, Joe Barlow, Congressman from San Antonio, was Reb's only serious opponent for the nomination. Barlow was a decent chap who subscribed to Ronald Reagan's eleventh commandment, "A Republican shall not speak ill of a fellow Republican." A colorless fellow, Barlow had difficulty generating excitement. He was conservative, but unlike his opponent, he offered few new ideas. Following his speech to the Texas tea party, the internal polling by McCoy's campaign showed Reb to have an insurmountable and growing lead over Barlow.

After winning the nomination in April, Reb and Marlenna took a much needed three-week vacation in Hawaii. They rented a beachfront estate on Maui, where Ravenna, Jeff, and the kids joined them for a week.

On their return to Dallas, Reb met with Hoppy, Jake Fillmore, and his campaign team to plan the general election campaign. They decided to follow the template for the primary campaign with few modifications. Reb's Democratic opponent was Dix Jenkins, a seven-term congressman from Austin and former state attorney general. Dix lacked both charisma and new ideas. In their two debates, Reb effectively parried Jenkins's efforts to criticize Reb's decision to sell Magnolia Petroleum & Chemical, and to tie him to the more unpopular policies of President Thurston's administration. In the debates and during his campaign rallies, Reb continued to hammer home the themes he had stressed during the primary campaign.

In October, Reb was proud and grateful to have President Thurston join him for a campaign rally that drew twenty-five thousand people in Houston. Maggie appeared tired and to have lost weight since he had last seen her, but Reb attributed her appearance to the strain of her job. He was unaware of her failing health. As the enthusiastic crowd stood, applauded, and cheered, Reb leaned over and said, "Madam President, they love you here in Texas. Your visit will put me over the top, for sure."

The president replied, "Don't be so modest, Reb, these folks are cheering mostly for you. I regret that you declined my offer to be my running mate in 2012, but I am thrilled you have jumped into the fray and are going to be the next governor of Texas. By the way, Ding Bell has briefed me on the Madison Committee's activities, and I think you have some excellent ideas. Next year, when our schedules permit, I would like to discuss how I can help you move your agenda forward."

"I appreciate your interest, Madam President, and look forward to meeting with you at your convenience."

Neither Reb nor the president knew that this was the last time they would see each other. The White House scheduled a meeting in Washington for the two of them to discuss the Madison Committee's proposed Second Bill of Rights, but President Thurston died before that meeting took place.

Three weeks after the president's visit, Rogers Edmund Burke McCoy was elected governor of Texas with 58 percent of the vote, and was sworn into office in January 2015. He and Marlenna prepared to move into the Governor's Mansion, where by law he was required to reside whenever he was in Austin. The lovely antebellum mansion, built in 1856, is situated adjacent to the state capitol. Nearly destroyed by fire in 2008, the $30 million project to restore the building was completed in 2012.

Following a spectacular inaugural dinner and ball attended by over a thousand people, the governor and first lady retired to the governor's suite for their first night in the mansion. Reb had been elated all evening, but most of all he was anticipating sharing a moment of intimacy with his wife. Marlenna looked ravishing in her gorgeous, strapless Carmen Marc Valvo gown in a rich ruby red from Neiman Marcus in Dallas, her favorite store for apparel. She was without doubt the most beautiful woman at the ball, and he loved dancing with her, but he had spent much of the evening accepting congratulations and best wishes. By the time they got to their bedroom well after midnight, he was tired, but eager to make love to his wife.

He had already shed his clothes when he embraced her from behind, began kissing her neck below the ear, and said, "Marlenna, darling, as always you were the most desirable, captivating creature I saw tonight. I loved the entire evening, but most of all I couldn't wait for us to be alone, so I could slip that beautiful dress off of you and make passionate love."

"Hmmm, that sounds like a wonderful idea, Governor. You know I've never had sex with a governor before."

"I am relieved beyond words to hear that, pretty. But tonight I plan to remedy that gap in your résumé."

With that Marlenna turned to face him and let her gown slide to the floor. She had nothing on but her bra, which Reb expertly removed. He breathed deeply the scent of her perfume and allowed his loving eyes to drink in her beauty. Even after all these years, the wondrous happiness she gave him could occasionally bring tears of joy to his eyes as happened now. He took her in his arms and eagerly kissed her open lips. As he led her by her hand to bed, he said, "Wonder what everyone would have thought if they had known the first lady of Texas had gone commando tonight?"

"Well, honey, I thought it would save you some time. Besides the gown was so tight, if I had to go to the bathroom during the evening, I could not have hiked the dress up high enough to pull down my thong."

"You are the sexiest woman alive, pretty, and if I loved you anymore, my heart would surely burst." With that, they made love, as they had countless times before, but as always it seemed as magical as their first time. Governor and Mrs. McCoy spent a blissful first night in the Governor's Mansion.

20

Among the fifty state chief executives, the governor of Texas constitutionally is one of the weakest. The Constitution of the state of Texas disperses power by making most important state offices elected rather than appointed positions. In addition to the governor, the lieutenant governor, attorney general, comptroller of public accounts, commissioner of agriculture, and commissioner of the land office are all elected statewide. Even the nine Texas Supreme Court justices are elected, as are the three members of the Texas Railroad Commission. Established in 1891, the TRRC regulates the state oil and gas industry, but, despite its name, no longer retains its original mandate to regulate railroads. Even members of the state board of education are chosen through regional elections.

The only major appointment made by the governor is the secretary of state, who oversees elections, but a two-thirds vote of the state senate is required to confirm the governor's nominee. The lieutenant governor arguably is more powerful than the governor. Elected independently of the governor, the lieutenant governor is the president of the state senate. In this capacity, the lieutenant governor has the power to make senate committee assignments and in the case of tie votes to cast the deciding vote on legislation. The governor's ability to get his legislative agenda passed largely depends on being able to work harmoniously with the lieutenant governor.

The governor also has little direct budget authority. The comptroller of public accounts is responsible for tax collection, accounting, and providing the legislature with the estimated state revenue for the biennial budget. The state budget must be balanced; therefore, the legislature may not appropriate expenditures in excess of the comptroller's revenue estimate. The legislature theoretically can overrule the comptroller's revenue estimate, but only by a four-fifths majority in both chambers. No comptroller has ever been overridden by the legislature.

Reb was unconcerned that the office of governor had limited powers. His overriding objective in running for office was to get the Texas Legislature to approve the Madison Committee's proposed Second Bill of Rights, and to submit a formal application to the U.S. Congress to call a constitutional convention. With a mandate from the voters and a good working relationship with the lieutenant governor, Reb succeeded in getting the state legislature to pass this application within two months of taking office. With this major initiative accomplished, he planned to commence lobbying his fellow governors to pursue a similar effort with their respective state legislatures. Not having extensive official responsibilities as governor, he had ample time to do so.

During his first Republican Governors Association meeting, Reb began his drive to get more states to join Texas in the effort to adopt the Second Bill of Rights. Among his peers, Reb's reputation in the business world preceded him, which gave him instant credibility, and being from the country's second biggest state brought him immediate prominence in the exclusive governors' club. In addition to these attributes, Reb's engaging personality and natural leadership qualities gave him star power. Before long, six fellow governors had bought into the Madison Committee agenda and each began actively working to have it passed by their respective legislatures.

In an April 2015 issue of *National Review*, a biweekly periodical of conservative opinion founded in 1955 by the late William F. Buckley, Jr., Reb was featured on the cover with the ghost of James Madison hovering in the background. The cover headline for the issue's feature story was, FATHER OF THE SECOND BILL OF RIGHTS: CAN THE STATES RESCUE THE CONSTITUTION? Reb felt the article was overly complimentary of him and did not give adequate credit to his fellow Madison Committee members, but he was grateful for the publicity and thoughtful critique of the proposed Second Bill of Rights. The story's author commented:

> It will be an uphill battle to get at least thirty-four states to petition Congress for a constitutional convention, especially since it has never been done before. Even if that hurdle is surmounted, Congress probably will rely on technicalities to avoid calling a convention. If the effort catches fire with the public, however, there is a chance it might succeed and that, in turn, might be the best and last chance to restore constitutional balance and pull the nation back from the fiscal abyss.

A few weeks after the *National Review* article appeared, Reb met with Jake Fillmore in the governor's office inside the state capitol building. He had been reelected chairman of the Republican Party of Texas, and for the past six months had been an ex officio member of the Madison Committee, attending its monthly meetings. When the two old friends turned to business, Reb said, "Jake, we're making excellent progress with the Madison Committee agenda. We obtained our legislature's approval sooner than I thought possible. That's been most helpful to me as I meet with my counterparts around the country. Already three other states have petitioned Congress to call a constitutional convention and six more legislatures are deliberating similar action."

"Yes, Governor," Jake now addressed Reb by his first name only when they were together socially, "your decision to make the Second Bill of Rights a centerpiece of your campaign accelerated the legislature's passage of a petition to Congress. That has generated wide coverage in newspapers and periodicals across the country. Of course, not all the editorials are favorable, but most are supportive, and many others are taking a wait-and-see posture for now."

"We need to make sure we don't lose our momentum, Jake. The Madison Committee's agenda becomes more popular the longer the nation's economic growth drifts along at a sluggish pace and the federal deficits continue to pile up. From my perspective, enacting the Second Bill of Rights is imperative. I'm planning to start discussions with several Democratic governors who might be receptive to our ideas. To further emphasize the commitment of Texas Republicans to reining in the federal government, I would like to change the party's official name to the Republican Constitution Party of Texas. I would also love to entice our friends across the aisle to rename their party the Democratic Constitution Party of Texas, but I realize that that is beyond my powers of persuasion to accomplish. The point is, I see this as an American issue and not limited to a particular party, but I want there to be no doubt where the Texas Republican Party stands regarding its commitment to limited government as established by the Constitution."

"I support your idea, Governor, but before a change can be made, I will have to take it to the state party's executive committee for discussion and a vote. We'll also need to get the congressional delegation and state elected officials on board. I expect Ding Bell and the lieutenant governor can help with that. The biggest hurdle, I suspect, will be obtaining the national Republican Party approval. I'm reasonably confident that that won't be an insurmountable problem if we lay the groundwork with the national leaders in advance of adopting the name change. How can anyone be opposed to the Constitution, especially a Republican?"

"That's exactly the point, Jake. I'd like you to do what has to be done to implement this change as soon as practical. Let me know how I can be of help. I'll also suggest to my fellow Republican governors that they consider making a similar change in their state party names. We both know this change is cosmetic, but adding 'Constitution' to the party's official name is symbolically important. It lets our citizens know precisely what is of paramount importance to Texas Republicans."

"I'll get on this right away, Governor. We also will want to roll out the new name to appropriate fanfare and tie it in with the legislature's application to Congress for a constitutional convention to consider the Second Bill of Rights. This will provide us a great opportunity to educate folks and get further coverage by the press and on the cable news channels."

"Thanks, Jake. I knew I could count on your support."

In the first six months of his term, in addition to pursuing the Madison Committee's agenda, Reb devoted significant time to working with the state board of education, mayors, and large businesses to establish weekend safe houses for disadvantaged youth living in inner-city and other depressed communities. A public private partnership called the Texas Opportunity for Disadvantaged Youth, or TOFDY, was established. Funding was provided through 'investments' made by participating companies that pledged to finance weekend safe houses and adopt inner-city schools. Pilot projects were planned for the state's seven largest cities. When TOFDY determined these were meeting established criteria, the program would be expanded to the next twenty largest cities and selected rural communities.

Participating companies each pledged to invest a minimum of one million dollars for building safe houses, and an equal amount over the next ten years for operating and maintenance costs. Several larger companies made up front investments of as much as $10 million. Charitable foundations also were solicited to participate, and the Marcoy Foundation invested $7 million with a commitment to donate an additional $700,000 per year for ten years. Total investment funds raised by June 2015 exceeded $250 million, which surpassed Reb's first-year goal.

Although there were a few early glitches, the TOFDY partnership met with immediate success. Educators, business executives, and city officials merged their respective talents, expertise, and egos harmoniously to focus on a common objective. The weekend safe houses took vulnerable children, ages eight to eighteen, off the streets from Friday afternoon until Sunday evening. In addition to mentoring and tutoring, courses in civics, moral values, self-responsibility, and interpersonal skills, as well as athletics and physical fitness were provided. Single mothers of TOFDY kids were offered day programs on the weekends to help them be better parents and to develop useful workplace skills. Objective metrics were established to measure progress, and there was regular interactive feedback between teachers who taught TOFDY children during the week and the weekend safe house professional counselors. It would take years to determine if the program was having a significant positive impact on the lives of TOFDY children, but early results were promising. Reb was well pleased with how this key initiative had quickly achieved enthusiastic support from TOFDY partners and popularity with TOFDY children and their parents.

Reb's other major campaign pledge was to improve border security between Texas and Mexico. His most worrisome concern was the potential for drug cartel violence in the Mexican border towns spreading into Texas, and the potential for terrorist attacks launched from Mexico. When he came into office, the Texas Rangers, the state police, and the attorney general all expressed profound concerns about the risk of widespread violence occurring along the border, most likely in El Paso, Laredo, or Brownsville. Of even greater concern was the threat of a terrorist attack, the most likely target being one or more of the several dams on the Rio Grande River. At least three incipient attacks had been thwarted in the past four years. Texas law enforcement believed the perpetrators were reconnoitering the dams to detect security vulnerabilities in preparation for a real attack in the future.

When Reb asked who was behind these attacks, he was told it could be Islamic fanatics or a Mexican Marxist terrorist group believed to be funded by Venezuela's Hugo Chavez and aligned with a drug cartel. The U.S. Department of Homeland Security, of course, was aware of these potential threats, but Texas officials did not believe adequate resources were deployed along the border or in undercover surveillance to protect against an attack. The federal government felt it had to balance aggressive border protection against its desire for smooth relations with the Mexican government. Reb believed if the choice was between smiley-face diplomacy or defending the border and protecting American lives, the latter were a far higher priority. He was also troubled by the increasing number of illegal aliens crossing the border for work, and the burden this placed on state schools, hospitals, and social service agencies.

Reb developed a two-pronged strategy to lobby Homeland Security for beefed-up security and border control, and to reach out to the Texas Hispanic community to build support and understanding, and gather input regarding the illegal alien problem. Reb welcomed immigrants from Mexico, but the United States had to be in control of its sovereign border and admit immigrants in an orderly, legal, and fair manner. Hispanic leaders were skeptical of Reb's outreach, but at least an open dialogue was established, which was more than he achieved with Homeland Security. Consequently, he introduced a bill in the state legislature similar to what Arizona had passed in

2010, and he requested additional funds for Texas law enforcement to devote more resources to protecting the border.

After six months as governor, Reb was generally pleased with the progress his administration had made thus far on his signature issues, with the exception of border security. By this time, he realized that the world of private business offered far more personal satisfaction than did the political world. A successful business executive is relentlessly focused on strategizing, gathering relevant information, deciding, taking prompt action, objectively measuring performance, and making appropriate changes if objectives are not met. An elected official, however, is focused on endlessly discussing, debating, cajoling, compromising, threatening, pleading, and horse trading to get anything done. And the process is exasperatingly slow. The inherent inefficiency of democracy was the price paid for self-governance and freedom. While Reb learned quickly the rules of the game and played it fairly well for being a novice, he did not enjoy it and was frustrated by it.

At the end of one particularly aggravating week, Reb returned to the Governor's Mansion and confided to Marlenna before dinner that he would not stand for reelection in 2018. Between now and then, he would faithfully serve the citizens of Texas, and dedicate every spare moment to proselytizing as many fellow governors as possible to champion the proposed Second Bill of Rights in their respective state legislatures. When his term was up, he would return to private life without regret, certain he had done his best.

"Pretty, I want to travel the world with you, read lots of interesting books, and make you in fact what you have been in my heart since I fell in love with you forty years ago: the sun around which my life orbits."

With tears welling in her eyes, Marlenna replied, "Oh, honey, you are an incurable romantic. Look what you've done. You made my mascara run. What am I going to do with you? I love you with all my heart. Now, let's have dinner and go to bed early so we can fool around."

21

Washington, DC
September 2015

Late in September 2015, just three months after assuming the presidency, Biff Fubarsky was both livid and filled with self-pity over the polling data his chief political advisor had briefed him on earlier that afternoon. His political honeymoon barely had lasted a fortnight, after his predecessor was laid to rest in Arlington National Cemetery. The presidential election was only thirteen months away, but his prospects for winning were dimming with each new poll. Only 40 percent of likely voters supported him for president against an unnamed Democratic opponent, and only 49 percent of Republicans favored his nomination. The most painful number in the poll results was that nearly 60 percent of likely voters viewed Biff as a caretaker, someone to keep the seat warm until a new president was elected.

President Fubarsky was the victim of several unfortunate circumstances. His predecessor Maggie Thurston had been popular, despite the continued weak economy, high unemployment numbers, and out-of-control federal spending. Americans had a warm feeling for their first woman president who was charismatic and exuded confidence and competence. Because of her personal popularity and gender, Democrats refrained from direct personal attacks on Thurston for fear they would redound to their detriment. Fubarsky had no such political immunity. With the election just over the horizon, Democrats ramped up with gusto their attacks on the dismal economic performance under Republican stewardship, counting on or hoping that the electorate would forget things were as bad as or worse than when they held the White House.

Fubarsky's biggest political liability was that the more people saw and heard him, the more they sized him up the way Jake Fillmore described him—a bombastic empty suit. If Biff had stepped forward within a month of assuming office and announced a bold plan for stimulating economic growth and cutting back government spending, and said he was carrying out President Thurston's plans had she lived, he might have garnered much goodwill with the public. Instead, Biff dithered, reveled in the trappings of power and office, and mumbled platitudes without substance.

The only accomplishment he had thus far was getting his choice to replace him as vice president approved by Congress. The Twenty-fifth Amendment, ratified a few years after President Kennedy's assassination, provides that whenever there is a vacancy in the office of vice president, the president will nominate a replacement who must be confirmed by majority vote of the House and the Senate. Biff didn't want anyone who might overshadow him in the job. Moreover, neither ambitious Republicans nor Democrats wanted a strong figure as vice president lest he or she parlay the position into national prominence and a possible future run for president. To get someone confirmed as vice president, the nominee would have to be seen as having no further political ambitions. Biff selected a seventy-two-year-old three-term senator who offended virtually no one and publicly announced he would serve out the term and retire. The nomination sailed through both houses.

President Fubarsky's political weakness had already attracted two challengers for the Republican nomination, a former governor and a conservative senator, who did not wait for Biff to announce whether he was running in 2016. Other challengers were waiting in the wings if Fubarsky's polls did not improve soon. Senior party leaders feared a bitter, internecine struggle for the nomination in which Fubarsky may or may not prevail, but the party would be divided going into the general election and headed for almost certain defeat. To avert this eventuality, several senior Republican senators got together and decided one of them should talk with the president to dissuade him from running.

Sen. Ding Bell, one of the president's closest and trusted associates from his time in the Senate, drew the short straw for this unenviable assignment. The president was expected to announce formally his candidacy no later than mid-October, so Ding had to meet with him promptly.

Ding was able to arrange a thirty-minute Oval Office meeting with the president the first week of October, ostensibly to discuss the Senate's fall legislative agenda. When Ding saw the president, he was startled at how tense and aged he appeared after only three months in the job. Biff was clearly in over his head, and the unfavorable poll numbers only exacerbated his agitation.

After briefly reviewing the Senate's legislative calendar, Ding said, "Mr. President, I understand you plan to announce your future plans next week. Before you do, I hoped to have the opportunity to share with you, in confidence, my perspective."

"Well, Ding, I have tentatively decided to run, but I have not discussed it with anyone other than Dolly. It's timely that I hear your thoughts, as you are someone I trust. The two concerns I have about running for election to a full term are the terrible polling numbers and, between you and me, the job is not as enjoyable as I always thought it would be. Funny how you can aspire to something all your life only to be terribly disappointed once you attain it."

Ding almost felt sorry for Biff, but his admission gave him an opening. "Mr. President, as you well know, the country faces enormous challenges at home and abroad, and needs a full-time president who is above the political fray. As you also know, there will be several formidable conservatives who will contest you for the party's nomination. In the end, you very likely will prevail, but the struggle will leave the party divided and consume most of your time that could otherwise be spent on the urgent problems the country faces."

"Ding, how can you suggest I run away from a fight? If I don't run, I will immediately be relegated to lame duck status and unable to get anything done."

"If I may respectfully disagree, Mr. President, your stature and popularity would skyrocket if you chose not to run. You would be seen as placing the country ahead of your personal ambition, and people on both sides of the political aisle would be more amenable to working with you to move your agenda forward. If you assume the mantle of statesman, you have a good chance of leaving a positive legacy and being held in esteem and affection by the American people. If you subject yourself to an ugly, drawn-out struggle for the nomination and ultimately lose either the primary or general election, you will probably be treated harshly by history. I don't like delivering this message so directly, but I figure every president needs to have a few people who will tell the truth, even if it isn't what he or she wants to hear."

"I appreciate your candid analysis, Ding. I briefly considered dropping out of the race, but discarded the idea after hearing from my political advisors. You have crystallized the issue for me and are probably correct. This job is not what I thought it would be, so why try to keep it for another four years? Dolly would be thrilled if I decided to retire. I will take your counsel under advisement, and I thank you for coming to see me."

Rising to leave, Ding said, "Thank you for your time, Mr. President. If there is anything else I can do for you, please call on me. Also, I want you to know that you will have my full support regardless of what you decide."

"I appreciate that, Ding. I know you to be a man of your word. It seems I had a lot more friends before I got this job. Glad to know you're still one of them."

As Ding reached the door to depart, he glanced back at the president and saw that he had swiveled his desk chair around to gaze pensively out on the White House south lawn and the Washington Monument in the distance.

22

President Fubarsky's announcement that he would not stand for election in 2016 surprised everyone, except the first lady and Ding Bell. The fight for the Republican nomination was suddenly wide open, and political pundits pontificated that at least a half dozen people would declare their candidacies with no clear favorite likely to emerge until after the Iowa caucuses in January 2016, and the first primary in New Hampshire a week later.

Newspaper reporters in Austin, Texas, immediately speculated whether Governor McCoy might run for president. When the question was put to Reb, he replied with total honesty, "I have not given the matter the slightest consideration."

When pressed to elaborate, he added, "I have no interest at this time in running for president. Only last year I was elected governor, so it seems to me to be premature to discuss running for another office. That's all I have to say on the subject, except that the Republican Party has many talented and qualified individuals, any one of whom has the potential to be an outstanding president."

For the moment, the press dropped the subject, but several op-ed columnists noted that Governor McCoy had not absolutely, irrevocably ruled out running for president. Of course, no savvy politician would foreclose any future options, so as to preserve flexibility of action if unforeseen circumstances altered the political landscape to his advantage. Reb truly had no interest in the presidency, but by not slamming the door shut, others might continue to view him as a potential candidate. This gave him additional leverage and influence with his fellow governors whom he was encouraging to embrace the Second Bill of Rights.

By mid-October, the name change to Texas Republican Constitution Party had been made official, and twelve state legislatures had petitioned Congress to call a constitutional convention to consider the Second Bill of Rights. Reb was assiduously working with eight other states to follow suit. Several states had modified or added amendments, but the core seven amendments drafted by the Madison Committee were incorporated in all the petitions submitted to Congress thus far.

In late October with just over two months until the Iowa caucuses, the Republican Governors Association held a meeting to determine if they could coalesce around one of their members to support for the presidential nomination. So far, four Republican senators and a former governor turned TV commentator had declared their candidacies, but no incumbent Republican governor had done so. Governors generally think senators don't make particularly capable presidents. They can be effective campaigners and speechmakers, but most are inept in executive administration, which is what the presidency requires.

After eliminating from consideration those who flatly refused to run under any circumstance, the twenty-six Republican governors voted by secret ballot in a round-robin elimination, which winnowed out the two governors with the fewest votes in each round. By the third round, Reb was the top vote-getter and after the sixth round, he had won by a decisive margin. The vote reflected the high regard Reb's peers had for him, and the fact that he had become the leader and public face of the initiative to restore limited federal government and adopt the Second Bill of Rights. If he ran for president, Reb could propel this issue into the forefront of the presidential election. Even if he failed to win the nomination, the candidate who did win would be compelled to make this issue a centerpiece of his or her campaign.

Reb expressed his sincere appreciation to his colleagues for their vote of confidence, and said he would decide whether to run within a couple weeks. Events were moving at a breakneck pace. Reb needed time for calm reflection before making such a momentous decision, and he had to discuss the matter with Marlenna. His instinctive reaction was to stay away from presidential politics, but he also was irrevocably committed to the Madison Committee agenda and could not responsibly turn his back on an opportunity that potentially could result in achieving its objectives. Within another month, five more states were expected to pass petitions to Congress, bringing the number to have done so to seventeen, half the number of states needed to call a constitutional convention.

A few days after the Republican governors met, Reb was not surprised that a story appeared in major papers across the country reporting that TEXAS GOVERNOR McCOY CHOICE OF REPUBLICAN PEERS FOR PRESIDENT. The story cited unnamed sources, but Reb knew one or more of his governor buddies were trying to build enthusiasm for his candidacy and to pressure him into running. A day later, the tea party announced that it was unimpressed with any of the Republicans who so far had entered the race, but if someone like Gov. McCoy decided to run, he would almost certainly win the tea party's endorsement.

The morning the tea party story appeared, Marlenna put down the paper, took a sip of her coffee, and said to her husband, "When you told me about the governors voting you their favorite candidate, it spoke highly of you, but I thought the idea of you running for president was ludicrous. Now, a story shows up every day touting you as a candidate. Two and a half years ago, the idea of politics never entered your mind. Then you ran for governor, and lightning struck. Less than a year into that job, please don't tell me you are giving serious consideration to running for president."

"Marlenna, a month ago I gave no thought to any further political ambition, other than serving out my term as governor. I also never anticipated that Maggie Thurston would die in office, or that Biff Fubarsky would decide against running for election to a full term. As you know, the reason I ran for governor was to advance the Madison Committee agenda. The progress made thus far has exceeded all expectations. We are on the verge of securing half the thirty-four states needed to petition Congress to call a constitutional convention, but it will be much more difficult to capture the next seventeen. If I were to run for president, even if I lost, we could bring this matter to center stage and increase the odds of securing the remaining states we need."

"But why does it have to be you, Reb? Why can't one of the other governors supporting the Second Bill of Rights run for president and make this his campaign issue?"

"If I don't run, perhaps someone else will step in and carry the banner. By now, I have become the public face of this initiative. As much as I don't relish the idea of running for office again, especially the presidency, I don't see how I can decline to do so having come this far."

"Reb, I love you and you are indispensable to me, but as wonderful as you are and as good a president you would no doubt be, you are not indispensable to the country. You know better than I that running for president is not for the fainthearted. It will be exponentially harder and dirtier than your run for governor. I read a column recently that said a definition of insanity is anyone who would subject himself, and his family, to running for national office. Media scrutiny and opponents' dirty tricks are constant and intense. The process is utterly demeaning. This columnist went on to write that one candidate who ran unsuccessfully some years ago indicated the experience was worse than undergoing a proctology exam with a splintered broomstick handle."

"Well, I guess anyone who runs for president should have an industrial drum of K-Y Jelly near at hand. Perhaps I am too obsessed with pushing the Second Bill of Rights, but I believe adoption of these amendments is essential to the future of the country. I didn't plan to get caught up in this. I am a reluctant citizen politician, but fate and a profound sense of duty compel me to see this through. I won't run for president, however, without you at my side."

"Oh, Reb, you know I won't stand in your way, and I will enthusiastically campaign with and for you. I can't believe how this Madison Committee could have completely taken over and changed our lives, but in my heart I know that if you choose to run, you will be motivated solely by your genuine love and concern for the country."

"Marlenna, darling, you're too marvelous for words. If I decide to run for president, once it's over, I'll take you anywhere and give you anything you want."

In a gently sardonic manner, Marlenna responded, "Even with your wife, you are already sounding like a professional politician. Promise me anything to get my support, hoping I'll forget your previous promises. Well, as I recall, cowboy, only a few months ago you romanced me with some malarkey that when your term as governor is over, we would travel the world together, always westward so we would never miss a sunset. Now that promise is no longer operative. Instead of foreswearing politics, you are going run for president. So it goes."

"Cut me some slack, pretty. If I do run, it is highly improbable I will win the nomination, much less the general election. I will not pander to the voters. Instead, I would lay out the stark reality facing this country and future generations if difficult decisions are not taken urgently. Nothing would be sugar-coated. The issues are freedom, solvency, and what our generation bequeaths to posterity. Based on history, however, voters don't like to hear hard truths, especially when other candidates are dishing out vapid happy talk. Who wants to listen to some saturnine sermonizer telling you to eat your vegetables and forget about having dessert? I am sure my opponents and the press will skewer me as a purveyor of doom and gloom, so vote for anybody else who promises to deliver free gold, frankincense, and myrrh."

"Well, I don't agree that you likely would lose with your message, Reb. I believe many Americans, probably a majority, belatedly have come to realize dramatic, almost revolutionary change is needed to save the country from an accelerating downward spiral. People hunger for someone to speak the truth and explain what needs to be done. You have great ideas that you articulate with passion, clarity, and sincerity."

"Whether or not I win is of no consequence. My purpose would be to convince the people and legislatures of at least thirty-eight states to ratify the Second Bill of Rights. If that can be achieved within the next one or two years, the American people will have reaffirmed liberty and limited government, placed the country on a path to solvency, and saved future generations from financial servitude."

"When I chided you about running for president, I was just being selfish. While I have trepidation about a presidential campaign, I want you to go for it if that's what you decide. Have you talked to Ding or Jake about this yet?"

"No, I wanted us to have this conversation before going any further. I will meet with Ding, Jake, Hopalong Cassidy, and Natalie Goldwin in a couple days. If they all agree the idea is not risible and are willing to sign on as my campaign brain trust, I'm going to go for it. The poet Robert Browning once wrote, 'Ah, but a man's reach should exceed his grasp, or what's a heaven for?' If I do this, pretty, it will be the second time in my life that I will have reached beyond my grasp. The first time was when I reached for you and grasped hold of heaven, the stuff of dreams. But the gods eventually demand retribution for blessings in the form of curses, thus I should stoically accept that the second time, I'll be reaching for hell and the stuff of nightmares."

"I love you, cowboy. I don't know any other girl whose husband quotes Robert Browning to her at breakfast."

23

Running for President
2016 Election

In early November, Reb met with Ding, Jake, Hoppy, Natalie, and Tai Li Ho at the Marcoy Foundation. New to the group was Ho, known to all as Tally Ho, which fit his profession, public opinion polling. Tally Ho was of Chinese ancestry but, save for his oriental features, was as American as anyone else at the meeting. His great-great grandfather emigrated from China to the U.S. in the 1860s to help build the transcontinental railroad, and his grandfather survived the 1906 San Francisco earthquake.

Tally Ho, thirty-eight years old, was a summa cum laude graduate of Cal Tech, with a degree in mathematics and a doctorate in computer science from Berkley. When Reb told Hoppy he was planning to run for president, Hoppy said the campaign should retain Tally Ho, the best pollster in the business. Hoppy explained that Tally Ho knew in detail the demographics and everything voters liked and disliked in each of the four hundred thirty-five congressional districts, and could recite this knowledge on demand from his photographic memory. Reb liked Tally

Ho immediately for his firm handshake, eye contact, directness, and quiet demeanor but unmistakable brilliance.

Reb called the meeting to order. "Thank you all for agreeing to join me in the most unique and in my case quixotic adventure in democracy: running for president of the United States. All of you except Tally Ho were with me during my successful run for governor just last year. Never did it occur to me until a couple weeks ago that I would ever run for president, but events, perhaps the tide of history, and my own free will have conspired to bring me to this decision. I would not attempt this challenge, however, without all of you on my team. Each of you has experience working on a national political campaign, whereas I don't. So I will depend on you for your candid, blunt advice on what to do and when to do it."

Pausing to sip a Diet Coke, Reb continued, "While I don't have much political experience, and none at the national level, you all deserve to know up front precisely why I am running. If limited to four words to explain my platform, they would be: freedom, solvency, security, and posterity. The federal government has far exceeded its constitutional limits thereby eroding personal freedom in exchange for increasing dependency, brought the country to the brink of insolvency, undermined long-term national security, and diminished what this generation of Americans will bequeath to posterity. We cannot successfully address these enormous challenges with tepid, incremental measures. To quote Abraham Lincoln, 'The dogmas of the quiet past are inadequate to the stormy present.' While I intend to put forward a number of proposals during the campaign, my central theme will be to argue for adoption of the proposed seven amendments known as the Second Bill of Rights, which I have been promoting since becoming governor. Do you think this message would appeal to the electorate? If so, what are the critical factors for a successful campaign?"

Ding spoke first. "Governor, I believe you have the message and proposals the voters need to hear. It is serious and sober, and it assumes the voters are adults, not children. The question is whether you or anyone can convince the voters to grant you a mandate to make the painful choices necessary to restore constitutional balance and fiscal sanity."

"That's the key issue, Ding," responded Reb. "Can we reach the average voter? After fifty years or more of the federal government becoming ever more involved in our day-to-day lives, we Americans almost have to relearn that there is an inverse correlation between individual liberty and dependency on an all-powerful national government. The more we have of one, the less we have of the other. What is the proper balance? Moreover, the states must reassert their sovereign rights in order to restore federalism to the federal government. When the Constitution was ratified, the sovereign states agreed to delegate limited and enumerated powers to the new federal government, with all other rights and powers reserved to the states or the people. So concerned were the Founders that the federal government might amass powers beyond those specifically granted to it, they insisted on the Ninth and Tenth Amendments being included in the Bill of Rights, which explicitly enshrined the concepts of federalism and limited government in the Constitution. Over the past seventy-five years, however, the Ninth and Tenth Amendments have been essentially ignored, and the federal republic established by the Framers has been transmogrified into a monolithic nation state. The best and perhaps last chance to curb federal power resides with the states, through collective pressure and constitutional amendments."

Tally Ho addressed Reb. "Governor, you articulate a rather sophisticated message that only the best informed voters will grasp. The American people are intelligent, and most possess common sense, but they are understandably cynical about government and politicians, and they are generally ignorant of their country's history. Furthermore, most voters have never known anything other than a huge federal government that meddles in all aspects of daily life and provides a variety of entitlements to about half the population. For many years, politicians of both parties have encouraged people to look to government to alleviate their problems when the going gets tough. In all the polls I have conducted, folks gripe about the nanny state, but when you get down to specifics, they aren't willing to give it up."

Reb soaked in what Tally Ho was telling him and appreciated the young man's matter-of-fact candor. Tally Ho was saying politely that Reb may have the right solution to the country's problems, but good luck selling it to the people.

At this point, Hoppy spoke up. "While I agree with Tally Ho's conclusions based on his polling, over time, public opinion can be changed. To do so will require a consistent, easily understood, plain-spoken message persistently delivered by a credible candidate. In barely a year's time, Governor, you have been so successful in selling the Madison Committee's proposed Second Bill of Rights that seventeen state legislatures have petitioned Congress for a constitutional convention. And I believe in time at least another seventeen will follow suit, which will all but ensure a convention is called. To reach enough voters to win the nomination and then the general election, we need to shape and test market your message."

"Hoppy, I get what you and Tally Ho are telling me," Reb responded. "I just want to be clear that while I am running to win, winning the presidency is not my primary objective. My paramount goal is to change dramatically and permanently the direction of this country, so future American generations can enjoy the blessings of liberty and opportunities for prosperity that all of us have enjoyed. I believe the proposed Second Bill of Rights is the vehicle for bringing about this change, and by running for president—win or lose—I can further that goal. I am willing to shape and test market my message, as you put it, to reach the hearts and minds of the electorate, but I will not engage in manipulation or pandering. It is long past time that the American people heard the truth, or at least what I believe to be the truth. They can then make an informed decision as to which direction they want the country to go in the future."

"Reb, I mean, Governor," interjected Jake, "no one here doubts your passion or commitment for your cause, and I know everyone here shares your vision. My concern is getting your message through the flak and distortion of your opponents and the media. We need to establish a rapid response team to counter immediately any bullshit. If we allow a lie or disinformation to stand unanswered for more than a twenty-four-hour news cycle, it will take hold in the public mind as being true unless and until proven false. Also, because you handle television interviews extremely well and are a straight talker, I recommend we expose you to as many interviews and debates as possible. A lot of candidates are afraid of interviews or debates, for fear they will go off message, or commit a verbal gaffe, or get confused by their previous lies. You don't have that problem. The more people get to see you and hear your message, the more folks will buy what you're selling. No offense, but you and your message are an acquired taste."

"No offense taken, Jake," replied Reb, who turned to Natalie and said, "How much money will be needed to be competitive in the primaries, and assuming we win the nomination, what will the general election cost?"

With a quick glance at her papers, Natalie answered, "The primary campaign is divided into three segments. The first segment includes the Iowa caucuses in January and the February primaries in New Hampshire, South Carolina, Nevada, Michigan, and Florida. To be competitive on television and cover all other campaign costs, we'll need to raise $20 million. The second segment spans March and April, with twenty-one states and about one thousand one hundred or almost half the delegates up for grabs. This will cost another $30 million, and much of that money will have to be committed by the end of February. The third segment extends from May till early June with nearly a thousand delegates at stake. During this time, another twenty-one states hold their primaries, including Texas, Ohio, Pennsylvania, Indiana, and North Carolina. If the nomination is not decided by the end of April, the third segment could burn another $25 million. If we win the nomination, the general election might require $700 million, possibly more."

"How difficult will it be to raise these huge sums of money, Natalie?"

"Well, Governor, if you win a couple or three early primaries, it will be easy. Political donors like to back likely winners, and winners attract plenty of free media exposure. I've read the tea party is planning to endorse you when you announce, which will be a big boost to the fundraising effort. I think we have a state-of-the-art fundraising operation via direct mail and the Internet. If you and Mrs. McCoy are willing to headline fundraising events, that will bring in substantial chunks of cash. The general election has an enormous price tag, but if we get to that bridge, I have no doubt we'll cross it."

Hoppy chimed in. "We need to frontload money and place our emphasis on winning one or more of the first primaries. Early momentum is crucial to having a realistic chance of winning the nomination. Playing catch up in this league is nearly impossible unless three or more candidates split the early primaries with no clear favorite emerging. The sooner you formally announce you are in the race, the better."

"Well, gentlemen and lady, I will announce November 8, one year to the day before the 2016 election. As I did when I ran for governor, Marlenna and I will provide $10 million of seed money, but half will be in the form of a loan. By the way, the campaign ground rules will be the same as the gubernatorial campaign: no personal attacks, no dirty tricks, and no dissembling."

"Governor," said Tally Ho, "it may not speak well of human nature, but polling data confirm that so-called personal attack ads are effective, which is why candidates spend lots of money on them. Undecided voters often end up voting for the candidate who appears to be the least sleazy. These ads also motivate supporters of a candidate, who delight in seeing the opposition eviscerated, to get out and vote for their hero. When all candidates stoop to running unsubstantiated, distorted attack ads, they tend to cancel each other out. While your position is noble, you will be disarming unilaterally, and that could be the difference between winning and losing in a close race."

"Tally Ho makes a valid point," said Hoppy. "In our run for governor last year, we did not resort to this tactic, and it didn't hurt us. In a presidential election the stakes are so high, virtually all modern campaigns either directly or through surrogates run attack ads, which are often vicious and dishonest. A not uncommon tactic is to run a scurrilous ad very late in the campaign alleging an unsubstantiated charge or blowing out of proportion some trivial youthful indiscretion. The timing of the ad does not leave the attacked candidate enough time to refute it."

Reb interrupted Hoppy. "Look, I'm not naïve. I realize by not engaging in this activity, I may place my candidacy at a disadvantage. So be it. I don't want to win on that basis. Now, I will vigorously defend against any falsehoods or misstatements about me or my positions. Also, I plan to run spots based on irrefutable facts that criticize and find fault with the positions of my opponents, but I will not tolerate attacks on personal character, period. My primary focus will not be on my opponents, but in conveying with specificity my ideas and policy proposals to the American people. Ding, Jake, what are your thoughts on this?"

Ding spoke first. "Governor, no candidate running for any office should be so desperate to win as to ever compromise his principles or personal integrity. Not always, but quite often, the voters are pretty good at assessing a candidate's character by the time they cast their vote, especially for president. You have my support, because we agree on the major issues, and I believe your ideas will touch a chord with the American people. You also provide a sharp contrast with the typical politician, which is part of your appeal. Engaging in gutter politics would blur away that favorable contrast and reduce you to being just another political hack in the eyes of the voters."

When Ding finished, Jake said, "I agree with Ding's remarks. My advice is to run a campaign as bold and unorthodox as are your ideas for changing the country's direction. Every presidential election is touted as a turning point in history, but most elections herald only a continuation of the past. If you can persuade the electorate to embrace the Second Bill of Rights, as well as your other initiatives, history will record next year's election as a watershed event, when the country decided to return to its founding principles of limited government, sane fiscal policy, and individual liberty."

Reb thanked everyone for their advice and insights and concluded the meeting. "I am honored and privileged to have such a distinguished team managing this campaign. Please always bear in mind that while I am the public face of the campaign, this race is not about an individual personality. I realize we have to sell me as well as our ideas to the public, but let's make sure we don't allow this to be turned into a personality cult. That would be anathema to the Founders' concept that concerned common citizens in a democratic republic have a civic duty to render public service. As so eloquently phrased in the Constitution's Preamble, this campaign is all about and only about securing the blessings of liberty to posterity."

24

After Reb announced in Dallas that he would run for the Republican presidential nomination, he and Marlenna immediately departed for Iowa, where they camped out campaigning for two weeks until Thanksgiving. The candidate and his wife also spent the first couple of weeks of December in Iowa, before moving on to New Hampshire, the site of the first presidential primary in which delegates to the party conventions would be chosen. After the Christmas break, Reb divided his time between the two states leading up to the mid-January Iowa caucuses, followed two weeks later by the New Hampshire primary.

Reb was amused by the quadrennial process by which the oldest and greatest democratic republic in the world went about selecting its presidential candidates. Iowa and New Hampshire have an absurdly disproportionate influence on this process, given that both are small states and neither one is a microcosm of the country. Between them, they have a population of 4.3 million people, 95 percent white, less than 2 percent black, 2.5 percent Hispanic, and 1 percent Asian. The country's population of over 300 million is 64 percent white, 12 percent black, 16 percent Hispanic, and 4.5 percent Asian. Because the Iowa caucuses are always held before the first presidential primary, and New Hampshire law mandates that it hold the first primary, these states are the first popularity contests for aspiring presidential candidates. Accordingly, the media devote enormous coverage to these events. As flawed as this process was, Reb concluded it was superior to the bad old days when party bigwigs convened in a smoke-filled room to decide amongst themselves who would be the party's presidential candidate.

Few candidates in modern times—Bill Clinton being an exception—have lost both Iowa and New Hampshire and gone on to win either the Democratic or Republican presidential nomination. These two states have catapulted unknown candidates to national prominence and sounded the political death knell for figures of national renown. The virtually unknown Jimmy Carter, a former one-term governor of Georgia, became a de facto resident of Iowa for a year before the 1976 caucuses and ended up being the top Democratic vote-getter after "uncommitted." This propelled him to his party's nomination and the presidency. On occasion, just failing to meet expectations can finish off a campaign. In New Hampshire's 1968 Democratic primary, at the height of the Vietnam War, President Lyndon Johnson narrowly defeated anti-war Sen. Eugene McCarthy, 49 percent to 42 percent. Such a strong showing by a challenger against a sitting president, revealed Johnson's deep unpopularity within his own party, and a month later he announced he would not stand for reelection.

Reb was the last candidate to enter the contest for the 2016 Republican nomination. Five others, within six weeks of President Thurston's state funeral, announced their candidacies and had been campaigning hard for several months, especially in Iowa. At first, Reb thought he should pass on Iowa, and perhaps New Hampshire, instead focusing his time on the next primary state, South Carolina. Both Hoppy and Jake vetoed this idea.

"Reb, you will not be perceived as a viable candidate if you skip either Iowa or New Hampshire," opined Jake. "We realize your late start places you at a disadvantage in the first two contests, but it would be preferable to play and lose than not to play at all. Expectations for you in both Iowa and New Hampshire will be low, and the putative frontrunners will ignore you to attack each other. Our strategy should be to aim for third or no worse than fourth place in Iowa, and finish second or third in New Hampshire."

"Well, Jake, we can't lose our way to the nomination."

"Governor," responded Hoppy, "you have a long-term advantage in this race. You start off as an underdog by having announced late, but being a frontrunner is a burden except at the finish line. It's sort of like Aesop's fable about the tortoise and the hare. We'll sneak up on 'em, and by the time they figure out we're a serious threat, it'll be too late. Tally Ho will run a tracking poll daily in Iowa and New Hampshire. Based on how you are doing, we'll leave the press with the impression you will come in one or two places below what our polls indicate. That way you outperform expectations and look like a surging candidate even though you don't win. We will invest significant resources in winning South Carolina and Florida, where conservative southern candidates are always popular. By then, the field probably will be winnowed down to three, with you number one or two. Your momentum and the campaign's financial war chest will place you in a good position to win a plurality of the delegates in play during the February and March primaries, which should give you an almost insurmountable lead making you appear the inevitable nominee."

"Okay," said Reb, "I'm convinced the strategy you guys propose is the way to go. I can road-test and fine-tune my campaign message in Iowa and New Hampshire. Also, by competing in those states, I can participate in any candidate debates, which will be important."

Within a few weeks, Reb had polished his basic campaign speech. In Waterloo, Iowa, a week into the campaign, he addressed a crowd of twenty-five-hundred folks, a third of whom waved tea party signs. His deep baritone voice, expressive and at times passionate, commanded attention and could be mesmerizing. Without a teleprompter and only occasionally glancing down at a few note cards, he said:

> "In the coming election, every public spirited citizen who loves his or her country and been blessed by her freedom and bounty should not vote for me or any other candidate. Nor should you vote for your self-interest. Instead, next November, I challenge each of you to vote for the future, vote for your grandchildren, great grandchildren, and all Americans yet unborn to ensure they may enjoy the blessings and opportunities of liberty bequeathed to us by our forefathers. Vote for the candidate you trust most to restore a Constitution of limited government, individual freedom, and financial solvency.

> "To paraphrase my great ancestor and namesake Edmund Burke, the great eighteenth-century British political philosopher and statesman, the Constitution, which governs American society, 'is indeed a contract, not only between those who are living, but between those who are living, those who are dead, and those who are to be born.' Each generation of Americans is charged with the solemn duty and obligation, as the Founding Fathers wrote in the Preamble to the Constitution to 'secure the Blessings of Liberty to ourselves and our Posterity.'

> "As Americans, we owe our allegiance not to any political party or ideology. Our allegiance is to the Constitution, individual liberty, and keeping faith with the generations who come after us. But my generation, our generation, has not kept faith with the future. Over many years and several generations, we have allowed the federal government to expand its powers far beyond those enumerated in the Constitution. In doing so, we the people have gradually exchanged a measure of our individual liberty for dependency, thereby subtly diminishing our character and dignity.

> "The cost of financing the vast expansion of the federal government has far exceeded its revenue from taxes. To finance its chronic annual budget deficits, the federal

government has incurred ruinous debt effectively condemning our grandchildren and their grandchildren to financial servitude. For any American generation to spend far beyond its means and leave the bill for future generations to pay is an unpardonable breach of trust. If our generation allows this to happen, we shall be rightly cursed for eternity by our forefathers and those who come after us. We will have broken the social contract and failed to pass on the blessings of liberty to posterity."

Reb next turned to what Hoppy derisively called the dreaded 'snooze, lose, or confuse the audience' part of his speech.

"I know numbers make people's eyes glaze over, but every citizen needs to understand the magnitude of the country's fiscal problem. In just the past eight years, since 2008, cumulative government budget deficits have doubled the gross federal debt to $20 trillion, nearly 110 percent of the nation's annual Gross Domestic Product. The average person cannot comprehend a billion dollars, much less a trillion dollars, which equals a thousand billion dollars. A time machine that traveled back in time one billion minutes, would place you on Earth just after the time of Christ, about 100 A.D.

"Even if the government generated a $100 billion surplus every year in the future and used it to retire debt, it would take 200 years to pay off the $20 trillion, and we would still owe the interest. Not included in the debt, however, are the estimated $100 trillion in unfunded liabilities related to entitlements such as Social Security and Medicare. This is the amount by which the forecast cost of future benefits, promised by the government, exceeds projected tax revenue. If we decided today to begin funding the $100 trillion in unfunded entitlement liabilities at the rate of $100 billion per year, it would take a thousand years to do so!

"Can there be any doubt that our generation has been on a spending spree that will bankrupt the country and saddle our heirs with enormous financial burdens, for which they will derive no benefit? The source of America's national security is her economic health and wealth, but enormous debts and a debased currency are rapidly eroding that security. Our problems are daunting, but not hopeless if we the people act promptly to restore limited government and reassert the sovereign rights of the states by amending the Constitution with a Second Bill of Rights."

Reb then summarized the Madison Committee's seven proposed amendments: 1) require a supermajority approval by Congress before incurring total debt in excess of 100 percent of GDP, 2) mandate that projected entitlement benefits always be fully funded for at least twenty-five years, 3) institute twelve-year term limits for members of Congress, 4) require a formal declaration of war by Congress if hostilities against a foreign enemy last beyond ninety days, 5) provide any state the right to secure its international borders if the federal government fails to do so, 6) clarify that the judiciary's role is limited to interpreting not making laws, 7) and require a constitutional convention every twenty-five years.

Reb concluded his speech:

"If we do not address the country's enormous financial challenges, future generations will be left to cope with and clean up the mess we leave to them. This should be unacceptable to every responsible adult American. Fundamental, almost revolutionary, change will be required to meet this challenge. Although important, merely changing our representatives in Washington is inadequate to the task. Experience has demonstrated the federal government is incapable of reforming itself. We must permanently restore the founding principles of a federal government with limited powers, and all other rights and powers reserved to the states and the people as established in the Ninth and Tenth Amendments of the Constitution.

"The only way to achieve this restoration is through constitutional amendments initiated by the states in a constitutional convention. At least thirty-four of the fifty state legislatures must apply to Congress to call a convention. Amendments approved in convention would become the law of the land when ratified by at least thirty-eight states. Already, twenty-two states have petitioned Congress for a convention. So far, Iowa is not one of those states. I urge you to let your governor and state legislators know you strongly support the proposed Second Bill of Rights. Whatever the outcome of next November's election, let us join together as Americans to restore a Constitution of limited government, financial solvency, and individual freedom. In so doing, like all generations that have gone before us, we also will have fulfilled the sacred trust of every generation to secure the blessings of liberty to posterity. Thank you."

Hoppy was not comfortable with the tone or content of Reb's basic speech. He feared it was over the average voter's head and did not mention any specific domestic or international policy proposals. Voters wanted to know what a President McCoy would do to grow the economy, reduce unemployment, lower deficit spending, balance the budget, secure the borders, strengthen international relations, and combat terrorism. Reb patiently told Hoppy that the Second Bill of Rights was the prerequisite to addressing all the economic issues. Once Reb established the Second Bill of Rights as a central campaign issue, on which other candidates would be compelled to take a position, he would then discuss specific policy proposals he would implement if he were to win the election.

Finally, after one lengthy debate with his campaign director, Reb said, "Look, Hoppy, have Tally Ho conduct some focus groups, polling folks from both parties and independents to see what they think about the need for a Second Bill of Rights and the case I make for it. If I'm sinking in the polls, or we get blown out in either Iowa or New Hampshire, I'll revamp my message to be more policy oriented. In the meantime, order enough copies of the *Second Bill of Rights* pamphlet, so we can distribute one to every person who attends a campaign event or rally. Let's also hand everyone a booklet copy of the Declaration of Independence and the Constitution."

25

Despite Hoppy's concerns, Reb was growing more relaxed and starting to enjoy the campaign ritual. At many events, Marlenna appeared, made brief remarks, and introduced her husband. She took a much more visible and prominent role in Reb's campaign than was typical of other candidates' spouses. Always animated, elegant, and beautiful, she possessed natural stage presence. Smiles lit up the wildly cheering crowds whenever she strode onto the stage, always to Frank Sinatra's rendition of "Too Marvelous for Words."

This was Reb's idea who arrived on stage to a loud medley of four Sinatra up-tempo recordings, "I've Got You Under My Skin," "You Make Me Feel So Young," "I Get a Kick Out of You," and "Fly Me to the Moon." The minute a rally ended, the venue was filled with the sound of ABBA singing "Thank You for the Music." Reb and Marlenna both loved music with an irresistible, finger-snapping beat and great lyrics. While his message was serious, he wanted everything else about a campaign event to put folks in a happy, upbeat frame of mind. The music helped to fire up the crowds.

Most unusual for the typical candidate, Reb insisted on punctuality. He hated to be late for a scheduled event, saying it was a sign of an undisciplined organization, and that it was disrespectful of the people who came to see and hear him. Their time was every bit as valuable as his.

By most accounts, Reb acquitted himself well in the first two town hall debates among the Republican candidates, one each in Iowa and New Hampshire. In the New Hampshire debate, the moderator asked Reb's colleagues what they thought of the proposed Second Bill of Rights. Three remarked that they had no particular objection, but that focusing on specific policies for getting America back on the right track was more important than betting everything on a "Hail Mary pass" to amend the Constitution. One candidate was dismissive of the idea saying, among other things, "The Constitution should not be tampered with lightly. The problem with government is not the Constitution, but the politicians we send to Washington. Electing conservative Republicans is the answer."

The debate moderator turned to Reb and said, "Governor McCoy, you have two minutes to respond."

Exuding conviction as always, Reb began:

> "History has proven time and again that when in the majority, neither political party has the capacity or the will to curb the federal government's appetite for power, or to rein in out-of-control spending. Our eighteenth-century Founding Fathers did a brilliant job crafting our Constitution and were savvy about the inherent nature and ambition of men to amass power at the expense of liberty. The Founders established a limited government of enumerated powers with checks and balances among competing interests to safeguard this experiment in self-government. Despite their genius, however, they could not foresee all the machinations and rationalizations men and women would devise over time to justify government's never ending expansion and spending. For all practical purposes, the United States government is insolvent, except for two facts: it can print money, which debases the currency, and its foreign creditors so far have not called in

their loans. We are on the way to becoming a banana republic, but without any bananas."

"Moreover, as government inexorably usurps power, we gradually surrender ever more of our individual liberty. The states and the individual, once crucial to the idea of a federal republic based on limited government, have been elbowed aside by the federal government. This has resulted in the steady drip of trickle-down tyranny. Worst of all, our generation will be the first in America's history that likely will not secure the blessings of liberty to posterity. Instead, we will pass off to future generations the enormous debts piled up by our irresponsible spending, thereby diminishing their opportunities to pursue happiness.

"This is unconscionable, but there is an alternative scenario. We the people must organize within our respective states to demand that our elected legislators petition Congress to call a convention to amend the Constitution with the proposed Second Bill of Rights. These seven amendments if ratified will restore a Constitution based on limited government, individual liberty, and financial solvency. Most importantly, our generation will have secured the blessings of liberty to posterity. Already twenty-two of the thirty-four states required have petitioned Congress to call a constitutional convention to debate the proposed Second Bill of Rights. I am confident at least twelve more state legislatures will approve similar petitions."

Reb was invited to address a joint session of the New Hampshire legislature on the Second Bill of Rights a few days before the primary. Two weeks later, New Hampshire became the twenty-third state to make an application to Congress calling for a constitutional convention. By then, Reb had finished a strong second in the Granite State's primary and was off to the Palmetto State of South Carolina where, as Hoppy predicted, he won his first primary.

Following the New Hampshire debate, money began to pour into the campaign. Natalie Goldwin could now saturate upcoming primary states with television ad buys, which was crucial, because they were bunched closely together making it impossible for Reb to spend much time in any state. Tally Ho's polling showed Reb's message to be steadily gaining favor with voters the more they heard him explain it, but they were also asking what specific actions would he propose to reduce the debt and deficits, reform entitlements, and create jobs.

Tally Ho's data were encouraging to Reb. Both Ding Bell and Jake Fillmore had told him before he decided to run that the key to success would be to offer voters a bold idea that they associated with him and to hammer it home consistently, persistently, repeatedly every day until the election. This he was doing, and it seemed to be gaining traction. Even Hoppy conceded he was mistaken in trying to divert Reb from making the Second Bill of Rights and posterity his central theme, but urged him to begin advocating policies that addressed key voter concerns.

The week after Reb won the Florida primary, nationally syndicated columnist Walter Rothmann wrote favorably on Reb's "implausible candidacy," describing him as "an accomplished, capable person, but a political novice, whose campaign is premised almost entirely on one issue, the proposed Second Bill of Rights. McCoy chastises the voters that they risk being the first generation of Americans to break faith with future generations by bequeathing to them an insolvent 'banana republic, but without any bananas' and the diminished liberty of the federal government's 'trickle-down tyranny.'" Rothmann continued:

> "Ironically, his message comes across as positive and upbeat. All we need to do is hold a constitutional convention, the first since 1787, and adopt the seven amendments known as the Second Bill of Rights. He just may achieve his objective. Thanks in large part to McCoy's labors, twenty-three states already have called for a convention; only eleven more are needed to require Congress to do so. This assumes, of course, that Congress does not evade on technical grounds its duty under Article V of the Constitution. Now, that would indeed be an act of tyranny, although not a surprise, because if ratified, the Second Bill of Rights would restore the Founders' concept of federalism and limited government, thereby sharply curtailing the power of all three branches of the federal

government. If it comes to pass, however, Governor McCoy will have won without bloodshed nothing less than the Second American Revolution."

Reb and the campaign high command appreciated Rothmann's column, but thought he was over the top describing the proposed Second Bill of Rights in terms of a Second American Revolution. Endeavoring to reinstate fundamental constitutional principles, from which the federal government had drifted away, was hardly revolutionary. From Reb's perspective, the Madison Committee had launched a counterrevolution against the progressive revolution, which began early in the twentieth century with adherents in both political parties. To advance their agenda of social reform at home and leadership on the world stage, progressives advocated greater concentration of power in the federal government, particularly the presidency, and embraced the "living Constitution" theory to justify their abandonment of a limited federal government with enumerated powers. The problem is that progressivism acknowledges virtually no limits or boundaries as to how far government may go to impose its programs and reforms for "the greater good" on a free society. Consequently, government never stops expanding or encroaching on individual liberty, and ultimately metastasizes into the bloated, overreaching, financially overextended, imperial nation-state we have today.

Rothmann's column declared Reb the frontrunner for the Republican nomination. After winning eighteen of the twenty-six state primaries and caucuses held during February and March, he had established a commanding lead, just one hundred fifty delegates shy of the one thousand two hundred needed to lock up the nomination. In every state, the tea party energized Republicans and independents in support of Reb's candidacy. The crowds were growing ever larger and enthusiastic. Up until Florida's primary, security for the governor and Marlenna was provided by three members of the Texas Rangers and local police. Often accompanied by Marlenna, Reb typically would leave the dais after his prepared remarks to shake hands with and exchange a word or two with supporters. With increasing frequency, the excited crowds would surge forward trying to touch the candidate and his wife, sometimes almost knocking them over. The Rangers had some harrowing moments when they feared Reb or Marlenna might be knocked off their feet and possibly trampled.

Reb never understood the obsessive, idolatrous fascination so many people had for entertainers, athletes, and political figures who had captured the public's imagination. Celebrity worship was beyond his comprehension. Of course, the media had instigated the build-up of Reb and Marlenna by featuring them on the covers of *Time* and *People* magazines. Other publications ran feature stories on them as well. The cynic in Reb told him the American media loved to build someone up, particularly a politician, as a hero or savior, for no reason other than to savor the melodrama and public disillusionment when they decided to tear down their creation.

He realized he was simply the latest political shooting star and that much of his appeal he attributed to his wife's star aura, which captivated both men and women. This he understood, because she had captivated him for forty years. There is nothing more breathtakingly lovely than a mature woman possessed of class, charm, and dazzling beauty. Marlenna was all of that. At an event in Louisiana, however, she was almost crushed by an adoring crowd, and Reb was about to insist that she not mingle with overenthusiastic supporters. She objected saying that they were in this together and would see it through together. Reb relented, because by the time the campaign left Louisiana, the Secret Service had assigned a protective detail to the McCoys. Secret Service protection was provided to all candidates once they appeared to have a distinct possibility of winning a major party's presidential nomination.

Each person protected by the Secret Service is assigned a code name by the White House Communications Agency, which agents use to communicate with each other the movements and whereabouts of the protected person to other agents. Being from Texas, Reb was assigned the code name "Lone Star." Marlenna's code name was "Movie Star," which she thought a bit pretentious. When she inquired about having her code name changed, she was asked if she preferred "Rock Star." She did not. Traditionally the code names for members of a protected family begin with the same letter, but an exception was made for the McCoys, because both code names contained the word "Star."

With primary victories in Indiana and North Carolina in early May, Reb wrapped up enough delegates to win the presidential nomination. He would be formally nominated at the Republican convention in Salt Lake City in August. Anticipating the victory, Hoppy had arranged for simultaneous grand parties in Charlotte and Indianapolis hotel ballrooms for campaign staff and key supporters. After a brief victory speech, Reb and Marlenna spent a couple hours at the Charlotte event being sure to speak to and thank virtually everyone in the room. They both had a gift for giving each person they spoke to their undivided attention, eliciting a smile or a laugh, and making them believe they were the only person in the room.

In his remarks at the start of the celebration, which were telecast live to Indianapolis and broadcast by many cable networks, Reb said:

> "Thank you, North Carolina, and thank you, Indiana, for putting us over the top. And thank you to all concerned Americans across this wonderful, bountiful country for your hard work and support of our campaign. As I said from the outset of this journey, our quest is not about me, and it is not about you. Our mission is to keep faith with our grandchildren, their grandchildren, and all future generations of Americans by securing the blessings of liberty to posterity. Toward that end, I just learned that today, Montana's legislature approved an application to Congress

to call a constitutional convention to consider the proposed Second Bill of Rights."

An enormous cheer erupted, after which Reb continued:

"With Montana, we now have twenty-six states that have petitioned Congress to call a convention. Only eight more to go, and we will reach the magic number of thirty-four. Keep your passion and energy at a high level. We have a lot of work to do between now and the election in November. Remember this election is not between Republicans and Democrats. This year we vote to restore the Constitution and America's future. Our platform is Freedom, Solvency, Security, and Posterity. Freedom Fever, Catch It! Thank you, and God Bless America."

Sustained applause, whistles, and cheers raised the rafters. Reb and Marlenna stood beaming and waving, soaking in the adulation. Others joined them on stage. Suddenly the crowd began chanting, "Restore America's Joy—Vote for the Real McCoy." After ten minutes, this chant was replaced with "Marlenna, Marlenna, Marlenna!" Following several minutes of this, Sinatra's "Too Marvelous for Words" filled the ballroom followed by ABBA's "Thank You for the Music."

Reb and Marlenna finally fell exhausted into their hotel bed at 1:00 a.m. With no events scheduled the next day, they slept in, awoke refreshed, and made love for the first time in over a week, after which they showered together, laughing and cooing like lovestruck college kids before having breakfast served in their suite around 8:45 a.m.

Over breakfast, Marlenna asked Reb, "Now that you've locked up the nomination, let's take some time off and go away someplace where we can have some privacy. It's been an exciting and mostly fun six months, but we are both exhausted and need a break."

"I'd love to, honey, but there are still seven primaries left over the next four weeks. I should make one- or two-day visits to all those states, so the voters there don't feel neglected. Why don't you go back to Dallas, relax, and spend time with Ravenna and the kids. I'll fly home in between my trips to the last primary states to be with you."

Since the New Hampshire primary, the campaign had leased a fourteen-passenger Gulfstream 550 business jet to fly Reb, Marlenna, campaign staff, and security personnel from state to state. Hoppy had advised Reb that when the general election campaign began after the nominating convention, they would lease a Boeing 757 commercial airliner to accommodate expanded campaign staff, dignitaries, and media people that accompany a modern presidential campaign like rock band groupies. Reb expressed concern that gallivanting around in such an aircraft would be too costly and ostentatious. He set aside his reservations, after Hoppy assured him there was no other practical way to crisscross the country and accommodate the number of press and media people that expected to be along for the ride, and Natalie said the campaign could afford the 757.

Marlenna said, "Okay, but don't forget you promised to be with me at the June fundraising gala for the Dallas Arts District." Marlenna had been the chairperson of this annual event the past two years, which was held in the Meyerson Symphony Center, designed by the world-renowned architect I.M. Pei. Between eight hundred and a thousand Dallas high-society types could be counted on to turn out for this glittering event. At $5,000 per ticket, the gala would raise $4-5 million for further development of the downtown Arts District."

"Yes, baby, we will attend the gala together. And remember this Sunday we are scheduled to be at Washington Military Academy to dedicate Madison Hall, and the following Sunday, I accepted an invitation to throw out the first pitch at a Texas Rangers home game. Right after your gala, we'll take off on our planned two-week vacation trip to Jackson Hole, Wyoming."

A few days later, the McCoys, Hoppy, Jake Fillmore, Tally Ho, and Secret Service personnel boarded the Gulfstream at Love Field in Dallas for the flight to Philadelphia and the WMAC event. Part of the flight time was spent discussing strategy for the general election campaign.

"As you know, Governor," began Hoppy, "to win the general election, we need to capture at least 270 of the 538 electoral votes. Tally Ho, give us a summary of your polling."

"We have 211 secure electoral votes. We will run the table across the south, the plains and the Rockies, except perhaps Colorado. I figure the Democrats have 193 electoral votes in their column. Their strength is in the Northeast, parts of the Midwest, and the Pacific coast. That leaves 134 electoral votes up for grabs, with 30 leaning our way, 45 leaning Democrat, and 59 tossups. Absent a big surprise, this shapes up as a very close election."

"Thanks, Tally Ho," began Reb, "Guess we will focus our effort on the leaning and tossup states."

"That's right, Governor," said Hoppy, "but I think we may want to devote time and money to a few of the so-called secure Democratic states, specifically California and Washington. Now, I don't expect in the end we can win them, but there are encouraging signs the Republican ticket may run stronger in those states this year than in recent elections. The Democrats can't run the slightest risk of losing California's 55 electoral votes, or even Washington's 12 electoral votes, and have any chance of winning the election. Making a serious play for California and Washington will force the Democrats to invest more resources there reducing what they otherwise could commit to tossup states. By the way, I believe there is not much chance the Democrats can take away any of our secure states, no matter how much they spend trying to do so."

"Reb, according to Tally Ho's data," Jake interjected, "you have an excellent chance to win a majority of the popular vote. Of course, it's the electoral vote that counts and that looks to be very close at this early stage of the campaign. Who you pick as your running mate could determine whether you win the election."

"Well, Jake," responded Reb, "my reading of history doesn't persuade me that VP candidates determine the outcome of elections. I believe people vote for president based almost entirely on who is at the top of the ticket. Be that as it may, I want a running mate who shares my views on the key issues, especially the Second Bill of Rights. My first choice is Georgia Governor Lillian Duzmore, whom I've come to know and like over the past year and a half. She early on supported the Second Bill of Rights and was successful in persuading the Georgia Legislature to petition Congress for a constitutional convention. I'd like you to ask her if she is willing to be considered and provide the necessary information for you to conduct an appropriate background check."

Lillian Dorothy Gish Duzmore, fifty-year-old, second-term governor of Georgia, was a conservative Republican and tea party favorite. She was named for her father's distant cousins, the famous Gish sisters, Lillian and Dorothy, who were movie stars at the dawn of cinema in the early twentieth century. Born and raised in Atlanta, Georgia, the governor was a graduate of Duke University. From college, she joined a small software company, eventually rose to be its president, and orchestrated its acquisition by Microsoft in 2002, which made her fabulously wealthy. Lillian entered politics in Georgia in 2006, and by 2010 was elected Georgia's first woman governor. She and her husband of twenty-five years, Benjamin "Duzzy" Duzmore, a writer of mystery novels, lived with their two teenage children in Atlanta. Like Marlenna, Governor Duzmore was a physical fitness buff who appeared to be younger than her age. She had thick blonde hair, which she wore in a stylishly short, layered cut that enhanced her delicate, pretty features.

Hoppy was not elated with Reb's idea. "Governor, Lillian Duzmore has a lot to recommend her, but except for her gender, she does not bring anything to the ticket that you don't already have. You are both southerners and conservative reformers. I think you should consider someone from the Senate who can bring you a state that is a tossup or leaning Democratic."

"Hoppy, I disagree," Jake said. "Reb is an insurgent candidate who is tolerated, but not fully embraced by the party establishment. He is in the mold of Reagan or Goldwater. If he takes a conventional choice to balance the ticket, he will dilute the credibility of his reform message. Washington is the problem, so adding some senior senator to the ticket will make him look like just another politician trying to triangulate. Duzmore is an outsider like Reb, she believes in the Second Bill of Rights, and being a woman, she will help us attract the largest voting bloc in the country."

Hoppy replied, "Look, I don't object to Governor Duzmore. You make some excellent points, Jake. In the end, it obviously is your decision, Governor. Probably the best advice is to pick someone you like, trust, and are comfortable with, and most importantly, is qualified to be president, if necessary."

After listening to Jake and Hoppy's interchange, Reb turned to his wife, who had walked forward from her seat in the aft cabin to listen in on the discussion, and asked, "Marlenna, what is your opinion about placing Lillian Duzmore on the ticket?"

Reb relied on Marlenna to offer her opinion before he made a major decision. He did not always follow her advice, but he trusted her judgment, could count on her candor, and knew her sole motivation was his best interest. Almost always, he solicited her opinion when they were alone, but now he wanted Jake and Hoppy to hear his wife's perspective.

Marlenna thought for a moment and then said, "I don't know Lillian well, mostly by reputation, news stories, and TV appearances. What I do know, I like. She is a dynamic speaker, extremely intelligent, assertive, yet feminine, unflappable, and thinks well on her feet. Attractive and relatively young, I imagine she would have broad appeal to both men and women. If anything, I suspect she is more conservative than you, Reb, but still in the mainstream. She articulates the need for a constitutional convention and the Second Bill of Rights nearly as well as you do. I've seen her deliver speeches that fire up the crowd. You and I haven't discussed prospective VP candidates before now, but I can't think of a better choice. In my humble opinion, a woman whose political philosophy is compatible with yours would be the ideal choice, and Lillian meets those criteria. Aren't you glad you asked my opinion?"

Hoppy was impressed with Marlenna's analysis and insight. He said, "Well, you all have overcome my initial reservations. Barring any unforeseen problems, I guess Lillian Duzmore is our running mate."

Jake remarked, "I like the sound of MCCOY–DUZMORE. It not only names the ticket, but it conveys a positive 'can do' image. We're gonna have some appealing campaign slogans: FOR PRESIDENT – VOTE FOR THE REAL MCCOY; FREEDOM, SOLVENCY, SECURITY, AND POSTERITY; RESTORE AMERICA'S JOY – VOTE FOR THE REAL MCCOY; FREEDOM FEVER – CATCH IT! and MCCOY–DUZMORE. By the way, Reb, where did you come up with 'Freedom Fever, Catch It!'?"

"Oh, some years ago, major league baseball ran an ad campaign using the slogan, 'Baseball Fever, Catch It!' Hope there is no copyright infringement. Look, clever slogans are great, but substance is better. I will be proud to have Lillian as my running mate. After you have the initial conversation to sound her out, Jake, I'll place a call to her. Tally Ho, please start testing Governor Duzmore in your polling, so we can determine which voter groups are most receptive to her. One last piece of business, Jake, find out what is required to get the party name changed at the convention to the Republican Constitution

Party. I know we will get a lot of flack about this, but I want to run nationally using the same name the party adopted in Texas."

"You're, right, Reb, this will cause a lot of the old guard heartburn, but you are the party's nominee and probably can force the name change through. I believe it will require a supermajority vote of the delegates, which should not be a serious problem. In the end, the party will want to unite behind its candidate."

"I trust you are correct, Jake. Republicans pay a lot of lip service to upholding the Constitution. I say make it part of the GOP's formal name. After all, the driving force behind my candidacy is the Second Bill of Rights and the reaffirmation of the Constitution."

"What if the Democrats do the same thing?" asked Hoppy.

Reb replied, "You and I know they won't, because it would be too restrictive as to the scope of government. That's also why many Republicans won't be happy about our changing the party's name. We'll now be forced to live up to our new name. But it would be great if the Democrats copied us. Imagine, if both American political parties made the Constitution their lode star, a lot would change for the better in the United States. Each party would pursue its ideology and policies within the boundaries laid out in the Constitution. We would still need the Second Bill of Rights, however, to keep politicians from backsliding. Whether or not one agrees with the old saying that laws are made to be broken, we should always keep faith with the supreme law of the land. Yet, too many politicians in both parties believe the Constitution is a malleable document that they are free to pull and stretch as far as the people and the courts will allow. We have to prevent the Constitution's elasticity from being stretched to absurdity."

"One last item, Governor, if I may," began Hoppy, "what role do you have in mind for President Fubarsky at the convention and during the campaign? His staff have been bugging me about ensuring he has a prominent role and is accorded all due respect."

"During evening prime time of the first day of the convention, I would like to see the president honored appropriately. I also want there to be a fitting tribute to President Thurston. As far as the campaign goes, I'm not sure how Fubarsky can be of much help. Whereas Thurston supported the Second Bill of Rights and, had she lived, would have thrown her political clout behind the idea of a constitutional convention, Fubarsky has ignored the issue. For the sake of courtesy and party unity, we can ask the president to join us for a few events in specific states where his popularity is high, but I don't want him out campaigning very much. The best thing he can do to support the campaign is to avoid doing anything that will hurt our chances."

With that, Reb and Marlenna returned to rear of the aircraft, buckled into their seats, and fell fast asleep holding hands until awakened by the pilot's announcement that they were beginning their descent into the Philadelphia area.

26

Reb's return to Washington Military Academy & College was filled with nostalgia. The last time he and Marlenna had been there was five years earlier. The campus was especially beautiful in spring with its pink and white dogwood and magnolia trees, fragrant lilacs, and vibrant yellow daffodils in full bloom. Of course, nothing and everything had changed in the nearly half century since Reb graduated in 1968.

The school's founder and first superintendent, Gen. Brubaker, and the first commandant, Gen. Maddendorf, passed away years ago. The standards, rituals, and traditions they had established survived, but the spit-and-polish military bearing appeared to Reb's eye to be less emphasized than back in his day. The biggest and most noticeable change was that WMAC was now co-ed. The campus looked much the same except for the Ionic-columned, Federalist-style brick building perched on the hill overlooking the parade field. Just completed, this was Madison Hall, a gift to WMAC from Reb and Marlenna. The upper level of the new facility was a mess hall that could easily accommodate the entire corps of cadets, which numbered a thousand at full strength. The main doors opened on Continental Drive, the primary campus avenue between WMAC's main gate and the main formation area, and where Reb had his unplanned encounter with Gen. Eisenhower over fifty years earlier. On the building's lower level, which featured large palladium windows facing on the parade field, was the James Madison Center for Constitutional History, which contained a library, large lecture hall, classrooms, and a stunning historical panorama of the founding of the Republic.

WMAC's superintendent, Maj. Gen. Horton Wainwright, met Reb and Marlenna at the main gate and escorted them to Madison Hall before attending Sunday chapel services with the corps of cadets. In full dress uniform, his tunic festooned with countless medals, Wainwright looked every bit a general with his erect bearing and confident demeanor. He shot an admiring albeit circumspect glance at Marlenna as he greeted them both warmly.

A man of courtly charm, the general said, "Mrs. McCoy, what a pleasure to have you grace us with your presence this lovely day. And Governor McCoy, welcome back to your alma mater. Congratulations on winning the Republican presidential nomination. You are the first alumnus of WMAC to attain such a high honor."

On the short walk to Madison Hall, Reb engaged the general in conversation about the school. When they reached the portico, the general commented, "I do hope you both have a favorable first impression of what your generous gift allowed us to build. I believe you will find the interior is even more spectacular than the exterior."

As they entered the large vestibule that led to the enormous mess hall, Reb told the general how elated he was with the facility. His and Marlenna's $9 million gift had funded the thirty-five-thousand-square-foot structure, which had been a dream seeking a benefactor for ten years. Over the years, directly and through their Marcoy Foundation, Reb and Marlenna had endowed scholarships at WMAC, but the gift of Madison Hall was almost double all their previous donations to the school. The WMAC board of trustees had encouraged the McCoys to name the building after themselves, but Reb insisted that it be named in honor of James Madison.

Following the private tour of Madison Hall, Gen. Wainwright, now joined by his wife, escorted Reb and Marlenna to the chapel. The corps of cadets was already there, standing in the rows of pews awaiting the arrival of the superintendent and his distinguished guests. Standing in the transept with her back to the chancel and facing the corps of cadets was the current regimental commander, Cadet First Captain Monica Bradley. Reb recalled how he stood precisely in the same spot, marked by a brass plate in the floor, when he was the first captain. Once Gen. Wainwright, his wife, and guests arrived at their front row pew and were seated, Cadet First Captain Bradley, the first woman to lead the corps of cadets, nodded her head and the entire corps, whose eyes were all focused on her, sat in unison and the nondenominational chapel service began.

Months before, when Reb's visit to WMAC was scheduled, he was asked to address the corps of cadets during the chapel service. Each Sunday, a faculty member or guest speaker spoke to the corps in chapel. The school chaplain desired to cover a different character-building topic each Sunday to avoid repetition. Reb had been given a list of topics to choose from and he selected courage. Following a gracious introduction by the chaplain, Reb left his pew and ascended the pulpit. There would be nary a hint of anything political in his remarks.

> "As a plebe over fifty years ago, I sat where you are gathered today. If there is only one indelible memory shared by every member of the Long Grey Line, it is WMAC's motto, 'Courage, Honor, Conquer.' It was not by accident that General Brubaker, WMAC's founder, placed courage first in the school motto.

"Winston Churchill once said, 'Courage is rightly esteemed the first of human qualities because it is the quality that guarantees all the others.' Now, Mr. Churchill was the epitome of valiant, intrepid, undaunted courage as the leader of Great Britain in its lonely struggle during the darkest days of World War II against Adolph Hitler's Germany. And yet I wondered how Mr. Churchill's hierarchy of virtues could place courage ahead of integrity or honor. Surely personal integrity was the foremost human virtue.

"Gradually, I came to realize that Mr. Churchill was absolutely correct. We have all heard the approving phrase, 'that person has the courage of his or her convictions.' Absent courage, we would have no convictions. Without courage, we would too often and too easily abandon integrity, honor, and all the other virtues whenever they were tested.

"It takes a measure of courage to stand up and do the right thing, to confront and speak out against injustice, to ignore misguided peer pressure, to be faithful to one's values and principles even when no one else is looking, and to overcome personal adversity. Sometimes doing the right thing is unpopular and can expose one to risk or ridicule, but with courage one will always make the right choice regardless of the consequences. We all know the difference between right and wrong, good and evil. Yet, we can be tempted occasionally to betray our conscience, because everybody else does it, or we don't think we will be caught, or it is expedient, or we find some other rationalization for not being true to ourselves. Whenever we fail to live up to our ideals, however, we are displaying a lack of courage.

"Many people think of courage as demonstrating physical bravery. That is an aspect of courage, but most physical courage, on a battlefield for instance, is a matter of suppressing one's overwhelming fear and doing what has to be done under extreme circumstances. Bravery in the face of physical danger certainly is a virtue of the highest order, especially when brave action will defend or protect comrades in arms or the defenseless. But the brave individual on a battlefield can be a complete coward in other life situations.

"The courage we all have to find within ourselves day after day typically is not physical courage, but the moral courage to remain true to all the other virtues and to persevere in the face of adversity. In this sense, courage is a conscious act of free will. Each of us has the power within to make courage the unshakable foundation by which we will live our lives, upholding our values and ideals, and defending the virtues we hold dear and wish to be judged by at all times.

"Winston Churchill was indeed wise when he said courage is the one and only virtue that guarantees all the others. No one else can instill within me or any of you the virtue of courage; it is a choice each of us must make individually every day of our lives. Never forget that common to every honorable man and woman is the virtue of courage. An anonymous wise man once said, 'When in doubt, always do the courageous thing.' Abiding always by that adage, you will never let yourself down."

Reb returned to his seat next to Marlenna who squeezed his hand and whispered her approval in his ear. Following the service, Gen. Wainwright complimented Reb on his remarks and asked if they could be published in the next cadet newsletter. Reb had no objection, but told the general he had spoken from notes and not a prepared text. Wainwright said that was no problem because Reb's talk had been recorded.

The McCoys, the Wainwrights, and the Secret Service detail strolled from the chapel along a brick walk lined with flowering dogwoods to Eisenhower Hall at the south end of the parade field. Here Reb and Marlenna could freshen up and relax for thirty minutes until the parade commenced. Following the parade, there would be a brief ribbon-cutting ceremony in front of Madison Hall as the new building was formally dedicated. While waiting for the parade to start, a handsome, elderly woman was introduced to Reb by Gen. Wainwright. Within a few seconds, he was elated to recognize her as Colonel Kelly Kernel, his Alternative History teacher during his senior year at WMAC. Although she was now an emeritus professor, Reb had requested that she join him and Marlenna to review the parade and attend the Madison Hall dedication ceremony.

"Colonel Kernel, what an honor and pleasure to see you again after so many years. You look wonderful."

"Governor McCoy, the honor is mine. Please call me Kelly." The years had been kind to Col. Kernel, now in her early eighties. Wearing a stylish navy dress and light jacket, she looked at least fifteen years younger, and was obviously both physically fit and mentally sharp. Reb introduced her to Marlenna.

"How pleased I am to meet you, Marlenna," said Col. Kernel. "As lovely as you appear on television, you are even more beautiful in person. I want you to know that it has been forty-eight years since your husband was my student, but I remember him, because he was the regimental commander and an excellent student. I am honored and touched that he would invite me to join you both today to review the parade in your honor."

"It is indeed my pleasure to meet you, Kelly," said Marlenna. "Reb has told me what a wonderful teacher you are."

Reb remarked, "Kelly, once Marlenna asked me where I came by my fascination with history, and I told her about you and the course you taught that the cadets affectionately called "Herstory." I've never forgotten your thesis that history is never inevitable, and that it's usually written by the winners. As a result, history is often incomplete in that it omits inconvenient facts and provides only one perspective."

"Well, Governor, nothing could gladden this retired teacher's heart more than to learn that the class I taught made a lasting impression on you and helped to encourage your lifelong love of history. Finding the truth about the past is difficult once 'establishment historians' determine the prism through which a historical figure or event will be viewed. Almost every historian has a point of view, which too often is shaped by the historian's personal life experience, ideology, or bias. Abraham Lincoln, for example, was one of America's most important figures, but he has been deified such that almost all the books written about him are hagiographies. But there are other legitimate interpretations and points of view of Lincoln's presidency that are ignored or dismissed by establishment historians. The truth, in my opinion, is that Lincoln had a brilliant mind and was our most eloquent president, but his reasoning and judgment, while well intentioned, were flawed and had horrific consequences for the country. This alternative perspective is never assessed by mainstream Lincoln and Civil War historians. My, my, I apologize for prattling on like this. You aren't here to listen to the crackpot theories of an old woman."

"Kelly, this is wonderful and fascinating for me," said Reb. "Your ideas are very stimulating. We must talk further at the luncheon following the building dedication."

Gen. Wainwright interrupted the conversation to inform Reb, Marlenna, and Kelly that it was time to go down to the parade field reviewing stand. Reb had insisted that his visit to WMAC was not a political event, but as the putative Republican presidential nominee, larger crowds than usual had gathered on and off the campus and the Philadelphia TV stations were on hand to film the event for the local evening news. The Secret Service was not pleased with the security set-up. Additional police had been called in to help manage traffic and the crowds. The parade field bleachers were behind the reviewing stand. A hill ascended behind the bleachers where onlookers could stand. There were at least one thousand five hundred visitors on campus on or near the parade field. All of them had passed through security.

Opposite the reviewing stand on the far side of the parade field was a ten-foot-high wrought iron fence along a line of fir trees. Another five hundred people were gathered outside the fence to watch the proceedings with local law enforcement personnel maintaining order. Reb and Marlenna would be out in the open from the time they walked down the steps of Eisenhower Hall, strolled to the reviewing stand, participated in the ceremony, and reviewed the parade. The Secret Service personnel posted at Eisenhower Hall alerted their colleagues in front of the parade bleachers and adjacent to the reviewing stand that Lone Star and Movie Star were on the move.

According to protocol, Wainwright and the governor led the way with Col. Kernel and Marlenna following close behind. Marlenna was smiling and waving to the crowd, some of whom shouted her name. In her figure-flattering, toffee-colored linen suit, she looked stunning and was the cynosure for all eyes. As the group approached the bleachers, a middle-aged bald man wearing glasses suddenly jumped a low brick wall along the walkway and headed toward Marlenna with something in his hand. Startled and not knowing his intentions, Marlenna instinctively called out to Reb who immediately turned around and lunged to block the unidentified man from reaching Marlenna. A split second later, a Secret Service agent grabbed the man in a hammerlock and deftly dragged him away.

Simultaneously, an agent positioned in a window on the upper floor of Eisenhower Hall with a bird's eye view of the entire area, spoke into his mike, "Movie Star threatened! Secure Lone Star!" A moment later, six agents surrounded Reb and Marlenna and were about to remove them from the area when Reb put up his hand and said, "Wait a minute. The guy meant no harm. Here is the rose he had in his hand and wanted to give to my wife. He was overly exuberant and out of order, but no harm, no foul. Let's not overreact and disrupt the parade any further."

With that, the agents reluctantly backed off. Their standard operating procedure was to whisk a protected person away from an apparent attack immediately to a secure location. Marlenna had remained calm throughout and told Reb she was just fine. They both inquired of Kelly if she was okay, and she was.

Reb turned to Gen. Wainwright and suggested he have the public address announcer remind all visitors to remain in their seats until the conclusion of the parade and Reb and Marlenna had departed the immediate vicinity. With that everyone in the bleachers settled back and Reb, Marlenna, the general, and Col. Kernel took their places on the reviewing stand, and the parade began.

The band played the national anthem. Marlenna and Kelly were each presented a spray of flowers, and Reb was presented a memorial sword by the general recognizing him as alumnus of the year. The cadet officers were ordered by Cadet 1st Captain Bradley to report to the reviewing stand and salute the dignitaries. A three-cannon battery positioned at the north end of the parade field fired off a 19-gun salute in Gov. McCoy's honor, after which the officers returned to their respective cadet companies.

First Capt. Bradley then approached the reviewing stand, saluted Reb with her saber and in a crisp, strong voice said, "Sir, permission to pass in review."

Reb responded so all could hear, "Pass in review."

The first captain did an about-face to face the corps of cadets and, in a confident voice of command clearly heard across the parade field, ordered, "Pass in review." The battalion commanders ordered their units to attention, right shoulder arms, and right face. The first captain and her regimental staff moved off smartly to take up position ahead of the band. On her command of forward march, the regimental staff and the band stepped off to begin the parade with the band playing a rousing march to which Reb could not help but tap his left foot to its beat. As each company approached the reviewing stand, its cadet captain ordered eyes right and saluted the dignitaries. The corps put on a great parade, maintaining excellent formation. When the color guard with the American flag marched by, tears welled up in Reb's eyes. He recalled how once he had been the first captain, and what a great feeling it was to see the corps of cadets on parade. Of course, as always, the band, which in the past had performed for presidents and the Queen of England, was magnificent.

As soon as the parade was over, but before the band stopped playing, the Secret Service formed a phalanx around Reb and Marlenna and hustled them down the walk and up the steps to Madison Hall for the dedication ceremony. Reb inquired as to the fate of the man who had caused the ruckus and was told he had been taken to local police headquarters for interrogation. Reb insisted that he deserved nothing more than a stern reprimand and insisted on confirmation that he had been released from custody. The lead agent assured Reb he would follow up on this.

Following Gen. Wainwright's brief dedicatory remarks, Marlenna cut the ribbon to Madison Hall, and the dignitaries, invited guests, and most of WMAC's faculty and staff entered the mess hall for a celebratory luncheon. Reb and Marlenna posed for a formal photograph that would later be enlarged and displayed permanently inside Madison Hall's main doors.

After lunch had concluded, Reb and Marlenna prepared to depart WMAC to fly back to Dallas. As Gen. Wainwright escorted them to the main gate, Reb said, "General, this has been a splendid day. Marlenna and I can't thank you enough for all your hospitality. We have loved every minute, except for that moment when one of Marlenna's crazed fans lost his self-control, but that turned out well for all concerned."

"I'm terribly sorry about that, Governor."

"General, please, I'm only kidding. That was not any fault of yours. The corps of cadets looked terrific. Please tell 1st Capt. Bradley how impressed I was with the parade. If you will be kind enough to oblige me, I have a request. Please cancel all routine demerits and marching tours any cadet received for minor infractions this past week, and extend Saturday and Sunday leave an additional two hours next weekend."

The general momentarily feigned grave concern but then smiled. "Governor, what you ask is most unusual, but because you are a former WMAC regimental commander and a most distinguished alumnus, I shall be pleased to grant your request. I have no doubt you will be extremely popular with the corps."

"One last thing, General, because she suggested it to me in the first place, please tell the corps of cadets that this dispensation is granted at Marlenna's request."

"With pleasure, Governor." Then turning to Marlenna, he said, "Marlenna, you are even more charming and lovely than your reputation. Mrs. Wainwright and I are honored to have had the pleasure of meeting you. You and the governor are welcome here at any time, and we hope the next time is in the not too distant future."

Reb thought to himself that this guy was smooth but sincere, and could have a future in politics or diplomacy.

Reb and Marlenna said their good-byes and got into the waiting limo for the ride to the airport. As they rode away, Col. Kernel remarked to Wainwright, "General, they are two wonderful people, down-to-earth, warm, and sincere. The governor, I believe, would make a fine president, and Marlenna a beautiful first lady. I hope the voters see them as I do."

"Colonel, I agree with you. This was the first time I met either of them in person. Over my career, I've dealt with quite a few big-shot politicians and their spouses. Too many are arrogant prima donnas, lacking both courtesy and gratitude, who expect everybody to kiss their backsides. The McCoys are nothing at all like that. They have the common touch and are a class act. I was especially impressed with the aplomb with which they both reacted to the security incident before the parade. In a situation like that, a person reacts instinctively; you can't fake it. What comes through is a person's true character."

"How right you are, General. Governor McCoy obviously knew what he was talking about when he delivered his excellent talk on courage in chapel today. I hope the cadets absorbed what he had to say."

27

A week after the McCoys returned to Dallas from WMAC, Reb found himself on the pitcher's mound at Rangers Ballpark in Arlington getting set to throw the ceremonial first pitch of a night game between the Texas Rangers and the New York Yankees. A crowd of forty thousand fans did not expect much, as most male politicians throw like girls, and often can't get the ball to the catcher behind home plate without bouncing it.

Reb, however, had been a high school pitcher for WMAC and was determined not to embarrass himself, or worse be teased mercilessly by Marlenna. They had arrived at the ballpark an hour and a half before game time for security reasons, and so he could warm up his ancient pitching arm in a secluded spot under the stands where Ranger players could take batting practice between innings during a game.

When Reb walked out to the mound a few minutes before game time and was announced to the crowd, there was polite cheering and applause. An unusually cool evening for late May, Reb was dressed in gray slacks, a Ranger jacket, and baseball cleats. When the Ranger catcher signaled he was ready, Reb went into a full wind-up and fired a strike that popped into the receiver's mitt. The radar gun registered the speed of his pitch on the scoreboard at 64 mph. Reb thought his pitch was terrific for a sixty-five-year-old, as he raised his arms in victory and waved to the fans. The crowd cheered loudly its approval and appreciation as the catcher ran out to present Reb the ball.

The president and part-owner of the Rangers, Nolan Ryan, a Hall of Famer, baseball's all-time strike-out king, and pitcher of a record seven no-hitters, jogged out to the mound grinning and presented Reb an oversized contract as the scoreboard flashed, "Sign him up!" Reb laughed and embraced Nolan as they walked to their box seats behind the Ranger dugout. Marlenna was beaming, waiting to give him a hug. "Nice job, cowboy. I bet the Yankees are glad you're not pitching tonight."

The game was televised nationally, and in the third inning Reb by invitation joined announcers Jon Miller and Joe Morgan in the broadcast booth to talk baseball in between pitches. Unceremoniously fired following the 2010 season, Miller and Morgan had been brought back to the Sunday Night Baseball broadcast booth a couple seasons later by popular demand.

The ebullient, good-natured Miller remarked, "Governor, you have the best pitching delivery I've ever seen for a politician. That was some fastball you pitched."

"What do you mean fastball, Jon? That was my changeup," Reb joked.

"Well, then, maybe Nolan Ryan should give you a big signing bonus and send you out to pitch. I noticed you're a southpaw, and I understand the Rangers are in need of left-handed pitching. Now, tell me, is it true you were named after Rogers Hornsby?"

"Indirectly I was. My grandfather believed Hornsby was the greatest hitter he ever saw. He named my father after Rogers, and my Dad passed the name on to me."

"How did you come to be known as Reb instead of Rogers?" asked Miller.

"My other given name is Edmund Burke, a distant ancestor on my mother's side of the family. My nickname derives from my initials, and for as long as I can remember, I've been called Reb."

"What team did Eddie Burke play for?" wondered Miller, a twinkle in his eye.

Playing along, Reb replied, "He never got out of the minor leagues, Jon. I understand he couldn't hit the curveball. Actually, Burke was a prominent eighteenth-century British politician. How that relates to baseball, I can't say."

Quickly responding, Miller said, "Well, Governor, you said he couldn't hit the curve-ball, but as a successful politician, he must have thrown a good spitball."

Laughing, Reb responded, "I never thought about it like that, Jon, but judging from the politicians I know, you're probably right."

"Tell me, Governor, because you are named after Rogers Hornsby, does that mean you think he was a greater second baseman than my dear friend Joe Morgan?" asked Miller, who loved to needle his broadcast partner. Morgan had starred for the Cincinnati Reds in the 1970s.

"Now, Jon, I didn't say that. I said my grandfather believed Hornsby to be the greatest hitter. He also thought Harry Caray was the greatest baseball broadcaster." Carey had been the voice of the St. Louis Cardinals for a quarter-century commencing in 1945.

Morgan laughing said, "All that Rogers Hornsby and I have in common are we both were second basemen and elected to the Hall of Fame. He was definitely a far better hitter than I was, although I'm not sure I agree he was the greatest of all time. Now, I do agree that Harry Caray was the best broadcaster."

Feigning hurt feelings, Miller said, "Gee, Joe, we've been partners for a lot of years, and now I learn you don't think I am the top broadcaster.

For the rest of the inning, McCoy, Miller, and Morgan continued their light-hearted banter about the action on the field. As the inning drew to a close, Miller said, "Governor McCoy, thank you so much for sharing some time with us. Best wishes to you during the upcoming campaign."

Reb and Marlenna left the game in the sixth inning and flew to Austin. Campaigning kept Reb away from Austin except for a day or two a month. The legislature was not in session, and the lieutenant governor was very capable in Reb's absence, so the state's business was not being neglected while he campaigned for president. After a few days in the Governor's Mansion, the McCoys returned to their home in Dallas to attend the Arts District gala hosted by Marlenna at the Meyerson Symphony Center.

The gala was a smashing success. In addition to the tickets sold, Marcoy Foundation made an anonymous challenge grant of $1 million. This gift was conditioned on being matched by pledges made during the gala. After plenty of wine and spirits, the wealthy and generous gala attendees pledged $1.5 million to more than match the anonymous grant. All told, after expenses, the gala raised a record $7million.

Although Reb received much attention, the glamorous star of the evening was Marlenna. She was absolutely gorgeous in her sexy, Giorgio Armani one shoulder, floor-length white gown. As hostess, she and Reb had the honor of the first dance, a foxtrot. As they glided beautifully around the dance floor, gazing happily into each other's eyes, Reb said, "Baby, you are always the most beautiful and desirable woman in any gathering. If the people here tonight were aware of your Secret Service code name, they would all certainly agree with me that you live up to it."

Marlenna laughed, flashed her perfect smile, and said. "Oooh, I'm glad you think so, darling, but I think we need to get your eyes checked."

If ever a couple were meant to be soul mates, one in spirit, bonded by eternal love, it had to be Reb and Marlenna McCoy. Part way through the dance, by prearrangement, the orchestra began a tango, and without missing a beat, the McCoys effortlessly shifted into the sensual dance step they had learned in Argentina many years before. The orchestra finished up with a lovely Viennese waltz that Reb and Marlenna executed perfectly. The crowd gathered around the dance floor, applauded warmly, and delivered a couple of whistles as Reb and Marlenna bowed graciously. Everyone who wished to dance now took the floor. Jake Fillmore impertinently cut in on Reb to claim the second dance with Marlenna.

After a few steps, Jake, an expert dancer, said, "Marlenna, I'm not hitting on you, but you are as ravishing tonight as when I first met you and Reb in Brazil over twenty-five years ago. How are the two of you bearing up under the intense fish bowl pressure of the campaign?"

While she had been accustomed all her life to receiving compliments on her looks, the only ones that mattered to her were her husband's. "Thank you, Jake. As to your question, I believe we are both doing well. I appreciate your interest. I'm sure looking forward to our vacation in Jackson Hole, though. We both need a break. The easy part is over. I'm worried that Reb will push himself too hard from now until the election. As you know, he runs at only one pace: full speed. The good news is after the convention in early August, there will be only three months to go. The bad news is there will still be three months to go."

"I will work with Hoppy to make certain we don't over schedule either of you. And if you think we need to ease up, tell me, and Hoppy and I will figure out how to get you both a little down time."

Reb had left the dance floor and was surrounded by Ding Bell and the other members of the Madison Committee. "Reb, this is a wonderful affair. It is also probably the last non-political event you will attend until after the election. By the way, assuming he is asked by a reporter, I understand Fubarsky will say some favorable things about the Second Bill of Rights at his next press conference. His support probably will be tepid, but that's better than having him oppose it."

"That's good to hear, Ding. Say, Duane, Pip, I've been noticing at recent campaign rallies a growing number of signs supporting the 9-10 party. How is that effort going? I hope it won't result in any competition or ill will with the self-described tea party folks."

Duane Darby and Pip Pippin had taken it upon themselves to recruit people at the grassroots level in several states to organize groups whose primary interest was limited constitutional government, and reaffirmation of the Ninth and Tenth Amendments. This was not difficult to do, and in states whose legislatures had petitioned Congress to call a constitutional convention, 9-10 party membership grew rapidly. The focus had now shifted to establish 9-10 party chapters in states that had not yet applied to Congress for a convention to consider the Second Bill of Rights.

Duane said, "No, Reb, there should not be any clash between the two grassroots efforts. They are compatible with each other. The tea party has a broader agenda around taxes, jobs, deficits, as well as a return to constitutional principles. The 9-10 party is focused exclusively on the latter issue and the Second Bill of Rights."

Nodding his head in agreement, Pip added, "We are already seeing 9-10 party rallies being held in state capitals that are resisting or dragging their feet on the Second Bill of Rights question. Our supporters are already pressuring state legislative candidates to pledge their support for a constitutional convention. If neither Democratic nor Republican candidate for a state seat provides a strong endorsement, the 9-10 party is planning to run a third party candidate. The 9-10ers also are pressuring candidates for the U.S. Congress to tell voters where they stand on calling a convention if we get thirty-four state petitions to do so."

"That's great to hear," said Reb. "I think the Madison Committee's idea to organize this effort in key states has a lot of potential. We are now up to twenty-nine states with petitions before Congress seeking a convention. I believe we can get to the magic number thirty-four by the election, or soon thereafter. That way, no matter whether I win or lose, Congress will be forced to call a convention. You appear concerned, Judge. What's bothering you?"

Responding to Reb's question, Judge Wyatt Solomon said, "Reb, I strongly recommend we not stop at thirty-four states. We should try to get thirty-eight to forty on board. We know Congress will resist calling a convention if it can find a plausible reason to do so. I understand several states have adopted petitions that have modified the Madison Committee's proposed amendments or added others. Congress may try to argue that it needs thirty-four identical petitions to be required to call a convention. Remember there is no precedent for this, and Congress has latitude to set the precise rules for triggering Article V."

"You're right, Wyatt," replied Ding, "We should not slack off after we gather in the thirty-fourth state. We will also need to bring intense public pressure to bear on Congress. We can't permit trivial objections to derail this effort."

Abby Abbeville interjected, "We should lay the groundwork for keeping the 9-10 party active after the election is over. That will ensure the media give the convention issue sustained coverage. It will also place pressure on congressmen and senators who pledged to call a convention to live up to their word."

"Good point, Abby," responded Reb. "We can't take anything for granted. There can be no letup. 'It ain't over till it's over,' as Yogi Berra once said. I'm very pleased with the Madison Committee's ongoing efforts. You all don't receive the credit you deserve. For better or worse, I've become the public face of the committee, but I know each of you has made an invaluable contribution to getting the Second Bill of Rights off the ground. Who would have predicted three years ago the progress we've achieved so far?"

Ding replied, "Reb, I think I speak for everyone when I say we are all grateful for what you have done to move the Madison Committee agenda forward beyond all expectations. I am honored just to be a part of this historic effort and happy to let you stand in the spotlight."

At that, Marlenna joined the group gaily saying, "Tsk, tsk, sweetheart, you promised me your undivided attention tonight. And here I find you no doubt discussing business and politics. There are many people here who have not yet had a chance to greet you. Excuse us, please."

Reb turned to his Madison Committee colleagues and said, "Abby, gentlemen, by your leave, I am unable to resist Marlenna. Please excuse me."

Judge Wyatt, exuding his southern courtly charm, dramatically took Marlenna's hand in his and kissed it. "My dear, please forgive us. Before the evening is over, allow me the pleasure of one dance with you."

With a coquettish smile, Marlenna replied, "Why, Judge, I would be utterly devastated if you did not save at least one dance for me."

Everybody enjoyed a hearty laugh, as Marlenna led her husband by the hand to the dance floor. On the way, she said, "Reb, darling, I've asked the orchestra to play one of your favorite Sinatra tunes. Since Frank had a previous engagement in the hereafter, you will have to sing the lyrics to me. I know you must be starved, but dinner will be served after this song. Oh, and before dinner, I want you to introduce Bishop O'Faherty who will deliver the benediction."

Reb marveled at how his wife efficiently attended to all the details of her event, while appearing not to have a care in the world and finding time to charm all her gala guests. The orchestra had just returned from a break when they reached the nearly deserted dance floor. As he could with most all of Sinatra's songs, within four or five notes Reb identified the tune as Jerome Kern's "The Way You Look Tonight." The orchestra was playing it to Nelson Riddle's superb arrangement written for Sinatra's 1964 Reprise recording. As he whirled his wife onto the dance floor, Reb began singing softly the lyrics to Marlenna:

> Someday, when I'm awfully low,
> When the world is cold,
> I will feel a glow
> Just thinking of you,
> And the way you look tonight.
>
> Yes, you're lovely
> With your smile so warm
> And your cheek so soft,
> There is nothing for me
> But to love you,
> And the way you look tonight.
>
> Lovely, never, ever change
> Keep that breathless charm,
> Won't you please arrange it
> 'Cause I love you
> Just the way you look tonight.
>
> Mmmm Mmmm, Mmmm Mmmm,
> Just the way you look tonight.

As the orchestra finished the tune, Reb held his wife close and said, "Keep that breathless charm, pretty. I love you."

"I love you too, cowboy, and always will. We've had a great ride together. Now, let's go eat, and don't forget to say something clever about the bishop."

Reb dutifully made a gracious introduction of the affable Bishop O'Faherty, head of the Catholic Diocese of Dallas and close family friend of the McCoys for over forty years. Following the bishop's benediction, Sen. Ding Bell stood to offer an affectionate toast to Reb and Marlenna. As one, the gala guests gave the McCoys a standing ovation, after which all were seated to enjoy a delicious five-course dinner.

Before the evening ended, Judge Wyatt got his chance to dance with Marlenna. Reb danced several more times with his wife, including one of her favorites, "YMCA," before they departed the gala.

The Dallas Morning News society page provided extensive coverage of the event, including many photos of various attendees. The featured color photo in the paper, of course, was of Reb, looking as if he were born to wear a tuxedo, and a smiling, ever photogenic Marlenna. Later that day, Reb and Marlenna departed for two weeks of rest and relaxation in Jackson Hole, the last time they would have more than one day off between July and the November election.

For their vacation, they rented a luxurious ranch owned by an old friend. The property was situated on a thousand acres of land and offered privacy, along with a spectacular view of the Teton Range, nine peaks in northwest Wyoming, each of which rises over twelve thousand feet above sea level. Everyday, they went hiking, horseback riding, or trout fishing. Reb caught up on his pleasure reading, and Marlenna, who had brought along her art materials, produced three miniature paintings, two portraits and one of the mountains.

While living in Brazil, Marlenna had taken up painting. She was quite talented, and, after a couple years, decided to specialize in miniatures that typically measured six by eight inches when framed. Her medium was either oil or acrylic, and her style was evocative of nineteenth-century French impressionism. Painting a miniature is arguably more challenging than a larger canvas, because it is a complete composition requiring delicate, precise strokes. A mistake on a larger canvas often can be painted over, but not so on a miniature. Marlenna painted landscapes but, as time went by, she increasingly specialized in portraits, usually of relatives and friends, which she gave to the subjects. Each work was signed "Marlenna" in the lower right corner of its custom frame. Anyone fortunate enough to receive a portrait painted by Marlenna treasured it as a most precious gift.

Reb loved Marlenna's art, but, despite repeated entreaties, he had never succeeded in getting her to do a self-portrait for him. She always resisted saying that would be an exercise in vanity. One day, he placed a favorite recent photograph of her on her pillow with a love note telling her how much it would mean to him if she would paint a portrait for him from the photo. By the end of their vacation, she surprised him with her self-portrait, which he thought captured her beauty perfectly. He noticed that starting on the left side of the frame and running around to the lower right corner she had painted "For the love of my life, Marlenna." Her gift brought tears to his eyes.

In Dallas art and social circles, virtually everyone knew Marlenna by her given name, just as Cher or Oprah or Madonna, on a much larger stage, is immediately recognizable by her first name. Rarely did anyone address her as Mrs. McCoy. Even little kids in their Highland Park neighborhood addressed her as Marlenna, which pleased her, but Reb thought a bit impudent. Those same kids addressed him as Mr. McCoy, or occasionally as Mr. Marlenna, which never failed to amuse him.

Hoppy and Jake only occasionally called or emailed Reb while he and Marlenna enjoyed their time alone together. He did talk to Lillian Duzmore after Jake told him she had reluctantly agreed to undergo a background check as a possible VP nominee.

"Lillian, this is Reb. How are you and Duzzy doing? Is Georgia going to live up to its nickname this summer and bring in a great crop of peaches? Nothing tastes better than a fresh, ripe peach."

"It's nice to hear your voice, Reb. Duz and I are doing just fine, and yes, we expect a bumper crop of peaches this year. How is Marlenna? Hope you both are getting tanned, rested, and ready, as Nixon used to say."

"We're doing great and couldn't ask for better weather. The fresh air, serenity, and nature's beauty are conducive to quiet reflection and healing the spirit. Lillian, let me get to the point. You are my first choice to be my running mate. Before you say anything, I want you to know I have no second choice."

"Reb, darling, you know how to flatter a girl. As much as I want you to be our next president, I have no ambition to be vice president of the United States. It's an impressive title, but a position without substance or authority."

Reb couldn't blame her. After all, he had declined Maggie Thurston's offer in 2012 to be her running mate for similar reasons.

"Look, I know someone with your take-charge personality is not accustomed to playing second fiddle, but please hear me out. I want a running mate whom I trust, and who is qualified to be president, shares my political philosophy, supports the Second Bill of Rights wholeheartedly, and is not a Washington insider. You meet all those criteria, Lillian. If we win, which is probably a long shot considering the message I will deliver to the American people, I will reorganize and downsize the bloated White House staff. There will no longer be a layer of so-called czars between the president and the cabinet departments. I would give you responsibility for overseeing half the departments, while the others would report directly to me. You would be a true executive, not just hanging around in case I have a stroke or drop dead."

"You make the job sound more interesting, but I need time to think it over and talk to my family. For anyone other than you, I wouldn't even consider this, Reb. When do you need an answer?"

"Thanks, Lillian, for giving this serious consideration. I would like to have your answer by July 1. In the meantime, please call me any time to discuss whatever issues or concerns might come to mind as you weigh your decision. Whether we win or not in November, I'm confident the two of us as a team can bring along the remaining states necessary to require Congress to call a constitutional convention. I know you agree with me that adoption of the Second Bill of Rights is far more important to the country's future than anything we could accomplish during four years in the White House. We can't let this opportunity slip our grasp, as it most certainly won't come again."

"I see through your clever ploy, Governor McCoy," replied Lillian with a laugh. "You are setting me up so I can't refuse your offer without feeling unpatriotic. That's not kosher."

"You're right, Lillian. But all's fair in love and war. This is all about the love we share for our country and the high stakes political war we must fight to secure the blessings of liberty to posterity."

"I'm beginning to understand how you managed to seduce Marlenna into marrying you, when she could have had her pick of any man. I'll call you soon with my answer, Reb."

He hung up the phone and reflected that Lillian had reacted just about how he thought she would. Her reluctance to run for VP only reinforced his conviction that she was the ideal choice. He also figured it was likely she would agree to be his running mate. Her charisma, energy, and commitment would be huge assets to the campaign.

The only other business during his vacation was a call from Ding Bell a couple days later. After exchanging pleasantries and a couple jokes, Ding said,

"I'm picking up intelligence corroborated by multiple sources that the campaign is going to be nasty and personal. There are many special interest groups and powerful people in all three branches of the federal government who are desperate to prevent a constitutional convention and the adoption of the Second Bill of Rights. Motivations run the gamut from protecting personal and institutional power to fear of a runaway convention to philosophical belief in big government. The opposition is prepared to engage in slanderous personal attacks against you in order to defeat you. The theory is if you are discredited, the push for a convention will collapse."

"Ding, our opponents' desperation ignores a stubborn fact. The widespread and growing popular demand for restoration of limited constitutional government is far bigger than me or any other individual. In any event, before I decided to run for governor, you, Jake, and Marlenna all warned me that politics is not beanbag. Untrue personal attacks are part and parcel of many campaigns. We just have to counter any calumny with the truth and have faith in the collective judgment of the electorate to sort out fact from fiction. If my opponent or his supporters goes negative, we'll do our best to refute promptly any lies, but I am not going to retaliate in kind."

"You're right to stick to the high road and focus on the issues, but I recommend you set up an anti-defamation unit inside the campaign that can act swiftly to counter any slander the opposition throws against the wall. An unchallenged and repeated lie will be accepted as true by many people, if it is not quickly shown to be untrue, especially since there usually is a scintilla of distorted truth wrapped in the larger lie to make it seem plausible. Wasn't it Mark Twain or Winston Churchill who remarked that a lie can travel halfway around the world while truth is pulling on its boots?"

"Okay, Ding, I accept your advice and will ask Hoppy to give this priority, so we aren't caught flatfooted. If our quest to have the Second Bill of Rights adopted is ultimately successful, a lot of power will flow away from

Washington and the federal government. The people whose power will be diminished by such an eventuality, I expect, will do most anything to keep it from happening. The stakes are high for them and even higher for the country's future. How many Americans throughout our history have given their lives in defense of this country? All I risk is having my integrity and reputation impugned in pursuit of what you and I and many others believe is essential to secure freedom's blessings for posterity. As long as my wife, family, and friends know the truth about me, I can live with whatever lies are leveled against me."

28

Between the party nominating conventions and the election, a modern presidential campaign moves at a frenetic pace. The candidates probably spend a third of their time inside an airplane crisscrossing the country to make speeches at events and rallies, attend fundraisers, grant countless interviews, and participate in debates. Behind the scenes, schedulers, advance men and women, state organizers, get-out-the-vote operatives, radio and TV ad producers, press handlers, pollsters, and many others work eighteen- to twenty-hour days under intense pressure. Underpinning this large, complex organization are the rainmakers who bring in enormous amounts of money via mail, telephone, and the Internet.

The candidate and the senior people directing the campaign must be immune to stress, able to cope with sudden change and off-the-wall surprises, adept at prioritization, and masters of tactics and strategy. Having a sense of humor is an important attribute for everyone involved, but the foundation of the campaign is teamwork, mutual trust, and commitment by all to the candidate and his vision for America.

Because presidential campaigns occur every four years, there are plenty of seasoned operatives available to staff key positions. Even so, the idea of starting up an operation from scratch that will raise and spend $700-800 million and go out of business, win or lose, within four months Reb considered both amazing and insane. He was the first presidential candidate in history to have been the CEO of a Fortune 500 multinational company. His outstanding executive ability and analytical skills enabled him to organize and lead a highly efficient, professional campaign, but no business he had ever managed provided him an experience remotely comparable to the unique nature of a presidential campaign.

The Democrats held their convention in San Francisco in mid-July. They nominated a fifty-six-year-old lawyer, Governor Conrad Bucknell of Pennsylvania, for president. Born to great wealth, Bucknell had previously been Pennsylvania's senior senator and was a liberal, but not an extreme ideologue. Reb did not know Bucknell, but based on Hoppy's in-depth briefing, the Democrats had chosen a formidable candidate. Bucknell's choice for his running mate was a complete shock to Reb. It was none other than his long ago high school summer sweetheart from Springfield, Lola Lovett. Following a career in academia culminating as president of Wooster College in Wooster, Ohio, Lola entered politics. She was now Ohio's senior U.S. senator and a committed liberal.

Except for exchanging a few letters while he was in Vietnam, Reb had not had contact with Lola since he enlisted in the army in 1968. He did not think his brief teen-age dalliance with her would be revealed to the public. He certainly was not going to mention it, and, presumably, Lola had no reason to do so either. Even if their long ago mutual infatuation did become public, he would suffer no embarrassment. On the contrary, Reb found the irony rather amusing. Still, he felt obliged to inform Marlenna.

Over breakfast the morning after the Democratic convention concluded, Reb said, "Marlenna, I want you to be the first to know that long, long ago, when I was in high school and years before I met you, I dated Lola Lovett."

"My, my," responded Marlenna, "actually, it would seem I am the third one to know. Small world, isn't it? She is quite attractive and no doubt was a very pretty young girl. How could such a nice liberal girl get involved with a Neanderthal conservative like you?"

"She's a Springfield girl, which is where we met. Neither of us was the least bit interested in politics at that age."

"What did interest you, darling, the birds and the bees? I'm just having a little fun with you. You owe me no explanation, but I'm glad you told me about your dark, secret past. To tell the truth, I think it's pretty cool. You must be the first presidential candidate in American history to have laid the opposing party's vice presidential candidate. At least we now know that conservatives and liberals have something in common. Maybe this signals the dawn of a new era of intimate bipartisanship."

Reb was not surprised that Marlenna found it all so amusing. Nevertheless, he was relieved to have this discussion behind him.

The Democrats had put on an impressive convention, and the Bucknell–Lovett ticket benefited from an expected jump in the polls. Tally Ho's post-convention polling showed the Democratic ticket ten points ahead of the not yet nominated Republican ticket. This lead would be erased following the Republican convention, Tally Ho confidently predicted. Reb was not so sure, but he was even more relieved that Lillian Duzmore finally had agreed to be his running mate. Had she declined, Reb almost certainly would have chosen a male running mate. In that event, the Democrats would have had an inherent advantage with women voters, especially among independents and moderates. With Lillian on the Republican ticket, this issue was neutralized.

❧ ⸻ ❧

The Republican convention hosted by Salt Lake City in August was a great success, judging by the wild enthusiasm of the delegates and the TV ratings. Reb got his way in the Rules Committee followed by an overwhelmingly favorable floor vote to change the party's name to the Republican Constitution Party. This generated interminable discussion and debate by the pundits and TV talking heads, which pleased Reb, even if much of the blather was negative, because it focused attention on the Constitution and the proposed Second Bill of Rights. He wanted this to be the central issue of the campaign.

Following a warm and glowing multi-media tribute to the late President Thurston on the convention's second night, President Fubarsky delivered a fine if typically long-winded speech. He rightly emphasized his administration's slow but steady progress defeating al Qaeda in detail in the western provinces of Pakistan and in Yemen on the Arabian Peninsula. He also recounted that several planned terrorist attacks on American soil had been prevented. The president, however, did not dwell on the U.S.' painfully high unemployment rate, enormous deficits, crushing debt burden, slow economic growth, and now rising inflation, other than to lay much of the blame on the Democrat-controlled House of Representatives. He did not comment at all on the deteriorating conditions along the southern border with Mexico, where it appeared a major terrorist incident was inevitable if remedial security measures were not taken in the immediate future.

Gov. Lillian Duzmore was a popular choice to be Reb's running mate, and she gave a terrific acceptance speech on the third night of the convention. The next night Reb gave his acceptance speech after being introduced by Sen. Ding Bell and Marlenna. Eleanor Roosevelt was the first spouse of a presidential nominee to address a party convention when she delivered a speech on behalf of her husband FDR at the 1940 Democratic convention. Spectacularly attired in a cinnamon fitted jersey dress by Roberto Cavalli that featured an asymmetrical neckline gathered by a gleaming metal ring, Marlenna paid homage in her brief remarks to Mrs. Roosevelt and quoted from her 1940 convention speech when she said, "This too is no ordinary time."

The nearly five thousand delegates and alternates stood and cheered Marlenna's every move and word. The demonstration went on for fifteen minutes. Hoppy began to worry that she would upstage her husband. Watching a TV monitor offstage, Reb was thrilled to see the genuine affection the throng had for his wife, whose incandescent smile and head-turning beauty were made for high-definition television.

Her winsome speech focused on Reb's integrity, kindness, and generosity. In closing, she said, "Ladies and gentlemen, please welcome my wonderful husband, an extraordinary leader for an extraordinary time, and your nominee to be the next president of the United States, Governor Reb McCoy!"

Reb bounded onto the stage and into his wife's open arms. He hugged her close and kissed her on the lips, but was careful to avoid an exaggerated lip lock as Al Gore had gauchely imposed on his wife at the Democratic convention in 2000. Ten minutes later after the cheering subsided and Marlenna had made her way offstage, Reb began his acceptance speech, which he had personally written and not shared beforehand even with Marlenna or Hoppy. Millions of American voters were gathered around their TV sets to hear Reb's prime time speech, which was aimed more at them than the party faithful in the arena where he spoke.

> "Ladies and gentlemen of the Republican Constitution Party, I am pleased and honored to accept your nomination to be president of the United States of America. Incorporating the word 'Constitution' in our party's formal name is not a frivolous change, as some cynics and skeptics maintain. Our overriding mission is to restore the

Constitution bequeathed to us by the Founding Fathers of limited government, individual liberty, and financial solvency.

"In his inauguration speech over fifty years ago, John F. Kennedy challenged all Americans to 'ask not what your country can do for you; ask what you can do for your country.' Unfortunately, over the intervening half century since President Kennedy's stirring summons, we Americans have incessantly asked more and more of our country. Consequently, the federal government has grown exponentially and expanded its powers far beyond the limits of the Constitution. In the process, we have seen budget deficits and the national debt spiral out of control as we fund the enormous obligations of the welfare state. Both political parties have been complicit in the centralization of power and control in the hands of the federal government.

"For nearly a century, the fundamental debate in American politics has been whether this country whose independence was won in a bloody revolution will remain a free society or become a welfare state. Our generation has been called to answer and cannot honorably evade this question: Is the Constitution of the United States of America a governing document that guarantees liberty or equality? We cannot have both, and we no longer can afford the latter. The more we become a society whose highest goal is equality, the more intrusive government will be of necessity, and individual liberty will be permanently diminished—perhaps one day extinguished—as we become increasingly dependent on government to provide for our needs. Liberty and equality are mutually exclusive.

"Society that esteems equality above liberty begets the soft tyranny of government paternalism and dependency that inevitably will undermine individual responsibility and vanquish the human spirit. In such a democratic society, individual citizens are spared, as Alexis de Tocqueville wrote, 'the trouble of thinking and the pain of living,' and instead become a 'herd of timid and industrious animals of which the government is the shepherd.' The Founding Fathers' great struggle for freedom was to attain individual liberty, not collective equality. Liberty frees man to dream, to be self-reliant, and to aspire to realize his or her individual potential and self-dignity.

"For my part, I stand with the Founding Fathers foursquare for liberty. The Constitution was intended to safeguard the rights our Creator has endowed in all men and women, among which are life, liberty, and the pursuit of happiness. Neither our Creator nor the Constitution endowed us with a right to equality or a guarantee of happiness. We each are blessed with free will to pursue happiness as we each see fit, constrained only by our individual talents and ambition, so long as we do not encroach upon another citizen's liberty.

"Now, so as not to be misunderstood, society has a moral and solemn obligation to provide for all those who cannot help themselves. America is a rich and generous country founded on Judeo-Christian values and principles of love and compassion for our fellow man. The poor, the disadvantaged, the halt, and the lame must be provided sustenance and care if they are unable to do so for themselves. Whenever possible, however, they should be afforded assistance and educational opportunities that may equip them to fulfill their potential and pursue their own happiness as independent citizens. This is a necessary duty and obligation of both private philanthropy and government.

"This generation of Americans is summoned not only to reaffirm liberty and disavow equality, except before the law, but also to place the nation on an irreversible path that will return the federal government to solvency. To say that the government spends money like drunken sailors is to defame sailors. Over the past seven years, the federal government's annual budget deficit has far exceeded one trillion dollars every year. The federal government spends $1.60 for every dollar it receives in revenue from taxes. Can anyone imagine running a business or personal budget on this basis? Anyone who did would be bankrupt within a year or two.

"Our national debt exceeds $20 trillion and grows every minute of every day. The unfunded future obligations for entitlements such as Social Security and Medicare exceed a hundred trillion dollars! No human being can comprehend numbers of this magnitude. A billion is one thousand millions. A trillion is one million millions. We are broke. If something can't go on forever, it won't.

"As government has blithely continued to expand its power and intrusiveness into our lives, and we have accepted benefits that we cannot hope to pay for during our lifetime, we have collectively lost our common sense. The late great twentieth-century Englishman G.K. Chesterton, prolific man of letters known in his time as The Apostle of Common Sense, once wrote: 'A society is in decay when common sense has become uncommon.' Citizens of America, can anyone gainsay that our society is in decay and that we have no one to blame but ourselves for having collectively lost or abandoned our common sense?

"The only way out of the country's fiscal death spiral is to cut radically government spending, to reform the entitlement programs so that each generation pays its own way, and to institute policies that will promote robust economic growth. Over the past quarter century, government has grown much faster than the private sector. In the future, we must unleash the inherent growth potential of our innovative free enterprise economy while simultaneously reducing the size of government. The Democratic Party forthrightly advocates increasing taxes. Raising taxes, however, will retard economic growth and increase unemployment. The government does not have a revenue problem; it has an out-of-control spending problem. The Republican Constitution Party advocates slashing spending and growing the economy, thereby increasing jobs and tax revenue to the government.

"Melancholy history offers few, if any, examples of men or women, having personally aggrandized power, voluntarily surrendering it. We cannot rely upon or expect our federal officials, elected or appointed, to restore limited government, individual liberty, or fiscal solvency. They have a vested interest in maintaining the status quo. Only the people of the several states through their state assemblies can muster the will to demand that Congress be petitioned to call a constitutional convention for the purpose of adopting seven amendments known as the Second Bill of Rights. It is in the hands of "we the people" to seize the initiative and restore the proper constitutional balance among the people, the sovereign states, and the federal government.

"The proposed Second Bill of Rights would not diminish the federal government's legitimate powers as enumerated in the Constitution. It would, however, clarify the limits of those powers without constraining the government's policy options. Among other things, the Second Bill of Rights, if ratified, would impose term limits on members of Congress; place the federal government on an irreversible path to fiscal solvency; and restore the sovereign states as key players in our federal republic as the Founders intended. Since the Civil War, the sovereign states, which created the federal government, have gradually been reduced to a minor role in the federal system, yet they are the only practical check on the national government.

"Already, twenty-nine state legislatures have petitioned Congress to call a constitutional convention. Once that number grows to thirty-four, Congress, under Article V of the Constitution, will be required to call such a convention. If the convention recommends adoption of the Second Bill of Rights, it will become the law of the land once ratified by thirty-eight states. This is America's best and perhaps only hope for reaffirming limited government of enumerated powers and individual liberty, as well as restoring fiscal solvency.

"The Preamble to the Constitution expressly states that among the reasons for its establishment is to secure the blessings of liberty to posterity. If we don't restore fiscal sanity to government, we will be the first generation of Americans to fail to secure the blessings of liberty to our grandchildren and their grandchildren. Instead, we will bequeath to them the curse of financial servitude that will require them to repay the debts our profligate generation has irresponsibly and thoughtlessly incurred. This will rob future generations of the opportunities to pursue happiness that we have enjoyed. It is incumbent on each generation to repay its public obligations and not leave them to burden future generations.

"This election may be our last chance to secure the blessings of liberty to posterity.

"I stand before you seeking the presidency for the express purpose of reaffirming liberty and limited constitutional government, and keeping faith with future American generations. Cast not your vote for your short-term self-interest, but for your grandchildren and future generations yet to be born who have no representation unless we keep faith with them as our ancestors kept faith with us. Our generation of Americans has a rendezvous with history we dare not shirk or evade. Let us not crucify America's future upon a cross of debt! Thank you and God bless America."

The speech lasted forty minutes including interruptions totaling twenty minutes for applause and cheers. The moment Reb said, "Let us not crucify America's future upon a cross of debt," an enormous roar erupted from the now standing crowd, a blizzard of confetti and thousands of balloons were released, and Marlenna dashed onto the stage to be at her husband's side holding his hand. They waved, smiled, and soaked up the outpouring of genuine affection from five thousand cheering, foot-stomping, and applauding supporters, at least half of whom were waving signs or placards saying: MCCOY–DUZMORE...FOR PRESIDENT–VOTE FOR THE REAL MCCOY... and FREEDOM FEVER–CATCH IT!

Soon Lillian and Duz Duzmore joined the McCoys on stage, followed by Ravenna, Jeff, and the six-year-old twin grandchildren. The twins raced for their grandfather and glamorous grandmother. Kyle was dressed in a navy sport jacket and red tie, while his sister Deanna wore a periwinkle ruffled dress and matching patent leather Mary Janes. When Ravenna joined her parents, wearing a teal version of her mother's dress, people might easily have mistaken her for Marlenna's younger sister, not her daughter. Millions of television viewers sitting at home, regardless of political sentiment, clearly observed that Ravenna and her children had inherited Marlenna's beauty gene.

As the partying on the convention floor went on and on, the television networks covering the event brought in their analysts to comment on Gov. McCoy's acceptance speech. On one network, the columnist Walter Rothmann remarked, "This was one of the finest political speeches I have heard, although I don't know how well it will be received by the public. It's not often that a politician quotes Alexis de Tocqueville or G.K. Chesterton or evokes William Jennings Bryan's famous 'Cross of Gold' speech delivered at the 1896 Democratic convention. No doubt McCoy's ending sentence, 'Let us not crucify America's future upon a cross of debt,' will be the one most remembered, but there were many other memorable phrases. However this speech goes over in Peoria and the rest of America, one thing is sure, Governor McCoy tonight spoke to America's voters as if they are mature, intelligent people. He spoke to them from the heart; he did not pander or grandstand; he summoned them to restore constitutional limited government, individual liberty, self-reliance, and fiscal solvency. Those are high-minded ideals. It remains to be seen if an election can be won on such a platform."

The television anchor person thanked Rothmann and then asked Donald Utopeville for his thoughts. Utopeville responded, "I agree with Walter's comments and would add this. Governor McCoy avoided any mention of specific policies he would advocate as president other than ratification of the proposed Second Bill of Rights and no tax increases. He would, however, take this country in a dramatically different direction than it has traveled over the past fifty years. He clearly has established that the welfare state as we know it is no longer affordable and the United States is effectively bankrupt. At some point, he will have to lay out the specific proposals he has for slashing deficits and reducing the debt. Every government program has a constituency, which will fight tooth and nail to preserve it. The policies implicit in cutting back government won't be widely popular."

Rothmann jumped in saying, "McCoy knows this, but tonight he challenged this generation of Americans to 'man up,' if you will, and think about its duty to bequeath the blessings of liberty, rather than financial servitude, to future generations. I think it was very astute the way he cited the Preamble to the Constitution to make the point that each generation has an obligation to pass on to the next generation a country that is at least as good as the one they inherited. This is not the run-of-the-mill rhetoric of platitudes we normally hear during a political campaign. He has painted a bleak future, but shows us the way to change that future for the better."

"No doubt McCoy has established the terms of the debate," replied Utopeville, "and he has faced head-on the fundamental issue: liberty versus equality, limited government versus a welfare state. He has framed it eloquently. It will be fascinating to see how Bucknell and the Democrats respond to McCoy's challenge. I bet there are not a few Republicans who are a little uncomfortable with their standard bearer who would cut or eliminate many of their cherished programs."

"I know how the Democrats or their surrogates will respond," said Rothmann. "They will attack McCoy personally to try and discredit him. While Bucknell is a strong candidate, McCoy has elevated the debate to a high plane and is appealing to the patriotism, honor, and conscience of Americans. It will be difficult to attack McCoy on the substance of his argument. Consequently, his opponents will try to destroy his reputation, thereby discrediting his ideas. It will be hard to do, but it is perhaps the Democrats' only hope for victory in November. The problem is, I suspect McCoy does not have many if any skeletons in his closet, or they would have been revealed by now, so the opposition will have to make something up and hope it sticks. Politics at the presidential level, especially with a potentially transformational candidate like McCoy threatening to upend the status quo, is a dirty business. But I suppose it is better than settling matters by armed force."

"On that note," interrupted the television anchor person, "we have to end this interesting dialogue and return to our regularly scheduled programming.

29

During Reb's acceptance speech, Tally Ho conducted eight simultaneous focus groups in cities across the country. He also began polling immediately following the speech. As he had predicted after the Democratic convention, the Republican ticket following its convention enjoyed a bounce in the polls and erased the Democrats' lead. The focus groups all reacted favorably to Reb's speech. The major concern voiced by focus group participants was the need for Reb to lay out specific policies for reducing government's size, reducing the national debt, and reforming entitlements.

Hoppy, Jake, and the senior campaign staff met with Reb a day after the party convention to review the campaign calendar. Much of the overall campaign strategy and travel schedule Reb delegated to Hoppy, trusting his political instincts and experience. Reb insisted, however, on visiting states that he thought were fertile territory for petitioning Congress for a constitutional convention, even if it was a long shot he would carry them in the election.

Reb wanted Hoppy to arrange for three debates with Bucknell, one each on domestic and international policy, and one on the proposed Second Bill of Rights. He also suggested one debate between Duzmore and Lovett. Reb told Hoppy he was willing to concede venue and format of the debates, as long as there were three on the topics he proposed. Reb also wanted ample time set aside to do television, radio, and newspaper interviews.

For everyone involved in the campaign, every day was one of nonstop, hyperactivity, which an outsider would describe as chaotic. From Labor Day through November 7, the eve of the election, the candidates did not pause for breath or respite. Like Reb and Marlenna, Lillian was indefatigable and a wonderful campaigner. Of course, she and Reb rarely saw each other as they campaigned separately to cover more territory, but they were in contact by phone or email daily. Reb trusted Lillian and did not control what she said in her speeches. After Labor Day, they did not stand on the same stage together until the final day of the campaign.

Over Hoppy's reservations, Reb insisted on closing out the campaign with a nostalgic whistle-stop tour by train. Reb's romance with trains began in his youth, and he knew all about Harry Truman's whistle-stop tour during his upset victory in the 1948 presidential campaign. Back then, railroads were the primary means of conveyance on long trips, and a large part of the U.S. population was clustered near a train depot. Hoppy was cool to the idea, because more locations in more heavily populated areas could be reached traveling by air. Nevertheless, The Real McCoy Express was scheduled to depart Philadelphia early October 26, following the third presidential debate. Its itinerary over the ensuing nine days was to include Pittsburgh, Cincinnati, Cleveland, Chicago, Denver, San Francisco, Seattle, and back to Chicago, with numerous small town stops along the way.

As it turned out, the media were captivated by the whistle-stop tour, and it received a great deal of favorable coverage. The train was made up of eight cars: a dining car, two coaches equipped with Wi-Fi for the working press, three sleepers for the press plus one for campaign aides, and last, Reb and Marlenna's private car. When the train pulled into a small town, Reb and Marlenna would greet the crowd from the rear platform of their private car and deliver a brief speech. Besides the debates, Reb thought the whistle-stop tour would be the most enjoyable aspect of the campaign.

Two weeks of contentious negotiations between Hoppy and his counterpart in Bucknell's campaign were required to nail down the debates. The presidential candidates would meet at two-week intervals beginning Tuesday, September 27. The final debate on October 25, two weeks before the election, would be on the Second Bill of Rights as Reb had insisted and would take place, appropriately, in Philadelphia's Independence Hall, the site of the Constitutional Convention of 1787. The first debate would be devoted to defense and international affairs, and the second debate would focus on domestic issues. Since the advent of televised presidential debates in 1960 between Kennedy and Nixon, Reb believed they were pivotal in helping voters choose a candidate.

By the time of the first debate on defense and foreign policy, Bucknell and McCoy were in a virtual tie. Fearing being labeled weak on defense, as several Democratic candidates in the past had been, Bucknell pledged not to cut the defense budget and criticized Reb for policy statements he had made indicating he would radically reduce defense spending. In the 2017 fiscal budget, defense accounted for nearly $900 billion, or 20 percent of the total federal budget.

When it was Reb's turn to respond to his opponent, he said:

> "If elected, I will reduce annual defense expenditures by one third, or $300 billion, over four years. The country's deficits and debt are unsustainable, as I have been preaching since the start of my campaign. There can be no sacred cows in the budget. We can reduce the resources devoted to defense without compromising America's fundamental security interests. In the future, we will rely increasingly on technology in lieu of manpower to project force abroad.

Any weapon systems developed to fight yesterday's conflicts and not suited to tomorrow's threats will be eliminated. Where we have troops stationed abroad, we will ask our allies to reimburse us 75 percent of the annual cost or we will return home. For years, there have been efforts to close unnecessary military bases in the U.S., but nothing ever happens. If elected, I will direct the Secretary of Defense to determine which U.S. military installations are superfluous and to begin a phase-out as soon as practical. Each vacated base will be put up for sale to the highest bidding private sector company that will create the most jobs in the community and cover the cost of environmental remediation. Finally, the military pension formula will be reduced prospectively from 2.5 percent to 2 percent of final pay for each year of active duty service."

Bucknell responded by saying McCoy's proposals would eviscerate the Defense Department and do irreparable harm to national security. Reb replied that the nation's enormous public debt, deficits, and painfully slow economic growth over the past six years were the country's biggest national security threats and had to be dealt with urgently.

On foreign policy, Reb laid out his ten priorities: secure the border with Mexico, expand free trade, restore a strong dollar, undertake no nation building, protect the world's sea lanes, permit no country to gain a military advantage in space, develop and deploy effective missile defense systems, defend against cyber attack, pursue long-term partnerships and alliances with democratic countries of South America, and adopt a firm, credible posture of 'don't tread on me' or our allies. Bucknell discussed his foreign policy views in general terms and offered few specifics.

Both men came across well on TV. They were attractive, confident, and obviously competent. McCoy, however, appeared more sincere and forthright than did Bucknell, who avoided taking a stand on many issues and came across as what he was, a politician, albeit a good one. Most of the liberal media called the debate a tie or gave Bucknell the edge. Conservative media opined that McCoy won hands down, but there was consternation over his proposed deep cuts in defense spending. Defense hawks in particular expressed hand-wringing angst over his position on the defense budget. Veterans groups spoke out against the proposed 20 percent reduction in future military pensions.

Tally Ho's post-debate polling showed that the voters liked both men, but thought Reb had won the debate. The Republican ticket took a lead in the polls by six points. Democrats were seeing similar results in their polls, and several anti-McCoy groups not affiliated with Bucknell's campaign decided it was time to go negative.

A story soon appeared in one of the supermarket tabloids saying that while living in Brazil, Reb had had an extramarital affair with a Brazilian woman that produced a child named Gisele. When the mother abandoned the child, so the story went, the McCoys adopted her. Reb laughed when he was informed of the story, but because the press was going crazy over it, the anti-defamation unit quickly got out the truth.

Now twenty-eight years old, married, and living in Rio de Janeiro, Brazil, Gisele was actually born two years before Reb and Marlenna were transferred to São Paulo in 1990. She was the daughter of the McCoys' Brazilian maid, a widow who died of an incurable renal disease a year before the McCoys returned to the U.S. in 1995, leaving the child an orphan at age six. Reb and Marlenna arranged to be named her legal guardians, rather than turn her out into the streets of São Paulo to fend for herself, which was the tragic fate of too many Brazilian children. Gisele lived with the McCoys in Dallas until her college graduation in 2009, when she decided to return to Brazil to pursue her career. She loved Marlenna and Reb as if they were her natural parents, and stayed in frequent contact with them. She was also close to Ravenna who considered Gisele her kid sister. Once the facts were made public, this ridiculous story quickly died and no lasting damage was done.

A week later, a video went viral across the Internet of Reb and Marlenna on a chaise lounge beside the backyard pool at their home in Dallas. Marlenna, reclining on her back, is working on her tan and looks incredibly sexy in her cobalt blue bikini. Reb appears fit and handsome in a polo shirt and shorts while applying lotion to Marlenna's legs. Her left foot propped against his chest, he obviously enjoys massaging the oil into her skin up the entire length of her beautiful gam. Later, they appear to be eating Jell-O with whipped cream. At one point, Reb spoons some whipped cream on his wife's bare left shoulder and leans over to lick it off, after which they engage in a passionate kiss. The final clip shows him suddenly standing up and rushing in the direction of the camera.

Two summers before he was elected governor, the video had been taken by a neighborhood teenager who was spying on them through the dense fir trees that Reb thought afforded their pool adequate privacy. Reb heard rustling in the trees and chased the kid off, but didn't think any more about it. After Reb was elected governor, security mandated that the stone wall that wrapped the back of the property be extended around the front of the house and a gate be installed at the driveway. After consulting with his neighbors to be sure they had no objections, he had a ten-foot-tall stone wall erected at his expense to secure the property.

There was nothing embarrassing in the video, although it was an invasion of privacy, and the McCoys would have preferred that it not be splashed across the Internet, but that's the way the modern world is. What it did show was how incredibly beautiful Marlenna was and how much she and Reb were attracted to each other. Of course, what man alive would not be attracted to Marlenna.

On *The Tonight Show* the day the video surfaced, Jay Leno in his opening monologue remarked, "Say, did you see the Internet video of Governor McCoy getting a bit amorous with a beautiful woman? This had to be a first.

Imagine a politician hitting on his wife instead of an intern." The studio audience laughed with gusto.

A few days after the video hit the Internet and bled over into the mainstream media, Marlenna was scheduled to appear on *The View*. To poke fun at herself, she decided, unbeknownst to Whoopi, Joy, Elizabeth, or Barbara, to go on stage dressed in a nun's habit. The ladies and the audience broke into prolonged laughter that brought tears to their eyes. Just before she sat down between Barbara and Joy, Marlenna doffed the habit to reveal she was wearing an adorable peridot, scoop-necked, cap-sleeved dress, hemmed slightly above the knee, and Jimmy Choo eelskin platform pumps. Marlenna sat down, quickly ran her fingers through her hair to restore its natural shape, and looked absolutely stunning.

She proceeded to charm the audience and the ladies of "The View," including Joy and Whoopi. At one point, Marlenna leaned over to Joy and said teasingly, "I don't care what you think of me, Joy, but I do hope you don't call me a bitch."

Joy and the crowd roared with laughter, as they all recalled Joy's nasty outburst some years earlier when she called a female Republican senate candidate by that pejorative appellation.

At another point, Whoopi asked Marlenna, "Do you think your husband has always been faithful?"

Taken momentarily aback, Marlenna recovered quickly to reply with her delightful laugh, "If Reb has ever been unfaithful, he is the best actor in the world. He has certainly given me more happiness than I ever thought possible to expect from marriage. We have both worked—that's not the way to phrase it—from the beginning, we both were committed to keeping the romance alive in our relationship, because it is a beautiful, enjoyable, physical expression of our love for each other and a key to our happiness. I guess some women and men can be fooled by their spouses, but there is a mutual trust, a bond between us that I would bet my life has not and cannot be broken. That may sound naïve or hokey, but if I had it to do all over again, I would marry Reb in a heartbeat."

Over the applause, Whoopi leaned in and commented, "And I have no doubt, honey, he would marry you again as well. He is a lucky man. How do you stay so young and beautiful?"

"Why, thank you, Whoopi. I am blessed, but appearance doesn't say anything about what's in your heart or soul. As important as romance and trust have been to our marriage, we also laugh a lot and go to church every Sunday, or at least once a week. We both are drawn closer to each other during and after Mass, and that sustains us through the next week if there are any bumps along the way. I know in today's world, religion is shunned or rejected by many people, but I am grateful that both my husband and I are spiritual and share a strong faith."

"Is your husband Catholic too?" asked Barbara.

"Yes, he converted to Catholicism fifteen years ago, although ever since we were married, he always attended church with me each Sunday."

"Did he convert to please you?" followed up Barbara.

"No, Reb's personal spiritual journey led him to the Church. I believe the English writer G.K. Chesterton, in particular his wonderful books, still in print, *The Everlasting Man* and *Orthodoxy*, had a major influence on him."

Elizabeth said, "I understand in an interview recently your husband said the secret to his successful marriage was that early in your relationship the two of you had a disagreement and you said to him, 'would you rather be right or be happy?' He reflected on that a moment and decided he preferred to be happy, and that depended on you being happy. Is that story true?"

"Oh, Reb tells that tale a lot. I'm sure I did say that to him half seriously. The truth is we each have always placed the other's happiness first, but in case of a tie, I win," replied Marlenna, laughing at herself.

The appearance was all piffle, but it endeared Marlenna to many women who had not yet seen or heard her. She touched a chord and came across as a warm, genuine person. Her charismatic charm matched her ineffable beauty.

Shortly after her appearance on *The View*, Marlenna was asked and agreed to appear on the covers of *Vogue* and *Cosmopolitan*. Before agreeing to *Cosmo's* proposal, she checked with Reb who gave his enthusiastic approval. When the *Cosmo* issue hit the newsstands, there was the ever photogenic Marlenna looking scrumptious with her distinctive hairstyle, expressive eyes, and perfect come hither smile. She was barely clad in a dynamite dress displaying lots of cleavage as all *Cosmo* cover girls do. The lead story on the cover was "Beauty's Not Just for the Young: Meet Marlenna at 62." In the article, Marlenna revealed that in her mid-fifties, she had relatively minor cosmetic surgery to eliminate loose skin under her chin and to repair a slightly drooping eyelid, but other than that everything was her original equipment. The writer pointed out the obvious that Marlenna's original equipment looked spectacular. Soon women around the country were taking their copies of *Vogue* or *Cosmo* to their hair stylists and asking for a "Marlenna cut."

The most brazen proposal was made by *Playboy*, which offered to pay her a million dollars to pose the way pretty girls do in that venerable men's magazine. *Playboy* assured her its pictures would be as tasteful and glamorous as the photos they had published many years before of the fabulously beautiful and sexy Vikki La Motta, then fifty-one years old and ex-wife of Jake "The Raging Bull" La Motta, a great middleweight boxing champion during the 1940s and early 1950s. While both amused and flattered, Marlenna firmly declined *Playboy's* offer, which Reb would not have approved of in any event.

The publicity Marlenna attracted had turned her into a national celebrity. Tally Ho's polling revealed her to be extremely popular with both men and women, regardless of political affiliation. He estimated her star power benefited the McCoy–Duzmore ticket by 2 to 4 percentage points, which could be decisive in a tight election. With the possible exception of Jackie Kennedy in 1960, no presidential candidate's spouse had ever had a significant affect, positive or negative, on the candidate's polling numbers. Reb, of course, was not in the least bit surprised that his wife was a huge asset to his campaign.

Just before the second debate, a New York tabloid ran a titillating headline, "GOP Candidate Dated Porn Star!" The story went on to report that Reb had dated a woman named April Showers in college who went on to Hollywood where she starred in several erotic films. Her most infamous X-rated film was *Paris in April* with her costar Rod "The Human Dildo" Paris. When Hoppy excitedly informed Reb of the news, he could not fathom what it was about. Deeper into the story, the source revealed that April Showers's real name was April Honeysuckle, who mentioned to a friend that she had dated Reb when they both lived in Houston. The paper ran an old racy photo of April promoting *Paris in April*, side by side with a more recent and slightly more demure picture of her. When he saw the photos, Reb saw that the years had been good to April, as she was still quite attractive.

Reb had not been in touch with April since he graduated from Rice in 1973 and went off to grad school at SMU. Apparently, some time later, the enterprising April lit out for California and got involved in the adult movie business. As he recalled April from all those years ago, Reb could imagine that her sultry looks and uninhibited enthusiasm for sex made her a natural for such movies. He surmised that April saw X-rated movies as a way to gain entrée into legitimate show business. Indeed it was, because under her real name she went on to become a successful producer of several popular TV sitcoms.

The campaign immediately put out a press release stating Reb had, in fact, dated Ms. Honeysuckle while he was an undergraduate student at Rice, but had not had any contact with her in over forty years and had no knowledge about her career. When asked, the press spokesperson stated truthfully that Gov. McCoy had never seen the movie, *Paris in April.*

The evening this story broke, Reb sat down with Marlenna to fill her in. As usual, Marlenna took it in stride and found the humor in it. "Well, cowboy, I've learned a lot about you during your run for president. First, you inform me you diddled the Democratic VP candidate. Now, I learn you once dated a porn queen. How many more women have you poked who are going to share the good news with the world?"

Reb groaned and replied, "Well, at least, there were none after I met and fell in love with you, pretty."

"Maybe if you lose the election," continued Marlenna playfully, "and after your term as governor, we could create a new film genre: geezer porn."

"Yeah, how about an X-rated remake of the old Hepburn–Fonda flick, with a slight name change, *Scum on Golden Pond*, starring Reb Scum and Marlenna Pond?"

Laughing, Marlenna replied, "Hey, how come you get top billing? Can we begin rehearsals tonight?"

Tally Ho informed Hoppy and Jake that the porno queen revelation had not had an adverse affect in the polls, but the internal polling data found that the cumulative effect of the negative allegations, even though untrue and quickly disproved, was raising doubts with some voters. Of course, that is what the opposition hoped for, and Hoppy was sure there would be more to come. The closer to the election an adverse story surfaced, the less time was available to refute it and for it to be forgotten. Because Reb would not engage in similar behavior, the voters assumed Bucknell must be without baggage or the Republicans would expose it. Hoppy admired his candidate's character, but was exasperated that he could not unleash some defensive dirty tricks.

The second debate on domestic policy generated several sharp exchanges between the two candidates. Reb was first to be asked for specific spending cuts he would pursue if elected. He began by saying that there had to be an almost revolutionary change in the culture of the federal government, and it had to start at the top with the president. If he were elected, he would reduce the White House staff by 33 percent, eliminate all so-called administrative czars, and have the cabinet departments report directly to him or to the vice president.

He then ran down a lengthy list of proposed spending cuts with a brief comment on each that included: reduce the number of federal workers by 10 percent, and reduce individual compensation in excess of $75,000 per year by 10 percent to save $35 billion per year; eliminate farm subsidies to large corporations saving $20 billion per year; eliminate the education and transportation departments, instead making direct block grants to states saving $15 billion per year; eliminate energy subsidies to save $20 billion per year; modify the Social Security cost-of-living adjustment formula, increase to 69 the age to receive full benefits, and offer the option of personalized accounts, saving $50 billion per year within five years; radically overhaul government-provided health care by issuing vouchers to future beneficiaries, regulating insurance companies but allowing them to operate in all states, capping liability for malpractice, contracting with private sector auditors to root out fraud and improve internal controls, with 10 percent of documented savings used to compensate auditors, and disburse Medicaid in block grants to states for aggregate annual healthcare savings of at least $160 billion. Combined with his proposed $300 billion in annual cuts to the defense budget, Reb estimated these cost-cutting proposals would generate annual taxpayer savings of at least $600 billion. Time did not permit him to mention all his cost reduction ideas, but he invited voters to go to his website for a full explication of how he would rein in the cost of government by $850 billion per year.

In addition, Reb proposed to simplify the personal income tax code by creating a progressive flat tax with four rates: 10, 15, 20, and 25 percent. Deductions would be limited to dependents, charitable donations, mortgage interest on loan balances up to a million dollars, and contributions to a qualified retirement plan. State income and property taxes would no longer be deductible for federal tax purposes. All federal subsidies and special tax breaks for private sector businesses would be eliminated except the research and development tax credit. The corporate tax rate, however, would be reduced from 35 to 17 percent, and profits earned abroad would no longer be taxable in the U.S., which would encourage U.S. multinational companies to repatriate overseas earnings for investment here at home. Reb argued his tax reforms would make the U.S. more competitive with other developed countries, thereby increasing domestic jobs and economic growth. The estimated near term annual reduction in revenue to the government of these tax reform proposals was $60-75 billion, but the benefits of higher economic growth would more than offset this cost within three years.

Reb then proposed a new business income tax credit. He said there would be no higher priority in his administration than the education of disadvantaged children. He intended to provide a national program modeled off the successful Texas Opportunity for Disadvantaged Youth program he had introduced as governor and was now up and running in all of Texas's major cities. He pointed out how this voluntary program brought the private sector and educators together to establish weekend safe houses for the most vulnerable children and to improve school facilities and curricula. Reb argued that neither business nor the nation could afford any longer to allow the enormous potential of underprivileged children go to waste. These children were potential customers, employees, and productive citizens. America's most important and fundamental moral challenge was to do everything possible to afford every child a realistic opportunity to pursue happiness, a right with which all men and women are endowed by their Creator.

He also argued that it should be left to the individual states to decide whether or not to extract oil and gas reserves on and off shore, provided they adhered to the highest standards of environmental safety. He pointed out that Alaska, the Gulf of Mexico, Pennsylvania, and South and North Dakota possess vast untapped oil and gas reserves, the development of which would greatly improve the country's trade deficit by reducing oil imports and generating substantial royalty income to federal and state governments. He also supported incentives such as subsidized interest rates to encourage expanded nuclear energy capacity, both large megawatt facilities and self-contained underground reactors that could provide power for small cities.

Finally, as his time expired, Reb stated that the dollar must be a strong and stable currency to protect Americans from erosion of their purchasing power and for it to continue as the world's reserve currency. Toward this end, Reb proposed fixing the dollar's value to a basket of commodities for purposes of settling government to government foreign exchange transactions. He argued against a return to the gold standard, as some had proposed, because it was impractical and too inflexible. A broader commodity index, however, that included gold as a component, could restore stability and confidence in the dollar, provided the U.S. government took serious and irreversible steps to reduce its debt and deficits.

The debate moderator invited Gov. Bucknell to respond. Without saying what he would do to restore fiscal responsibility to government, he launched into an attack on Reb's proposals. Bucknell said:

> "From what we have just heard, if Governor McCoy had his way, he would overturn the longstanding contract between the federal government and the American people. Entire government programs would be slashed and some eliminated. He would radically revamp the entitlement

programs, leaving many elderly citizens without the safety net and dignity they have been promised in their retirement years. He even resurrects the discredited and risky idea of personalized or privatized Social Security accounts. Adding insult to injury, while average citizens would bear most of the burden of cuts in government services, Governor McCoy proposes a huge tax break for big business. Where is the justice and equity in that?

"Obviously the deficit must be reduced. First, we should focus on eliminating waste, fraud, and abuse. This is always talked about, but nothing is ever done about it. In my administration, this would be our primary focus, but we can't solve the government's fiscal problem only by cutting government spending. We also need to increase taxes on those who have benefited most from America's bounty. And we should also introduce a federal value-added tax to raise additional revenue. Governor McCoy, however, asks nothing of the wealthiest among us. In fact, he would cut taxes on the most profitable corporations, thereby providing a windfall gain to their wealthy shareholders."

Bucknell went on in this vein, never getting specific about what he would do to reform government spending, until his allotted time expired. It was now Reb's turn to rebut Bucknell.

"Governor Bucknell suggests that the cost of government can be brought under control simply by cutting that favorite triumvirate: waste, fraud, and abuse. Politicians have been extolling the virtues of this so-called strategy for years without material or lasting results. Fraud is certainly an enormous problem within the federal government, particularly within the Medicare system. I propose to attack this not with empty rhetoric, but by contracting a small army of professional auditors and investigative attorneys who will be paid a modest retainer fee with most of their compensation contingent on ferreting out and eliminating fraud. This is an investment I am confident will pay extraordinary dividends to taxpayers.

"My opponent offers few specifics on how he will rein in the cost of entitlements, but is quick to criticize my proposals falsely saying they will harm senior citizens. Anyone currently retired or over fifty-five years old will see only modest changes in their Social Security. The revised formula for calculating cost-of-living adjustments will not be as generous as in the past, but benefits will not be cut. Younger workers will have to work longer and receive lower benefits than their parents, but they will have at least ten to fifteen working years to build up private savings to augment their Social Security income.

"Governor Bucknell dismisses the idea of offering younger workers the option of placing a portion of their Social Security taxes in a personalized investment account. This can be structured in a way so as to minimize long-term investment risk, but offers the potential for higher investment returns than the government will pay. Best of all, a personalized account at the time of death can be passed on to a spouse or children. I am always amazed when Democrats berate this idea, especially since they proudly and erroneously proclaim they are the only party that looks out for African Americans. Unfortunately, the average lifespan for blacks is about six years shorter than for all other Americans. This means that African Americans, on average, benefit less from Social Security than other citizens, because they die at a younger age. In effect, African Americans subsidize everyone else's Social Security. This is indefensible. If personalized Social Security accounts were an available option, people fated to die relatively young would at least have a nest egg to pass on to their loved ones.

"Governor Bucknell advocates raising taxes to reduce the deficit. If I believed that would be effective, I would support higher taxes. The best and most efficient way to cut the deficit, apart from cutting spending, is to stimulate robust economic growth. The U.S. has been hamstrung by slow, occasionally negative, growth for eight years. Our unemployment rate still hovers above 9 percent. Raising taxes in this environment would only slow growth further. Given the fragile economy, the idea of a value-added tax on top of the income tax would throw the country into a deep recession, perhaps a depression. I agree with Winston Churchill's observation that, 'for a nation to tax itself into prosperity is like a man standing in a bucket trying to lift himself up by the handle.' To begin to solve our fiscal crisis, we need to slash government spending and stimulate the economy. Simplifying the personal income tax code and reducing corporate income taxes will give the economy a much needed shot in the arm. Strong economic growth will lead to more people being gainfully employed and increased revenue going to the federal government."

Each candidate was allowed five minutes for a closing statement. Based on a coin toss, Bucknell went first and competently summed up his position while attacking a number of Reb's proposals. Before the debate, Reb had outlined in his mind what he would say in closing. When Bucknell finished, Reb made the following statement:

> "In his wonderful and insightful book, *Democracy in America*, written nearly two hundred years ago, the Frenchman Alexis de Tocqueville wrote, 'The American Republic will endure until the day Congress discovers that it can bribe the public with the public's money.'
>
> "For the past half century, we the people and the politicians of both parties whom we have elected to represent us have engaged in an unsustainable spending orgy of guns, butter, and entitlements. In the process we have constructed an economic paper empire on a foundation of public debt that is no more stable or durable than a sand castle on a beach at low tide.
>
> "We have spent our way down a blind canyon to a precipice that stares into the abyss of fiscal ruin and political instability. Not since the country's founding has America's national security and future been so gravely threatened. There is no easy way out of our predicament. There are but two choices. Either we as a nation plunge soon or sooner, because there no longer is a later, into the abyss, or we turn away from this fate and end the financial profligacy that has brought us to this pass.
>
> "In the past, when the country's security was threatened, we faced an armed enemy. From Bunker Hill to Yorktown, from Pearl Harbor to D-Day, our American ancestors always unflinchingly mustered the courage, fortitude, and perseverance necessary to defeat our enemies with our blood and treasure. Today, the country's future is not challenged by an armed enemy on a foreign battlefield. No, America now faces a more daunting threat that will require not physical courage, but moral courage, because our enemy is reflected in a mirror.
>
> "We the people must return to the democratic republic of limited government inherited from our forefathers that was built on the bedrock virtues of thrift, self-reliance, honesty, and magnanimity. We, America's prodigal generation, are hereby called to restore America's freedom,

solvency, and security, and to bequeath the blessings of liberty to posterity. This we are honor bound to do if not for ourselves, then for all those Americans who come after us. Let us not fail to do our duty just as our ancestors never failed in their times of trial to fulfill their duty to themselves and future generations. Thank you."

30

The second presidential debate was won decisively by Reb, despite the tough medicine he prescribed to cure the country's fiscal ills. The political pundits were nonplussed by the apparent reaction of the voters. The Republican Constitution ticket opened a ten-point lead in a national poll of likely voters. Tally Ho's internal polling for the McCoy campaign indicated an eight-point lead, but Hoppy and Jake knew that lead could be erased within a week's time. They were worried about a surprise "scandal" being made public in the last few weeks before the election.

Both Bucknell and his running mate, Lola Lovett, stepped up their condemnation of McCoy's policy proposals trying to stir up fear among the electorate, but this was to be expected from a candidate trailing late in the campaign.

In the third week of October, an obscure political action committee with ample funding to run a television attack ad nationally charged that while CEO of Magnolia Petroleum & Chemical, McCoy had mismanaged the company forcing its sale, causing the elimination of many jobs, while he left with a golden parachute exceeding a hundred million dollars. The ad ended with a solemn and deep-voiced male announcer intoning, "This is the real McCoy nobody knows. Is this the kind of executive leadership America deserves or needs? Put America first in November. Vote Bucknell–Lovett."

The campaign's anti-defamation unit had anticipated an attack along these lines. Within days, the McCoy campaign ran an ad in all major media markets pointing out graphically that during the decade Reb was Magnolia's CEO, sales and profits doubled and quadrupled, respectively, and the stock price nearly tripled. When it became clear to Magnolia's management and directors that its employees and shareholders would be better served over the long term by a merger, Gov. McCoy shrewdly negotiated deals that protected jobs and realized top dollar for shareholders. True, as a large stockholder, McCoy left with a nine-figure payday, half of which he and his wife promptly donated to their charitable foundation. The ad closed with an upbeat female announcer saying, "This is the real McCoy every American needs to know, because he offers the real world business experience and successful leadership that is necessary to rescue the federal government from bankruptcy. Remember: McCoy–Duzmore. Freedom Fever – Catch It!"

Hoppy figured the attack on Reb's time as CEO of Magnolia would fire up voters who already had decided or were inclined to vote against him, but it probably would not be a significant factor with truly undecided voters. Tally Ho's polling showed an uptick in the Bucknell–Lovett ticket's popularity, but the McCoy–Duzmore lead was still outside the margin for error.

Of much greater concern was a story in the press a week later alleging that while serving in Vietnam, Reb was charged with disobeying a superior officer's direct order, a court-martial offense. As soon as the planted story appeared, ads went up on television and the Internet raising the question: "Is a man who disobeyed military orders on the battlefield qualified to be America's commander-in-chief?" The ad closed by saying, "Now we know why Gov. McCoy almost never refers to his military record, which, for honorable veterans, typically is a source of pride."

Throughout the campaign, just as he had done during his run for governor, he had intentionally downplayed his time in the army believing it was unseemly for politicians to wrap themselves in the flag of military service and patriotism. Moreover, his stint in the army when he was a teenager nearly fifty years ago, in his opinion, was not germane to his qualifications for office. Still, he was surprised and angered by this particular attack, which directly impugned his honor, and thought it revealed how desperate the Democrats were.

Hoppy and Jake believed this charge, if not refuted, could cost Reb a lot of votes among veterans and jeopardize the election. They immediately phoned Reb, who was campaigning on the West Coast, to discuss the allegation and decide how to respond to press inquiries. This bombshell was smothering the campaign's message.

To Hoppy's direct question as to the veracity of the allegation, Reb responded, "I did in fact disobey what I believed was an *unlawful* order to shoot innocent women, children, and elderly civilians in cold blood. I'll never forget that moment as long as I live. Following an investigation, I was exonerated. Fortunately for me, the story of the My Lai massacre in March 1968 belatedly became public in November 1969, while I was awaiting court-martial. Immediately, all charges against me were dropped, because it was evident an inexperienced martinet of a lieutenant had ordered me and my troops to massacre civilians, just as happened at My Lai."

Hoppy said, "Governor, I think we ought to get your story out to the press right away. It would probably be best if you held a press conference and shot down this absurd allegation. In fact, the truth is you were a hero who displayed mature judgment and the courage to do the right thing at great risk to yourself. All Americans love a story like this, and I love it when we can stick an opponent's dirty trick right up his ass."

Jake reflected on this and said, "I'd like to offer another approach for dealing with this. In three days, Reb, you are scheduled to address the Veterans of Foreign Wars. Originally, you were going to explain more fully your proposals for cutting the defense budget and military pensions. Why not also use the occasion to show this allegation to be the less than half truth it is? In the meantime, we will alert the press that you will confront this serious charge at the VFW convention, which will attract maximum media coverage."

"I like your idea, Jake," replied Reb. Hoppy signaled his support as well.

When Reb took the stage at the VFW event a few days later, the anger and discontent of the audience was palpable, although Reb did receive polite if brief applause when he was introduced. He first addressed the charge he had disobeyed direct orders in Vietnam, telling the veterans and nearly a hundred reporters what he had told Hoppy and Jake a couple days earlier. He also said he had requested the Defense Department to release his entire service record, including all relevant documents pertaining to the incident in which he disobeyed orders.

Next, Reb discussed his proposed deep cuts in the defense budget.

> "As president, I will not compromise America's national security, but it is imperative that we reorganize and downsize our military because the country is broke. I will challenge the military chiefs to set aside parochialism and work as a unified team to restructure the armed forces using far fewer resources while continuing to fulfill their mission of defending the United States. We no longer can afford to maintain a military establishment that can fight multiple wars simultaneously.
>
> "This leads me to another controversial proposal I have made to cut military pensions. Given the negative reaction to this idea, I almost think our military personnel would rather risk life and limb for their country on the battlefield than to accept a pension reduction for future service that will help their country get its fiscal house in order. For years,

military personnel, most of whom enter active duty between the ages of eighteen and twenty-two, have been able to retire after twenty years of service with an inflation adjusted pension equal to 50 percent of active duty pay. This pension formula is far more generous than any private sector plan of which I am aware. Under my proposal, an individual who enlisted in the military tomorrow would have to serve twenty-five years to receive a 50 percent pension. This is still a very generous retirement annuity for someone in their mid-forties.

"The foundation of our long-term national security has always been a fiscally sound government and a strong, growing economy. The men and women at the end of the spear bear the burden of battle in defending our great country, but what stands behind them is the might of America's superior technology and vast wealth. If we continue much longer running up trillion-dollar budget deficits on top of the $20 trillion in public debt the nation already has borrowed, and the $100 trillion in unfunded entitlement promises, soon we will no longer be a military superpower. The most serious war we face today is here at home, struggling to rein in our overspending. As in all America's shooting wars, we will rely on the military to do its part in the war here at home to restore fiscal solvency."

The applause Reb received at the conclusion of his remarks was much more enthusiastic than that which greeted him. He actually received a standing ovation, but sensed many remained skeptical of his proposed draconian cuts in the military's budget. This was borne out in a poll undertaken by Tally Ho several days later in which only 56 percent of veterans supported the Republican Constitution ticket. This did not auger well, because in most elections, the Republican candidate can count on winning 60–65 percent the veteran vote.

The media fact-checked Reb's version of the charge he disobeyed orders in Vietnam, and all but the most far left outlets acknowledged he had done the right thing. Several newspapers, Internet blogs, and cable news channels actually portrayed him as hero.

Duane Darby was livid over the disingenuous attack on his old friend and determined to create a political action committee to raise funds for an ad telling the true story of Reb's military record in Vietnam. Reb was unaware Duane was doing this. Duane knew Reb did not want to discuss, much less boast, about his war service. Nevertheless, Duane felt the American people needed to learn the truth about his dear friend who had heroically saved his life and the lives of many others on a godforsaken mountain in Vietnam many years ago. The political commercial featured Duane and several of Reb's other comrades in arms. They presented a factual account of his action that earned him the Distinguished Service Cross, the nation's second highest medal for valor. It also covered the full context of Reb's disobedience of orders, even though that incident occurred after Duane had returned stateside to recover from his battle wounds. He was able to locate several guys from Reb's platoon who witnessed that episode, and they told a moving story. All this was tastefully portrayed in a sixty-second commercial that ran nationwide.

Any objective person who saw the ad would conclude that Reb was an outstanding soldier who had displayed courage and character under enemy fire, and also when his commanding officer gave him an unlawful order. These are qualities most Americans want in their president. Reb suspected Duane was behind the commercial, but neither he nor Duane ever brought the subject up in conversation. Reb would have preferred not to have his military service made a campaign issue, but since his opponents injected it into the campaign, he was grateful his friends and supporters had set the record straight on his behalf.

Less than two weeks before the election, Reb and Conrad Bucknell met in debate for the final time in Philadelphia's Independence Hall on October 25. According to Tally Ho, the race had tightened, although Reb was still slightly ahead. More worrisome to Tally Ho than the popularity contest was the state-by-state breakdown, which indicated the McCoy Duzmore ticket was lagging in the only vote that counted, the Electoral College. Reb needed 270 electoral votes to win the presidency. If the election were held the day of the final debate, Tally Ho could be sure his candidate would win only 220 of the 270 electoral votes he needed.

The good news was states with 68 electoral votes were still too close to call. The bad news was that the Bucknell Lovett ticket had 250 electoral votes virtually locked up. The arithmetic was simple: Bucknell needed 20 more electoral votes to win, whereas McCoy needed 50 of the 68 still on the table. As Tally Ho pointed out, it was shaping up as one of those rare elections in which the candidate who wins the popular vote could lose the election.

Reb knew the last time that happened was in 2000, and prior to that, one had to go all the way back to 1888 when the incumbent president, Grover Cleveland, won the popular vote, but lost the electoral vote and the presidency to Benjamin Harrison. Cleveland avenged his loss four years later when he defeated Harrison, winning both the popular and electoral votes, to recapture the White House, the only president to serve two non-consecutive terms.

In 2000, Al Gore won the popular vote, but lost the electoral vote to George Bush when the latter narrowly won Florida by a margin of 537 votes. Gore tried every possible gambit to overturn the Florida vote, but in the end failed to do so. Ironically, Gore would have won the presidency and Florida's outcome would have been moot had he carried his home state of Tennessee. Reb could not recall any major party candidate ever losing his home state even when defeated in a landslide election. The people who knew Al Gore best concluded his opponent was the better candidate by a margin of more than eighty thousand votes. Reb thought this was an interesting insight that went virtually unmentioned in the bitter aftermath of that election. Reb vowed to himself that he would not challenge a controversial close vote in any state, even if the outcome of the election hung in balance. He did not lust for the presidency enough to subject the country to such a melodrama that would undermine the legitimacy of whoever ultimately won.

The day of the debate, Hoppy, Jake, and Tally Ho met with Reb and reviewed the polling data. Hoppy stated the obvious when he said, "Well, Governor, not to put any pressure on you, but a lot is riding on tonight's debate."

"Thanks for sharing that with me, Hoppy."

"Reb," spoke up Jake, "you have done very well in the previous debates. Tonight's topic is the constitutional convention and the Second Bill of Rights, which are the heart of your campaign. I'd say you've got Bucknell right where you want him."

"There's no question that I am eager to debate the subject," replied Reb, "but usually it is advantageous to be on the attack, as Bucknell surely will be, instead of being on the defensive. I will try to maneuver him into having to come up with an alternative to the Second Bill of Rights rather than simply attack it. I will have to establish that the status quo is no longer sustainable."

Tally Ho appeared to be deep in thought, which he usually was. "Governor, following the first two debates, you benefited from a bump up in the polls at Bucknell's expense. I see no reason for that not to happen again. Not that you can tailor your remarks to the undecided states, but if we can win tonight's debate, that might pull you ahead in those states. Four of those tossup states have petitioned Congress for a constitutional convention, so those voters should be disposed toward voting for you. I believe we have a reasonable chance to win most of the tossup states, and perhaps a few of the states currently in Bucknell's column are drifting toward you. Most surprisingly, Illinois is looking shaky for Bucknell. If we can wrench Illinois away from the Democrats, we will win for sure."

Hoppy said, "The itinerary for the cross country train tour will take us into Illinois twice, so we will have ample time to campaign across the state, which should improve the odds of pulling off an upset and winning 20 electoral votes. The problem is the Democratic machine controls Chicago and Cook County with an iron grip. They always wait for the Republican downstate counties to report their election results, so the Chicago machine knows how many votes they need to carry the state. Almost always the Democrats carry the state. Whoever said life is for the living never visited Chicago, where elections, at least, are for both the quick and the dead. So I won't get my hopes up too much, but we ought to give Bucknell a run for his money and force him to spend valuable time in Illinois the last week of the campaign."

That evening the debate moderator directed the first question to Reb, asking why he believed a constitutional convention was necessary. Anticipating the question, he launched into his prepared remarks.

> "I am both honored and humbled to be here tonight in Independence Hall where the Constitution was drafted by our Founding Fathers two hundred twenty-nine years ago. They created a democratic republic of limited government with enumerated powers. Being brilliant and savvy men of the world, they understood the propensity of many men to acquire and wield power over others. Therefore, the Founders endeavored to establish checks and balances that would ensure no undue concentration of power in any person, office, or branch of government.
>
> "It is important to remember that the Constitution and the federal government were created by the original thirteen sovereign states. Following heated debate in their respective ratifying conventions, the states voted to establish a republic whereby limited and specific powers as set forth in the new Constitution were delegated by the states to the federal government. The new government worked pretty much as the Founders envisioned early on, but with the passage of time and the events of history, power increasingly and ineluctably became concentrated in the federal government at the expense of the states. This process has accelerated

over the past seventy-five years, and today we the people are governed by a federal government that has aggrandized unto itself virtually unlimited and intrusive powers that have diminished individual liberty and emasculated the states.

"One purpose for establishing the Constitution, as stated in its Preamble, was to create a more perfect union. The Founders realized perfection in the affairs of free men is an ideal always to be pursued but never attainable. Therefore, the Founders made provision in Article V of the Constitution for amendments that the people might deem prudent and necessary in the future. Indeed, the first Congress proposed and the states ratified soon thereafter the first ten amendments known as the Bill of Rights. Since then, there have been only seventeen other amendments to the Constitution, all of which originated in Congress.

"The original states that ratified the Constitution feared, with good reason, the usurpation of powers by the federal government beyond those specifically delegated to it and, therefore, insisted on the Bill of Rights as a condition of ratification. The Bill of Rights, as we all know, guaranteed certain rights to the people by explicitly prohibiting the federal government from abridging them. Congress may make no law that: establishes or prohibits the free exercise of religion; abridges freedom of speech or of the press; denies freedom of assembly or the right to petition the government to redress grievances; infringes on the right to keep and bear arms; permits issuance of warrants without probable cause; deprives a citizen of life, liberty, or property without due process of law; or denies the accused of a speedy trial before an impartial jury. Given the relentless growth in the scope and power of the federal government and the numerous court battles citizens have fought defending these rights, does anyone believe they would be secure today without the Bill of Rights?

"The Ninth and Tenth Amendments are two of the most important amendments in the Bill of Rights. The Ninth Amendment states that the enumeration of certain specific rights shall not be construed as denying other rights retained by the people. The Tenth Amendment states that powers not delegated to the federal government by the Constitution, nor prohibited by it to the states, are reserved to the states or the people. These two amendments could not be more explicit in asserting that the federal government's powers are limited, yet both these amendments have been essentially disregarded by the government without objection by the courts. The unrestrained federal government we have today could not have happened had the Ninth and Tenth Amendments been respected and upheld.

"The checks and balances established by the Founders have been blurred, if not altogether erased. The federal government has grown so large and omnipotent that individual liberty has been gradually diminished and the sovereign states no longer serve as a counterbalance to the federal government. Moreover, the checks and balances among the three branches of government have been eroded, as Congress has ceded enormous power to the Executive, and the courts have generally upheld the government's expansion of power. In effect, rather than checking each other, all three branches effectively have conspired to enable the federal government to expand its reach and power with virtually no restraint. In the process, the government has run up staggering deficits, debt, and unfunded entitlement promises that will bankrupt the country and saddle future generations with the bill. In that event, our generation will have swindled future generations yet unborn of their posterity by condemning them to financial servitude.

"If we are to restore limited government, fiscal solvency, and individual liberty, there is no viable option other than the adoption of the amendments we call the Second Bill of Rights. If ratified, these amendments will restore the proper balance of power among the federal government, the sovereign states, and the people, as well as place the nation on a path to fiscal sobriety. Most importantly, our generation will have kept faith with the Founders' promise as stated in the Constitution's Preamble to secure the blessings of liberty to posterity.

"Congress is institutionally incapable of proposing amendments that would circumscribe its powers and prerogatives. Men and women in high office rarely, if ever, voluntarily yield their grasp of power. Fortunately, Article V provides that upon the application of two-thirds, or thirty-four, of the states, Congress shall call a constitutional convention to consider amendments. Amendments approved by a majority of states in convention will be referred to all the states for ratification. Upon ratification by three-fourths, or thirty-eight, of the states, amendments will be adopted and become part of the Constitution.

"Thirty states thus far have petitioned Congress to call a convention, and at least seven others have petitions pending in their state legislatures. We are on the threshold of Congress being required to call a constitutional convention, which is auspicious news for all freedom-loving Americans. A constitutional convention, I contend, is America's best and perhaps last chance to reaffirm liberty and limited government, and to restore the nation to solvency.

"To answer the question I was asked earlier: why I believe a constitutional convention is necessary, I reply for all the reasons I've just recited. There is one other reason. There has not been a constitutional convention since 1787, two hundred twenty-nine years ago. Surely it is not too soon to convene another."

Now, it was Bucknell's turn to speak.

"Governor McCoy as usual makes his case eloquently, but I disagree with his premise, as well as his remedy. We can't return to a simple government of limited powers that existed in the eighteenth and nineteenth centuries. The size of America's population, its diversity and demographics, advances in technology, and the role of the United States in world affairs make it impractical not to have a strong, powerful federal government. And for all the criticism of an overreaching government, America remains the freest country on earth. The urgent problems we face today are a sluggish economy and government deficits. These issues must be our highest priority, but limiting the federal government's power to address them would only make matters worse.

"The polls suggest the country is split on whether a constitutional convention is a good idea, and only 45 percent of those polled strongly support the proposed Second Bill of Rights. The Founding Fathers created a masterful Constitution that has stood the test of time and proven to be sufficiently flexible to accommodate the enormous changes in society and the country over the past two hundred years. I say, why fix something that isn't broken? There is a tremendous risk that a constitutional convention could approve all manner of amendments that reflect the passions of the moment, but would be unpopular or unworkable in the future. This is a risk not worth taking, in my view.

"Rather than tinker with the Constitution, which in the political realm is comparable to revising the Bible in the theological realm, we should focus our energy on solving the debt crisis and growing the economy thereby reducing unemployment. These problems can be tackled without amending the Constitution. In fact, time spent debating constitutional amendments that probably won't be adopted would divert us from the immediate challenges we face as a nation. In this election, the voters should choose those candidates who are committed to solving difficult problems, have the best ideas for doing so, and are willing to work with colleagues on both sides of the political aisle to reach compromise solutions."

The debate moderator turned to Reb and said, "Governor McCoy, you have two minutes to respond."

Reb glanced at the notes he had made during Bucknell's remarks and began his rebuttal.

"The principles of liberty and limited government are constant. They don't change because of societal or technological change. Limited government does not mean weak government, nor does it mean returning to the government we had in 1816 or 1916. What we have in 2016, however, is unlimited government. Every crisis, every problem that arises becomes yet another rationale for expanding the federal government. As government seizes more power and control over our affairs, there is a commensurate and inevitable decline in individual liberty. We may be the freest country on earth, but we are not as free as we should be or used to be.

"I agree with Governor Bucknell that the Constitution is not broken. But too many of the politicians elected and sworn to uphold the Constitution have irresponsibly and recklessly allowed government to expand far beyond its proper limits and to spend the country to the brink of bankruptcy. For decades, Congress and presidents of both parties have seen this fiscal train wreck coming and done nothing to avert it. Bitter, intractable partisanship makes meaningful reform impossible. Whenever one side tries to address entitlements, the other side yells foul. It is next to impossible to cut, much less eliminate, any government program.

"To believe our elected politicians will rein in government or permanently cut spending is the naïve triumph of hope over hard experience. One way to change this culture is to amend the Constitution by adopting the Second Bill of Rights. The other way to bring about behavior change is to wait for the inevitable financial collapse and ensuing depression. I prefer a few constitutional amendments to the alternative scenario.

"Finally, Governor Bucknell expressed his concern that a constitutional convention might run amok and pass ill advised amendments, or perhaps establish a new government. This notion betrays a lack of trust and confidence in the wisdom and common sense of the American people. The government belongs to the people, and I have great faith and confidence in their collective judgment. Too many members of Congress seem to believe the government belongs to them. Instead of acting as public servants, they behave as our public masters. Incidentally, if a constitutional convention were to approve a silly amendment, thirty-eight states would be required to ratify it. I am confident there will always be at least thirteen states possessed of wise and sober judgment that would not ratify a foolish amendment."

The remainder of the debate focused on the specific amendments in the proposed Second Bill of Rights. Interestingly, as each amendment was discussed, Bucknell did not take serious exception to any, yet he adamantly opposed the idea of convening a constitutional convention. Reb surmised that Bucknell did not want to appear inflexible or unreasonable on any particular amendment, but his apparently contradictory objection to a convention was driven by his legitimate fear that this would diminish the federal government's power. No doubt his fear was shared by virtually all Democrats and not a few Republicans.

As the debate drew to a close, the moderator asked Reb why the Second Bill of Rights was limited to seven amendments, and if there were any others he would like to see included.

Reb responded:

"The Madison Committee, which drafted the proposed Bill of Rights about three years ago, considered other amendments, but settled on the seven we've just discussed. We concluded the Constitution should not be cluttered up with a laundry list of amendments. Ideally, the Constitution should not deal with policy matters that legitimately fall within the purview of Congress and the Executive. Nor did we want to restrict the government's legitimate enumerated powers as defined in the Constitution. Our objective was to further perfect the Founders' master work by lending clarity to the proper scope and reach of government and to end the deleterious practice of elective careerism by instituting term limits for members of Congress. The country and the government are best served by citizen legislators committed to temporary public service instead of permanent incumbency.

"Several of the states that have petitioned Congress to call a convention have modified the Second Bill of Rights, others have proposed additional amendments. I think that is great and expect the constitutional convention to debate and decide on the final amendments to be sent to the states for ratification. I remain satisfied with the Second Bill of Rights as drafted. The only addition I might propose today would be an amendment prohibiting Congress from imposing unfunded mandates on the states or rescuing bankrupt states with financial bailouts. Unfunded mandates are unfair, and, in my view, unconstitutional. If the federal government, pursuant to its legitimate constitutional authority, chooses to mandate that the states take some action, the funds to do so should be provided by the government not the states. Finally, a state that has shortsightedly mismanaged its affairs to the point it is facing financial collapse should be required to work out its problems without financial assistance from the federal government."

Bucknell felt compelled to interrupt, saying:

"We can't allow a state to fail just as we did not allow GM to fail. The government provides financial aid to affected states when a hurricane hits or an oil spill occurs. There is no reason not to provide aid if a state cannot meet its financial obligations."

Reb responded:

"The financial bailout of an insolvent state creates a moral hazard and is probably unconstitutional. If states know the federal government will come to their financial rescue, what incentive do they have to act responsibly? How is it fair to Americans residing in financially sound states such as South Dakota, Indiana, or Texas, to name just three, to use U.S. taxpayer money to bail out, say, California or any other state? To compare a natural disaster to a state bailout is inappropriate. A natural disaster is unpredictable and outside a state's or anyone's control. It is an act of God. The bankruptcy of a state, however, is a manmade political disaster. Because state politicians created the disaster, they and their constituents should be held accountable for fixing it, not the rest of the American people. Finally, if the feds start bailing out states, whatever sovereignty they retain would be snuffed out, because the feds would effectively take over the state and place it in receivership. This, I submit, would violate the Constitution."

Reb was relieved when the debate ended. He was critical of his performance and felt he had done better in the earlier debates. But he could now look forward to the whistle-stop campaign by train and the end of the long campaign.

31

The waning days of the campaign were a frenzy of movement, activities, and speeches. The itinerary for the whistle-stop tour would take Reb and Marlenna to a number of states that were considering, but had not yet formally petitioned Congress to call a constitutional convention to consider the Second Bill of Rights. Achieving this objective, in his mind, took precedence over winning the presidency. He realized that almost all his ideas for reducing spending and reforming entitlements would not happen unless the Second Bill of Rights was adopted thereby compelling Congress and whoever was president to act.

Reb hoped to engender a groundswell of public and legislative support for the Second Bill of Rights in at least four more states to reach the magic number of thirty-four necessary to require Congress to call a convention. As it became increasingly clear this would be achieved, several prominent, long serving members of Congress began making bellicose statements that applications approved by thirty-four state legislatures was not sufficient to call a convention. Both houses of Congress would have to review each state's application and establish what rules and criteria must be met in order to convene a convention. Of course, this being a matter of great consequence, Congress would need to hold hearings. Because there were so many other priorities on the docket, the issue of a constitutional convention probably would languish in limbo for a long time.

Reb was troubled, but not surprised by the attitude of a few old dinosaurs doing everything possible to hang onto their power and prerogatives. For now, he decided it was not worth reacting publicly. Following the election, however, and as soon as thirty-four states had submitted formal applications to Congress, he would orchestrate a strategy to bring public pressure to bear on Congress to act. The tea party and the 9-10 party initiated by the Madison Committee would be the key to this effort.

At dawn the day after the final debate, the whistle-stop tour got underway with Reb and Marlenna ensconced in a luxurious private railroad car at the end of the train. The campaign had rented a Pullman car, number 7503, built in 1914 for the chief executive of the Pennsylvania Railroad. The car recently had been rebuilt and could travel up to 110 miles per hour behind a modern locomotive. The interior had been restored to its original splendor, including elegant wood paneling, a working fireplace in the parlor, a master suite featuring a full-size bed, marble bath with nickel fixtures and a shower, a full-size dining room table with adjacent kitchenette, and additional sleeping quarters to be used by staff and Secret Service personnel. The rear of the car had an open vestibule that permitted Reb to speak to crowds at stops along the way without leaving the car.

Advance campaign personnel were on hand at each scheduled stop touting the impending visit of the Republican Constitution Party's presidential candidate to build enthusiasm and ensure plenty of people were on hand when the FREEDOM FEVER – CATCH IT! Express pulled into the depot. At each stop, the candidate spoke for no more than fifteen minutes after being introduced by Marlenna, who always received a rock star greeting. Reb usually took several questions from the crowd, which displayed his humor, directness, and confidence in dealing with unscripted questions. The whistle-stop tour got off to an auspicious start.

Two days after the last debate, in his weekly column, Walter Rothmann endorsed Reb for the presidency:

> The country is fortunate to have two estimable men running for president this year. Either one is qualified for the job, to the extent any one person is fully prepared for the most powerful and difficult job in America, if not the world. This presidential campaign has been marked by uncommonly serious debate over the gathering fiscal storm that threatens the nation's future. Procrastination is no longer an option. Nor can we any longer tolerate political happy talk or doubletalk. Upon this election, like none other in my memory, hangs the future of America.
>
> Will we rein in government's feckless, reckless spending, thereby curbing our dependency on the nanny state, or will we demand the restoration of limited government and individual liberty, which implies greater self-reliance? If we choose the former, we will surely face in the foreseeable future financial collapse and potential political instability that will be devastating, not only for those who are most vulnerable, but for the cohesion of the country. If we choose the latter, our generation will endure bearable sacrifice, but we will have salvaged our honor by passing on to future generations of Americans the reasonable prospect of being free and able to pursue their happiness without an undue burden of debt inherited from their ancestors.
>
> Gov. Conrad Bucknell has sounded an uncertain trumpet. At times, he speaks in visionary terms, but at heart, he essentially wants to maintain the welfare state, only tinkering around the edges. Gov. Reb McCoy, however, has bluntly and at times eloquently stated the bleak fiscal situation the country faces. While he refuses to sugarcoat the magnitude of the problem, he offers a path to solvency and a bright future if the people choose it. He is a change agent who will shake up the status quo. He has elevated and framed the crisis America faces not only in constitutional, but also existential terms. Reasonable people may not agree with all the specific solutions McCoy has put forth for

addressing our impending national bankruptcy, but he at least proposes serious ideas for radically reforming a government in urgent need of reform.

The looming financial crisis has understandably received most of the media coverage during the campaign, but McCoy has also brought attention to the other historical turning point confronting the United States. Within a decade, China, and twenty years later India, will surpass the United Sates in terms of GDP, thereby ending our century-long preeminence as the world's largest economy. This will have momentous consequences, as McCoy has pointed out, and will require a reassessment of the appropriate role the United States should play in this brave, new world. McCoy has intimated the United Sates ought to model itself as a super Switzerland, but strongly allied with Europe and our own hemisphere, particularly Brazil.

His decade of experience as CEO of a major multinational company, his strategic vision, and his grasp of the fundamental reform the United States must undertake today in order to safeguard the nation's future prosperity in a rapidly changing world make McCoy the best choice for president to lead the country through the perilous times ahead.

McCoy has made the proposed Second Bill of Rights the centerpiece of his campaign. He has made a compelling case why this is a prerequisite to reforming government. Without it, there is scant hope the federal government will reform itself. What only a year ago virtually every political pundit predicted would sink without a trace into the mire of history may become reality. The odds now are better than even a second constitutional convention will be called, perhaps in 2017. Ratification of the Second Bill of Rights would be the most momentous and salubrious reaffirmation of liberty since the miracle in Philadelphia during the summer of 1787, and would auger well for the country's future. If that happens, Reb McCoy would deserve his country's gratitude, and the peal of a second liberty bell should be heard throughout the land."

After perusing Rothmann's column, Reb turned to Hoppy, who had decided to accompany the candidate on the whistle-stop tour, and said, "Well, it's great to have Rothmann in our corner. He's a pretty influential guy.

But I doubt he will offset the endorsements Bucknell has received from *The New York Times*, *The Washington Post*, and *The Los Angeles Times*."

"Governor," replied Hoppy, "anybody who reads the editorial pages of those papers is not going to vote for you anyway. Besides, you have the endorsement of a majority of the newspapers in between the East Coast and the left coast, and *The Wall Street Journal* is backing you. On the other hand, *The Springfield Sun*, your adopted hometown paper, has backed Bucknell. I think they like Lola Lovett better than you."

Reb laughed. He had insisted that the train stop in Springfield, Ohio, on its way north from Cincinnati to Columbus. Because Ohio was still too close to call and its 18 electoral votes were crucial to victory, the campaign allocated one-and-a-half days to the state during the whistle-stop tour.

"We should be in Springfield in another hour, Hoppy. Maybe my speech will change the editorial board's mind. What do you think?"

"Fat chance, Governor. But maybe you can win over some of the voters leaning Democratic. Who do the good folks of Springfield and Clark County love more: their favorite native daughter, Lola, or their favorite adopted son?"

The Secret Service had not liked the idea of the whistle-stop tour, because it complicated their mission of protecting Lone Star. In any campaign, the daily schedule of the candidate has to be made public to the press several days in advance, so people can be informed about and attend the rallies. When traveling by aircraft or in a vehicle, it is easier for the Secret Service to control the environment. A train, however, is more difficult to protect, because it travels a predetermined fixed route and is out in the open. Also, when the whistle-stop express pulls into a depot, the candidate is exposed on three sides to a potential assassin, because he addresses the folks gathered to greet him on the open vestibule at the rear of the private car.

Most campaign events are held in an enclosed space, or a sports arena, which is easier to secure.

There was heightened concern for Lone Star, because, over the previous two weeks, several non-specific threats against him had been received that implied an attack might be attempted somewhere along the route of the whistle-stop tour. The Secret Service never knew how serious a threat was and, therefore, had to treat all as deadly serious. Accordingly, local law enforcement was alerted to be on hand in force at each scheduled stop, the rails ahead of the train were scouted, and investigators in Washington did all they could to anticipate an attack and if possible run to ground would-be attackers.

The lead agent responsible for protecting Reb requested an additional agent be assigned to his protective detail for the duration of the whistle-stop tour. This brought the contingent of agents protecting the candidate and his wife to six. At the lead agent's insistence, Reb reluctantly agreed to wear a protective bullet-resistant vest under his shirt and suit jacket whenever he appeared on the rear platform to deliver a speech. On these occasions, Marlenna was asked to remain inside the car, so the agents could focus their entire attention on Lone Star. If an attack were attempted at a whistle stop, it would probably occur early to midway through his speech when he was most exposed and all attention was focused on him. If he made it through the speech without incident, he would ask Marlenna to make a quick appearance, wave to the crowd, and retreat into the railroad car. The sides and windows of the ninety-ton car were bulletproof, and its undercarriage could withstand the blast of a substantial explosive device.

Apart from security personnel, only Hoppy was made aware of the threats. Reb decided not to tell Marlenna to avoid causing her distress, although she was immediately perplexed, then concerned when he told her she would not precede or accompany him on the car's vestibule during his remarks. On schedule at 11:30 a.m., the train pulled into Springfield stopping on the east side of Fountain Square in the heart of downtown. Alongside the train was a six-story upscale hotel. On the west side of the square stood the imposing three-story, brick-and-stone City Hall and Market Building, erected in 1890 and converted into a museum of history a quarter century ago. An enormous Romanesque structure a city block long with a one-hundred-fifty-foot clock tower at its east end fronting Fountain Square, it was the tallest building in the city.

An overflow crowd numbering perhaps six thousand filled the entire square between the buildings spilling across the railroad tracks behind the train. Police officers were everywhere. Three Secret Service agents were strategically positioned around the area, two were standing at the rear of the private rail car, and the lead agent was just inside the car. A sweep of the City Building and the hotel had been completed an hour before the train arrived and those buildings had been ordered evacuated until the train departed.

At 11:35 a.m. following the mayor's introduction, Reb stepped out onto the open vestibule's platform to uproarious cheers that continued for several minutes. Realizing his requests to stop their cheering were futile, he simply began his remarks over the train's public address system.

> "Thank you, Springfield. It is wonderful to be back in America's heartland and the hometown of my adolescence. Judging by your warm greeting, I assume you all are not from the local newspaper."

Boos and groans erupted as Reb publicly tweaked the paper for endorsing his opponent. Continuing, he said:

> "As most of you know, as a young boy I lived with my grandmother on her farm she named Hillcrest on Limestone Street, just south of I-70. I went to grade school here, rode a horse we kept on the farm, and played baseball in the summer, perhaps with some of you.
> "I believe you also know it's been reported that I dated my vice presidential opponent, Senator Lola Lovett, when we were in high school. Because Lola was born and raised

here, I can understand why she is very popular in these parts. But I wish to remind you that both candidates on the Republican Constitution Party ticket have connections to Springfield. Not only did I spend much of my youth here, but my running mate, Governor Lillian Gish Duzmore, is a distant cousin and namesake of one of Springfield's most famous native daughters. As some of you may know, the original Lillian Gish was one of the first great Hollywood stars during the era of silent movies. From my perspective, both presidential tickets have strong sentimental ties to Springfield. Therefore, rather than cast your vote based on sentimental reasons, vote for the ticket with the best ideas for restoring limited government and liberty, and bequeathing to your grandchildren and their grandchildren an America as wonderful as the country we inherited from our ancestors."

As Reb spoke, an unseen figure high above the crowd positioned himself by a window inside the City Building clock tower on the floor just below the east-facing clock. He was a professional assassin equipped with a high-powered sniper rifle and scope now aimed at his target, Gov. Reb McCoy. Over a period of eight years, the sniper had killed at least sixteen men and one woman on three continents. His usual fee was one million dollars deposited into a numbered Swiss bank account. The sniper had never failed to kill his target and had never been arrested, even for a traffic violation.

The sniper never knew and didn't care who contracted for his services, or why they wanted a target eliminated. Most of his targets were men involved in a criminal enterprise that probably was in competition with whoever sought out his services. Only three victims were politicians, all mid-level figures in third world countries. Until now, he had never hired out to kill an American politician. Where his victims were concerned, he was bereft of emotion, concern, or remorse, except after the one woman he had killed. When he had sighted her in his scope, he nearly aborted the hit. From then on, he refused any contract to kill a woman.

He always dealt through a trusted middleman with whom he never socialized or acknowledged if their paths crossed in public. When he was wanted for a job, the middleman would contact the sniper via an innocuous email that contained the time and place they were to meet. His assignments were usually received in the confessional of a large Catholic Church in a major city. The middleman assumed the role of priest, and the sniper was the penitent.

On being informed his target was the Republican Constitution Party presidential nominee, the sniper demurred. The handler replied, "I understand, my son. If you confess to this sin, your penance will be *Hail Mary* twice."

The sniper understood this to mean he would be paid twice his usual fee, or two million dollars. He responded to his "priest" handler, "Yes, Father, I accept my penance."

With that, the "priest" handler passed a slip of paper under the confessional screen to the sniper, which contained the words, "during whistle-stop train tour, site of your choosing, schedule typically made public three days in advance."

After stepping out of the confessional and making the sign of the cross while bowing his head before the altar, the sniper exited the church and promptly disposed of the now shredded note. Two weeks later and two days before the campaign train was scheduled to arrive in Springfield, the sniper was there to formulate his plan. He was a survivor in a most dangerous profession because of his meticulous attention to detail.

The city was abuzz with talk and excitement about the candidate's visit. The sniper easily learned precisely where the train would stop and the crowd would gather. After casing the City Building, which sat adjacent to the railroad tracks, he determined that an upper floor of its clock tower, which for years had been closed above the third floor and accessible only to maintenance personnel when necessary, provided the best vantage point for taking out the target who would be in the sniper's direct line of fire while standing on the platform of the open vestibule during his speech. After completing his reconnaissance of the City Building and surrounding area, the sniper departed for Columbus where he stayed in a hotel finalizing his action plan until returning to Springfield late on the night before the hit.

The sniper had chosen Springfield to fulfill his contract, because it was a medium-size town with a smaller police force than a large city like Cleveland or Chicago. The set-up was not ideal, because there was only one possible escape route, the same one he would use to gain access to the clock tower. The sniper assumed five Secret Service agents would accompany the target. Three would be body men who would never stray far from the candidate and his wife. The remaining two would be somewhere on the square and likely would rush the east tower after he got off his shot. The sniper figured to make his escape before the agents could reach him, and even if they did, he thought there was an even chance he could take them both out before they took him down. He expected the local police to be in chaos trying to control a panicked crowd and not focused on the assassin.

The City Building had been swept, evacuated, and locked up the day before McCoy's arrival. But the local police neglected to post a guard at the west entrance. That night the sniper disabled the lock in a manner that would not be detected, climbed the west tower to the third floor and gained access to a ladder leading to the narrow, four-foot-high passageway that ran the four-hundred-fifty-foot length of the building under its pitched roof. Wearing an outer coat, he carried with him his rifle in two pieces, a scope, a small handgun with silencer, glass cutters, two suction cups, four oatmeal cookies and a candy bar, two bottles of water, two Ziploc bags, and a large trash bag. He carried no identification on his person, having left counterfeit documents in his locked rental vehicle parked three blocks away. He arrived at the east tower on the floor beneath the clocks at midnight and settled in for the nearly twelve-hour wait until his target's train pulled into town.

The Secret Service asked the police to sweep the building once again, especially the clock tower, an hour before the FREEDOM FEVER – CATCH IT! Express arrived. A young officer was ordered to carry out this assignment. The officer went to the top floor of the clock tower and began working his way down floor by floor. When he reached the floor beneath the clocks, he almost passed by the room where the sniper was located, because, unlike the other rooms, its door was locked. After a moment's hesitation, he took his pass key and opened the door. The moment he stepped into the room, the sniper shot the officer between the eyes with his silenced handgun, killing him instantly.

After dragging the officer's body into the room and securing the door, the sniper grabbed his radio and read his nametag. He had overheard the officer communicating with his police captain twice. With a natural ability to imitate speech patterns, the sniper was confident he could convince the captain he was Officer Bates.

"Bates, advise your position and security status. Over," barked the captain.

The sniper replied, "Captain, Bates here. I'm descending from second floor to ground floor. Clock tower secure. Over."

"Okay, Bates. When you've completed your sweep, report to the north side of square and join other officers there on the perimeter. Over."

"Roger that, Captain. Over and out."

The sniper held his breath a moment to listen for any suspicion the captain might express. There was none. He left the radio on to hear the communications among the police officers on the ground, so he could be alerted if there were any sign he had been detected.

Ten minutes later, the captain bellowed, "Bates, have you cleared the building? You should have reported in by now. Over."

Thinking fast, the sniper grabbed Bates's radio and answered, "Sorry, Captain. Thought I heard something on the ground floor in the museum, so I investigated. Everything is secure. Will exit west door shortly and move to the square. Over."

After a pause, the captain said, "Okay, get moving. The train has arrived. Over."

"Yes, sir, Captain. Over and out."

The sniper heaved a sigh of relief and returned to his position at the window. He had cut out and removed a small section of glass at the bottom right corner of the window using the glass cutters and the suction cups. Through the open space he aimed his rifle. He wanted to wait till McCoy had spoken for several minutes before taking him out. He could hear his voice over the loudspeakers, but couldn't make out the words. The room was getting pretty rank. Having been holed up there for nearly twelve hours, he had had to defecate in the plastic trash bag, and urinate several times into the Ziploc bags and the now empty water bottles.

McCoy was obviously now into the substance of his speech. Every so often he would gesticulate with his arms to emphasize a point. He had the entire crowd's rapt attention and was apparently a very good speaker. He appeared to speak without notes, which impressed the sniper. Now was the time to complete his assignment. As he aimed, the sniper realized he would not have a head shot. The roof of the rail car extended over the vestibule platform forming a canopy. Because Reb was tall, the canopy obscured his head from the sniper. The only sure way to kill someone was with a head shot, but this was not an option. The sniper would have to aim for the torso and try to time his shot when McCoy raised his right arm to gesture to the crowd.

The moment came twelve minutes into Reb's speech. The sniper aimed down at his target. It was a steep angle shot, but from the distance of about two hundred feet, he could not miss. He squeezed the trigger.

A loud crack suddenly echoed throughout the square below. Simultaneously, Reb was lifted off his feet and knocked to his left almost off the rail car's platform. The Secret Service agent closest to Reb spoke urgently into his mouthpiece, "Lone Star down! Lone Star down!"

There was instant pandemonium, the crowd scattering in all directions as if there had been a jail break. The local police had their hands full trying to keep people under some semblance of control.

The three Secret Service agents closest to Reb rushed to him and pulled him into the railroad car. Marlenna leapt to his side. The lead agent radioed to the engineer to start the train. The deputy agent, who was across the square in front of the hotel, could tell from the direction Reb fell that the shot had to have come from the City Building. He looked up at the clock tower and thought he saw movement in a window just below the east clock. He ordered his two colleagues positioned on the square to enter the City Building's main doors and ascend the clock tower. The deputy agent then ran at full speed the city block distance to the west end of the building to prevent the shooter from trying to escape via that exit.

When he got there, he saw that only two matronly meter maids were posted at the west exit to keep anyone from entering the building. Because the police captain believed Officer Bates had swept and secured the building, and he needed all his police officers on duty in or near Fountain Square, no armed officers were stationed there who could assist the deputy agent. While disabling the door lock, he ordered the meter maids to call for reinforcements and then entered the building. The elevator had been secured. The deputy agent dashed up the stairs to the third floor and saw the ladder that accessed the attic.

By the time the deputy agent reached the west end of the third floor, the agents climbing the clock tower on the east end reached the sniper's lair. They found only the body of Officer Bates, the sniper's bodily excretions, and the rifle. Before the agents had reached the third floor, the sniper had descended the tower and entered the narrow passageway that ran the length of the roof above the third floor to the building's west end.

Dormer windows allowed intermittent natural light into the passageway. The deputy agent heard the sniper hurrying toward him and hid in the niche of a dormer window. When the sniper was thirty feet away, the deputy agent shouted, "Halt! Secret Service! Drop your weapon! On the floor, face down, hands on your head!"

The sniper instantly realized there was a sixth agent on McCoy's Secret Service detail. He fired two shots from his silenced handgun that missed. Before he could fire again, the deputy agent stepped out of the dormer recess and shot the sniper dead. He had wanted the sniper alive, but had no choice. As the sniper collapsed to the floor, the other two agents arrived on the scene.

While the sniper was tracked down, Reb was taken to the bedroom suite in the private rail car and placed on the bed. He was in severe but bearable pain. Marlenna hovered over him trying to give comfort and hold herself together. Reb looked up at her, smiled and said, "Hey, baby, why the tears, are you okay?"

"Oh, Reb, of course I'm okay. But we have to find out how badly you're hurt."

"I feel like a horse kicked me in the ribs. I guess whoever did this isn't voting for me."

Marlenna was relieved he was making light of the situation trying to ease her anxiety. When she sat down beside him on the bed, her dress slid up above her knee, and Reb immediately placed his hand on her thigh gently rubbing her skin. This was a relief, because, under the circumstances, if he noticed her leg, she was quite sure he was not terribly hurt.

After moving a half mile, the train was considered far enough from the scene of the attack and a possible second shooter that it was ordered to stop. A paramedic attended to Reb. His jacket, shirt, and bullet-resistant vest were removed. The rifle bullet had penetrated the outer layers of his protective vest, which dispersed and dissipated its force. Reb suffered mild blunt force trauma leaving him severely bruised and probably with two cracked ribs. Without the vest, he would certainly have been killed. X-rays and a more thorough medical examination to determine the extent of any internal injuries would be required to confirm the paramedic's diagnosis. An ambulance was on the scene by now to transport Reb and Marlenna to a nearby hospital.

On the way to the hospital, Reb asked the lead agent accompanying him, "Was anyone else hurt?"

The lead agent replied, "Yes, sir. I'm sorry to report that a local police officer, Rick Bates, was killed by the sniper."

Reb wanted to know the details and asked for information on the officer's family.

ER doctors confirmed that Reb had suffered one cracked and one bruised rib, but no internal bleeding or other injuries. He would be in pain for several weeks and have to be taped tight around the torso, but with over-the-counter painkillers, he would be able to resume campaigning. Marlenna was prescribed an anti-anxiety drug to calm her nerves.

Reb called in Hoppy, and they decided to board the train, cancel the rest of that day's stops, and head directly for Chicago. He would resume the whistle-stop tour there. A press release was put out along with a couple photos of Reb smiling and flashing the A-OK sign. Before departing Springfield, Reb insisted on talking to the police chief to inquire if he could visit the downed officer's widow. The chief said the young mother of two children was understandably in shock, but thought the governor's gesture was very thoughtful and gracious.

The Secret Service agents commandeered a police SUV and drove Reb and Marlenna to the home of Officer Bates. Reb paid his respects to Mrs. Bates and told her how sorry he was that her husband had sacrificed his life courageously trying to defend the life of a stranger.

Mrs. Bates, a lovely twenty-six-year-old woman, now widowed with children ages four and six, replied through her tears, "Thank you, Governor McCoy and Mrs. McCoy. You are very kind to take the time to pay your respects. We always knew that being a police officer was at times a dangerous profession, but Rick loved his work. He also admired you very much, Governor. The radio reported that you were shot. Is that true? Are you okay?"

By now Reb and Marlenna were fighting back tears. This young woman, still in shock trying to absorb the devastating news her husband had been killed in the line of duty, was concerned about the well-being of the stranger standing before her.

Reb said, "I'll be fine, Mrs. Bates. Is there anything we can do for you?"

"No. Thank you so much for your concern. It's somehow comforting to meet the man Rick was helping to protect and knowing that you care."

"May God bless you, Mrs. Bates. I will leave a phone number that will place you in direct contact with me if I can be of any help."

As they left the Bates home, Reb asked the police chief if he thought Mrs. Bates needed any financial help. The chief replied that she had a good job with Honda in Marysville, Ohio. Also, there would be insurance, a modest widow's pension, and a fundraiser to set up a trust for the children's care and education. Reb told the chief he and Marlenna would be donating $250,000 to the trust fund, but he asked that Mrs. Bates not be told. The chief expressed his appreciation for such a generous gesture and assured Reb the gift would remain anonymous. A check arrived a few days later.

The press worldwide headlined the attempted assassination. There was much speculation about who might order such an audacious attack and what their motive might be. The answer probably would never be known. The sniper's identity documents found in his rental vehicle were fraudulent, and there was nothing to link him to his "priest" handler. The trail went cold. Both wealthy, powerful liberals committed to big government and wealthy, powerful conservatives opposed to deep cuts in the military feared Reb's election. Wall Street and European bankers probably viewed Reb as a threat to their interests. There also was conjecture that Mexican drug kingpins believed that if Reb won the White House, he would secure the border with Mexico, thereby severely curtailing the illicit drug business.

The sniper was described as swarthy, approximately age forty, and obviously having been in superb physical condition. In addition to the bullet that killed him, the autopsy revealed what probably were two old bullet wounds, one in the left leg and another in the right lower abdomen. Perhaps the sniper had served in a military service.

The FBI, CIA, and Interpol were enlisted to determine the true identity of the sniper and find out who his associates were. Apart from his fingerprints and a plane ticket found in the rented vehicle that would have taken him from Columbus to New York, there wasn't much to go on. Interpol reviewed its unsolved assassinations to see if there were similarities in modus operandi, but nothing concrete turned up. Inside the sniper's pocket was found $5,000 in cash and a safety deposit box key that was traced to a bank in Baltimore. The safety deposit box had been rented under an assumed name and contained information on a numbered Swiss bank account that had a balance in excess of $9 million. Deposits totaling $19 million had been made over a number of years, each for a million dollars, except the last, which was for $2 million. Investigators hit a deadend with this discovery.

Of course, as soon as the sniper's "priest" handler read the newspapers about the failed contract hit, he arranged to destroy his computer hard drive and establish a new email account. He was confident there was nothing to tie him to the sniper or the case. The group that ordered the hit approached him through a cutout to discuss making another attempt on McCoy's life, but the "priest" handler said that would be far too risky, because the candidate's protection for the remainder of the campaign would be elevated almost to the level afforded a president.

Reb never speculated aloud on who might have tried to kill him. He knew he was a threat to many powerful interests at either end of the political spectrum who benefited from maintaining the status quo. The Second Bill of Rights, if ratified, would reorder radically the balance of government power. In that event, many politicians and special interests would see their power and wealth greatly diminished. Moreover, if elected, Reb's stated policy proposals for curbing government spending would likewise gore a lot of powerful oxen. Reb had no desire to be a martyr to his crusade to secure liberty's blessings for posterity, but he also would not be scared off or otherwise deterred from his mission.

32

By the time the train reached Chicago nine days before the election, Marlenna and Reb's doctor convinced him to cancel the whistle-stop tour. The rocking motion of the train aggravated his rib-cage pain, and the bedroom suite and bathroom in the private car did not offer enough space for him to maneuver comfortably. His recovery and comfort would be facilitated by staying in hotel suites and traveling by air to campaign events. Hoppy and the staff immediately began to revise the campaign itinerary for the last week, but endeavored to schedule appearances at as many places as practical where the train had been scheduled to stop.

Reb left the revised itinerary in Hoppy's hands, except that he wanted to attend the funeral for Officer Bates in Springfield without any press attention. Four days after the attempted assassination, Officer Bates was laid to rest in beautiful Ferncliff Cemetery where Reb's maternal grandparents were buried near a memorial marker honoring his parents. Reb and Marlenna attended the private church service and the interment without attracting public attention. A local reporter spotted Reb in the back of the church and tried to approach him at the cemetery, but the Secret Service held him at bay. Immediately after the funeral, Reb flew off to the next campaign event.

Before returning to Springfield for the funeral, Reb sat down for an extended interview with Katie Chicklet, the CBS news anchorwoman. Her first question to him was, "Governor McCoy, do you have any idea who would want to have you killed? And how has the experience affected you?"

"To your first question, I have no idea. I can only speculate that some individual or group feels threatened by the possibility I might be elected. After all, I have left no doubt that I plan to shake up the status quo. Anyone fully invested in the status quo probably doesn't relish having me become president. Regarding your second question, the experience has left me with one bruised and one cracked rib that are still pretty painful, but I feel better every day and am sprinting to the finish line. I was lucky, and I'm thankful I was wearing a protective vest."

"Do you think there was a conspiracy behind the attempt on your life?"

"Well, the hit man was obviously a professional. Therefore, someone hired him. Two or more people involved in planning and carrying out a criminal activity would seem to fit the definition of conspiracy."

Sensing that McCoy didn't want to discuss this topic any further, Ms. Chicklet changed the subject. "Governor, what do you find so wrong with the Constitution that has served the country so well for so long that compels you to advocate making major changes to it?"

Reb replied, "I think the Constitution is a marvelous document, and I find no fault with it. I do find fault, however, with all the politicians elected to uphold the Constitution who have failed to so. The Founders and the original sovereign states established a limited federal government of enumerated powers with all other powers residing with the people or the states. Today, we have a federal government of virtually unlimited powers intruding relentlessly in most every aspect of daily life without regard for the Constitution. Consequently, there is an imbalance in the Republic whereby the federal government usurps more and more power at the expense of the states and individual liberty. Moreover, the government has spent and promised so far beyond its means, we are headed for financial collapse if we don't take hold of our fiscal affairs. The amendments proposed in the Second Bill of Rights aim to further perfect the Union the Founders created by reaffirming their governing principles."

"But you propose adding seven amendments to the Constitution. And to do so, you have been campaigning hard to see that a constitutional convention is called to consider these amendments. All previous amendments originated within Congress. Why do we need a constitutional convention, and what would prevent it from throwing out the Constitution and replacing it with something else?"

"Well, Katie, we need a constitutional convention, because the Congress will never initiate the amendments I believe are necessary to reign in government power and spending. Congress is the fox in the Constitution's hen house, if you will. A fox can't restrain itself from going after the hens, just as Congress can't restrain itself by voluntarily surrendering any of its power. The fox and the Congress are obeying, respectively, their genetic and institutional instincts. It would be futile to try to change the nature of a fox or of Congress. The only practical way to amend the Constitution with the Second Bill of Rights is through a convention of the states. It's theoretically possible, but highly improbable, that a convention would try to replace the Constitution. Even if it voted to do so, three-fourths of the states would have to ratify any changes recommended by the convention in order to become the law of the land."

"Why do we need seven amendments, and if they were all adopted, wouldn't that result in a federal government that is too weak?"

"The seven amendments that constitute the proposed Second Bill of Rights would not in any way limit or undermine the legitimate powers of the federal government. They would merely clarify the boundaries of those powers and reinforce individual liberty. They also would restore the sovereign states to a position where they can act as an effective check on the federal government. There is virtually no check today on the federal government's reach and power. The legislative and executive branches encourage, aid, and abet the federal government's relentless expansion and the courts generally don't interfere. Who is there to stand up to Congress, or the president, or the federal courts? Even the so-called mainstream press has essentially abdicated its once proud role acting as an independent check on government, because most journalists believe in a monolithic federal government. The Second Bill of Rights would make it possible to restore proper constitutional balance and secure liberty's blessings to posterity."

"Many people contend that the real motive behind the proposed Second Bill of Rights is to drive a stake through the heart of liberalism and progressivism, and to enshrine conservative values in our Constitution. How do you respond to that?" Ms. Chicklet asked.

"I fear progressivism is driving a stake through the heart of our democratic republic by bending, twisting, and stretching the Constitution to the breaking point. I view myself as conservative, but most of all, I am a constitutionalist. Even if one concedes progressives are well intentioned and have many good ideas, the problem is that progressivism places virtually no limits on what government legitimately can do. That not only diminishes individual liberty, replacing it with an ethos of dependency, but it has taken the country to the verge of bankruptcy. This has undermined our national security and cast a shadow on the prosperity of future generations of Americans. And both parties are culpable. I have no problem with progressive, conservative, or moderate politicians, as long as all politicians legislate and govern within the framework of limited government established by the Constitution."

"You say you would not raise taxes to deal with the country's deficits. Does that mean you would rely exclusively on spending cuts to balance the budget? If so, isn't that inherently unfair?"

"The only chance we have to restore financial solvency is to cut spending, reform entitlements, and grow the economy. Raising taxes in a sluggish economy with unemployment above 8 percent for eight years now would be counterproductive. For years the economy grew fast enough, on average, to keep up with increased government spending. But those days have been gone for over a decade now. Robust, sustained economic growth is a win-win for government. It puts people back to work, thus reducing expenditures on unemployment benefits, food stamps, Medicaid, and welfare, while increasing tax revenue. In my opinion, the only time it makes economic sense to consider raising taxes is when the economy is booming to the point of becoming overheated. We need to reform the tax system, eliminate crony capitalism, and stabilize the dollar.

"Do you believe Social Security is constitutional?"

"Yes. The Supreme Court has said it is. Social Security is a great program that needs to be reformed and made better. It provides dignity and independence to senior citizens and allows them to retire while they are still young enough to enjoy life. It also largely relieves many children of the worry and financial burden of providing for their elderly parents. But the benefit structure can no longer be sustained. To save the program, the benefit formula will have to be made less generous, and the retirement age needs to be increased consistent with the longer average lifespan of Americans. These changes will make Social Security actuarially sound. We all have to live within our means, even the federal government."

"You have been quoted as saying that the closest thing to eternal life here on earth is a federal government program. Name one federal program you would cancel and why."

"There are many that should be canceled or scaled back, but one that makes no sense to me is the ethanol subsidy program, which really subsidizes crony capitalism for no benefit to the taxpayers. In fact, it hurts people, especially those who are economically disadvantaged. This is all wrapped in the cloak of developing renewable energy to wean us off fossil fuels and save the planet. Deriving ethanol from corn is inefficient. Some experts claim the energy required to produce a gallon of ethanol exceeds its energy output. Other experts say there is a net positive energy output, but it is insignificant. Without government subsidies, most of which go to huge corporations, and mandates to blend ethanol with gasoline, this program would not be economically viable. Worst of all, we are misdirecting farmland away from producing corn for food to growing corn for fuel. This raises the cost of food to consumers. Finally, U.S.-produced ethanol will never displace more than 5 percent of our gasoline consumption, and it generates its own pollutants that may be as bad as fossil fuel emissions. Anyone who is informed and honest knows this all to be true, but politically the ethanol subsidies are untouchable."

"Why are they untouchable?"

"Because farmers and big agribusinesses in farm states like the subsidies, and senators from those states trade votes for programs supported by senators from other states in exchange for perpetuating the ethanol program. Also, Iowa has enormous influence on the presidential nominating process. Few candidates who want to do well in Iowa pledge to kill the ethanol program. I learned that firsthand when I lost the Iowa caucus."

"Brazil has a successful ethanol industry. Why can't the U.S. replicate what they have done?"

"Brazil's ethanol industry, which also is heavily subsidized by the Brazilian government, dates back at least forty years when it was a struggling third world country with very little indigenous oil. Ethanol was a way to reduce oil imports, which had to be paid for with precious hard currency. Instead of corn, Brazil uses sugarcane to produce ethanol. This is a more efficient process than corn-based ethanol. Even so, without government subsidies, Brazil's ethanol is not competitive with gasoline, especially now that Brazil has discovered and is exploiting huge offshore oil reserves. By the way, the combination of using sugarcane as the feedstock, plus relatively cheap land and labor, makes Brazil's ethanol, delivered in the U.S., much cheaper than American ethanol. But the U.S. government imposes a tariff of fifty-four cents per gallon on ethanol imported from Brazil to protect our subsidized domestic producers. If ethanol is so important to our energy future, why not buy it from the low-cost producer, so our farmland devoted to ethanol can revert to food crop production? The answer is that the U.S. ethanol program is a political and crony capitalist boondoggle. Government industrial planning almost always results in an inefficient allocation of capital and resources."

After a couple more questions from Ms. Chicklet, the interview ended. With the cameras and microphones turned off, Katie leaned toward Reb and said, "Thank you again, Governor, for granting me this interview and giving me so much of your time. Also, I must say that while I may not see eye to eye with you politically, it is refreshing to have a politician, especially one standing for election, answer directly the questions asked without evasion or digression."

"Well, Katie," Reb replied, "until a couple years ago my entire adult life was spent in business, not politics. In the business world of my experience, direct, straightforward communication, both verbal and written, was essential to success. Like you, I wish this was a trait common to all politicians."

❧──❧

In his last column before the election, Donald Utopeville wrote:

Since I began writing this column forty-four years ago, I have covered eleven presidential elections. Next week, for the first time, I will cast my vote for a Republican to be America's next president. Actually, I will vote for a Republican Constitutionalist, Gov. Reb McCoy. My decision did not come easily. Gov. McCoy's opponent, Democratic Gov. Conrad Bucknell, is a fine candidate and probably would make a good president in a less troubled time, but McCoy has a surer grasp of the dire problems facing the country and a bolder strategy for dealing with them.

I am a proud lifelong progressive who believes government can and should institute social programs for disadvantaged citizens to provide them an opportunity to attain the American dream. Gov. McCoy would not agree with my expansive view of government, as he believes in a more limited federal government. But I do agree with him that the most urgent crisis we confront is reducing our monstrous deficits, debt, and unfunded liabilities to a sustainable level. If we don't soon restore America's fiscal solvency, financial and economic collapse are inevitable. This is not a prognostication; this is a certainty.

In that event, all Americans will suffer, but especially those whom progressives in particular have championed and done so much to lift up to a better life. Moreover, if America continues on its present fiscal course, we will be guilty of robbing future Americans yet unborn of the opportunity to live the American dream so many of us enjoy and take for granted as our birthright. A just society not only has a responsibility to look after its poor and disadvantaged citizens, it also has a fiduciary responsibility to future generations. We will fail to meet both responsibilities if America's fiscal crisis is not brought under control.

The fact is our social programs can't be sustained without a vibrant economy, and government can't continue to spend far more than it collects in tax revenue. Borrowing to finance deficits resulting from excessive spending can't go on indefinitely. McCoy understands this and has a plan for putting the nation on a track to solvency and economic growth. I say let's give him a chance.

I have journeyed from skepticism to indifference and finally to all-out support of the seven proposed constitutional amendments collectively referred to as the Second Bill of Rights. McCoy has championed this cause throughout his brief career in politics employing logic and common sense in a persistent, persuasive manner.

Gov. Reb McCoy is a man of courage, principle, and conviction. He comprehends America's grim fiscal reality and unflinchingly confronts it with the bold, perhaps revolutionary, actions necessary to reclaim our national solvency. He never obfuscates or minimizes the challenges we face as a country, nor does he waste time attempting to assign political blame for our predicament. Instead, he is focused on finding solutions to our problems. As McCoy points out, we all share responsibility for having created our fiscal plight. Therefore, we are all responsible for resolving it. Gov. McCoy's character and experience make him the right person at the right place and time to lead America at this critical juncture in the nation's history."

As the highly respected dean of the country's liberal opinion leaders, Utopeville's endorsement of McCoy caused quite a stir in journalistic and political circles. Reb tossed *The San Francisco Chronicle* on the table, turned to Hoppy and Jake, who had joined him early that morning to review the day's calendar, and said, "Mr. Utopeville has had an epiphany. Never did I expect to receive his endorsement."

Jake responded, "Let's just hope he doesn't turn off any of your conservative supporters who usually have contempt for liberals like Utopeville. Getting his endorsement could hurt more than it helps."

"Aw, Jake," said Hoppy, "you're much too cynical. This endorsement makes Reb acceptable to those Democrats who may be tempted to vote for the governor, but need someone on their team to tell them he is not the devil."

Tally Ho entered the room, a suite atop the Fairmont Hotel on Nob Hill that offered a spectacular view of the Golden Gate Bridge and San Francisco Bay. He had brought with him updated polling data, which he distributed to the three other men. "Gentlemen, I am certain the governor will win the popular vote by 52 to 48 percent. That will translate into a winning margin of at least five million votes. The problem is the electoral vote stubbornly remains fluid, although moving in our direction."

"What's the hard electoral vote count?" asked Hoppy.

"We have 251 electoral votes locked up. Bucknell has 244, down from 250 in his column prior to the last debate. There are three states too close to call that will decide the election, Ohio, Illinois, and New Mexico. If we carry Illinois, or we win Ohio and New Mexico, we win the election. Bucknell can win only if he captures both Illinois and Ohio. If I had to bet, I'd say we win Ohio, and Bucknell wins New Mexico. Illinois is a coin toss."

Hoppy interjected, "If Illinois is that tight, it will go to Bucknell."

"Yeah, in Cook County the deceased continue to vote from the grave, but only if they are registered Democrats," noted Jake dryly.

Reb turned to his pollster. "Tally Ho, how can we win the popular vote by such a significant margin and not win a majority of the electoral vote?"

"That's an interesting question, Governor. A 52 to 48 popular vote victory typically would translate into 300 or more electoral votes, well above the 270 needed to win the election. This election cycle is unprecedented in modern times. Both parties are winning the states they are expected to win, but you are winning your states by larger margins than Republican candidates usually do. At the same time, you are losing by smaller than normal margins in the Democratic states, especially New York and California. These two anomalies are driving up your overall popular vote, but not helping you in the electoral vote."

Hoppy spoke up, "Governor, it seems to me we should concentrate our time and energy from now till the election on Illinois, Ohio, and to a lesser extent, New Mexico. I recommend both you and Lillian camp out in these three states, and that we flood the airwaves with television commercials. Natalie assures me we have plenty of cash on hand and more pours in every day from the Internet. Of course, Bucknell and Lovett also have a pretty good pollster and will probably be doing the same thing. The good citizens of Illinois, Ohio, and New Mexico will feel like they have been invaded."

Thus, the 2016 election campaign's last few days witnessed both presidential and vice presidential candidates crisscrossing the Land of Lincoln, the Buckeye State, and the Land of Enchantment in a final push to secure the electoral votes needed for victory. Reb closed out the campaign in Cleveland, Ohio, where he spoke to a fired up crowd of twenty-five thousand people. In his wind-up speech, he touched on all the themes he had been discussing since announcing his candidacy a long year ago, but he also was reflective.

"The long and winding presidential campaign blessedly draws to a close. You no doubt are as relieved as I am. Tomorrow the American voters have their say. For the fifty-eighth time since the ratification of the Constitution, the people will choose who shall be their president for the coming four years and the transition of power will be peaceful and orderly.

"I have read various articles in recent years that either deny American Exceptionalism, claim it to be dead, or argue America is no more or less exceptional than any other country. I reject all of these opinions, which I believe are rooted in a fundamental misunderstanding that equates exceptionalism with superiority. This is not true. America is exceptional, because it is uncommon, unique, but that is not a claim to being superior or better than any other country.

"The great Englishman G.K. Chesterton, a man of genius and perspicacity, once said, 'America is the only nation in the world that is founded on a creed.' Chesterton went on to say, 'That creed is set forth with dogmatic and even theological lucidity in the Declaration of Independence.' As we all know, the Declaration states that it is a self-evident truth that 'all men are created equal,' and are 'endowed by their Creator with certain unalienable rights,' among which 'are life, liberty, and the pursuit of happiness.' This is what makes America exceptional. No other nation was founded on the idea that men derive their fundamental rights not from the authority of the state, or a hereditary monarch, but from God. To secure these God-given rights, our forefathers instituted a government that derives its just powers from the consent of the governed.

"This was then and remains today astonishing, dare I say exceptional. On this continent far from the Old World, this nation was settled by immigrants fleeing religious or political persecution, or seeking a better life. National identity in all other countries of the world is rooted in history, community, and ethnicity. America's identity is rooted in an idea, a creed that extols liberty, egalitarianism, individualism, self-reliance, free enterprise, and the open frontier, where no citizen is better than another and all men and women are equal before the law. There is no rigid class structure determined by birth in America. An American's opportunity is limited only by his or her ambition, industry, and talent. All of this defines American Exceptionalism.

"The rights we enjoy as free men, although granted by our Creator, cannot be taken for granted. Freedom is not free. It has been often remarked that safeguarding freedom requires eternal vigilance. Most people think that protecting freedom is to defend it against foreign enemies. But today the greatest threat to our freedom and individual liberty is an ever expanding, intrusive, and insolvent federal government, which I have discussed at length throughout this campaign. We have over many decades gradually exchanged some of our individual liberty for increasing dependence on an increasingly bloated government that is fiscally unsound.

"If our generation were writing the last chapter in America's history, perhaps it would not matter how much we spend and promise beyond the country's ability to pay, because no one would have to bear the burden of our profligacy. Live for today, and party like there is no tomorrow. But we are not the last American generation. We have a solemn duty and obligation to pass on the blessings of liberty to posterity. This is the American social contract that links all past, present, and future generations and must never be broken. If we don't urgently rein in government spending and reform entitlements, we will unjustly condemn future generations to struggle to repay the national debt incurred for our benefit and gratification. The first responsibility of freedom is to safeguard it for posterity.

"While the challenge we face is daunting, we can successfully meet it. After all, we created it; therefore, we can fix it, provided we the people exercise our free will and choose to do so. I have set forth a number of specific policy proposals for restoring limited government and fiscal solvency, which I will not repeat here. The best way to restore a proper constitutional balance in the government of our affairs, regain control of our public finances, and reaffirm liberty would be to ratify the Second Bill of Rights.

"Perhaps the most important vote Ohioans cast tomorrow will be for your state legislators. Vote for those candidates who support the proposed Second Bill of Rights and a petition to Congress calling for a constitutional convention. So far thirty state legislatures have so petitioned Congress. Thirty-four states are required to call a convention. Let's make Ohio one of the thirty-four.

"Cast your vote tomorrow not for your personal short-term interests, but on behalf of Americans unborn who have no vote or representation. Cast your vote to secure the blessings of liberty to our posterity. Freedom fever – catch it! Thank you, and God bless America."

ABBA's "Thank You for the Music" boomed across the outdoor stadium filled with cheering and applauding Republican Constitution Party faithful. Marlenna joined Reb on the stage as they waved to the adoring crowd. After the final campaign event, the McCoys immediately departed for the airport and flew directly to Dallas where they would cast their votes the next day, greet well wishers, and await the election returns.

Marlenna was relieved the campaign was finally over. She was worried about her husband who had allowed himself too little time to recuperate from the failed attempt on his life. While in good spirits, he was obviously exhausted and still in pain, although he did not talk about it.

Once their aircraft was aloft, Marlenna snuggled up close to Reb and said, "Honey, we both need to get away for some peace, quiet, and relaxation. You haven't fully recovered from your injuries, because you haven't given yourself a chance to heal. You're not a kid anymore except in your own mind, but your body is sixty-six years old. Promise me, regardless of the election outcome, we'll go lie on a beach somewhere for two weeks."

"Baby, I know I've been pushing it, but I couldn't take time off or appear to be an invalid during the last two weeks of the campaign. I want to get away as much as you do, just the two of us. Why don't you pick out a romantic place in Florida on the beach?"

"Okay, cowboy. I'll start working on it tomorrow after we vote."

Before Marlenna finished her sentence, Reb was sound asleep, which pleased her greatly.

33

Shortly after 3:00 a.m. East Coast time on November 9, the Drudge Report flashed a headline on its Internet site: "OT!" Beneath this sports abbreviation for overtime, Drudge reported: ELECTION IS DEADHEAT. One of the New York broadsheets ran a banner headline: It AIN'T OVER – THE FAT LADY DOESN'T SING! The headline filling the width of the front page of *The Dallas Morning News* simply read: DEADLOCKED.

McCoy–Duzmore and Bucknell–Lovett improbably had divided the electoral vote evenly, each winning 269. The Republican Constitution ticket, just as Tally Ho had predicted, won 52 percent of the national popular vote, beating the Democratic ticket by over five million votes. The only vote that counts, however, is the electoral vote, and if no candidate captures a majority, as provided in the Constitution, it falls to the House of Representatives to elect the president. The Senate chooses the vice president. Not since 1824 had a presidential election been decided by Congress.

The press was clamoring for a statement from the candidates. Reb called a 7:30 a.m. meeting of his senior staff at Dallas campaign headquarters. Lillian Duzmore and her top aides joined via videoconference from Atlanta. Everyone except Reb, who had gotten five hours sleep during the night, appeared tired, disheveled, and bleary-eyed from staying up all night and perhaps a bit too much tippling.

Reb called the meeting to order and said, "Well, folks, I didn't expect this outcome, but I have to say Tally Ho's final polling data signaled a tie was possible if Illinois and New Mexico went to Bucknell and we carried Ohio, which is what happened. Not having a decision is a disappointment, especially after the tremendous effort all of you and the entire team gave to the campaign. But while we didn't win, we also didn't lose. It looks like the House of Representatives will decide who will be the next president, and the Senate will select the vice president. The new Congress won't convene until January 9, 2017, two months from now. The new administration is to be sworn in on January 20, so Congress won't have much time, given that it usually moves at the pace of cold molasses, to get its act together."

"Governor," interrupted Hoppy, "I think there were some flagrant voting irregularities in Illinois and New Mexico. Depending on the results of an investigation, we may want to challenge those results. If we were to prevail in either state, we would have the electoral votes needed to win outright and avoid kicking the decision to the House. Tally Ho, tell us what you think about the Illinois and New Mexico results."

Always polite and deferential, Tally Ho said, "Governor McCoy, Governor Duzmore, in New Mexico we lost by barely four thousand votes out of nearly nine hundred thousand total votes cast. There are anecdotal reports of some possible irregularities with voting machines in Bernalillo County, which is Albuquerque. Similar problems have occurred in previous elections going back to 2000, but in none of those elections would changing New Mexico's reported vote alter the outcome of the national election. Therefore, election results were never challenged. In Illinois, it appears there were egregious problems in Cook County, which is no surprise. Several heavily Democratic Chicago precincts reported vote totals exceeding the number of registered voters. Because we swept the downstate Illinois counties by huge margins, the Cook County political machine had to work overtime to round up or make up enough votes to tip the state to the Democrats. That's why Illinois was the last state to be called at 3:00 a.m. this morning. Out of six million total votes, we lost by fewer than six thousand."

Hoppy turned to Reb. "Governor, I have spoken to legal counsel and been advised that obtaining a recount in New Mexico probably would be difficult unless the final vote shows we lost by less than half a percentage point. In that event, an automatic recount is triggered. In Illinois, the law is murky. There is no mandatory recount requirement in the case of a close election. We would have to demonstrate probable voter fraud that would satisfy an Illinois court, which will be difficult to do. But I am convinced we could uncover blatant fraud in Cook County and share it with the press to create doubt in the public's mind as to the election's legitimacy. This might bring pressure to bear on a state judge to order a recount. In my gut, I know we won Illinois, and if the Cook County machine had not stolen it from us you would be president-elect."

"I don't want to initiate a challenge of the Illinois vote," responded Reb, "either in a judicial court or the court of public opinion. You are no doubt correct, Hoppy, in assuming there was skullduggery in Illinois, but if someone wants to contest the election result that will be up to a private citizen or the authorities in Illinois to do so. My campaign will not be officially or unofficially involved in such activity. Remember what a fiasco the 2000 election became after Gore challenged the Florida vote. Ultimately, as you will recall, an appeal was made to the U.S. Supreme Court, which essentially held in favor of Bush. The Democrats were embittered about the outcome, as the Republicans would have been had the ruling gone the other way. The Court's reputation was tainted by that spectacle.

"I'm not willing to put the country through such an ordeal. I'll follow Nixon's example. In 1960, there was compelling evidence that fraudulent votes in both Illinois and Texas put those states in Kennedy's column. Had Nixon carried those states, he would have won the election despite narrowly losing the popular vote. But Nixon decided to put the country's interest ahead of his ambition, something for which he is given scant credit. We'll leave it to the House of Representatives to decide who will be the next president."

"Governor," replied Hoppy, "your point is well taken, but if we believe there was outright fraud in the Cook County vote and we don't challenge it, aren't we complicit in undermining the integrity of a presidential election? Aren't the voters of Illinois and America entitled to a fair election? As the aggrieved party, shouldn't you demand a recount in Illinois?"

Reb always encouraged people to speak their mind, and Hoppy never disappointed him, which was one reason he held him in high esteem and trusted him implicitly. Reb faced the video screen and said, "Lillian, I would like to hear your perspective on this matter."

"As usual, Hoppy's point-of-view merits serious consideration," began Lillian. "On balance, however, I agree with you, Reb, that we should not contest Illinois, because if we do, Bucknell certainly will fight us tooth and nail, which will be an ugly replay of Florida 2000. If carrying Illinois had lifted him above 270 electoral votes, perhaps I would have a different view, but we can still win in the Congress. Elections should not be decided by lawyers or in courts. We really don't have a national presidential election; we have fifty independent state elections plus the District of Columbia. Each state is responsible for ensuring its election is honest. Perhaps the Republican Constitution Party in Illinois should lead a reform movement there to clean up the system so future elections are fair and square, but contesting yesterday's election that didn't go our way would make us appear to be self-serving sore losers."

Jake joined the discussion, saying, "Reb, I am sympathetic to your and Lillian's position, but I wouldn't be too optimistic about your chances in the House, because it is controlled by Democrats. Now, in the Senate where the Republicans are in the majority—and the vice president will be chosen based on a simple majority vote—Lillian almost certainly will win."

"True, the Democrats run the House, but the vote will be by state," replied Reb. "Each state's congressional delegation will caucus to decide whether to support me or Bucknell. That means California with fifty-three congressmen and Texas with thirty-six each cast one vote for president, just like Delaware and South Dakota, which have just one congressman apiece. I've added up the results of the election, and McCoy–Duzmore won twenty-eight states. Bucknell–Lovett won twenty-two states. They also won the District of Columbia, but it has no vote in the House. If each state's congressional delegation votes consistent with that state's popular vote for president, we would win. We can even lose two states that voted for us and still win twenty-six to twenty-four in the House."

"But, Governor," interjected Hoppy, "there is a distinct possibility four congressional delegations from states you won easily will vote for Bucknell, which would give him the twenty-six votes he needs to become president. Delaware, South Dakota, and Wyoming each has one Democratic congressman. They were all reelected with more votes than you won in their respective states. Nebraska, which you also won handily, has three congressmen, one Republican and two Democrats. Any Democratic congressman who votes for you will be ostracized by his Democratic colleagues and probably stripped of his seniority, including a committee chairmanship if he holds one. The pressure on these people will be intense, and in the end I bet they will protect their status in the House, defy the will of their constituents who voted by wide margins for you, and hope all is forgiven or forgotten when they stand for reelection two years from now."

"If Bucknell can flip four states that we won," replied Reb, "aren't there at least two states he carried in the election whose congressional delegations would support us?"

"That is most unlikely," responded Hoppy. "Democrats outnumber Republicans in every congressional delegation from the twenty-two states Bucknell won. Speaker LaRue controls the House Democratic caucus with an iron grip a Russian tsar would envy. I'm certain none of her members would dare cross her."

Hoppy was referring to the charismatic, larger than life, occasionally outrageous Lashette LaRue. Born Bobbie Jo LaRue in Enid, Oklahoma, she moved with her family as a young girl to Southern California. Blossoming precociously into a voluptuous woman with heroic hooters, a wasp waist, and long, long legs, Bobbie Jo aspired to be an actress. After an "interview" on a Hollywood casting couch, a lecherous movie producer cast her in a B-western movie, changed her name to Lashette, and ordered her to dye her hair black. She played the role of a cowgirl following in the footsteps of her "grandfather," the late Lash LaRue, an old-time movie cowboy who used an eighteen-foot bullwhip to subdue desperados. Lashette's acting potential was underwhelming, but she attracted wolf whistles wherever she appeared. With her raven bangs, scarlet red lipstick, and stunning figure, she reminded old timers of the 1950s pinup girl Bettie Page.

After several sexpot B-movies and torrid affairs with her leading men, she married a wealthy Hollywood agent, became a lawyer, and entered politics. A committed liberal, she won a seat in Congress in 1996, and rose through the ranks relying on her street smarts and God-given assets preserved through the miracle of cosmetic surgery. With her name, personality, and appearance, it was almost foretold that she would one day be elected the House Democratic Whip, responsible for rounding up and counting votes, twisting arms, and keeping the House Democrats in line. Always attired in tight-fitting clothes that emphasized her bosom and cleavage, she became known as the House Dominatrix, and was admiringly said to have not only the biggest boobs in Congress but the biggest balls as well. Formidable, respected, and popular in a predominantly male environment, at age fifty-two, Lashette was elected Speaker of the House when the Democrats took over from the Republicans following the 2014 election.

"I agree with Hoppy," opined Jake, "Lashette may look like a floozy, but she is one savvy politician. I can't imagine any Democrat voting for you in the House, unless Lashette decides she doesn't want to be the number two Democrat in Washington. Right now, she is hands-down the most powerful and influential Democratic politician in the country, but that would change if Bucknell becomes president. I suspect, however, she will deliver the presidency to Bucknell in exchange for his commitment to support her highest priority issues. I think our goose will be cooked in the House."

"So be it," replied Reb, "but it will be awkward if Bucknell is elected president by the House and Lillian is elected vice president by the Senate. I don't know how you feel about that, Lillian, but if you agree, I would propose to Bucknell that he and I jointly recommend to the Senate that they hold in abeyance the vote for vice president until the House decides who will be president, and then elect the president's running mate to the vice presidency."

Immediately Lillian said, "I agree completely, Reb. The president and vice president should be of the same party. In fact, if you were to lose in the House, I would inform the Senate that I would not serve as vice president under Bucknell, because it would be unfair to him and frankly to me as well.

A vice president must enthusiastically support the president in public. Because our political views are so far apart, I could not support most of Bucknell's agenda if he becomes president."

"Our chances of winning appear pretty bleak," opined Reb, "but there is excellent news in a number of state legislative election results. Tally Ho, please give us a brief rundown."

Tally Ho shuffled through his papers a moment and said, "In eight states that have taken no action until now on the Second Bill of Rights, the Republican Constitution Party won outright majorities in both legislative chambers. The winning candidates ran on a platform supporting a constitutional convention. Six of these states also have a newly elected or incumbent Republican governor."

"Thanks, Tally Ho. Before the election, I spoke with each of the Republican gubernatorial candidates and the sitting governors. All have assured me they will encourage their respective legislatures to take up the Second Bill of Rights matter early in next year's legislative session. This is the silver lining in the cloudy national election results. In all probability, we soon will have at least thirty-four states with petitions before Congress seeking a constitutional convention to consider the Second Bill of Rights."

"That's great news, Reb," said Jake, "but remember, the House of Representatives is controlled by the Democrats, and Lashette is on record saying she opposes a constitutional convention and will try to block it on technicalities."

"We'll face that challenge once we get thirty-four states with formal petitions before Congress," replied Reb. "Ding Bell tells me the Senate, after much debate and hand-wringing, will ultimately honor the petitions of the states and call for a convention. That will place enormous pressure on the House, plus we will keep up the public pressure through the tea party and the 9-10 party. If the Democrats ignore the petitions of thirty-four or more states, they will do so in direct violation of Article V of the Constitution. Speaker LaRue, I hope, is too shrewd to take the country down such a perilous path. Well, I need to get ready for a 9:00 a.m. press conference. Thank you all. We'll reconvene after Governor Bucknell and President Fubarsky's press conferences later today."

Hoppy had arranged for the nationally televised press conference to be held in a large auditorium on the SMU campus, conveniently located only a few miles from the McCoy residence. The room was packed with TV and print media journalists from the U.S. and Europe. Reb knew most of the people arrayed before him, as they had covered his campaign since the primaries. Unlike many politicians, Reb enjoyed parrying with the press. Reb began with a brief statement and then invited questions.

> "Good morning, ladies and gentlemen. The people have spoken and their collective wisdom is that the House of Representatives should decide who will be our next president, and that the Senate should select the next vice president. I don't know whether the American voters yesterday said Governor Bucknell and I are both so outstanding, or that we are both so awful, they can't choose between us.
>
> "The Constitution's Framers contemplated the possibility of a hung election, so the newly elected House and Senate will decide the question in early January. Until now, only two elections in our history have had to be decided by Congress, in 1800 and again in 1824, so this is an event rarer than the periodic appearance of Halley's comet. I look forward to Congress exercising its will, and I shall gladly accept whatever it decides. I'll be pleased to take your questions. Yes, David."

David Scribner, a senior correspondent with *The New York Times*, stood and asked, "Governor, given that you won the popular vote by a decisive margin of more than five million votes, do you believe the electoral college is obsolete and should be abolished?"

> "No, I don't. The press and the pollsters focus on the national opinion polls and many people understandably

think the candidate with the most popular votes wins. A presidential election is not a national election, rather it is fifty individual state elections, plus an election in the District of Columbia, all held on the same day. Each state has an electoral vote equal to the number of its congressional districts, which are apportioned based on population, plus its two senators. Because every state has two senators and at least one congressman, no state has fewer than three electoral votes. The most populous state, California, has fifty-three congressional districts plus its two senators for a total of fifty-five electoral votes.

"Adding up the state by state elections, Governor Bucknell won twenty-two states plus the District of Columbia having 269 electoral votes. I won twenty-eight states also having 269 electoral votes. Because neither of us won an absolute majority of the electoral votes, the House must decide the winner.

"The Constitution established a republic, a confederation of states, not a national government. In my judgment, a simple national popular vote would be an inappropriate way to choose the president of our republic. It is rare, however, that the winner of the national popular vote does not also win the electoral vote. This is an exceptional year."

"If I may follow up, sir, when the electoral vote contradicts the popular vote, isn't the democratic will of the people ignored? And if that is true, shouldn't the Electoral College be abolished to avoid the circumstance we have today?"

"Well, David, I disagree with the premise of your question. The people's will is expressed and honored within their respective states. Because each state has two senators regardless of population, from time to time, there will be a presidential election outcome in which the electoral vote winner may lose the national popular vote. Again, we were founded as a republic of sovereign states, which has been a consistent theme throughout my campaign. By the way, relying on just the national popular vote to choose a president may not always produce ideal results. A wildly popular regional candidate might focus his or her campaign on running up the popular vote as high as possible within that region and essentially ignore the rest of the country. In office, that president might disproportionately emphasize policies that benefit his or her region to the detriment of the rest of the country. A president should represent the entire country and the Electoral College system compels candidates to campaign for votes in most all states of the Union. Yes, Mandy."

Mandy Wellborn of Fox News stood and said, "I understand your position on the Electoral College, Governor, but when no candidate wins a majority of the electoral vote thereby throwing the election into the House, isn't the one-state-one-vote procedure undemocratic?"

"Because of wide population disparities among states, Mandy, one could argue treating each state equally is undemocratic. At the risk of repetition, please bear in mind that the United States is not a democracy; it is a democratic federal republic. The Constitution in numerous ways intended for the individual sovereign states that created the federal government to have equal power regardless of population or geographic size. The Senate, for example, was intentionally structured so that each state has equal representation. And in the rare event that a presidential election must be decided by the House, each state has an equal vote. California with fifty-three congressmen has the same weight as Delaware with its lone congressman. The candidate winning twenty-six state congressional delegations, whether they represent the smallest or largest twenty-six states, wins the presidency. These are the rules that have been in place for more than two centuries, and I accept them. No matter how the election turns out, I will not advocate any change in how presidents are elected. Any alternative system devised will doubtless have drawbacks that might be worse than the current system."

Reb called on an Associated Press reporter next who rose and said, "Governor, do you think the congressional delegations from states that voted for you or voted for Governor Bucknell are honor bound to cast their vote in the House for the candidate that won their respective states?"

"Obviously, I would like to see the twenty-eight congressional delegations from states that I won vote for me in the House, but unlike the Electoral College, congressmen have no moral, legal, or political obligation to vote for me or for Governor Bucknell. Nevertheless, I should think how their state voted in the presidential election would be an important consideration in a House member's decision. Congressmen are elected to represent their constituents' interests, and to exercise their independent judgment."

A foreign correspondent was recognized and asked, "Governor McCoy, where is the Electoral College located and what does it do?"

"Good question. It does not have an address, or a campus, or a football team. When the American people voted yesterday, they did not actually vote for me or for Governor Bucknell. Oh, our names appeared on the ballot, but voters actually voted for a slate of electors pledged to support either me or my opponent. Those electors were chosen in each state using procedures adopted by the various state legislatures and the District of Columbia. Typically, electors are chosen by the state political parties and are long time, loyal party activists. The number of electors in each state for each candidate is equal to the number of congressmen and senators representing that state.

"In December, the winning slate of electors in each state will meet in its state capital and formally vote for the candidate who won the state's popular vote. This is the first time votes actually will be cast for me or Governor Bucknell. Although the electors don't meet as a group, this event occurring simultaneously in the fifty states and DC is called the Electoral College. Each state certifies its electoral vote and sends it to the vice president in his capacity as president of the senate. In January, the votes are formally counted by Congress. We seem to have turned this press conference into a civics lesson."

Reb next called on Janis Holmes of *The Washington Post* who asked, "There are reports of voter irregularities in Illinois and New Mexico. Will you challenge these results or demand a recount?"

"No, I will not. It is up to each state to oversee its elections, ensure they are fair, and certify the results. No one in my campaign will directly or indirectly challenge the results in any state."

"If I may follow up, sir, there have been suggestions by members of Governor Bucknell's campaign that they are considering a challenge in one or more of the states you won. What is your reaction?"

"That is a decision Governor Bucknell will have to make. It won't change my position just stated. Should my opponent contest the outcome in any state McCoy Duzmore carried, I will take all available steps to ensure the challenge is conducted in a fair, unbiased manner. Next question."

A CNN reporter shouted above his colleagues, "Governor, will you lobby members of Congress to support you in the House in exchange for political favors or cabinet appointments?"

"No. That would demean both the presidency and Congress. If I won the White House on that basis, it would undermine my legitimacy and moral authority. I don't want the job badly enough to play those games. By now, every congressman knows Governor Bucknell's and my positions on the issues, and they know who won their state. There is nothing more to say that has not already been said. As soon as the new Congress is sworn in, each state's congressional delegation should caucus and decide which candidate their state will support for president. I'll take one last question."

Reb called on an ABC reporter who asked, "Governor, if you end up losing the election, what will be the impact on your effort to have a constitutional convention called to ratify the proposed Second Bill of Rights?"

Reb thought for a moment and replied:

"I am optimistic that whether or not I am elected president, in the near future, Congress will have the constitutional duty to call a convention. This effort does not depend on me or whether I become president. Thirty of the thirty-four states needed have petitioned Congress for a convention to consider the Second Bill of Rights. Based on yesterday's state legislative election results, I am confident that early next year we will surpass the magic number of thirty-four states. As I have said consistently and repeatedly throughout the campaign, adoption of the Second Bill of

Rights is imperative if we are to alter permanently the Washington political ethos, restore limited government, reaffirm individual liberty, regain fiscal solvency, and secure liberty's blessings to posterity. Thank you all very much."

Later that day, Bucknell held a press conference. The main news he made was to squelch talk of challenging any state's election results. Apparently, he concluded that doing so would not be popular, since McCoy had said unequivocally his campaign would not challenge Illinois or New Mexico. Bucknell knew there were problems in both states, especially Illinois. He was relieved that McCoy took the position he did, although if their situations were reversed, Bucknell would challenge Illinois's election results the minute the polls closed. Moreover, Bucknell decided he needed to appear presidential, because Lashette LaRue had informed him she was virtually certain four congressional delegations from states that had voted for McCoy would support Bucknell in the House vote. This meant he was on the threshold of snatching victory from the jaws of defeat and being elected president, thereby fulfilling his lifelong obsession.

President Fubarsky addressed the nation that evening. He wanted to calm any fears or anxiety among the people or the financial markets, which were easily unnerved by uncertainty. Fubarsky assured the country that, while it was rare for a presidential election not to produce a definitive result, the Constitution contemplated this eventuality. He said Speaker LaRue had assured him that resolving the election would be the first item on the House agenda. Fubarsky concluded his brief statement saying that if the new president did not have sufficient time to form his government by the time he was inaugurated on January 20, the outgoing administration's cabinet heads and other senior political appointees would remain in office to ensure continuity of government and a smooth transition.

As it happened, Speaker LaRue had to overcome the resistance—or perhaps it was merely a bluff—of the congressman from Wyoming, one of the four states she needed to go against the will of its people and vote for Bucknell. Delaware, Nebraska, and South Dakota quickly pledged to defy the judgment of their constituents back home and support Bucknell. With Wyoming, LaRue could deliver twenty-six states and the presidency to Bucknell.

Wyoming's lone congressman, Tom Hedonjoy, was playing hard to get with Lashette. Reelected to his fourth term, the thirty-eight-year-old Hedonjoy was a bachelor and man about town. He lived the good life. Whenever he was seen out enjoying the nightly pleasures available in Washington, he seemed always to be accompanied by one or two beautiful women. Popular among his House colleagues, and nobody's fool, Hedonjoy reminded old hands of Charlie Wilson, the charismatic Texas congressman who garnered fame as a ladies' man and champion of the Afghans in their ultimately successful struggle against Soviet occupation in the 1980s. Hedonjoy shrewdly assessed that he had leverage over Speaker LaRue, and he planned to exploit this to his advantage.

After some preliminary sparring by telephone, Lashette invited Hedonjoy to her office in the Capitol two weeks after the election for a one-on-one meeting. She wanted to know his asking price to vote for Bucknell.

Hedonjoy was escorted into the Speaker's elegant, chandeliered office and the door closed behind him. He inhaled the sweet scent of stargazer lilies, noticed the huge fireplace with carved marble mantelpiece, and admired the view of the Mall looking toward the Washington Monument. His three-room cramped office suite in the Rayburn House Office Building was a dump compared to this.

Coming immediately to the point, Lashette asked, "Okay, Tom, we both know why I asked you here. What do you need in order to vote for Bucknell?"

Tom had always found Lashette to be an incredibly desirable woman. The combination of her physical attributes, sensuality, and power acted as an aphrodisiac on him. He liked Lashette's direct style and fantasized that she was terrific in the sack.

"Lashette, I won 68 percent of Wyoming's congressional vote a couple weeks ago, while McCoy defeated Bucknell 61 percent to 39 percent. Most of the folks who voted for me also voted for McCoy. I'm having a difficult time rationalizing how I can vote for Bucknell under these circumstances."

Lashette liked Hedonjoy, despite all the stories, most of which were true, about his drinking and womanizing. He was a handsome, charming rake, and he was a capable politician with potential for higher office. She understood his vote was for sale. The only question was price.

"Look, Tom, you have to decide if you are on the team or not. You've got a bright future in the party if you don't get caught up in a scandal over your personal life. Your constituents love you, and you are clever enough to explain why you voted for Bucknell, assuming you do. In any case, by the time the next election rolls around, few people will remember how you voted for president. For god's sake, you won more than two-thirds of the vote. What do you want?"

"Three things, Lashette. I want a seat on the House Appropriations Committee. I also need a commitment to move legislation to the House floor for a vote that will provide cattle ranchers relief for the rising cost of feed because of the insane ethanol subsidies."

"Okay, I can make both those things happen. What's the third thing?"

"I want to spend an evening with you, Lashette."

Accustomed to being flirted with and propositioned all her life, a knowing smile crossed Lashette's inviting lips. So this is what he wanted. The guy had chutzpah. Did he have a bet with his buddies that he could screw Lashette? She had had a couple of brief affairs and a few flings with congressional colleagues over the years, but not since she had risen to a position of leadership.

Following a pregnant pause, she responded, "You would vote for McCoy if you don't get a chance to lay Lashette, Congressman?"

Hedonjoy smiled and suavely replied, "I didn't ask you to go to bed with me, Lashette, as delightful as that thought is. I simply asked that you share an evening with me. Whatever does or doesn't happen is up to you."

"We've got a deal, Tom. I'll count on your vote for Bucknell. But if I ever hear a whisper about the third item on your list being part of the deal to secure your vote, I'll make your life miserable."

"Lashette, believe it or not, despite my somewhat high public profile, I am a discreet guy. I would never do anything to tarnish your reputation. You know me to be a man of my word."

"Okay, Congressman Hedonjoy," replied Lashette, standing to signal the end of their meeting, "we have a deal. In a week or so, after the House recesses for Thanksgiving, call me on my private cell phone to arrange an evening where we can socialize and get to know each other better. I suggest we not be seen in public together, so I'll invite you to my residence at the Ritz Carlton for dinner."

As he moved toward the door to leave, Tom said, "I look forward to that Lashette. See you soon."

As she watched him depart, Lashette couldn't help but laugh to herself. Actually, the guy intrigued her. Younger men always did, since she had turned forty a dozen years ago. If this became known to history, she mused, would it be considered a corrupt bargain like the deal Speaker of the House Henry

Clay made with John Quincy Adams in 1825? Allegedly in exchange for being appointed Secretary of State, Clay supported Adams for the presidency over Andrew Jackson, who had won a plurality of both the popular and electoral votes in the 1824 election. Lashette thought to herself, 'Oh, the things I do for liberalism.'

34

Immediately after Thanksgiving, Reb and Marlenna departed for Florida for a two-week vacation. Reb's good friend and predecessor as CEO of Magnolia placed his oceanfront estate on Jupiter Island at their disposal. A secluded property with two guest houses in addition to the main residence, it accommodated the Secret Service agents who would continue to protect the McCoys until the presidential election was decided in the House of Representatives. The agents were unobtrusive, affording Reb and Marlenna the privacy and normalcy they craved, but rarely had enjoyed during the intense election campaign.

Marlenna, a voracious reader, luxuriated in the sand and sun, while perusing another *New York Times* bestseller on her Kindle, which was never far from her side. Reb spent time in the outdoor Jacuzzi solving the daily crossword puzzle with a view of the beach, the Atlantic, and his wife. By the time he had been there a week, he felt no further discomfort in his rib cage and the huge bruise on his right side had begun to disappear.

Hoppy stayed in touch daily, but only to keep Reb abreast of developments. President Fubarsky had suggested to Speaker LaRue that Bucknell and McCoy be invited to address the full House of Representatives before it voted for president, and she embraced the idea. A coin toss would determine who spoke first. The candidate to speak second would wait in an isolated room off the House floor, so he would not hear what his opponent was saying. Each candidate was to limit his remarks to no more than fifteen minutes. Reb agreed to these arrangements, although he thought whatever remarks he and Bucknell made would be a waste of breath, because it would be clear to everyone before Christmas how the House would vote.

As November turned to December, Hoppy called late one afternoon to report, as expected, that the Delaware, Nebraska, and South Dakota congressional delegations had announced they would vote for Bucknell. The congressman from Wyoming, Tom Hedonjoy, coyly said he didn't know how he would vote. A self-promoter and publicity hound, Hedonjoy craved the spotlight, and now that he was the deciding vote in the House, he was enjoying the attention and notoriety.

After providing this update, Hoppy said, "While these developments were not unexpected, they are still disheartening. Bucknell appears to have twenty-five House votes locked up, you have twenty-four sure votes, and Wyoming's congressman, Tom Hedonjoy, is technically undecided. It looks like the best we can hope for is a tie, which would force the House to continue voting until the tie is broken. I suspect, however, that in the end Hedonjoy will vote for Bucknell."

"I think you're right, Hoppy. From what I gather reading the papers here, Lashette LaRue seems too laid back not to be confident that Hedonjoy will vote with his party when the chips are down. He's probably already committed to her that he will vote for Bucknell, so she is indulging his ego by letting him game the media. Besides, from her point-of-view, keeping the drama and suspense alive until the House actually votes is good theater."

"Well, Governor, it's a shame to lose like this having come so close. By the way, the Chicago papers are investigating the Cook County votes and are raising troubling questions. Sure you don't want to challenge the Illinois vote?"

"Hoppy, you know my position on that matter, and it hasn't changed. Besides, the Electoral College meets next week and the state results will be certified. Unless there is a faithless Democratic elector who votes for me, despite having pledged to support Bucknell, thereby giving me 270 electoral votes, we've lost. That's not going to happen and in any event, I wouldn't want to win or lose that way. We both knew going in that this would be a close election, although perhaps not as close as it turned out to be, and that only one guy could win. I'm amazed and gratified at how well we did in the popular vote and the state legislative elections. This gives me confidence that there will be a constitutional convention in the next year or so, and the Second Bill of Rights ultimately may be ratified. That is far more important to the country's future than winning the presidency."

"I guess you're right, Governor. For what it's worth, both Walter Rothmann and Donald Utopeville wrote columns this week to the effect that any congressional delegation that overturns the popular vote for president in their state is committing a breach of faith."

"Oh, I don't know if I agree with that, Hoppy. Delaware, Nebraska, South Dakota, and Wyoming all voted for the Republican Constitution Party presidential ticket, but simultaneously they also voted for Democrats to represent them in Congress. In so doing, the voters in those states said they trust the judgment of the congressmen they elected over their opponents. If the congressional delegations from those states decide to vote for Bucknell for president, they are simply exercising the judgment the voters entrusted to them. I'm not sure how that can be construed as a breach of faith.

"Hoppy, I've got a pretty lady eager for me to take a stroll on the beach with her. It's an offer I can't refuse. I'll talk to you soon."

As he shut off his cell phone, Marlenna grabbed him by the hand and led him down on the beach to walk just beyond reach of the surf. "What did Hoppy have to report?" she asked.

"He was just confirming that the fat lady won't miss her curtain call when the House votes next month. Bucknell will be the next president."

"If it's certain that Bucknell will win, why bother with the charade of having you both address the House before the vote?'

"I suppose it's a matter of form and courtesy. Following an inconclusive, controversial election, it could help to unify the country. I view it as an opportunity to make a valedictory address."

As had been their quotidian afternoon routine since arriving on Jupiter Island, they strolled hand in hand for a mile or more, stopping occasionally to steal a kiss, listening to the waves and the plaintive wail of sea gulls, before turning back as dusk began to eclipse the late autumn sunlight.

At the end of their vacation, the McCoys flew to Austin, where they stayed in the Governor's Mansion through the holidays. Ravenna, Jeff, and the twins joined them to celebrate Christmas. Lillian and Duz Duzmore, Jake Fillmore, Ding Bell, Duane Darby, Wyatt Solomon, Pip Pippin, Abigail Abbeville, Hopalong Cassidy, and senior campaign staff, along with their spouses, attended a private New Year's party Reb and Marlenna hosted at the mansion. The Madison Committee members were invited, because Reb was grateful for their active support of the Second Bill of Rights initiative during the campaign, and he intended to resume regular meetings of the Committee in 2017. There would be no let-up in the effort to induce at least four more states to petition Congress for a constitutional convention.

On Wednesday, January 11, 2017, Reb and Bucknell addressed the House of Representatives in prime time. Marlenna and Mrs. Bucknell sat in the gallery and were given a warm welcome when introduced. Marlenna looked scrumptuous in a magenta jacquard suit by Tahari with ruffled collar, puffed shoulders, and three-quarter sleeves. As always, the camera loved her. Reb won the coin toss and elected to speak following Bucknell.

While the putative president-elect spoke, Reb waited with Ding Bell on the Senate side of the Capitol in S-211, The Lyndon Baines Johnson Room, named for the former Senate Majority Leader, later vice president and president of the United States. The ornate room featured elaborate fresco paintings on the ceiling and walls by Constantino Brumidi, the Italian artist who had emigrated from Rome to the U.S. in 1852. Brumidi's most famous fresco in the Capitol is the enormous and spectacular Apotheosis of George Washington painted on the dome of the Capitol's rotunda. Before seeking political asylum in America at the age of forty-seven, Brumidi had been employed by Pope Gregory XVI as a fresco artist for the Vatican.

After admiring the artwork in S-211, Reb remarked to Ding, "How many artists do you think have painted frescoes for the Vatican and the U.S. Capitol? Brumidi was but one of millions of immigrants who fled their homeland for America seeking freedom and a better life. With his brilliant talent, Brumidi made a unique, enduring, and wonderful contribution to his adopted country. Rome's loss was America's gain. That story has been repeated millions of times during our history."

Ding responded, "Brumidi's work can be found throughout the Capitol, which adds greatly to the interior majesty and beauty of this great building."

As Ding spoke, the House Sergeant at Arms entered the room to escort Reb to the House Chamber. When they arrived at the doorway into the

House, the Sergeant at Arms announced in a rich baritone voice, "Madam Speaker, the governor of the great state of Texas, the Honorable Rogers Edmund Burke McCoy."

As they had done for Gov. Bucknell, all the House members rose, turned toward the center aisle and gave Reb a rousing welcome of sustained applause, cheers and occasional whistles. Reb shook hands and exchanged greetings with members on both sides of the aisle as he proceeded toward the rostrum. There he greeted and shook hands with Speaker LaRue and the Republican House Minority Leader before turning to face the still standing and applauding House members and visitors in the gallery where Marlenna also was standing and applauding her husband.

After several minutes of the Speaker repeatedly wielding her gavel while calling the House to order, the chamber finally quieted enough for Reb to begin to speak. As with most of his major speeches, he relied only on a few notes, as he had committed his remarks to memory. Although well aware he did not have Winston Churchill's gift for dramatic oratory, Reb had copied Churchill's technique of memorizing important speeches, believing that a speech delivered or performed, rather than read from a prepared text, had greater emotional impact and verisimilitude. The teleprompter did not exist in Churchill's time, but Reb could not imagine the great man ever using one. Reb eschewed the teleprompter saying it robbed a speaker of spontaneity and an emotional connection with his audience. Reading off a teleprompter was like reading off the written page, except the speaker's head was tilted up instead of down.

> "Madam Speaker, members of Congress, distinguished guests, ladies and gentlemen, you honor me with this opportunity to address the United States House of Representatives. Although the congressional delegations from each of the fifty states will not cast their votes for president until tomorrow, based on reliable press reports and interviews, it is evident that the House will elect Governor Conrad Bucknell the forty-seventh president of

the United States. I have genuine respect and admiration for Governor Bucknell. He has been a worthy, honorable opponent, and I believe his character, integrity, and life experience make him well qualified to be president. While we disagree politically on many issues, I congratulate him and offer him my sincere best wishes."

The members rose to applaud Reb's gracious remarks. They all recognized, as did the people watching on television all across the country, that McCoy was a class act, a man who harbored no bitterness over losing such a close race. Many watching from home who had voted for Bucknell in November were now wondering whether they had made the right choice, especially since Bucknell's speech, which Reb had not heard, was self-serving, political, and focused on why he was a better choice for president than McCoy. The contrast between Bucknell's political stump speech and McCoy's elevated tone was stark. He continued:

"As the election is over except for tomorrow's final vote count in this historic chamber, I shall not comment on specific policies I advocate nor attempt to persuade you to vote for me. In any event, everyone by now knows where I stand on the issues. Instead, I wish to discuss America's future, which I believe to be in great peril.

"Our nation faces three impending and potentially existential crises that threaten to undermine the foundation of our Republic. The Constitution established by the Founding Fathers, which united individual sovereign states into a single nation, is imperiled by the relentless expansion of the federal government's power, the imminent threat of financial insolvency, and the rapidly deteriorating security along our border with Mexico. If we the people do not mobilize promptly to address these crises, we will face catastrophe and our generation will be the first in history to fail to secure the blessings of liberty to future generations of Americans yet unborn.

"The federal government has incessantly expanded its scope, size, and power over the past eight decades at the expense of individual liberty. The Constitution created a limited government of enumerated powers with all other powers reserved to the states or the people, but today government too often expands its reach without even considering whether its actions are within constitutional bounds. There always is a favored constituency or creative rationalization to justify any particular or expedient action government takes to dispense favors or interpose its will over the individual citizen, but is every action constitutionally appropriate? When all such government actions are aggregated, federal power becomes so predominant that individual liberty inevitably is diminished. When government becomes virtually omnipotent, can liberty long endure?

"I submit that the federal government has assumed too central a role and too great a power in American society such that it is no longer servant to the people but is now master of the people. The flame of liberty is being gradually extinguished by a soft trickle down tyranny. Benevolent despotism is still despotism. As my eighteenth-century British ancestor Edmund Burke wrote, 'The true danger is when liberty is nibbled away, for expedients and by parts.'

"Our liberty is also threatened by national insolvency, which is largely a byproduct of leviathan government and its insatiable appetite for spending. With annual budget deficits exceeding $1 trillion over the past eight years, an ever growing national debt currently exceeding $20 trillion, and unfunded entitlement liabilities in excess of $100 trillion, we have squandered our national patrimony and are on the road to financial perdition. Everyone in this Congress knows these facts and the nation's inevitable fate if we don't change course, yet internecine politics paralyzes government from taking the urgent, essential, and sweeping actions necessary to avoid the impending fiscal catastrophe. Each of you no doubt is convinced you are doing the right thing by your constituents and the country, but with Congress the whole is sadly less than the sum of the parts.

"The only way out of our national predicament is to slash spending, reform entitlements, and embrace pro-growth economic policies aimed at sustained economic expansion of 4 percent per year. Robust economic growth will reduce unemployment, enlarge the economic pie, and increase tax revenues flowing into the government. Economic growth and a commitment to smaller government will engender confidence within the country and around the world, and will reverse the trend away from the dollar as the world's reserve currency.

"For years, our burgeoning debts and deficits have resulted in the debasement of our currency and a lowering of our standard of living. In the words of Daniel Webster of Massachusetts, one of the immortal members of this body and the Senate during the nineteenth century, and whose words are engraved on the marble walls of this House, 'A disordered currency is one of the greatest political evils.'

"Finally, we face a malignant danger along the two-thousand-mile border we share with our neighbor, friend, and ally, Mexico. The Mexican government no longer controls a vast swath of its northern territory contiguous with the United States. It is bad enough that for years the U.S. government has not controlled rampant illegal immigration from Mexico, but now the fratricidal war within the Mexican drug cartel is spilling over into the United States. There also are credible reports of an alliance between elements of Hezbollah, the Lebanon-based Middle East terrorist group, and the Mexican druglords, which is a direct threat to the United States.

"The most fundamental reason for government to exist is to protect its citizens and its sovereign borders. A nation that fails to control and secure its sovereign borders cannot long survive. It is ironic that the federal government eternally seeks to extend its power beyond its constitutional limits, yet fails to discharge rigorously its constitutional obligation to 'provide for the common defense.' Texas and other border states will be forced to fill the vacuum created by the federal government's failure to devote adequate resources to secure the border with Mexico. This could lead to a constitutional crisis if violence continues to increase and the federal government does not fulfill its constitutional duty.

"To restore limited government, turn the nation away from the financial abyss, and secure our borders, it is no secret that I believe the federal government requires outside intervention in the form of a constitutional convention to consider seven amendments known as the Second Bill of Rights. These amendments would not curb the federal government's legitimate powers, but would clarify the limit and extent of those powers, mandate that the nation be restored to financial solvency, and provide states constitutional authority to defend international borders if the federal government fails to do so.

"By the middle of this year, I am confident that at least thirty-four state legislatures will have formally petitioned Congress to call a constitutional convention under Article V of the Constitution. I trust the Congress will act promptly to fulfill its duty by calling a convention. This may be our last opportunity to restore limited constitutional government, reaffirm freedom, sustain the Union, and secure the blessings of liberty to posterity, which each American generation is honor bound to do as set forth in the Preamble to the Constitution.

"The daunting challenges America faces are predictable, self-inflicted, and therefore curable, but time is of the essence. We must act with all due celerity. All that is required of this Congress and the American people is courage, patriotism, and perseverance. Let us exercise our free will to choose a future for America that keeps faith with ourselves, as well as all those who came before us and most importantly, those who will come after us.

"Thank you for your time, and pray that America may be ever deserving of God's grace and mercy."

The members of Congress stood in unison and gave Reb prolonged, polite, although somewhat reserved applause. They realized he had just delivered an important address that illuminated hard truths confronting America, but many took umbrage at receiving a public lecture, especially by an invited guest. Many, including Speaker LaRue, were viscerally opposed to the idea of a constitutional convention and a Second Bill of Rights, correctly perceiving such an eventuality a threat to their power and careers.

While accepting the applause, Reb waved and blew a kiss to Marlenna in the gallery, who was smiling and applauding her husband with enthusiasm. Reb's gesture toward his wife was a breach of protocol. He was blissfully ignorant of this, but had he known about it, he still would have blown Marlenna a kiss. By now, it was obvious to the general public that Reb and Marlenna were truly in love with and committed to each other. Their marriage was not superficial or a matter of convenience as with many politicians.

The anchor on Fox News asked Walter Rothmann to share his insights on the event just concluded. "Governor Bucknell must be feeling pretty low right now. Of the two men who addressed Congress and the nation tonight, Governor McCoy clearly came across as the more presidential, yet Bucknell will become our next president. Bucknell's remarks were forgettable and pedestrian, whereas McCoy, as usual, spoke with passion and eloquence about what he labeled the three 'existential' crises facing the country. His message was somber, but he spoke the truth and offered a way for Congress to redeem itself through nothing less than an 'outside intervention.' McCoy never fails to advocate for a constitutional convention and the Second Bill of Rights, and his prime time speech tonight to a national audience very likely brings that closer to reality."

"Do you think any minds were changed by the two speeches we heard tonight?" asked the anchor.

"Oh, I imagine a lot of minds were changed," replied Rothmann, "and most of those changed minds have deserted Bucknell to support McCoy. But no votes in Congress were changed, and that's all that counts now. No House Democrat who has publicly or privately pledged to the Speaker that he or she will vote for Bucknell will renege on that pledge. And were the positions reversed, neither would any Republican congressman vote for the other party's presidential candidate, certainly not over one speech. The best man or woman doesn't always win. That's a hard reality of life, as well as politics."

35

Dallas, Texas
March 2017

Two months after President Bucknell's inauguration, the Madison Committee gathered for dinner in a private dining room at Milano's restaurant in Dallas. Reb organized the occasion to celebrate the New Mexico Legislature's application to Congress to call a constitutional convention to consider adoption of the Second Bill of Rights. The magic number of thirty-four, or two-thirds, of the fifty states had now formally petitioned Congress, and at least two other states were expected to follow suit in the next few weeks. The legislatures in all twenty-eight states that had voted for McCoy, plus six legislatures in states Bucknell carried petitioned Congress for a convention.

After everyone was seated and each glass was poured with a St. Innocent pinot noir, one of Reb's favorite Willamette Valley wineries, Sen. Ding Bell rose to say, "I propose a toast to the Madison Committee and its esteemed chairman, the governor of the great state of Texas and the people's choice for president, Reb McCoy."

After shouts of "Hear, Hear," Reb thanked Ding and said, "This was a team effort. All of you should take enormous pride in achieving this milestone. I understand over five million copies of our *Second Bill of Rights* pamphlet were distributed or mailed during the past year. Another million copies were downloaded from the Internet. The grassroots 9-10 party, now established in every state, was launched by you and has been instrumental in developing support for a constitutional convention. These initiatives were instrumental in our success. Nearly every sentient adult American by now has heard of the Second Bill of Rights and the broad-based popular support for a constitutional convention. Various opinion polls indicate that 48 to 53 percent of those polled favor the Second Bill of Rights, 25 to 30 percent are opposed, and about 20 percent are undecided or have no opinion. The momentum is with us, but our biggest challenge now is getting Congress to act on the state petitions and call a convention. Ding, what is your assessment of the mood on Capitol Hill?"

"The outlook is mixed. I believe the Senate, where the Republicans hold a slim majority, will vote to call for a convention within the next three months. This issue is not subject to filibuster, but because a few Republican senators adamantly oppose a constitutional convention, we will need several Democrats to obtain a majority. I've already received commitments from enough Democratic senators to ensure we win."

"From what I read and hear, the problem will be in the House," interjected Pip Pippin.

"This is true," responded Ding. "Speaker LaRue is dead set against a convention and the Second Bill of Rights. As of today, she has more than enough Democratic congressmen plus at least ten Republicans who will vote against a convention. Enormous public pressure is the best hope for peeling away twenty members of her caucus to vote for a convention. Similar pressure must be brought to bear on the ten wayward Republicans."

"On what basis can the House in good faith deny the applications from thirty-four, soon to be thirty-six, states to call a convention?" asked Wyatt Solomon.

"As I understand it," replied Ding, "Lashette argues that Article V of the Constitution is silent on what rules and procedures appertain to calling a convention, and there is no precedent to follow. Therefore, it is up to Congress to determine when a convention will be called, and whether the state applications are valid. She contends that at least thirty-four state petitions must be identical to trigger a convention. Because of variations in several of the state applications, so far there are only twenty-seven virtually identical petitions."

"That's preposterous, Ding," harrumphed Wyatt. "Nothing in Article V says the petitions have to be identical. Moreover, I've reviewed every state petition and the variations are trivial. A couple states revised the term limits amendment from twelve years' total congressional service to a maximum of twelve years in each house. Two states want to allow military action for up to a hundred and eighty days instead of ninety days before Congress must declare war in order to continue hostilities. One state advocates a balanced budget amendment and an amendment prohibiting unfunded congressional mandates on the states. Five states would require a constitutional convention to be held at thirty- instead of twenty-five-year intervals. None of these are differences of substance. In any case, once a convention is in session it may consider any amendment proposed by a delegate. Any proposed amendment approved by a majority of the state delegations in convention would be referred to the states for ratification. Speaker LaRue's position doesn't pass the laugh test."

"Except for the fact, Wyatt," responded Reb, "she controls enough votes in the House to block a convention. I know the president has no constitutional authority regarding this matter, but if he were to say publicly he favored a convention and did some arm twisting with fellow Democrats in Congress, Lashette probably would feel compelled to change her position. At the end of our third campaign debate, Bucknell conceded that while he didn't think the Second Bill of Rights was necessary, he had no objection to a constitutional convention if enough states saw the need for one."

"Well, Reb," replied Ding, "the scuttlebutt I hear is that Lashette got Bucknell's commitment to oppose a constitutional convention, in return for which she ensured four congressional delegations from states that voted for you would support Bucknell in the House election. Bucknell is president because of Lashette, so I'm certain he will not renege on his commitment to her."

Abby Abbeville asked, "Why is Speaker LaRue, as well as virtually all the Democrats, so strongly opposed to a constitutional convention?"

Pip replied, "Career politicians and those addicted to big government fear a constitutional convention, because it threatens their power. Progressives believe government can solve society's problems and remedy injustice. And many Republicans believe in massive military spending and various pork barrel projects. If a convention is called and approves the amendments we know as the Second Bill of Rights, and thirty-eight or more states ratified them, the federal government's power would be sharply curtailed, and the careers of many politicians would come to an abrupt end. This is anathema to politicians like Lashette LaRue."

"It seems to me," offered Duane Darby, "that if Congress willfully disregards the state petitions for a convention on such dubious grounds as just described by Judge Wyatt, that would constitute a direct violation of the Constitution. Couldn't the aggrieved states appeal to the Supreme Court to order Congress to live up to its constitutional duty?"

"It would be a fool's errand to predict what the Supreme Court might do," said Wyatt, "but I suspect the Court would decide it had no jurisdiction in this matter. Article V vests exclusive power to call a convention with the legislative branch. Normally, the Court will not intervene in a constitutional dispute between the states and Congress unless it is a dispute over law."

Reb said, "We can't sit idly by and let Congress betray its constitutional duty. We need to encourage the tea party and 9-10 party activists to organize rallies around the country, and in DC. Cable news pundits and columnists sympathetic to the idea of a constitutional convention should be urged to keep this issue in the public eye. I will also talk to the governors of those states, which submitted petitions that don't conform with the other states' petitions to determine the feasibility of having the original petitions altered and resubmitted. This may be difficult in states where the petitions were adopted by a narrow vote."

Ding added, "So as not to appear completely obstructionist, Lashette has established an ad-hoc House committee to review the state petitions and determine the rules and procedures for calling a convention. She has appointed a majority of the members of this committee, including its chairman, Congressman Strank, a vociferous opponent of a convention and the Second Bill of Rights."

There was an audible groan around the table. A. Portnoy Strank was the most rebarbative personality in Congress. A short, pot-bellied, slovenly man with uncombed hair and usually attired in a wrinkled suit and food-stained tie, Strank's disposition was perpetually disagreeable. In fact, he seemed happy only when he was in a bad mood. He was sarcastic, rude, condescending, and tactless. Colleagues in his own party detested him, and everyone assumed his first initial stood for "Asshole." How he kept his seat in Congress for thirty years was a mystery, because he treated his California constituents the same way he treated his congressional colleagues. But Strank was ruthless, smart, shrewd, and brought home rashers of federal bacon to his district. He usually ran unopposed for reelection.

Ding continued, "I think the Strank committee is a sham intended to stall for time, hoping the issue will fade away. The grapevine informs me that if the House can defer a vote on calling a convention until the current congressional term expires at the end of 2018, Lashette will rule that all the petitions will have to be resubmitted by the state legislatures before the next Congress will take up the matter. This will effectively kill any possibility of a convention."

Wyatt suggested, "Reb, I think it would be a good idea for you to debate Strank on one of the major Sunday morning news programs. Given his enormous ego, he would eagerly accept such a challenge. I am sure on substance, style, and demeanor you would win a debate with Strank. It's easy to goad him into a self-righteous tirade marked by personal attacks, waving arms, and flying spittle."

"I am happy to debate Portnoy," replied Reb, "but even if I won in the court of public opinion, I don't think it would change any votes in Congress. Let's try to get the media to pressure Strank to let the public know when his committee will complete its work. The best time to challenge him to a debate is after it becomes obvious he and Lashette are dragging their feet. Also, we need to work with the states that have submitted petitions to pressure their respective congressional delegations to demand that a convention be called. I have already spoken to each member of the Texas delegation about this. But unless and until the Senate acts, Strank can stall with impunity arguing that both houses of Congress must approve a resolution calling for a convention. What do you think, Ding?"

"I agree the best way to ratchet up pressure on the House is for the Senate to pass a resolution calling for a convention. Then it will be obvious that Lashette and the House Democrats are defying the will of the states. I am confident I can get this on the Senate's agenda before the end of March."

Duane asked, "What if all efforts to pressure Congress to call a convention fail? What do we do then?"

"Let's hope we never feel compelled to cross that bridge, Duane, because I fear that bridge crosses the Rubicon," replied Reb enigmatically.

Duane turned to Wyatt and asked, "Could thirty-four or more states call a convention without congressional sanction? If such a convention submitted amendments for ratification to all the states and they were adopted by at least thirty-eight, would they be the law of the land?"

"I'm afraid not, Duane," replied Wyatt. "Article V of the Constitution specifically states that Congress shall call a convention upon receiving applications from two-thirds of the state legislatures. Therefore, the states have no direct authority to call a convention, but it also is clear that Congress is obligated to do so once it has determined that the applications from thirty-four states have been duly authorized by each state legislature. If LaRue, Strank, and the House fail to act after the Senate passes a convention resolution, I believe that will precipitate a constitutional crisis. That would take the country into uncharted territory and potential disaster. Speaker LaRue and the House are playing with fire that may turn into an out-of-control conflagration."

36

Pursuant to the applications from thirty-four states, the Senate narrowly passed a resolution in April, just as Ding Bell predicted, calling for a constitutional convention to be held in September 2017 in Philadelphia. Consistent with the Madison Committee's proposed 34th amendment to the Constitution, it called for the Chief Justice of the Supreme Court to preside over the convention and directed each state to designate from three to five convention delegates, with no more than one of a state's delegates holding elective office. The resolution provided for delegates to be chosen via popular vote in each state based on a slate of candidates proposed by the state legislatures. Any amendments approved in convention were to be submitted to each state legislature for ratification. If at least thirty-eight states ratified an amendment, it would immediately become the law of the land.

The Senate convention resolution was forwarded to the House of Representatives, where it was referred to Democratic Rep. Strank's committee for consideration. At a press conference a few days later, Speaker LaRue was asked when the House would take up the Senate resolution.

She responded that the Strank committee was reviewing the entire matter, and she expected it would make a recommendation to the full House in due course. The Speaker would not be pinned down to a date by which the House would act, saying there were many important matters of public business the House had to deal with and a constitutional convention was not the most urgent.

Lashette was a shrewd politician who rarely, if ever, made a public verbal gaffe. She never would say outright that she opposed a constitutional convention, but did comment that she was not yet convinced one was necessary, and that all the state petitions had to be carefully reviewed before any action could occur. It was up to Strank to ensure a fair and deliberate process as there was no need to act in haste. After all, there had not been a constitutional convention in two hundred thirty years.

In Austin, the press asked Gov. McCoy to comment on the Senate's action.

> "I am gratified that the Senate has acted favorably on the thirty-four, soon to be thirty-six, state applications submitted to Congress calling for a constitutional convention. The Senate's action is a vote for liberty and recognition of the fact that the states are indispensable to our republican form of government as established by the Constitution. I trust the House will see the wisdom of the Senate's action and promptly pass a similar resolution, so a constitutional convention may be called later this year."

In Washington, DC, the press sought comment from Rep. Strank, who uncharacteristically was avoiding the TV cameras. He finally agreed to take questions from the media on the issue two days after Reb made his remarks.

"Mr. Strank, will your committee and the House follow the Senate's lead and honor the state petitions for a constitutional convention?"

Strank bristled and replied:

> "As all of you ought to know, the Senate and the House are separate legislative bodies that act independently. In order for there to be a constitutional convention, both

houses of Congress will have to agree on the terms of a resolution calling for such a convention. Neither I nor my House colleagues will be pressured to follow what the Senate has done. Calling a constitutional convention is a serious step and deserves thoughtful deliberation. There is no precedent for a convention since the Constitution went into effect in 1789. We need to review each state's petition to determine it was properly adopted. If my committee votes to proceed with a convention, we will have to establish how a convention will be structured."

"When will your committee take action, Mr. Strank?"

"How do I know when we will act?" snapped Strank. "We only began to review all the pertinent documents and to hear testimony from constitutional scholars a few weeks ago. We will take action when we are ready to do so and not before. Good day."

This was classic Strank: surly, condescending, and abrupt.

On a Sunday in May, all the morning news programs agreed to televise jointly a live debate between Rep. Strank and Gov. McCoy on the prospects for a convention and the proposed Second Bill of Rights. Bob Shafter of CBS News was designated by the networks to moderate the debate. As Reb expected, Strank agreed to debate with alacrity, supremely confident in his intellectual prowess and ability to intimidate. For his part, Reb was eager to keep the issue at the forefront of the news hoping this would increase public support and pressure the House to act.

After providing viewers a summary of the seven proposed amendments known as the Second Bill of Rights and the requirement that at least thirty-four states had to petition Congress in order for a convention to be called, Shafter addressed his first question to Strank.

"Congressman Strank, given that thirty-six states, two more than required under Article V of the Constitution, have applied to Congress to call a constitutional convention, and the Senate has adopted a resolution in favor of such a convention, why is the House apparently resisting comparable action?"

"I reject the premise of your question, Bob. The House has created an ad-hoc committee, which I chair, to review this matter and come forward with a recommendation. We are taking a deliberate approach as there is no compelling reason to act in haste. This is the first time the states have applied contemporaneously for a convention to consider amendments. All the existing twenty-seven amendments to the Constitution were originated in the Congress and sent to the states for ratification. I believe, as do many of my colleagues, that we must take our time to make sure we get this right."

"What are the key issues your committee is considering?" Shafter followed up.

"Well, first, are the state petitions in proper order? Must there be thirty-four identical petitions to call a convention? If so, we have only twenty-seven petitions that are identical; nine others are different in various ways. If a convention is called by Congress, should its mandate be limited to consideration of specific amendments, or can it approve any and all manner of amendments? What should be the process for the states to ratify amendments approved in convention? These are not trivial matters and require time to think through. We are dealing potentially with fundamental changes to our Constitution and form of government."

Shafter turned to Reb and asked, "Governor McCoy, do you disagree with anything Congressman Strank just said?"

"I agree with Mr. Strank that if a constitutional convention approved the proposed Second Bill of Rights and it was ratified by the states, the federal government would be fundamentally changed. In that event, we would return to a government of limited and enumerated powers, reaffirm individual liberty, restore fiscal sanity, and secure the blessings of liberty to posterity. I disagree, however, with several of the matters Mr. Strank argues the Congress must address. The thirty-six states that have applied to Congress to call a constitutional convention have each deliberated and voted on this in their respective legislatures. There is no justification for Congress to second guess the states. The fact that not all the applications are identical has no bearing on the issue. Article V of the Constitution says nothing about the applications being identical. It merely states that Congress shall call a convention for proposing amendments on receiving applications from two-thirds of the state legislatures. In any event, the differences among the state petitions are not that significant. Finally, Congress has no authority to limit what amendments a convention might consider. It seems to me the Framers intended for Congress to be a clearinghouse to receive applications from the states and to establish administrative parameters such as time and place of a convention, who will preside, the procedure states will follow to name delegates to the convention, and the ratification process. The Senate got it right in its resolution. I believe the House should adopt the Senate's resolution, so we can move forward with a convention later this year."

Strank's indignation over Reb's critique and unsolicited advice as to how the House should conduct its business was reflected in his body language. Before he could jump in to tear McCoy a new one, however, Shafter asked Reb a follow-up question, "Governor, some people allege this whole business of a constitutional convention and a Second Bill of Rights is a conservative stratagem to end all the New Deal, Great Society, and other social programs that progressives have championed for many years. How do you respond to that?"

"That bogus charge is an effort to scare people by distorting the truth, because opponents have no credible arguments against the Second Bill of Rights. Many, though not all, opponents of this initiative are progressives who correctly see these amendments as curtailing federal government power and control, which are essential to achieving the liberal agenda. But many so-called conservatives also oppose the proposed amendments fearing that the defense budget and the president's ability to defend the country will be compromised. I reject both these arguments as being without merit. None of the seven proposed amendments that comprise the Second Bill of Rights diminishes the legitimate, specified powers delegated to the federal government by the Constitution. These proposed amendments merely clarify the limits of those enumerated powers.

"I am a constitutional conservative, but many liberal initiatives, in principle, are worthy ideas and are part of the country's social fabric. The problem is neither Democratic nor Republican politicians impose any limits on federal spending or the powers of government. Over time, we have spent the country into virtual bankruptcy and diminished individual liberty with a vast entitlement and regulatory state. This must be reversed or the country faces certain financial catastrophe in the foreseeable future. The Second Bill of Rights would compel the federal government to rein in its power and reckless spending. Unfortunately, for many years, the Congress has demonstrated repeatedly that it is inherently incapable of reforming itself or behaving in a fiscally responsible manner. Fortunately, the Framers provided in Article V a way for the people and the states to amend the Constitution when they feel compelled to do so."

Shafter now asked the obviously agitated Strank for a response.

"With all due respect to the governor, I won't presume to tell him how to govern the state of Texas, and he has no business telling me how Congress should handle this question. It is up to Congress to interpret the meaning and intent of Article V of the Constitution. We will not be a rubber stamp for the Senate or anyone else. I also take exception to the governor's repeated assertion here and elsewhere that the federal government acts as if it has unlimited power. The government reflects the will of the people through their elected senators and representatives. The government's just powers and laws derive from majority votes by both houses of Congress, approval of the president, and review by the Supreme Court."

In mid-tirade, Shafter interrupted Strank. "Congressman, do you approve of any of the proposed amendments?"

Strank blurted out his response:

"As a matter of fact, I don't. We don't need to make major changes to the Constitution that has served the country so well for over two centuries. I agree with those who believe the Second Bill of Rights is intended to weaken the government and roll back the social safety net programs that help our most vulnerable citizens. Having said that, I don't prejudge the issue of whether a convention should be called. And the House will not be pressured or bullied into taking hasty action on this gravely important issue."

"Would you like to respond to Congressman Strank, Governor?"

In a calm, measured tone, Reb replied:

> "Yes, thank you. Mr. Strank has just said that the government's powers reflect the will of the people and are determined by whatever a majority of both houses of Congress, subject to the president's approval, say those powers are. He and many of his colleagues have made similar statements in the past. This is the crux of the problem with government today. In effect, Mr. Strank argues that we are a nation governed by an elite handful of men and women, whereas I contend the American people are or should be governed by law, specifically the Constitution.
>
> "In a country of 320 million citizens, it takes only two hundred eighteen congressmen, sixty senators because of the Senate's filibuster rules, and one president to pass laws. Think about it. Only two hundred seventy-nine individuals can regulate our lives, dispense favors to preferred constituents, and impose their will on the people. These elite elected officials are sworn to uphold the Constitution, but as Mr. Strank has informed us, he and his colleagues believe they can do most anything they wish, irrespective of what the Constitution says, if they can muster a bare congressional majority and the approval of the president. I don't care how well intentioned they may be, a land governed by the whims of men and women and not the law of the land will end up surrendering its freedom to tyranny. I believe it is imperative that we urgently restore limited constitutional government and fiscal responsibility. Ratification of the Second Bill of Rights is crucial to achieving those goals.
>
> "Following the Philadelphia convention in 1787, but before the Constitution was ratified, Thomas Jefferson wrote to a friend saying, 'The natural progress of things is for liberty to yield and government to gain ground.' He did not write those words in an approving vein, rather he was warning that freedom required the eternal vigilance of free men or it might be forever lost. Mr. Jefferson could not have imagined the extent to which the federal government's

powers would become virtually unlimited over the past century, or that the Constitution could be interpreted in such an elastic and expansive manner as to be a nearly impotent check on government."

As Reb finished and without waiting for Shafter to ask him for comment, the feisty Strank launched into his emotional rebuttal:

"Governor McCoy apparently thinks the Constitution should be strictly interpreted, as if nothing has changed since it was written in the eighteenth century. But we live in the twenty-first century. While Thomas Jefferson might not have imagined the size and scope of today's federal government, he was a genius and if he were to return today, I'm certain he would immediately grasp the need for larger government to accommodate a modern, diverse, and complex society of over 300 million people. Many of the programs government has instituted over the past century are aimed at helping Americans at the bottom of the economic ladder who have no opportunity to realize the American dream. Governor McCoy would have us return to the good old days when government allowed rampant, unfettered capitalism that enriched a few and held down everybody else."

Reb responded:

"Mr. Strank seems to impugn the motives of everyone outside of government. I am skeptical of too much power concentrated in any institution, but especially in government. Power begets power, and too much power ultimately corrupts. Only the people and the states can check excessive government encroachment into our lives. Americans are a generous and rich people. We should always provide for those who can't help themselves. No one wants to return to a survival of the fittest nation, but we can no longer give government a blank check. We are bankrupt and the debts our generation has incurred will be left for future generations to pay. Is that responsible government?

"The best way to create individual opportunity is to embrace policies that support a growing economy and provide good education for everyone. It is the innovation and free enterprise of the private sector that has lifted millions upon millions of Americans out of poverty and produced this country's fabulous wealth that has allowed government to finance all its social programs. But government is spending faster than the private economy can grow. In fact, government too often inhibits economic growth. We must restore a proper balance between the larger needs of society and safeguarding individual liberty. Liberty means accepting that many people will make bad choices, but it is their God-given, free will right to do so. Progressives want to tell people what they can or cannot do for their own good. This is oversimplified, but freedom demands individual responsibility and accountability. The entitlement, nanny state stifles individual ambition, initiative, and self-responsibility. Looking to and depending on government for virtually everything erodes the individual's dignity and diminishes liberty."

Without waiting to be prompted, Strank replied sharply, as if his raised voice proved the truth of his opinion:

"Only government can protect the least among us and curb the rapacious greed of amoral businessmen and impersonal corporations. We cannot achieve a fair, just, and truly free society without pursuing a policy of egalitarianism and the only institution in society that can advance that goal is the federal government."

Shafter said, "Thank you, Congressman Strank. Governor McCoy, you have the last word."

"Egalitarianism, according to Mr. Strank and his fellow progressives, is primarily about achieving equal outcomes. In truth, an egalitarian society is one that celebrates individual liberty by ensuring all citizens enjoy equal rights, not equal outcomes through redistribution of wealth. All Americans should be guaranteed equal political, legal, property, and religious rights. But men and women are not equal in their talents, ambition, or industry, so we should not even desire a false utopia of equal outcomes. In fact, utopia can be achieved only through government tyranny and denying certain citizens the exercise of their legitimate rights. I don't want to return to the eighteenth or even the twentieth century, but I firmly believe the principles of individual liberty embodied in the Constitution are as relevant today as they were two hundred thirty years ago. Mr. Strank implies the Constitution is a relic of a bygone era. If the Constitution lacks the flexibility to accommodate modern

> times, Congress should amend it, not disregard it. I
> challenge Mr. Strank and Congress to fulfill their duty under
> Article V by honoring the states' petitions and calling a
> constitutional convention."

The American people were rarely treated to a substantive public debate on a transcendent issue. Most so-called debates degenerated into name calling, unsubstantiated charges, and triviality. Both Strank and McCoy effectively defended their respective positions, but Reb appeared to win the argument over whether Congress should call a constitutional convention. Strank had a weak hand and knew it. The most important debate benefit from Reb's point-of-view was the national media coverage, which kept the spotlight on the constitutional convention for several days.

In June, the Republican governors held their semi-annual meeting in Denver. There was much anger directed at the federal government over a number of issues. All twenty-six governors in attendance expressed outrage over the recent decision by Washington to prevent California from going into default on its debt. How was it fair much less constitutional for the government to have the taxpayers of forty-nine states bail out a state that had for years conducted its fiscal affairs as irresponsibly as did California? Would other states like Illinois and New York be given similar aid? Why should taxpaying citizens of states that are responsible in managing their budgets be obliged to rescue failed states? The bankrupt states were the result of manmade or politician made disasters, not a natural disaster like an earthquake, tsunami, hurricane, or tornado. It did not go unnoticed that California and the other states mentioned as possible recipients of a financial bailout had all voted for President Bucknell.

There was also grumbling among the governors over regulations issued by the EPA that had not been legislated by Congress and imposed draconian rules regarding carbon emissions that would be costly and hurt economic growth. Reb referred to these regulations issued by unelected bureaucrats as regulation without representation. Other unfunded mandates also were the target of gubernatorial anger.

The issue that riled up everyone, however, was the intransigence of Congress in refusing to pass a resolution calling a constitutional convention. Several of the more strident governors suggested that the states and the people might be forced to consider secession in order to get Washington's attention. Most of the assembled governors, including Reb, dismissed this idea, but the seed was planted. What recourse did the states have in the face of a government that recognized no limits on its power, was spending the country into oblivion, and disregarded the rights of sovereign states? No one had a good answer, but a solid majority of the governors said secession was not the solution. That had been tried once before and came to a sad, sanguinary end.

A few weeks after the Republican governors met, Walter Rothmann wrote a column that could have been sourced only by one of the attending governors, for it revealed the closed-door discussion of secession as a possible last resort to force the federal government to address the constitutional convention issue and other state grievances. The impact of Rothmann's column was like a "fire bell in the night," the phrase Thomas Jefferson used in 1820 to express his fear that the Union might not long survive following the difficult and heated debate over Missouri entering the Union as a slave state.

Rothmann wrote:

> "Unlike the Missouri Compromise two centuries ago, which probably saved the nation from splitting apart in 1820, and postponed the Civil War nearly two generations, the recent startling talk among sitting governors about secession has nothing to do with slavery. Today, many states are increasingly exasperated with a federal government that acknowledges no limit on its powers and exhibits no capacity to control its spending. The issue that most

exemplifies the frustration of the states is Congress's obstinate unwillingness to call a constitutional convention despite having received applications for a convention from over two-thirds of the state legislatures as required by the Constitution. On any specific law Congress enacts, there can be principled disagreement as to its constitutionality, but there appears to be no constitutional basis for Congress to refuse to call a constitutional convention. If one requires a smoking gun to be persuaded that Congress stands in breach of the Constitution, this is it. Talk of secession may be idle and reckless, but what recourse do the states and the people have in the face of a Congress that cavalierly disregards its sworn constitutional duty?"

For a week following Rothmann's "fire bell in the night" column, virtually every syndicated radio talk show host made the constitutional convention, the proposed Second Bill of Rights, and secession the primary topics of discussion, stirring up a firestorm of vitriol aimed at Congress. Much of the Constitution was arcane to many people, but Article V's perspicuity was evident to the average man in the street.

Rothmann's column provoked the press to seek out Reb for elaboration on what was discussed at the recent Republican governors meeting. In response to a reporter's inquiry as to the accuracy of Rothmann's piece, Reb responded, "Walter Rothmann has a well-deserved reputation for getting his facts straight and placing them in proper context. All reporters and journalists should aspire to his standard of professionalism."

Another reporter asked, "Who initiated the discussion of secession, Governor? Was it you, and do you support secession?"

"I won't comment on what was said at a private, confidential meeting among my fellow Republican governors, other than to say I did not introduce the topic of secession. I'll also add that this topic came up, in my opinion, out of frustration and exasperation, not as a serious policy recommendation. I don't support secession except as a last resort in the event the federal government became oppressive and usurped the rights and protections guaranteed by the Constitution to the states and the people."

A third reporter chimed in, "Do you believe the states have a right to secede from the Union, Governor?"

"I have no further comment on this matter. Thank you."

Speaker LaRue remained opposed to a constitutional convention, but she realized she had to get this story off the front page and shift the spotlight away from Congress. Following the July 4 recess, Lashette summoned Strank to her office, where they decided to have his committee and the full House pass a resolution establishing the required parameters for calling a convention. The House resolution, however, was substantially different than the Senate resolution, which required the matter to go to conference between selected members of each chamber in order to reconcile differences. The House's action appeared to be constructive, and Lashette cynically hailed the resolution as supporting a convention in principle. She knew, however, that the House Senate conferees would not achieve reconciliation, because Strank and the other House members she appointed to the conference committee would not agree to alter their resolution.

Ding Bell immediately saw through Lashette's ploy and promptly informed Reb. They agreed the best course of action for now was to refrain from public criticism of the House resolution and allow the conference committee a reasonable period of time to work out a deal. As Reb reflected on Lashette's strategy, he had to admire her panache and hard ball politics, but he also began to give serious thought to the preposterous idea that a credible threat of secession might be the only recourse available to the states to bring Congress to its senses.

37

Baton Rouge, Louisiana
October 2017

By autumn 2017, Congress had yet to agree on a resolution calling for a constitutional convention. By then, the federal debt had surpassed $21 trillion, not including federal guarantees of the bonds issued by the states of California, New York, and Illinois. EPA regulations never voted on by Congress went into effect on October 1 at the start of the federal government's fiscal year imposing enormous costs on many manufacturing enterprises and threatening economic growth. The economies of Louisiana and Texas were also hard hit by the lengthy delays that oil exploration companies experienced trying to obtain offshore drilling permits from the Department of Energy. This kept thousands of people out of work and exacerbated the country's reliance on oil imports.

In Texas, border residents were becoming increasingly worried and fearful about the rampant drug wars that had recently spilled over on the U.S. side of the Rio Grande River. In El Paso, three innocent Americans were shot and killed in their homes by stray gunfire from two warring

Juarez gangs. Gov. McCoy had ordered the Texas National Guard to deploy a regiment stationed in Lubbock to El Paso to reinforce the regiment based there. He also ordered the San Antonio regiment to redeploy to Laredo where violence in Nuevo Laredo across the river was rapidly getting out of the Mexican government's ability to control.

Reb personally had made repeated appeals to the director of Homeland Security and President Bucknell for additional border agents and military personnel, but received only token help. The U.S. government was attempting to work out a diplomatic arrangement with Mexico to allow American forces to patrol and use force as necessary along a twenty-five-mile-wide corridor inside Mexico's border to apprehend or destroy the drug gangs. Progress on this front was slow, as Mexico's political leaders feared being perceived as surrendering sovereignty to the gringos to the north. Many Mexicans on both sides of the border were still fired with resentment over the vast territory the U.S. won in the Mexican War fought more than one hundred seventy years ago.

Of more pressing concern to Reb were classified reports he was receiving from the Texas Rangers about an association between the Mexican drug cartel and Arab extremist groups including Hezbollah, a Muslim paramilitary organization based in Lebanon and supported by Iran and Syria. Hezbollah was originated to expel Israel from Lebanon and ultimately to destroy Israel. It is a formidable military organization well armed with rockets and other weaponry. Following Israel's attack on Iran's nuclear facilities just prior to President Thurston taking office in 2013, Iran, Hezbollah, and other terrorist groups swore revenge against the U.S., which was presumed to have orchestrated Israel's attack. Nearly five years had passed since that event without any successful terrorist attack carried out on American soil, but the news that Hezbollah might be operating in Mexico in cooperation with the drug cartels was alarming to Reb. Homeland Security, however, did not think there was any significant Hezbollah presence in Mexico and had no actionable intelligence it was planning to carry out an attack. This offered Reb no peace-of-mind, because he found the reports provided by the Texas Rangers to be credible even though they had not uncovered any specific plans by Hezbollah.

Against this backdrop, Reb agreed to an invitation from his counterparts in Oklahoma and Louisiana to a secret meeting to discuss matters of mutual interest. Belle Chevalier, governor of Louisiana, offered to host the get-together in Baton Rouge.

Belle's aristocratic ancestors on her father's side had fled France during the French Revolution's Reign of Terror and settled in Louisiana ten years before the Louisiana Purchase in 1803. She inherited the family sugar plantation in her early thirties, sold it twenty years later, reportedly for $20 million, and entered politics. Never married, Belle reputedly had many suitors attracted to her petite figure, pretty smile, and old-style southern charm. She was an astute businesswoman and had successfully navigated Louisiana's notoriously corrupt politics without sullying her reputation. Now serving her second term as governor, she was more popular than ever. Reb admired her style and respected her quick, analytical mind.

The governor of Oklahoma was Travis Maxwell who had made a fortune in commercial real estate before turning his attention and considerable intellect to Oklahoma politics. A graduate of West Point, he served in Army Special Forces for eight years including a tour of duty in the Middle East during the first Iraq war to liberate Kuwait in 1991. Now fifty years old, Maxwell was a square-jawed, physically fit outdoorsman who loved hunting and fishing. He was a man's man and found humor in most everything.

The three governors met in the Louisiana Governor's Mansion, a twenty-five-thousand-square-foot structure situated on eight beautifully landscaped acres in Baton Rouge. Built in Greek revival architectural style and featuring

Doric columns on three sides, the home had twelve bedrooms, eighteen bathrooms, and appeared to date from the antebellum period, although it was built in 1963, a century after the War Between the States.

Reb and Maxwell happened to arrive together for a scheduled 7:00 p.m. dinner and were ushered into the mansion's rotunda where presently Belle descended the dramatic circular staircase in a figure-flattering dark green suit. With her green eyes and dark red hair, Reb thought she resembled Maureen O'Hara. While her father's ancestry was French, Belle's mother obviously was of Irish descent.

Maxwell teasingly remarked, "Gee, Belle, living here in Tara as you do, I'm disappointed that you aren't dressed in a crinoline to receive your gentlemen callers."

"Frankly, my dear Travis, I don't give a damn about your disappointment. Now, give this true southern Belle an affectionate kiss on the cheek."

Travis did as he was instructed, whereupon, Belle turned her charm on Reb. "Why, Reb, darling, I do declare you get more handsome as time goes by. Are you still happily married to that gorgeous Marlenna? Oh, silly me, how could you not be? If ever she lets you go, promise you'll look me up."

Reb approached Belle, gave her a warm embrace and said, "How could I ever compete against all your suitors, sweetheart? You are still the Belle of the ball."

The three friends shared a good laugh, as Belle escorted Travis and Reb into the enormous dining room where Belle made sure her honored guests noticed three large paintings from her private collection. One depicts the main American and French characters involved in negotiating the Louisiana Purchase in 1803, probably the only work of art in which both Thomas Jefferson and Napoleon are depicted. The two never met, and one cannot imagine two more opposite historical figures having in common only their mutual greatness. The second painting is of the 1815 Battle of New Orleans where Gen. Andrew Jackson became an enduring American hero by defeating the British in the last engagement of the War of 1812, often described as America's second war of independence. The third work, Belle's favorite, portrays Gen. Washington and French Gen. Rochambeau accepting the surrender of British Gen. Lord Cornwallis at the Battle of Yorktown in 1781. In the distance can be seen the fleet of French Adm. de Grasse who defeated the British fleet at Chesapeake Bay, thereby blocking Cornwallis from escaping the capture of his army. Yorktown was the last battle of the American Revolution.

As she no doubt did whenever she had guests in this room, Belle remarked, "Without the support of the French Army and Navy, the American colonies could not have won independence from Britain. And without Napoleon's desperate need for cash to finance his European military adventures, who knows if or when America would have acquired the Louisiana Territory, which more than doubled the size of the United States. I am proud to be of French blood and America should be forever grateful to France. George Washington and Thomas Jefferson certainly were. Unfortunately, few school children today know anything about their country's history."

Reb replied, "Regrettably, too few adult Americans know much about their country's history."

Reb pulled out Belle's chair at the head of the table, and after she was seated, Reb and Travis took their places on either side of her. Travis poured wine from the decanter at his side and proposed a toast, "To our lovely hostess, Madame Belle Chevalier, governor of the great state of Louisiana. Viva la France!"

Reb said, "Hear, Hear, and long live the United States of America and the Constitution by which it is governed," as they touched each other's glasses and Belle beamed.

To ensure their privacy, Belle had given the wait staff the night off and arranged for each dinner course to be delivered by dumbwaiter from the mansion's subterranean kitchen. Pressing a floor buzzer beneath the table, she could alert the kitchen to send up the next course. Belle personally cleared the table after each course, took the china to the dumbwaiter, and returned with the next course. Reb was amused by this and couldn't refrain from remarking, "Belle, you are a wonderful waitress. I've never before been waited on by a governor. I'll bet you get great tips."

"I have a no tipping policy, darling, but I'll expect similar service from you when you invite me to Austin for a visit."

After Belle served the second course, she turned to the purpose of the meeting. "Reb, Travis and I are grateful you would join us this evening. Like you, we too are profoundly concerned about the direction of the country. If nothing dramatic is done soon, I fear we will suffer a financial collapse, the aftermath of which might result in the federal government assuming dictatorial powers. Until recently, we were guardedly optimistic that Congress would do its duty and call a constitutional convention, which hopefully would result in the Second Bill of Rights being ratified by at least thirty-eight states."

Under Belle's and Travis's leadership, Louisiana and Oklahoma's Legislatures submitted applications for a convention to Congress only months after Texas had done so. Reb was grateful for their unflagging support of the Second Bill of Rights. They also had been instrumental in getting the GOP to change its name to the Republican Constitution Party, and endorsed his run for president right after he announced his candidacy.

Belle continued, "We all know neither the Congress nor the federal bureaucracy can change from within. It's not in their DNA. Oh, there are a few people on Capitol Hill who know what needs to be done and are prepared to do it, but not enough to make a majority or even a critical mass. The government and its elected officials are addicted to spending and power. Absent an outside force, there appears no way to undo this Gordian knot. Travis and I liken it to dealing with a spouse or parent who has an alcohol or drug addiction. Often in such situations, there is an intervention in which the loved one is compelled by family and friends to face up to his or her addiction and immediately begin therapy. In the case of the federal government, we may need an exorcist to exorcize its demonic appetite for spending and power."

Belle paused to clear the second course plates and retrieve the entrée, a delectable Cajun snapper. While she did so, Travis refilled the wine glasses and said, "At our recent GOP Governors Association meeting, Belle and I, as you will recall, were among five governors who proposed that we consider organizing several states to secede from the Union. I know most of our fellow governors, perhaps you as well, thought we were nuts. But we live in nutty times, and I believe we must shake the foundation of the Republic if the federal government refuses to heed the Constitution or deal responsibly with the debt and deficits. I know it may sound absurd, but I've reluctantly concluded that we need to break up the Republic in order to save it."

Reb was not surprised that this was the topic Travis and Belle had in mind when he was invited to join them in Baton Rouge. And since his last conversation with Ding Bell, Reb had started to mull over the idea of secession, but he was not ready to commit to such a course of action. Not by nature an impulsive man, Reb had been a highly successful business executive, because he took bold decisions only after calculating the risks, quantifying and limiting the downside, and establishing that the upside payoff potential justified the bet. So far, from nearly every angle, he saw secession as a bad bet.

Commenting half in jest, Reb said, "So much for my earlier toast of long life to the USA and the Constitution. Are we a conspiracy of three plotting against the United States government? Look, since the governors' meeting and the transparent effort by the House of Representatives to forestall a constitutional convention, I have given some thought to the idea of secession. But so far, I'm having trouble getting beyond the arguments against secession, which are formidable. As we both know, this was tried once before over a hundred fifty years ago with entirely unfortunate results, except that slavery was abolished. If several states were to convince their citizens to vote overwhelmingly for secession, how would the feds react? The seceding states would be portrayed by the press as traitors, creating a backlash in favor of the federal government that would encourage it to increase centralized power."

Belle replied, "Reb, secession may be a desperate, last gasp attempt at bringing the American people and the political hacks in Washington to their senses, but can we not resort to it if all else fails? If we are going to lose our freedom, drown in an ocean of national debt, and shackle future generations in financial servitude, what have we got to lose? If Congress does not call a convention by year end, I believe we have to act early in 2018. If we can pull it off, at least the states that secede might have a reasonable chance to pass on the blessings of liberty to the great grandchildren of their citizens."

Travis interjected, "The only way secession can have a chance of succeeding is if a big state is involved, like Texas. Relatively small states like Oklahoma and Louisiana, either alone or together, would not be taken seriously. Any hope for success also depends on a figure of national stature, widely respected, and trusted by the people, to lead the revolution. Such a person is you, Reb."

"You both are serious about this, aren't you?" Reb asked rhetorically. "Assuming for the moment that the federal government would not use force to suppress secession and restore the Union, have you thought through all the enormous issues that would have to be addressed? First and foremost, you have to convince the people why secession is justified by laying out a bill of particulars against the U.S. government. In my view, only if a super majority, say, two-thirds of the electorate voted for secession, would it have legitimacy."

"Whoa, pardner," interrupted Travis, "I doubt you can get a two-thirds vote in favor of motherhood and cherry pie. If such a high hurdle were established to approve secession, there is virtually no chance it could be met in any state."

"Look, if a state seceded based on a narrow majority of its citizens," responded Reb, "I don't think it would appear legitimate. In fact, the minority would scream with justification that a tyranny of a narrow majority is forcing them to secede from their country. In my opinion, you would have to obtain no less than three-fifths or 60 percent of the vote for secession to have political legitimacy."

Travis said, "Okay, I take your point. I actually believe if a referendum on secession were held in Oklahoma today, it would receive more than 60 percent of the vote."

Belle added, "Louisianans hold a lingering resentment of the federal government primarily over its handling of the BP oil spill's aftermath, the moratorium on offshore drilling, and now the constitutional convention issue. At this moment, I'd wager that a secession referendum would win very close to 60 percent of the vote."

Reb continued, "Assuming a referendum on secession received 60 percent popular approval in our three states, a constitutional convention would have to be called immediately to establish a new republic and to adopt, presumably, the U.S. Constitution and the Second Bill of Rights. This would have to be ratified by the states joining the new republic. Elections would have to be held, laws enacted, and the new government staffed. Because the U.S. recognizes dual nationality, residents of seceding states would have the option of retaining both U.S. citizenship and becoming citizens of the new republic. Those who retain their U.S. citizenship would still be subject to U.S. laws and income taxes, and also subject to the laws and income taxes levied by the new republic. For several years at least, the U.S. would have to be permitted the continued use of its federal property and facilities within the new republic. Perhaps in time, a treaty could be negotiated, whereby the new republic could purchase federal land and facilities from the United States. The U.S. may reasonably demand that the new republic assume responsibility for a pro rata share of its national debt. A currency would have to be established. Diplomatic recognition of the new republic would be essential to establish its sovereignty and acceptance in the family of nations. Trade treaties would have to be negotiated. Social Security and Medicare programs would have to be instituted for the new republic's citizens not eligible under the U.S. plans. This all adds up to a daunting task, even if secession can be done peacefully."

"Reb, Travis and I have discussed many of the points you raise, but we need a contingency plan if Congress denies the states a constitutional convention. In that event, the threat of secession is our only option or else our states will go down the drain with the rest of the country. We don't want to secede, but the federal government is compelling us to explore that option. Our hope is that a serious threat of secession will catalyze Congress to restrain spending radically and call a convention."

"Belle, we can't threaten secession unless we are prepared to follow through," responded Reb. "We dare not run a bluff and hope it's not called."

Travis said, "Reb, neither Belle nor I have any intention of bluffing. If this idea moves forward, we have to plan and prepare to secede if the government fails to fulfill its constitutional obligations by a date certain. This is not a negotiating ploy. But unless you are willing to join with us, secession is not feasible. You are a national figure, the face of the Second Bill of Rights, the winner of the popular vote in the last presidential election, and the governor of Texas, the most important state after California."

As Belle graciously served generous portions of Creole bread pudding with whiskey sauce, Reb said, "Out of curiosity, what would be the name of the new republic, and how many states do think might seek to join?"

"I've considered that question," replied Belle. "How does Oklatexiana or Louisitexahoma grab you? Just kidding. Since Texas once was an independent republic and would be by far the largest state in the new nation, its name should be the Constitutional Republic of Texas. The CRT's capital and seat of government would be Austin, which would be carved out as the District of the Republic, or DR. You have a magnificent state capitol building that would be ideal for the CRP Congress. Oklahoma and Louisiana would also be founding states of the CRT."

Nodding his head in agreement, Travis said, "The only thing I would add is that, because Texas's size would be so overwhelming, it should subdivide into four or five states so as not to dominate Oklahoma and Louisiana. As for any other state joining the CRT, I would only require that it have a shared border with a CRT state. The new republic should be contiguous, because geographic separation would be difficult to govern and defend."

Reb said, "The treaty that admitted Texas to the Union in 1845, provided for the possibility of the former republic being divided into five separate states, so that establishes a basis for doing so in the new CRT. I think no other states should be encouraged to join the CRT, because that would further inflame passions in the U.S. Our goal is not to overthrow or even undermine the United States government. The people of the CRT would have simply withdrawn their consent to be governed any longer by the United States. We should, however, encourage states sympathetic to our cause to express their moral solidarity, which might deter the U.S. government from using force to defeat us. If we were to secede, it can be done only on a peaceful basis without animosity or rancor. There can be no Fort Sumter or any other hostile provocation. That won't guarantee how the U.S. will react, but we must endeavor to emulate Gandhi or Martin Luther King, Jr., in abjuring violence."

"There are many states that would support the CRT cause," remarked Belle. "Where do we go from here?"

Travis responded, "I think we should continue these discussions and start to involve others in planning how this would be carried out in the event we decide to seek approval of our citizens to secede. At some point, we need to conduct polling to determine how the folks in our states feel about secession. We also should establish a deadline by which we will act if Congress has not called a convention."

Reb answered, "I think for now we should discuss this matter only among ourselves. The more people we involve the more certain it is that it will become public information; that alone could force Congress to dig in its heels and piously announce it will not succumb to threats or blackmail. We have already seen the media frenzy over Walter Rothmann's recent column. I view this as a theoretical discussion and am not committed at this time to take any active steps toward secession. Of course, that could change based on future events. If we were to take this fateful step, have we each weighed it against the duty and obligation we have to the citizens of our respective states who have entrusted us with high office? Are we ready to forfeit the reputations we have established over a lifetime to be accused of infamy and treason for eternity? Are our loved ones joined with us in supporting us however matters turn out? Do we, like the signers of the Declaration of Independence, 'mutually pledge to each other our Lives, our Fortunes, and our sacred Honor?' These are some of the questions running through my mind, which I cannot answer at this moment."

Travis reflected on the questions Reb posed and replied, "I believe we have more reason to secede from the Union than the Founding Fathers had to secede from Great Britain in 1776. In fact, rather than our states seceding from the Union, I view the federal government as having seceded from the Constitution. My patriotism, my fidelity is to the Constitution. If we decide we must proceed with secession, I personally am prepared to pledge to each of you and the citizens of the sovereign state of Oklahoma my life, my fortune, and my sacred honor."

Reb looked at his watch. "Belle, the meal was delicious and the conversation stimulating to say the least, but I'll have to excuse myself to get back to Austin tonight. I suggest we meet again next month to assess the situation at that time and determine what action is appropriate."

Reb rose from the table and said good-bye to Belle and Travis, who both thanked him again for traveling to Baton Rouge on short notice to meet with them.

After Reb departed, Travis asked, "Do you think Reb will decide to pursue secession if Congress does not act by the end of the year?"

"I can't answer that," replied Belle. "I doubt he will, unless he is convinced there is absolutely no other option. Everything depends on events we cannot predict or control. I do know that he will not take such a fateful step without discussing it at length with the Madison Committee, and obtaining Marlenna's counsel. The future of America and freedom may well turn on the perspective of the beautiful, bright, and beloved wife of the governor of Texas, and her role in this drama likely will never appear in the history books. I'll say this. I can't think of two other Americans in whose integrity and judgment I have more faith."

38

In the weeks following Reb's meeting with Governors Chevalier and Maxwell, Marlenna could not help but notice the change in Reb's demeanor. He carried out his official duties with his usual verve, but when they were alone together, he seemed withdrawn and weighed down by a heavy burden. He also was staying up late into the night reading various books on the Civil War, Secession, Abraham Lincoln, and the Constitution.

He was still affectionate and attentive, but the usual conversation, banter, good-natured teasing, and love play they normally shared were missing. Concerned over what had her husband so preoccupied, Marlenna resolved to cajole him into telling her what was eating at him.

As if he was reading her mind, Reb initiated a conversation with her one evening after dinner in late October. "Marlenna, I haven't been very good company lately and for that I apologize. I've needed the last few weeks to think through a decision of enormous consequence from which there will be no turning back once it is taken. But before taking irrevocable action, I must have your input and hopefully your imprimatur."

"The gravity of your voice concerns me, darling, but I'm relieved and eager to learn what has been occupying your thoughts the past few weeks, ever since you returned from your meeting with Belle Chevalier and Travis Maxwell."

"I did not foresee four years ago that our lives and anticipated quiet retirement would change in such a profound, radical, and permanent way simply by agreeing to chair the Madison Committee. That seemingly innocuous decision led to my late-in-life entry into politics, election as Texas's governor, and an implausible run for president last year. I came reluctantly to the public arena with no motivation other than a sense of civic duty and my lifelong love of America. I have now reluctantly come to the most foreboding decision of my life. Despite great trepidation, I am certain my decision is correct, unavoidable, and impelled by the inexorable tide of history."

"Darling, will you please tell me what on earth you have decided? The suspense is killing me."

"If Congress does not call a constitutional convention by the end of 2017, I will endeavor to persuade the people of Texas to secede from the United States and establish an independent constitutional republic. I see no other recourse available to shock Congress into fulfilling its constitutional duty."

For a breathless moment, Marlenna sat in stunned disbelief, but then her words poured out. "Reb, I'm nearly speechless. You will be vilified and labeled a traitor. I fully support your position on the constitutional convention and the Second Bill of Rights. No one would have imagined that in just four years, thirty-six states would petition Congress to call a convention, and you were the driving force behind the success of that effort. If Congress doesn't act, however, why shouldn't it be left to the voters in 2018 to elect representatives pledged to call a convention? You have steadfastly argued since you went into politics that the federal government has aggrandized to itself powers not authorized by the Constitution. Isn't secession a violation of the Constitution? How can you advocate an unconstitutional act, while you admonish the federal government for doing the same thing?"

Struggling now to maintain her composure, Marlenna continued. "Besides all that, I love you, and I couldn't bear to see your reputation destroyed. You are as patriotic and honorable as any person I've ever known, and your love of country is obvious to anyone who knows you. My god, you served with valor in Vietnam when you easily could have avoided the draft with a student deferment. The thought of you being viciously attacked for being a traitor sickens me. Please awaken me from this nightmare and tell me you are joking."

Tears were now streaming down Marlenna's cheeks. Nothing devastated Reb more than to see his wife upset, especially when he was to blame for her tears.

"Pretty, please don't cry."

"Don't cry? A year ago you were very nearly murdered by a professional assassin while running for president. Now you want to lead an effort to break up the country. If you aren't hanged as a traitor, any number of pseudo-patriotic lunatics will try to kill you, and one of them probably will get the job done. Is there any wonder why I am crying?"

"Marlenna, honey, please hear me out. Secession is not unconstitutional, despite what Mr. Lincoln argued. The Supreme Court ruled it illegal after the Civil War, but that was a questionable ruling according to Wyatt Solomon. If we wait till the 2018 off-year election, as you suggest, the constitutional convention issue probably will have been relegated to the dustbin of history, overtaken by unforeseen yet inevitable future events. This has been the pattern with every previous unconstitutional expansion of government power. Defenders of the Constitution rail against each new encroachment on liberty, but within a year or two it is generally forgotten and accepted as a fait accompli. The country now is at a tipping point. If the states and the people supinely accept Congress's dereliction of duty on the convention issue, can anyone imagine an effective restraint on federal government power in the future? We must draw a line in the sand and say here is where we stand in defense of limited government, individual liberty, and fiscal responsibility."

"And what about the dishonor you will bring down upon your good name? You are more popular today than you were a year ago because of the classy, statesmanlike way you conducted yourself following the election. You have a deep reservoir of political capital with the American public, which you are about to squander."

"My reputation is of small consequence compared with what I believe is right and necessary to secure the future of Texas and America. Given what is at stake, true dishonor would be to stand aside for fear of damage to my reputation. Political capital is a highly perishable asset. I might as well spend mine in pursuit of a noble objective."

"Have you thought about Ravenna and your grandchildren? They adore you. What will be the effect on Kyle and Deanna, when children taunt them that their grandfather is a traitor?"

"We will sit down with Ravenna, Jeff, and the kids and lay everything out for them. Whatever names people may throw at me, you know I will never be a traitor. Never will I betray or start a war against America. And I will never pass state secrets to America's enemies. Those are acts of treason. If Texas were to vote to secede from the Union, it would be withdrawing its consent to be governed by the United States, and going its separate way in peace and friendship. There is growing sympathy and support for secession in a number of states. Oklahoma and Louisiana are already a hotbed of secessionist sentiment."

"Well, why not let Belle and Travis lead the way in breaking up the country?" asked Marlenna. "Why must you be the one who is out front? Over the last four years, you have done more than anyone else to keep the dream of the Second Bill of Rights alive. It's time for someone else to step forward to lead the fight for a constitutional convention."

"For secession and establishment of a new republic to be taken seriously and have any chance of convincing Congress to do its sworn duty, more than two states will have to secede and one will have to be a large state. Whether together or alone, Oklahoma and Louisiana could not pull it off. Texas is the key to the venture, and that means I must be personally involved. I believe in and am committed to the Second Bill of Rights and a constitutional convention as the best and perhaps last chance to return America to its constitutional first principles. To abandon the field and become a bystander now would be an act of moral cowardice. I'm not sure whether the man makes the times or the times make the man. In truth, each shapes and influences the other. At a particular place and point in time, I became unwittingly a pawn in the endless pageant of history, and at every subsequent turn since, I chose of my own free will to remain an actor in that pageant without knowing my ultimate destiny. I am firm in the belief, however, that there is no more true and honorable pursuit than the reaffirmation of liberty, no matter the personal cost. I desperately need you to understand and believe in what I must do."

He gently wrapped Marlenna in his long, strong arms, kissed her forehead, inhaled the lovely scent of her hair, and said, "You know I love and adore you, pretty."

"I too love you very much, Reb. You obviously have thought this all through and make a sound case for your position. With a saddened heart, I give you my unconditional support, but I fear you are about to unleash powerful forces that you can't control and can't defeat. If memory serves,

Shakespeare wrote, 'the better part of valor is discretion.' I wish you could take that adage to heart."

"No doubt Shakespeare was—and still is—right in most life circumstances. In the current circumstance, however, I believe honor and the lesser part of valor trump discretion. I recall Barry Goldwater's famous quote from his acceptance speech at the 1964 Republican convention: 'Extremism in the defense of liberty is no vice. And moderation in the pursuit of justice is no virtue.' There's not much discretion in that remark. Remember my speech on courage to the corps of cadets in chapel last year when we visited WMAC to dedicate Madison Hall? I would be a hypocrite if I now failed to do my duty as my conscience dictates. Our great American experiment in democracy has again arrived at a critical turning point. A combination of destiny, design, and acquiescence has conspired to place me at the center of events. Fate has wielded its insidious, irresistible power to ensnare me in history's improbable, unfolding drama, allowing no honorable escape."

39

Texas v. White

On the first Saturday in November 2017, the tea party and the 9-10 party held a long planned joint rally on the Mall in front of the Lincoln Memorial in Washington, DC. On a balmy Indian summer day, an estimated crowd of four hundred fifty thousand attended. When the event had originally been organized, the agenda was to focus on federal spending and the deficit, as well as the Ninth and Tenth Amendments. In the months leading up to the rally, however, Congress's failure to call a constitutional convention increasingly became the central issue of the moment.

The parade of speakers, many household names, others not, discussed the Second Bill of Rights and the Congress's constitutional obligation to honor the thirty-six state applications for a convention. The enormous crowd was well-behaved and polite, as it loudly cheered the speakers, a few of whom, including the governors of Oklahoma and Louisiana, suggested that if Congress did not act, the only recourse left to the states might be to consider secession. The crowd exhibited enthusiastic support for the idea of disunion and repeatedly chanted, "Give Us a Convention or We'll Demand Secession," a demand that certainly had never been heard before at the hallowed site of the Lincoln Memorial. There were also chants of the McCoy–Duzmore campaign slogan, "Freedom Fever – Catch It!" Neither Lillian nor Reb attended the DC rally, but media correspondents from around the country and several from Europe were there to cover it.

A poll taken the week before the rally indicated 35 percent of Americans believed secession would be justified if Congress did not call a convention; 30 percent rejected secession under any circumstance; 20 percent said secession was unacceptable at this time; 15 percent were undecided. The most remarkable and surprising results of this poll were that the word secession had not been uttered in political discourse as recently as six months ago, yet potentially a 55 percent majority of Americans might support secession under certain circumstances. In the week following the rally, another poll revealed an even larger majority possibly favoring secession if the federal government didn't address the convention matter and the ongoing budget deficits.

Politicians, journalists, and commentators were startled at this sudden grass-roots eruption in support of secession. Many hyperventilated that the country was on the verge of revolution and perhaps civil war. Various columnists and radio talk show hosts, both on the left and the right, avidly supported and encouraged secession for different reasons. A significant minority of liberals argued that purging the country of states whose citizens do not support the national government and its enlightened progressivism would be healthy, as it would eliminate the obstacles to fulfilling the utopian dream of a just society. A number of conservatives opined that secession would provide the opportunity to establish a new republic of limited government and individual liberty more aligned with the Founding Fathers' vision. Interestingly, the idea of secession made strange bedfellows of many liberals and conservatives who argued the Civil War had established for all time that the nation was indivisible and disunion would result in another civil war. Those in this group also claimed America's national security would be irreparably and perhaps fatally damaged if any states were to breakaway. Therefore, secession would be an act of treason by those who advocated it.

The columnist Donald Utopeville aligned himself with those who opposed secession and thought that any such talk was both silly and dangerous. In his opinion piece a few days after the DC rally, he wrote:

> The question of secession was settled decisively when the Union finally subdued the Confederacy in 1865, following a tragic, bloody, four-year civil war. Four years later in 1869, the U.S. Supreme Court in *Texas v. White*, ruled that the Union was indissoluble. Chief Justice Salmon P. Chase, writing for the majority, argued that the colonies united as states in 1777 under the 'Articles of Confederation and perpetual Union.' The Articles subsequently were succeeded by the Constitution in 1789, which was established to form a 'more perfect Union.' Chase wrote, "What can be indissoluble if a perpetual union, made more perfect, is not?" According to the Court, admission of a State into the Union was final. "There was no place for reconsideration or revocation, except through revolution or through consent of the States."
>
> While I believe secession to be illegal and unacceptable, the Congress of the United States is responsible for this subject being a serious topic of discussion. For no credible reason, Congress has stubbornly refused to honor the applications of thirty-six states to call a constitutional convention to consider the proposed seven amendments known as the Second Bill of Rights. This is a flagrant violation of Article V of the Constitution. The growing anger and frustration of states and citizens who support a convention is understandable and begs the question: What recourse do the people have when the federal government fails to abide by the Constitution? The Supreme Court has said it has no jurisdiction to resolve the matter, because the Constitution grants Congress exclusive power to call a constitutional convention. It would seem the only legitimate recourse available to the people is to wait until the next election, which won't occur for another year. In the

meantime, they should express their opinion loudly, clearly, and with civility to their elected representatives.

After reading Utopeville's column, Reb telephoned Judge Wyatt Solomon to ask him if he agreed that the question of secession's illegality and unconstitutionality had been settled once and for all.

"Governor, I don't believe the Supreme Court had judicial standing to rule on the matter of secession as it did in *Texas v. White*. Moreover, I think the Court's reasoning was flawed, lacked objectivity, and failed to consider many sound arguments that support a sovereign state's right to secede peacefully from the Union."

"Well, Wyatt, tell me why you disagree with *Texas v. White*."

"Why? Are you planning to secede from the Union, Reb?"

"It may depend on what you tell me about the right of a state to secede."

"With all the talk of secession recently, I have been rereading a few books I have on the subject. Many years ago in law school, I was assigned to a debate team that argued the case for secession. To begin with, the original thirteen colonies were individually chartered by the English Crown. While they were subject to the authority of the Crown, they were each sovereign and independent of each other. When the colonies declared their independence in 1776, they did so as free and independent states. History remembers this as the American Revolution, but it was also a declaration of secession from Great Britain. In fact, when King George III ratified the Treaty of Paris in 1784, formally ending the Revolutionary War, the treaty mentioned each colony by name and stated that the thirteen colonies were henceforth 'free, sovereign, and independent States.'"

Reb interrupted Wyatt to ask, "But once the colonies seceded from Great Britain by declaring their independence in 1776, didn't they independently and voluntarily enter into the Articles of Confederation, which was a perpetual Union?"

"Yes, the Articles were perpetual for all of about twelve years or until the Constitution was ratified, whereupon the states seceded from the Articles and adopted the Constitution in 1789. Unlike the Articles, the word perpetual is not mentioned in the Constitution. The Framers fervently hoped the new republic would last in perpetuity, but realists that they were, none expected it to last forever. Several of the states in their ratifying conventions adopted the Constitution, but reserved the right to resume the powers delegated to the federal government. I have in hand, as we speak, *The Federalist No. 35* in which Madison wrote:

> 'Each State, in ratifying the Constitution, is considered as a sovereign body, independent of all others, and only to be bound by its own voluntary act. In this relation, then, the new Constitution will, if established, be a *federal*, and not a *national* constitution.'

"Elsewhere in the same essay, he wrote:

> 'The Constitution is to be founded on the assent and ratification of the people of America…not as individuals composing one entire nation, but as composing the distinct and independent States to which they respectively belong…establishing the Constitution, will not be a *national*, but a *federal* act.'"

Reb responded, "But the Preamble begins, 'We the People of the United States.' That seems to contradict the idea that independent sovereign states voluntarily entered into a federation."

"As originally drafted, that language read: 'We the People of New Hampshire, Massachusetts, Connecticut, etcetera.' For the sake of brevity and more elegant prose, the names of the states were deleted in the final version. But the Constitution was ratified by conventions held in each sovereign state as stipulated under Article VII. In *The Federalist No. 45*, Madison wrote, 'The powers delegated by the proposed Constitution to the federal government are few and defined. Those which remain in the State governments are numerous and indefinite.' This did not allay the reservations of a number of suspicious and prescient delegates to the state ratifying conventions, particularly New York, Virginia, and Rhode Island, who feared that in time the new federal government might usurp powers beyond those delegated to it. This is why, soon after the Constitution went into effect, they adopted the Bill of Rights, which included the Tenth Amendment: 'The powers not delegated to the United States by the Constitution, nor prohibited by it to the States, are reserved to the States respectively, or to the people.' The Constitution is silent on the matter of secession; therefore, the sovereign states have an implicit right to secede."

"So, Wyatt, you're telling me that the North's defeat of the South in the Civil War did not establish secession as illegal?"

"No, not unless you believe that might makes right. The North imposed its will on the South and restored the Union, but that says nothing about whether secession is legitimate or illegitimate. In judging history, too often we think the side that prevailed by force of arms was not only the winner, but the just and the righteous."

"Wait a minute, Wyatt. Abraham Lincoln is revered above all other Americans, save Washington, because he fought and won the Civil War, thereby restoring the Union and freeing the slaves. You're telling me that that grand achievement was not just and righteous?"

"Lincoln gained eternal honor and glory for ending slavery in America, the only country on earth that declared all men are created equal and endowed by their Creator with unalienable rights to life, liberty, and the pursuit of happiness. The irony that escapes most people is that Lincoln had no intention of ending slavery at the start of the war. As the war dragged on, however, he found it politically and militarily expedient to emancipate slaves in the Confederate states where he had no power to do so, but not in Union states where he presumably had such power, which I find rather cynical. Slavery was not ended throughout the country until the Thirteenth

Amendment was adopted in December 1865, eight months after the war ended and Lincoln was assassinated. Lincoln's primary if not sole reason for waging all-out war against the Confederacy was to restore the Union. Astounding proof of this is the fact that in an effort to woo the departed states back into the fold in 1861, he supported a proposed 13th amendment that would have guaranteed slavery in perpetuity wherever it was then legal in the United States. This reprehensible idea, which actually was ratified by three Union states, was quietly dropped when the South gave no sign it would rejoin the Union and the war began. Think what Mr. Lincoln's legacy would have been had that amendment been adopted."

"Lincoln was a brilliant man steeped in history and political theory, why did he believe secession was illegal?"

"I can't answer that, but I am sure Pip Pippin can. In fact, he told me recently his next book, which he is writing now, will focus on the causes of the Civil War."

"Okay, Wyatt, let's go back to *Texas v. White*. You have explained why you think the Supreme Court's ruling was wrong, but, right or wrong, doesn't the Court have the last word on what is or is not constitutional?"

"Well, for one thing, judicial ethics require a judge to be impartial and dispassionately objective. Chief Justice Chase was a staunch Union man and served in Lincoln's cabinet as treasury secretary before Lincoln appointed him to the Court in 1864. Chase had been deeply involved in shaping government policy and financing the war. You could argue that Chase had a vested interest in the outcome of the case insofar as the decision would affect Lincoln's and his historical legacy. Imagine if, four years after an awful civil war that saw over six hundred thousand die, the Supreme Court ruled that secession was not prohibited by the Constitution. Such a ruling would have had the effect of declaring Lincoln's war to restore the Union unconstitutional. Chase should have perceived there might be reasonable doubt as to his impartiality and disqualified himself from the case. Instead, he wrote the majority opinion."

"Despite Chase's alleged lack of objectivity, does the Court's decision in *Texas v. White* establish secession to be unconstitutional?"

Wyatt reflected a moment and then said, "I believe the Court didn't have standing to rule on the question of secession, because secession is not a matter pursuant to the Constitution. It does not explicitly prohibit secession; therefore, the right to secede resides with the states. Frankly, I am surprised in the aftermath of the Civil War that there was no constitutional amendment adopted prohibiting secession. In my considered judgment, absent such an amendment, the Court's ruling in *Texas v. White* was outside its purview. It was legislating from the bench rather than interpreting the Constitution as written."

40

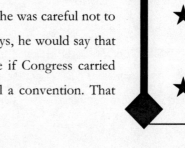

Over the next several days following his conversation with Wyatt, Reb telephoned each of the other Madison Committee members to inform them he planned to devote the next meeting to the question of secession. While Abby and Duane were shocked that Reb took the question seriously enough to explore it further, Ding, Jake, Pip, and of course Wyatt were already thinking along these lines. In planning the meeting agenda, Reb asked Wyatt to summarize their recent phone call with the full committee, and requested Pip to provide additional historical perspective on the causes of the War of Secession and Lincoln's decisions. He did not reveal to anyone besides Marlenna that he had already decided to back secession if Congress did not take appropriate action by year end.

As the days passed, the national media, cable TV, and talk radio became increasingly obsessed with the subject of secession. Whenever Reb could not avoid the press clamoring for him to grant interviews, he was careful not to exacerbate the situation. In various ways, he would say that any talk of secession would evaporate if Congress carried out its constitutional obligation to call a convention. That simple act would make all talk of secession moot. But he refused to be lured into the media's favorite game of pitting prominent political figures against each other by goading them into leveling accusations or hurling epithets. That was not his style, and he knew it would not advance the debate. Everyone by now knew exactly where he stood on the constitutional convention question. Reb believed in the sound advice he had been given years before about resolving a contentious matter: never bluff or threaten, but speak your mind, bide your time, act only when necessary, and never look back or apologize.

For her part, Speaker of the House Lashette LaRue said secession was unconstitutional or certainly illegal, and any public official who did not disavow such talk and label it irresponsible was fanning the flames of a possible crisis. When asked why the Congress had not acted on the state applications for a convention, she would only say that the matter was being dealt with in the House-Senate Conference Committee, and when they reached a decision, it would be voted on by both chambers.

She typically would end her press conferences saying in a smiling, seductive voice, "Look, people, the Congress will not act before it's time. Despite all the media hoopla and the instigation of certain individuals who would like to incite discord and perhaps disunion, there is no reason to place the matter of a convention ahead of other much more urgent public business. We have not had a constitutional convention in two hundred thirty years. There is no reason to rush into another one without careful reflection. While I cannot speak for the Senate, as long as I am Speaker, the House of Representatives will not be intimidated or pressured into taking action on any matter until it is timely to do so. Have a great day! Thank you."

Reb knew that Lashette had no intention of allowing the conference committee to vote out a convention resolution. Ding Bell had told him the House conferees were not budging from their position, and their Senate counterparts were unwilling to accept the House position. Because each legislative branch had the same number of conferees, the committee had reached an impasse. Ding also knew that two senators on the conference committee detested the idea of a convention, fearing it would strip them and the federal government of power, so it was virtually certain no convention would be called before the 2018 election.

Louisiana's Gov. Chevalier and Oklahoma's Gov. Maxwell contacted Reb during this time to reaffirm their pledge to support him and Texas if her citizens decided to secede. Reb told them both that it was premature to discuss such a possibility, but pressure was building to take some action if Congress persisted in stonewalling a constitutional convention. He had also heard from twenty other governors whose states had petitioned Congress for a convention, saying they would publicly offer loud vocal support of any action Texas or other states might take, but did not believe they could win sufficient support for a declaration of secession in their respective states. Reb felt like the guy who was urged by a buddy to get into a fight while his buddy offered to hold his coat.

By mid-November 2017, however, Reb's attention was focused on the security threat along the Texas border with Mexico. For several years, the Texas Department of Public Safety, at Reb's behest, had ramped up its resources and efforts aimed at penetrating and taking down the Mexican drug cartels now operating ever more brazenly in the Texas border towns. There also was alarming intelligence that pointed to a planned terrorist attack probably involving cartel members and Hezbollah agents operating in Mexico and possibly in Texas. As he had been doing for some months now, Reb and the Department of Public Safety passed on this intelligence to Homeland Security and the FBI.

Concerns and tempers were already rising across Texas, because the violence that had long plagued the Mexico border towns was spilling over with increasing frequency into El Paso, Laredo, Del Rio, and Brownsville. In the past three months, a number of innocent bystanders, including several young children, had been killed in all four cities in the crossfire between rival drug gangs. Reb believed that this activity might be prelude to a larger, more deadly planned attack. The cartels reputedly had a contract out on Reb because of his unrelenting pursuit of gang members operating inside Texas. This information was not shared with the public, nor did Reb tell Marlenna about it. The Department of Public Safety and the Texas Rangers, however, took the threat seriously and beefed up Reb's security detail as inconspicuously as possible.

Newspaper editorials across the state and public opinion were growing more fearful and angry with the federal government for not taking more visible action to strengthen border security. Reb had already deployed additional Texas National Guard units on or near the border in strategic locations, but there was not much else he could do. His sense of foreboding grew day-by-day as intelligence poured in that something was afoot that pointed to a major attack, but there were no specifics as to when, where, or how it would occur.

The rising anger with Congress for not calling a constitutional convention and growing fear over inadequate border security were inciting secession fever among many otherwise laid-back Texans, and the fever was beginning to spread to the Texas Legislature. Nothing concentrates the mind of a politician like an aroused constituency. Reb became concerned that if a terrorist attack was carried out on Texas soil resulting in significant casualties, there would be enormous outrage with the federal government for failing to protect the border and an emotional demand for secession. If that happened, he would no longer be leading and shaping public opinion, but contending with an angry mob while scrambling to manage events in an orderly manner. This was not a pleasant thought.

41

During the fall of 2017, the director of Central Intelligence ordered the CIA's highly classified Special Activities Division, the primary action arm of the National Clandestine Service, to undertake promptly a covert mission inside Mexico. SAD tasked its Special Operations Group, or SOG, to develop and implement immediately a top-secret action plan to determine if, when, and where Hezbollah and a Mexican drug cartel might launch a terrorist attack on the U.S. from Mexico, and, if possible, eliminate or degrade the threat. It was imperative that the identity of the mission's sponsor not be exposed to ensure plausible deniability for senior officials of the U.S. government.

SOG is considered by its foreign counterparts to be the premiere special operations force in the world for conducting espionage and unconventional warfare. Its elite paramilitary operations officers are trained to engage in direct-action raids, sabotage, psychological operations, and assassination. They can operate in any environment with limited support. SOG recruits most of its paramilitary operations officers from the elite Special Ops Forces of the

U.S. military. For the most sensitive operations, SOG uses its Cobra agents who are not formally CIA employees. Cobra agents wear no identification or clothing that could associate them with the U.S. government. If a Cobra operative is compromised or captured, the U.S. government in most cases will disavow any knowledge of the individual.

The National Clandestine Service has wide latitude for action. While it reports to the CIA director and the president, they typically have no direct knowledge of SOG's activities other than the intelligence it gathers that merits their attention. Its annual budget is appropriated as a lump sum by Congress and its details are not known to either senators or representatives, or the president. SOG is charged with carrying out clandestine missions in furtherance of the United States' vital national security interests. Independence from direct oversight by elected officials effectively grants SOG license to do most anything its leaders deem necessary and appropriate to protect and defend the United States. While concentration of such virtually unchecked power is at odds with the precepts of a democratic republic, this has been the cold, hard nature of espionage in a dangerous world ever since World War II.

SOG's classified operational history indicates that it faithfully endeavors to discharge its essential and dangerous mission in a responsible manner. Of course, SOG's self-assessment cannot be independently corroborated.

Most people mistakenly believe that the National Clandestine Service operates only in foreign countries, but it also conducts espionage against foreign enemies within the United States, usually in conjunction with the FBI, although occasionally on its own. There are agents located inside the U.S. who are not based at CIA's Langley, Virginia, headquarters or its training facilities. Safe houses exist in various American cities and front companies are used to afford cover to Cobra agents. Contacts between SOG and Cobra operatives are always done verbally, so there can never be a paper, wiretap, computer, or cyber trail.

Grant Serrano, a Cobra agent based in San Antonio, had been working for SOG for nearly twelve years. His father's ancestors were Spaniards who settled in what is today New Mexico a century before Mexico won its independence from Spain in 1821. His mother's great grandfather, Jeremy Dalton, had been a colonel on Gen. Ulysses S. Grant's staff throughout the Civil War. After the war, Col. Dalton wrote a private memoir of his service with the revered general, which had been handed down from one generation to the next. Serrano's mother named her only son after Grant. When he turned eighteen, his mother gave him a prized family heirloom also handed down from Col. Dalton. It was a medallion struck in 1870 that depicted, from right to left, front to back, the profiles of Washington, Lincoln, and Grant. Below each likeness was a facsimile of their respective signatures, while above, from left to right, were the words, "DEFENDER. MARTYR. FATHER."

As signified by this rare medallion, these three men during the late nineteenth century were considered America's greatest and indispensable leaders, a venerated trinity of heroes. Washington no doubt was the foremost Founder and the Father of his country. Lincoln was martyred to the cause of Union as virtually the last battle casualty of the Civil War, shot on Good Friday in 1865, and thereafter elevated to sainthood in the eyes of many. Grant was indeed the defender of the Union, for without him it is unlikely Mr. Lincoln could have won his war or his most honored place in American history.

Grant Serrano was an avid reader from an early age. He loved American history in general with a particular interest in the Civil War and the career of his namesake, Gen. Grant. Serrano's academic and athletic achievements in high school won him a scholarship to Harvard in 1995, where he excelled in the classroom and on the gridiron, leading the Crimson to an Ivy League championship his senior year. On graduation, Grant was accepted into the army's officer training program, after which he was assigned to a Special Forces unit and later recruited into Delta Force, the Army's elite and secretive counterterrorism unit. Following five years of Army service, which included an eighteen-month tour of duty in Afghanistan fighting the Taliban and al Qaeda, Grant was recruited by the CIA to be a SOG paramilitary operations officer.

Fluent in four languages including Spanish and Arabic, Serrano had a distinguished record of military and clandestine service to his country. He had undertaken all manner of missions from espionage to assassinations over the years. He had been awarded the Silver Star for valor by the army, and the Distinguished Intelligence Cross, the CIA's highest medal for valor. He had also endured fifteen months in the hell hole of a Turkish prison after being charged with espionage in Istanbul by the Turkish secret police. He denied the charges, which of course were true, but as a Cobra agent, he was on his own without help from his government. He finally was freed only after the Australian government intervened on his behalf, at the behest of the CIA. Serrano was permanently banned from Turkey, which suited him just fine. One of SOG's most valuable and experienced assets, five years after joining SOG, he was made a Cobra agent. The career he had chosen was not conducive to having a family. His first and only marriage ended in divorce, because the Firm or Company, as the CIA is known among its employees, always had to come first.

Since 2015, Serrano had been based in San Antonio. His cover was director of operations of a CIA front company that manufactured and assembled components for the automobile industry in several *maquiladora* plants located inside Mexico. A *maquiladora* facility is permitted to import products and materials duty-free, assemble them into finished products, which are then exported to the U.S. or another country. These operations provide good, legitimate jobs for Mexicans, and offer SOG agents an excellent cover to conduct espionage activities in Mexico against the drug cartels. With his thick black hair, dark complexion, and thorough knowledge of the local culture, Serrano passed easily for a Mexican, enabling him to move around the country without attracting notice or suspicion. He had built a network of informants and was providing valuable intelligence to his superiors that had helped break up several cartels and apprehend their leaders.

Serrano's SOG controller met him in San Antonio at a safe house and told him independent intelligence sources had revealed Hezbollah, which had been known to be operating inside Mexico for several years, was plotting a terrorist attack on the U.S. by year end or early in 2018, probably in Texas. One or more of the top drug cartels was believed to be aiding and abetting Hezbollah. Serrano was directed to focus all his effort on finding out details of the plot. A dedicated warrior and patriot, who would do anything he possibly could to foil a terrorist plot against the U.S., Grant told his handler he would immediately focus all his attention on this matter. In fact, he even had a few leads that might provide clues as to what nefarious plot was being hatched across the border between the drug bosses and Hezbollah.

42

Dallas, Texas
November 2017

A week before Thanksgiving, the Madison Committee convened in the Marcoy Foundation's tenth floor conference room. Reb had chosen this venue for privacy reasons, because meeting at the Rosewood Mansion likely would attract nosy reporters. All committee members were in attendance, as was Jake Fillmore.

Reb opened the meeting. "If we reflect on where we were when this committee first met four-and-a-half years ago on the anniversary of James Madison's birth, I am certain we all would agree that to have predicted then what we have so far achieved would have been considered preposterous. And yet for all the progress we have made, it may be lost if Congress does not exercise its constitutional responsibility to call a convention to consider the Second Bill of Rights."

Reb then asked Sen. Ding Bell for a status report on the constitutional convention question before Congress. "The House-Senate Conference Committee almost certainly will not reach any agreement, because most of its members are viscerally opposed to the idea for reasons we all know. The House leadership in particular, from Lashette LaRue on down, is adamantly against a convention and virtually impervious to public opinion. Lashette intends to drag her feet and take her chances on losing control of the House in the November 2018 elections. By then, she is betting this matter will have faded into the background, just another passing fad, supplanted by another major issue of the moment. After the election, win or lose, I understand she plans to pass a resolution during the lame duck session requiring that the applications calling for a convention be revalidated and resubmitted by the state legislatures to the new Congress. I believe this will be the death knell for a constitutional convention."

"Based on Ding's assessment," said Reb, "we have to assume Congress will fail to act in the near future. In that event, what do we do next? Do we accept defeat, not to mention a flagrant breach of the Constitution, and simply say we gave it our best, so it goes? Or do we owe it to the country and future generations to determine if there is an alternate course of action available to us? As you all know from my recent phone conversations with each of you, I am giving serious consideration to joining with the governors of Oklahoma and Louisiana and placing before the citizens of our three states a referendum on secession.

"Some of you have expressed understandable reservations about such a course of action. After all, we came together, because we were fearful that America's future and its constitutional principles of limited government and individual liberty were in serious jeopardy. Now, here I am suggesting the country should break apart. We all know how that worked out the last time it was tried. The purpose of today's meeting is to improve our understanding of what led to the Civil War, how Abraham Lincoln responded to that crisis, and whether he made the right choices. You've all seen a memorandum based on notes from my recent discussion with Wyatt in which he persuasively argues the legal case for secession. Today, I've asked Pip Pippin to provide his historical perspective on the causes and consequences of the Civil War and secession with particular emphasis on Lincoln's decisions. With this information, I hope we as a committee can apply the experience and lessons of the past to the situation we face today and reach a consensus on what we should do next. Pip, please proceed."

"Thank you, Governor. First, I agree with Wyatt that secession is not unconstitutional, notwithstanding the outcome of the Civil War. In short, I believe Lincoln was wrong on the fundamental question he faced in his presidency, and it had tragic consequences for the country."

"Wait a minute, Pip," interrupted Duane Darby, "how can you say Lincoln was wrong? He saved the Union and ensured that the natural rights articulated in the Declaration of Independence truly apply to all men, not just white men, by ending slavery, which obviously is how my ancestors and I gained our liberty."

"Duane, the one tremendous and perhaps only positive outcome of the Civil War was the end of the iniquitous institution of slavery. The question is did it have to be achieved at such a staggeringly high cost? Lincoln did not wage war to end slavery. Slavery was the primary cause of the South's secession, but it was not the cause of the war. The North fought the war to restore the Union, and it was Lincoln's decision alone to wage that war. Before I analyze Lincoln's decisions, let me start with a brief overview of the root causes of the institution of slavery in America and how it led to the Civil War."

Pip paused to sip his coffee and then resumed, "There have been thousands upon thousands of books written about the Civil War, and thousands more written on Abraham Lincoln. To summarize the history of slavery, secession, and the war in a few minutes can only fail to do justice to this enormous subject of inquiry, but I'll give it a try. Shortly after the Virginia colony was established in the early 1600s, England introduced

African slavery into America. While there were slaves in most of the colonies, the institution took root in the South, because slave labor was economical in raising cash crops such as tobacco, cotton, sugarcane, and rice, which could thrive only in the soil and climate there. By 1800, there were about nine hundred thousand slaves in the U.S., with seven hundred thousand toiling in the South. The only states without any slaves were Maine, Massachusetts, and Vermont. Sixty years later on the eve of the Civil War, there were four million slaves in the U.S., nearly 90 percent of them in the eleven states that would secede from the Union and form the Confederacy.

"What drove this growth in the slave population? The primary reason was Eli Whitney's cotton gin, a device that mechanically removes the seeds from cotton. This 1793 invention revolutionized the speed at which cotton could be harvested. As a consequence, the global demand for cotton in the first half of the nineteenth century skyrocketed. A labor intensive cash crop, the expanding cotton plantations required more land and slaves to support increased production. By 1860, the South produced two-thirds of the world's cotton. The textile industry of England and the New England states depended on southern cotton to feed their mills. Although probably no more than a quarter of southern families owned slaves, the South's antebellum economy was dependent on slave labor, and those free whites who did not own slaves benefited from slavery, as did the textile manufacturers in England and the U.S. Unintentionally, the marvelous invention of the cotton gin was a root cause of the Union break up in 1861, because it accelerated the growth of slavery in the South, which divided the nation into two distinct sections with ultimately irreconcilable cultures. Absent the cotton gin, slavery might have gradually withered away or at least not have become the foundation of the South's economy and culture.

"The cumulative effect of many events during the forty-year period prior to the Civil War, or War of Secession, drove the slave-free North and the

South further apart. Several crises during that time could have resulted in war, but compromises were worked out to postpone the day of reckoning. I believe two major factors leading to secession were the rise of the abolitionist movement in the North and the posture of many protestant ministers in the South. Abolitionists railed against slavery and they had a righteous cause. How could slavery continue to exist in a country based on the principles espoused in the Declaration? The abolitionists had newspapers to spread their message, and an increasing number of citizens in the slave-free states became anti-slavery if not outright abolitionist. In the decade running up to secession, the outcry in the North over slavery grew ever louder, and religious leaders became increasingly outspoken from the pulpit on the evils of slavery.

"And then there was the fanatical abolitionist John Brown who resorted to violence against pro-slavery men in 'Bleeding Kansas' in 1856. In 1859, Brown tried unsuccessfully to seize a federal armory at Harpers Ferry, Virginia, with the idea of inciting an insurrection by arming slaves and carrying the cause of abolition against southern slave masters. On the other end of the spectrum, there was mild-mannered Harriett Beecher Stowe whose book, *Uncle Tom's Cabin*, published in 1852, made a powerful emotional appeal for the end of slavery by vividly describing its horrors. The book sold over three hundred thousand copies, which was unheard of in the nineteenth century, and had an incalculable impact on northern public opinion.

"So, the South increasingly felt threatened by abolitionist rhetoric and the incessant condemnation of its economic system and way of life by many northerners, despite the fact the Constitution, without using the term slave, made the 'peculiar institution' legal. Naturally, whites in Dixie became defensive and resentful about the fulminations against slavery emanating from the North. Moreover, many southern preachers used the pulpit to defend and justify slavery, which reinforced the belief by most southerners, especially slave owners, that slavery was moral and condoned by the Bible. In retrospect, it is incredible that any Protestant clergyman could take the position that slavery was consistent with Christian values. Back then, people in general were more devout than they are today, so what one's minister had to say carried great weight.

"There were, of course, many other events that helped to bring about secession, but I believe the advent of the cotton gin, the cumulative pressure by northern abolitionists, and southern pride in a way of life they had known for over two centuries were the root causes that ultimately resulted in disunion."

"That's an interesting analysis, Pip," interjected Wyatt, "but what about the tariff issue, Lincoln's election, and states' rights? Weren't they all reasons the southern states decided to leave the Union?"

"I'll address each of those points, Wyatt. It's true that the tariff had been a bone of contention with the southern states for many years. In fact, in 1832, South Carolina voted to nullify the so-called 'Tariff of Abominations' before backing down in the face of President Jackson's threat to use the military to force compliance with the law. Subsequently, Congress reached an accommodation with the South on the level of the tariff. At the time of the War of Secession, the U.S. government raised 90 percent of its revenue from the tariff. The burden fell disproportionately on the agrarian southern states, because they had little manufacturing capacity and either had to purchase high priced equipment from northern manufacturers, or import from England equipment subject to the tariff. By the time of secession in 1860, however, the tariff was a secondary issue. Actually, the tariff was one major reason the North went to war. The South generated half the federal government's tariff income, which was lost as a result of secession. Moreover, the North did not want to see Charleston, New Orleans, and Mobile become free ports, as this would hurt northern manufacturing interests, which could not compete with foreign imports without the tariff's price umbrella.

"Lincoln's election, in my opinion, was more like the last straw than a primary cause for secession. The Republican Party and Lincoln were pledged to prohibit the extension of slavery beyond those states where it was then permitted. Most slaveholders recognized slavery was not economically viable in the plains, Rocky Mountain, or southwestern states and territories. Nevertheless, prohibiting slavery in those regions offended southern pride, and was one more example of the North demonstrating its contempt for the southern way of life. Southerners realized, however, that as new free soil states were admitted to the Union, their representation in Congress soon would be inadequate to fend off legislation limiting or even abolishing slavery. In order to preserve their way of life, from their perspective, secession was the only option.

"I agree that the issue of states' rights was a primary cause of secession in the case of the four states that seceded in response to President Lincoln's reaction to the firing on Fort Sumter in April 1861. I'll come back to this later. States' rights, however, was not a determining factor with the first seven states that seceded and established the Confederate States of America during the interregnum between Lincoln's election in November 1860 and his inauguration in March 1861. Those states, which included South Carolina, Georgia, Florida, Alabama, Mississippi, Louisiana, and Texas, seceded over slavery and the fear of U.S. interference in their social and economic system. Lincoln had pledged not to make any effort to abolish slavery where it existed and even supported a constitutional amendment to that effect, but the South did not trust him and by then the die was cast.

"Lincoln's immediate predecessor James Buchanan is reviled by history as the country's worst president. Buchanan is proof you can't always judge a man's capability by his résumé. Before being elected president, Buchanan had spent two decades in Congress, both the House and the Senate, and had served as minister to Russia, ambassador to England, and U.S. secretary of state. Promoted beyond his competence, Buchanan was an ineffectual chief executive, but by 1857 when he assumed the presidency, there was little or nothing he could do to avert the looming crisis. The accumulation of events over the preceding decade had made it clear that compromise between irreconcilable positions was no longer possible. By the time the first seven southern states seceded, Buchanan was a lame duck awaiting Lincoln's arrival.

"For all Buchanan's shortcomings, however, Lincoln might have done well to heed the wisdom and insight his predecessor displayed in his December 1860 annual message to Congress, when the southern states were about to secede. Buchanan opposed secession and considered it impermissible under the Constitution, but it is worth quoting at length from his message, excerpts of which I brought with me."

Pip flipped through his papers until he found the one he was looking for and then said, "Buchanan asked rhetorically of Congress, 'Has the Constitution delegated to Congress the power to coerce a State into submission, which…has withdrawn from the Union?' He goes on,

> 'After much serious reflection I have arrived at the conclusion that no such power has been delegated to Congress, or any other department of the Federal Government. It is manifest upon an inspection of the Constitution that this is not among the specific and enumerated powers granted to Congress…So far from this power having been delegated to Congress, it was expressly refused by the Convention, which framed the Constitution.'

"Lincoln obviously, and in my opinion regrettably, did not agree with Buchanan's reading of the Constitution."

Wyatt chimed in saying, "Buchanan was absolutely correct. On two separate occasions during the 1787 convention, the Framers voted against granting Congress the power to use military force to coerce a state into submission or compel its obedience. The only authority granted by the

Constitution to use military force in a state is found in Article IV, Section 4, which says the United States shall protect each state against invasion and, on application of a state legislature, domestic violence. Secession has nothing to do with an invasion or domestic violence."

"I would like to read," continued Pip, "one more pertinent passage from Buchanan's message to Congress in which he said,

> 'The fact is that our Union rests upon public opinion, and can never be cemented by the blood of its citizens shed in civil war. If it cannot live in the affections of the people, it must one day perish. Congress possesses many means of preserving it by conciliation, but the sword was not placed in their hand to preserve it by force.'

"There could be no greater contrast between the outgoing and incoming presidents than their respective views on how to deal with secession."

"It seems to me, Pip, that you and Wyatt have omitted one important provision of the Constitution that did not escape Mr. Lincoln's notice," said Duane, as he paged through his pocket copy of the Constitution. "Article IV, Section 4, also says that the United States shall guarantee every state a republican form of government. This was one of Lincoln's justifications for the war."

Pip replied, "Yes, Lincoln did make that one of his arguments for going to war. The problem is the Confederate States of America, or CSA, adopted a constitution that was nearly identical to the U.S. Constitution, so the seceded states in fact did have a republican form of government. It's true that the CSA constitution guaranteed slavery, but so did the U.S. Constitution of 1787. Moreover, Lincoln supported an amendment that would guarantee slavery could never be abolished in states where it was legal."

Sitting at one end of the twenty-five-foot oval conference table, reputedly made out of a single piece of polished Cuban mahogany, sat Jake Fillmore sans suit coat, slumped in his chair and appearing disinterested, but actually taking in every word. He sat up, turned toward Pip, and said, "Professor, I've learned more history in the past twenty minutes than in my entire life, probably, because I slept through all my college history seminars. As a descendant of the thirteenth president, Millard Fillmore, a man who excelled at mediocrity, I always took comfort in the belief that James Buchanan fell below Fillmore in the presidential rankings. But after hearing what you quoted from his 1860 speech to Congress, it seems to me he was a sagacious man. On the other hand, you seem to suggest that old Abe Lincoln might be a bit overrated. That comes as a great shock to me, because everything I can remember reading about Lincoln places him on a pedestal as our greatest president, even ahead of Washington. Why don't you worship at Lincoln's altar like virtually every other historian?"

"That's a good and timely question, Jake. Abraham Lincoln is an American deity, revered for his poetic eloquence, martyrdom, and winning the War of Secession, which reunified a nation torn asunder and ended slavery. Justly honored for his honesty, integrity, and humanity, he is forever memorialized in a massive Greek temple at one end of the National Mall in Washington, DC. Within that temple is a nineteen-foot statue of the great man seated in somber contemplation. If using the same scale the sculptor had posed him standing, the statue would be twenty-eight feet tall, more than four times larger than life. Most but not all the countless books about Lincoln are not biographies but hagiographies. And yet he was a mortal man, a politician, who was good and decent, but, in my humble opinion, made enormous and tragic misjudgments. I am not out to tear down Lincoln; rather I have tried to analyze objectively the decisions he made during a terrible time in American history.

"Of all our presidents, Lincoln came from the most humble circumstances, with the possible exception of Herbert Hoover. He truly was a self-made man, and his intellect may have been greater than that of any other president save Thomas Jefferson. He was a complex man: humble but ambitious, kind but ruthless, melancholic, yet always ready to tell a humorous story that often illustrated a larger point. His personal and public life were marked by unspeakable tragedy. His mother died when he was nine, and two of his four sons died, one at age four, another at age twelve while he was president. As president, he conducted a war that resulted in six hundred twenty thousand deaths on both sides of the conflict. That death toll represented 2 percent of the U.S. population. For perspective, if the U.S. were to lose 2 percent of its current population in a war today, there would be nearly six-and-a-half million deaths. The lives lost in the War of Secession nearly equaled total U.S. deaths in World Wars I and II, Korea, and Vietnam."

"One thing is certain in my mind," continued Pip, "the Civil War or War of Secession was Mr. Lincoln's war. He could have ended it at anytime by agreeing to let the South go its separate way, but did not do so. Any leader who presides over such a costly war will go down in his country's history as either a hero or a villain. History's final verdict generally depends on whether or not the warlord wins. Mr. Lincoln's hero status appears eternally secure, but it is still worth asking: Was the war justified, and could it or should it have been avoided?"

Abby Abbeville interrupted to say, "Pip, we've all read Wyatt's persuasive case for secession's legality, but what were Lincoln's arguments against it? By all accounts, he was a brilliant lawyer. How did he come to such a different conclusion?"

Pip replied, "Lincoln argued and believed that admission of a state into the Union was irrevocable. According to Lincoln, there were only two legitimate ways for a state to leave the Union: It could depart with the approval of the other states, or its citizens could exercise their natural law right of revolution against an oppressive, tyrannical government. He believed the Constitution and the Union are perpetual, and rejected the idea that there is a legal right of secession, because that would permit a minority to go its separate way whenever it disagreed with the majority. Democracy is premised on the principle that all the people, including the minority, must accept the will of the majority, provided the majority does not deny the minority its natural and legal rights. At the next election, the minority will have the opportunity to test its ideas again and see if they can command the support of a majority. If the minority withdrew its consent to be governed by the majority every time it lost an election, there would be anarchy. Lincoln equated the Union with the Constitution. There could not be one without the other. Paradoxically, he justified his manifest violations of the Constitution as being necessary to save the Union without which he believed the Constitution could not be preserved."

"Hold on, Pip," interjected Wyatt. "Thomas Jefferson wrote, and I am recalling from memory, 'If any state in the Union will declare that it prefers separation…to a continuance in Union…I have no hesitation in saying, let us separate.' Should Lincoln's judgment take precedence over Jefferson's? Also, Congressman Lincoln, thirteen years before he became president, said in a speech in the House of Representatives, 'Any people anywhere, being inclined and having the power, have the right to rise up, and shake off the existing government, and form a new one that suits them better.' This contradicts his later view that secession is unconstitutional. And this notion of the Union literally being perpetual is poppycock.

"The Constitution and the Union are perpetual in the same way a corporation is a perpetual entity. In that context, perpetual means there is no termination date, but we all know that most corporations sooner or later go bankrupt, are liquidated, or merged out of existence. Likewise, the Union is perpetual in that it has no expiration date, but that does not mean it might not peacefully break up or be dissolved at some time after its formation. As I've previously noted, the Articles of Confederation established a perpetual

Union, but the original thirteen sovereign states seceded from that confederation and entered into a new confederation under the Constitution."

Pip replied, "Wyatt, you have a fair point on the matter of perpetuity. Regarding the abandonment of the Articles for the Constitution, Lincoln would have said that all the then states agreed to ratify the Constitution; therefore, the Union was preserved under a new governing document. With respect to Lincoln's remark to Congress that you cited, he was referring to the intrinsic right of any people to revolt against an oppressive government that violates natural law. But he drew a distinction between revolution and secession. He believed there was no right of secession from a duly constituted democratic government by the minority, simply because it disagrees with the majority on an election or policy outcome. In his opinion, secession would result in anarchy and destroy the experiment in democratic self-government."

At this point, Reb leaned forward and said, "If I understand Lincoln's position, it is okay for the people to rise up in armed revolt against the government, and if they have the strength to defeat that government, they can go off and set up a new government acceptable to them. On the other hand, peaceful, voluntary secession is illegal, and the secessionists must be compelled to rejoin the Union, by force if necessary. It seems to me Lincoln made the argument for the divine right of kings. England's King George III, in effect, told the colonies they could not secede in peace, but if they rose up in armed revolt and defeated his army, they could go their separate way. That is the antithesis of freedom and democracy, where the people have the right of self-determination and must give their consent to be governed. Instead of a federal republic established by a voluntary confederation of sovereign states, Lincoln apparently believed the Constitution established a national government in which the states surrendered all sovereignty on joining the

Union. His concept of the Constitution rejected what the Founders intended and believed they created."

Pip replied, "Personally, I find the arguments and historical evidence that support the right of secession to be more persuasive than Lincoln's arguments against secession. I believe the right of secession should be available to the sovereign states as a last line of defense against an overreaching government that exceeds its constitutional authority and usurps the rights of the people. Among my fellow historians, however, the overwhelming majority support Lincoln's view on secession. Of course, the foremost reason people take Lincoln's side is because he won the argument by imposing his will on the South by force of arms. In so doing, he egregiously violated the Constitution he swore an oath to uphold and in the process, over six hundred thousand men perished."

Ding asked Pip, "You seem to lay blame for the War of Secession entirely on Lincoln's shoulders. But didn't the South fire the first shot by attacking Fort Sumter, the federal garrison in Charleston harbor?"

"Let's take a moment to consider that event and whether it justified the all out war that ensued. When Lincoln took office on March 4, 1861, seven states in the Lower South had already seceded and established the Confederacy. A few weeks before he was inaugurated, four states in the Upper South plus Missouri held conventions and all voted to stay in the Union, but they wanted the seceded states to be allowed to depart undisturbed. During the first month of the new administration, the CSA sent envoys to Washington to meet with Lincoln to arrange the orderly transfer of Fort Pickens in Pensacola, Florida, and Fort Sumter to the CSA, and to establish diplomatic relations. The South had already seized without incident a number of federal forts in CSA territory. The CSA also declared the Union would have free transit of the Mississippi River, which was a vital strategic interest of the North. Lincoln refused to meet with the CSA envoys, because that would imply the CSA was a sovereign nation, and he refused to acknowledge secession. During this time, other CSA representatives were meeting with Lincoln's secretary of state, William Seward, trying to work out a peaceful resolution of the federal forts guarding two important southern ports.

"Seward was a man of enormous ego who thought he should have been president. As the senior cabinet secretary, it is supposed he fancied himself a de facto prime minister who would be the power behind the throne. He did not reckon that his boss, who he thought at best inexperienced and unsophisticated, would take a firm hand of his government and make all important policy decisions. During the Fort Sumter crisis, Seward was assuring the southern delegates with whom he met that there would be no attempt by the Union to provision the fort, and that it would be abandoned. This, however, was the opposite of Lincoln's policy, which was to hold and supply Fort Sumter. It is not certain whether Seward was operating as a free agent without Lincoln's knowledge, or if the president was apprised of Seward's activities. If the latter, Lincoln was engaging in deception, which when discovered would provoke the South to fire the first shot, providing Lincoln his casus belli. Even if Lincoln was unaware of the message Seward was conveying to the CSA representatives, the South would still perceive it had been deceived with the same result.

"What Lincoln's intent was is not certain, but he needed the South to initiate hostilities so the North would have the moral justification to declare the seceded states in rebellion and commence military action to restore the Union. Having declared its sovereignty and independence, the CSA could not allow Fort Sumter, which controlled all shipping in and out of Charleston's harbor, to remain in Union hands. For his part, Lincoln, who had made restoring the Union his paramount objective, could not surrender Sumter without giving away the game and effectively recognizing the CSA.

"The fatal moment arrived April 12, 1861. After the Sumter commander refused a formal surrender demand by the senior Confederate commander in Charleston, the Confederates commenced an artillery barrage that lasted thirty-four hours. Running out of ammunition and food, the garrison surrendered on April 14. The barrage had started some fires, but no major damage was inflicted. Amazingly, no Union soldier was killed in the attack."

With incredulousness, Abby remarked, "You mean to tell me that the Civil War was started because of a military bombardment in which no one was killed?"

"Hell, there were more killed at Chappaquiddick," commented Jake, sardonically referring to the tragic 1969 accident on Martha's Vineyard in which a young woman passenger in a car driven by Sen. Edward Kennedy was killed when he drove off a bridge.

Pip responded, "Yes, the bloodless battle for Fort Sumter unleashed the dogs of war. On April 15, Lincoln declared the seven Confederate states in rebellion and ordered the Union states to raise seventy-five thousand troops. This act provoked the Upper South states of Arkansas, Tennessee, North Carolina, and Virginia, which had all voted to stay in the Union only a few weeks earlier, to secede from the Union and join the Confederacy. This was a strategic disaster for Lincoln and the Union. Virginia's departure was a staggering blow. Six of the first twelve U.S. presidents were Virginians, including the Father of the country, the Author of the Declaration, and the Father of the Constitution. Moreover, Virginia bordered the District of Columbia, which exposed the seat of government to risk of direct attack. The Confederacy suddenly had expanded from seven to eleven states and had nearly doubled its population. In response to Lincoln's troop call up, the CSA called for one hundred thousand volunteers."

"Lincoln was a master of the English language," remarked Wyatt, "yet he insisted on claiming the seceded states were in a state of rebellion or insurrection. Those words refer to an attempted overthrow of an existing government and replacing it with another. The states that joined the Confederacy never had any intention of deposing the federal government. Those states simply desired to leave the Union peacefully and establish a government more suitable to them."

"You're right," replied Pip, "but Lincoln had to mischaracterize secession as rebellion, because under rules of international diplomacy a rebellion is a civil war within a nation against its legitimate government and not a war between two independent countries. If he acknowledged that the southern states had seceded, he would be effectively recognizing the Confederacy as a sovereign nation. He desperately wanted to prevent other countries, particularly any European power, from granting the Confederacy diplomatic recognition. Had England or France, for example, recognized the Confederacy, Lincoln's moral justification for war would have been compromised and might have resulted in an alliance between the Confederacy and a European power that could have altered the war's outcome. Remember, without France's military aid during the Revolution, the fledgling United States could not have prevailed against England. The Confederacy's assiduous efforts to win an important ally never bore fruit.

"By the way, Wyatt, you earlier commented that the issue of states' rights was a primary cause of the War of Secession. Well, the four states that seceded after Lincoln issued his call for troops did so primarily out of sympathy for the right of the states that had preceded them into the Confederacy to secede from the Union."

Duane asked Pip, "After the South fired on Fort Sumter, what other option did Lincoln have, given his belief that secession was unconstitutional and the Union was perpetual?"

"One can never know the destination of the road not taken. But it does not require 20/20 hindsight to imagine that Lincoln might have pursued an entirely different course of action. On assuming office, he could have embraced Buchanan's sound reasoning that the Constitution did not grant the federal government the power to compel a state to remain in the Union, and allowed the seven states that had seceded while Buchanan was still president to go in peace. Then, Lincoln could have devoted his considerable intellect, political skills, and powers of persuasion to holding the rest of the Union together. He might have instituted a voluntary program, granting manumission in exchange for compensation to slave owners located in Union states, which could have been financed with government bonds. Instead of issuing government debt to finance 80 percent of the cost of the war, as in fact happened, bonds could have been used to end slavery gradually in the Union. Former slaves could have been provided basic education and training in a trade, along with forty acres and a mule, so they could become self-reliant, productive citizens.

"The Union without the seven states of the Deep South would still have been a transcontinental nation stretching from sea to sea, and an industrial powerhouse. Over time, it is likely that slavery would have died out in the Confederacy, because the rest of the world would treat it as a pariah nation. As Lincoln knew, in 1861, the most despotic, authoritarian country in the world, Tsarist Russia, freed its serfs. Six years after the Civil War, in 1871, Brazil freed all children born to slaves. By 1888, Brazil formally abolished slavery, the last country in the Western world to do so. There is no reason not to think that the Confederacy also would have abandoned slavery, probably long before Brazil did so. Moreover, the Confederacy might have broken apart. The future of Texas would have been better served in the Union than the Confederacy. Had Lincoln chosen peace instead of war, perhaps Texas's greatest hero Sam Houston, who lived until 1863, and strongly opposed secession, might have been a powerful symbol around which to rally for a reversal of secession. In fact, once slavery faded away in the Confederacy, it might have sought reunification.

"Obviously, all this is conjecture, but had Lincoln chosen peace over war, history would never have heard of Gettysburg, Chickamauga, Antietam, The Wilderness, Chancellorsville, or Shiloh. The total killed or wounded on both sides in each of these titanic Civil War battles was at least twenty thousand. The three-day Battle of Gettysburg witnessed thirty-three thousand total casualties. Antietam's casualties exceeded twenty-three thousand, with more Americans killed during that one-day battle than any other day in the country's history. At Chickamauga, there were over twenty-eight thousand casualties in thirty-six hours hours. For perspective, total American casualties during the amphibious landing and subsequent battle for Iwo Jima in 1945 during World War II were comparable to Chickamauga, but were incurred over a period of thirty-six days. After the carnage at Shiloh, as Gen. Grant wrote in his memoirs, there were so many fallen troops from both armies it was possible to walk the battlefield in any direction stepping on the dead without touching the ground, and the water of an adjacent pond turned red from blood.

"Moreover, had Mr. Lincoln opted for peace, there would have been no need for him to trash the Constitution. He launched a war, raised an army and authorized the funds to support it, and suspended habeas corpus without prior authorization of Congress as required by the Constitution. He did all this, yet did not call Congress into emergency session for three months, at which time it authorized his actions retroactively. He violated the right of freedom of the press by shutting down hundreds of anti-war newspapers and issued an arrest warrant for the Chief Justice of the United States, the head of a coequal branch of government, who had ruled against the suspension of habeas corpus, which Lincoln disregarded. Fortunately, Lincoln's long-time friend and bodyguard, Ward Hill Lamon, had the good judgment not to execute the warrant. To save the Union, Lincoln became a dictator and disregarded the Constitution.

"Ironically, Lincoln was fastidious in not interfering with slavery, because it was protected by the Constitution. Early in the war in 1861, his military commander in the Department of the West declared martial law in Missouri, which had remained in the Union, but because of its over one hundred thousand slaves, had many secessionist sympathizers. The commander emancipated Missouri's slaves, but Lincoln revoked the proclamation fearing it could provoke the departure of Kentucky and Maryland, which, along with Missouri, were the only Union states with major slave populations. This is further proof that Lincoln fought for Union, not to end slavery.

"As the war dragged on, the battle losses escalated, and the South gave no indication of capitulating, he announced his Emancipation Proclamation in September 1862 after the Battle of Antietam. The proclamation would free all slaves in states still in rebellion as of January 1863, but no seceded state took the bait. Another reason for the proclamation was to induce European nations that opposed slavery not to recognize the Confederacy. In this, Lincoln was successful."

Reb commented that, "Based on all you have shared with us, Pip, I conclude that Mr. Lincoln, despite his great intellect, persuasive reason, elegant prose, and soaring oratory, engaged in casuistry to justify his position on secession and the war. His obsession with restoring the Union, in his mind, justified any action he deemed necessary to bring that about including a horrible fratricidal war and subversion of the Constitution. No doubt he was sincere, but was he wise and just?"

Pip replied, "Lincoln did not live to write his memoirs, but if he had, he likely would have eloquently justified or rationalized all his decisions. But when I see his gaunt, careworn appearance and the haunted look in his eyes in photographs near the end of his life, I can't help but wonder if he realized that the war had been a horrifically tragic mistake. In his second inaugural address, he attributed the cause of the war to the Almighty who had taken retribution on America to expiate the sin of slavery. Lincoln was not deeply religious, nor was he cynical. That he would invoke God as the cause and justification of the war, I believe, was an unconscious effort to alleviate the overwhelming guilt and remorse he must have felt over the enormous loss of blood and treasure that had been inflicted on the nation. It was not God, however, but the free will of men, Lincoln foremost among them, who unleashed the terrible scourge of civil war."

"After the first major battles of the war with their horrific losses, why didn't Lincoln change course?" asked Abby. "I always was taught that the first rule when you find yourself in a hole is to stop digging."

Pip replied, "There is a macabre logic to war. Once a nation has incurred staggering losses, it feels compelled to risk and sacrifice ever more lives so that those who have already paid the ultimate price did not die in vain. The only thing worse than fighting and winning a war is fighting and losing it. In the War of Secession, each side believed fervently its cause was righteous. Lincoln knew he had every advantage on paper and if nothing else, in a war of attrition, the South could not win. The Union's population was more than double the South's, and excluding slaves, its advantage was four to one. The North also had 80 percent of U.S. industry, two-thirds of the guns, and two-thirds of the railroad mileage. The North's railroad network was a strategic asset and possibly the determining factor in winning the war, because it permitted the efficient and rapid long distance deployment of troops, cannons, supplies, horses, and fodder to the battlefield. Moreover, the North's industrialists and bankers had ample cash to purchase the government bonds issued to finance most of the war effort. The South, on the other hand, was cash poor, because its capital was invested primarily in illiquid land and slaves.

"The South's only hope was to seize the initiative whenever possible and hold off the Union Army's superior force long enough for the North's civilian population to grow weary and withdraw political support for continuing the war. This almost happened. As late as August of 1864, Lincoln was certain he would not be reelected that November, but in early September Gen. Sherman captured Atlanta and began his March to the Sea. This electrifying news buoyed the North's flagging spirits and assured Lincoln's reelection. By April 1865, Gen. Lee surrendered to Gen. Grant at Appomattox, effectively ending the war."

As Pip finished, and seeing there were no further questions, Reb said, "Thank you, Pip, for your excellent disquisition on perhaps the most important epoch in America's history that, one hundred fifty years later, remains fascinating and controversial. I believe we needed this historical background and analysis to help us as we contemplate secession in the twenty-first century. Obviously, there is no comparison between the circumstances we face today and those that led to secession in the nineteenth century. We may not be in complete agreement as to the right of a state to secede, but the way I see it, the federal government effectively has seceded from the Constitution. What other option do the people of any state have to remedy this usurpation of power? I concede that secession would be a last desperate act by people willing to risk literally everything for freedom with virtually no hope of prevailing in the end. That is a pretty good description of insanity, except that our cause is to restore constitutionally limited government, reaffirm individual liberty, and secure those blessings to posterity. The Founding Fathers nearly a quarter millennium ago took a similarly desperate and courageous act in support of the same cause against the longest of odds and miraculously prevailed. If three states were to secede peacefully and gain broad national public support for their cause, the federal government might be compelled to redress their grievances rather than draw the sword against them."

As Reb paused for a reaction, Jake spoke, "Didn't Lincoln establish the precedent for dealing with secession? Could any president after him allow secession to stand without being impeached?"

"Well, for one thing, Jake," replied Reb, "if I have any say in it, secession in the twenty-first century would be peaceful. There would be no Fort Sumter."

"Jake raises the key question," said Wyatt. "Would President Bucknell, faced with the threat or the fact of secession, follow Lincoln or Buchanan's example?"

Ding jumped in saying, "One of history's unanswerable questions is what would Lincoln have done had the South not fired on Fort Sumter? If states that seceded today refused to be provoked into hostile action, what would the federal government do? I can't imagine the American military shooting unarmed, peaceful citizens in cold blood. The Internet and TV would be all over something like that, causing an outpouring of opprobrium against the United States and exposing all its pious talk about freedom and human rights as utter hypocrisy. Even the Soviet Union broke up peacefully when communism crumbled in 1991. Hell, the British have consented to devolution in Scotland and Wales. People either have the right of self-determination or they don't, and no one outside the U.S. will care a whit about whether secession is legal or not."

"To advocate secession runs counter to my patriotic instincts and my better judgment," said Reb. "There are occasions in life, however, when the best available course of action is terrible, but inaction is worse. If you are strolling down the street and come upon two thugs assaulting a helpless woman, do you avert your eyes and pass on by as if nothing is wrong, or do you risk your own well-being by trying to help the victim? And what if you call the authorities, and it turns out the thugs are cops? In the situation before us, the woman being assaulted represents the Constitution, and her assailants represent the elected officials sworn to uphold and protect her. As much as this entire business is disagreeable for all of us, I see no honorable alternative but to do everything possible, regardless of any potential personal risk, to save the Constitution."

Duane leaned forward and said, "But Reb, while I fully believe in our cause, the chance that secession can succeed, based on historical experience, is between slim and none."

"You may be right, Duane," responded Reb. "Allow me to try another analogy on you. Assume the person you love most in your life, God forbid, is stricken with a terrible disease that will be fatal unless cured quickly. Further assume that the only known potential cure is controversial and has worked in only 5 percent of cases where it has been tried. Medical insurance won't cover the experimental treatment, the cost of which will virtually wipe out your net worth. Will you pay for the long-shot remedy to save your loved one? Of course, you will and without hesitation. I have concluded that secession—while controversial and a long shot—is the last and only chance we have to restore the Constitution to health and reassert the sovereign rights of states in our federal system, which Mr. Lincoln virtually eradicated a century and a half ago."

The room fell silent and Reb was about to adjourn the meeting when Duane said, "I came here today opposed to secession, but based on all I've heard this afternoon, I leave convinced there is no other alternative available to us. The irony of a black man supporting secession is not lost on me. But unlike in 1860 and 1861 when the South seceded to defend the indefensible institution of slavery, this time around supporters of secession will have the moral high ground."

43

As the Madison Committee meeting broke up and members departed, Ding and Jake remained to have a word with Reb. The three friends sat down and Ding spoke first, "Reb, do you realize what you are getting yourself into if you pursue secession? At best, you will be accused of perfidy; at worst you will be portrayed as a traitor. You have already done more than anyone could have thought possible to advance the Second Bill of Rights and garner support from thirty-six state legislatures across the country to petition Congress for a convention. Secession will be labeled by many in the media as lunacy, and anyone supporting lunacy must be a lunatic. You don't deserve that and I would hate to see it happen. Have you discussed this with Marlenna?"

"Ding, I appreciate your concern for me and, yes, I have talked it over with Marlenna. She is not keen on what I propose to do for reasons similar to yours, but she is supportive if this is my decision. Look, I have no martyr complex. Quietly serving out my last year as governor, concentrating on my education initiative, Texas Opportunity for Disadvantaged Youth, and silently fading away into retirement doing whatever Marlenna wants to do is how I would like my future to unfold. But the way the cards have been dealt and so far played, I have an obligation to the country to play out the hand. There is no way I can quit or back off now; we have come too far. We have reached a critical juncture in the country's history in which it must choose its destiny. Do we continue on the disastrous course we have been headed for decades, or do we return to our founding constitutional principles?"

Jake responded, "No one doubts your sincerity or commitment, Reb, and I fully support what you are trying to achieve, but there are times when you have to know when to hold 'em and when to fold 'em. Going down the road of secession is like betting the ranch on a busted straight with the seven of diamonds your high card. It's a guaranteed losing hand. What little most people know about secession is all bad. People revere Lincoln as America's quintessential hero, the political messiah who saved the country, ended slavery, bludgeoned the South into submission, and made secession tantamount to treason."

Before Reb could reply, Ding waved his iPOD and added, "While waiting for our colleagues to depart, I got a tweet from my chief of staff suggesting I tune in to MSNBC. Your old buddy, Portnoy Strank was being interviewed. The host goaded him into saying that 'freedom of speech allowed the little people to blow off steam all they want about secession, but any elected official fomenting secession violates his or her oath of office, is unpatriotic, and may be advocating treason.' The guest following Strank was none other than Jean Fondue, still thought by many to have been a traitor for her support of Ho Chi Minh and the commies during the Vietnam War. Fondue agreed with and praised Strank's caustic remarks. That's the sort of crap that will be thrown in your face if you continue to pursue secession."

Reb remarked, "Poor old Portnoy would not be happy if he wasn't angry, nasty, and engaging in extreme hyperbole. What about his violation of his oath of office by refusing to honor the states' applications seeking a convention thereby contravening Article V of the Constitution? His condescending characterization of average Americans as little people is rather revealing but not surprising. As for Ms. Fondue, she was not a popular girl among the GIs during my time in Vietnam, and the stench of her behavior then has stuck to her ever since. Don't bring up her name in conversation with Duane Darby. He'll go ballistic even after all these years."

"Strank is a 24/7 asshole," snapped Jake in disgust, "Perhaps his potty training experience as a child was traumatic, leaving him scarred for life. As for Hanoi Jean, it's beyond ironic she would be pontificating on the virtue of patriotism and the wickedness of treason. Now, that's chutzpah. At the height of the Vietnam War, didn't she visit Hanoi where she happily posed for a photo sitting behind an antiaircraft battery, pretending to shoot at American warplanes? I also read somewhere that while meeting American POWs, one slipped her a note he expected she would take to the American military authorities when she got home. Instead, she ratted him out to his brutal captors who beat him to a pulp and threw him into solitary confinement. Opposing the war is one thing, but what she did really was treason."

With a trace of exasperation, Reb said, "Look, the vapid views of Strank and Fondue are not worthy of consideration. Regarding your earlier comments, I don't disagree with what you both have said, and I know you have my personal interest at heart. But what is at stake is infinitely more important than any one individual's personal reputation or well-being. If I could honorably delegate this to someone else, I would do so. After listening to Pip and Wyatt, none of us believes secession is treasonous or even unconstitutional. We must relentlessly carry our message to the people by every means available. Several recent polls indicate a plurality of Americans supports secession under certain circumstances. Secession may be a bad bet, but this is the last hand of the last game.

"If Congress gets away with stiffing the states on a constitutional convention, there will be no hope of checking the federal government's power until the inevitable day of reckoning arrives when the financial house of cards collapses. We have one chance to get through to Congress and that is for Texas, Oklahoma, and Louisiana to threaten to secede. If as I expect our bluff is called, we must be prepared to go through with it. Unlike the South's secession in 1860, this time around our motives are altruistic, and I'm confident it can be done without risk of a civil war. Secession then was to preserve slavery, hardly a noble cause. The justification for secession today is the federal government's 'secession' from the Constitution."

Ding responded, "Secession in the nineteenth century was simple and straightforward, because there were no entitlement programs like we have today. How as a practical matter can a state disentangle itself from the bear hug embrace of the federal government? It has grown so big and become so intrusive in most every citizen's daily life, I don't see how a state could extricate itself from the Union without harming many, perhaps most, of its citizens dependent on entitlement programs. Reb, I recall you telling me how this beautiful table was brought into this tenth floor conference room. It is far too big to fit in an elevator. During construction but before the exterior wall was completed on this floor, you had a crane hoist the table into this room, after which the building was completed. This table is trapped inside this room and this building, which, as a practical matter, pretty well describes the situation of a state relative to the federal government."

"The problem with your analogy, Ding, is that the table is inanimate, lacks free will, and has no rights. The citizens of a sovereign state, however, have life, liberty, and the right to self-determination. Belle Chevalier, Travis Maxwell, and I have had several meetings since we first met in Baton Rouge to think through the details of secession. We have taken to referring to ourselves as the 'Three Secessketeers.' The approach we are taking to address the many daunting hurdles before us is to remember the wisdom imparted to me early in my career from the best and most unflappable boss I ever had at Magnolia. Whenever his subordinate department heads would bellyache about the technical, production, marketing, and other challenges they faced, he would calmly remind them that 'what we've got here is an abundance of opportunities cleverly disguised as problems. Let's go out and realize those opportunities.' His pep talk didn't solve any specific problem, but it's amazing how important attitude is in overcoming obstacles."

Observing Ding and Jake's growing impatience, Reb continued, "One thing we 'Three Secessketeers' have decided, assuming our respective legislatures go along, is to hold a popular plebiscite on the same day in each state so the people can vote directly for or against secession. If the referendum wins at least 60 percent of the vote in each state, each legislature will vote formally to adopt articles of secession and to call a convention to draft a constitution. The constitution we anticipate being adopted is the 1787 Constitution as amended plus the Second Bill of Rights. Once each state ratifies the constitution in convention, the Constitutional Republic of Texas will be proclaimed. If any state falls short of 60 percent in favor of secession, all three states will abandon any further effort to depart the Union."

Ding asked, "If the vote were held today, what would be the likely outcome? And when would you hold the vote?"

Reb responded, "Today, Belle and Travis are confident secession would surpass the 60 percent threshold in their states. Texas probably would fall short by two to five points, but the plebiscite is not being held today. If Congress fails to call a convention by December 31, 2017, we plan to hold a plebiscite on the first Tuesday after the first Monday in February 2018, which will be the sixth. By that time, we are confident support for secession in

Texas will top 60 percent. If the referendum carries in all three states, the Louisiana, Oklahoma, and Texas state legislatures are expected to ratify the plebiscite results and call a constitutional convention a few days later.

"On March 2, the 182nd anniversary of Texas's declaration of independence from Mexico, secession from the U.S. will be formally declared and the new republic established. A general election for the CRT House, Senate, and president will be held March 6. The first CRT Congress and president will serve an abbreviated term until the end of 2019, and focus on start-up legislation, revenue measures, and a budget. Beginning in November 2019 and every two years thereafter, elections will be held."

"That's an ambitious schedule," commented Jake. "Is a three-state republic viable? The size and population of Texas will dominate the CRT. Why would Louisiana and Oklahoma want to play second fiddle to Texas?"

"Regarding the schedule, Jake, we will have everything ready to go by the time of the plebiscite in February. We don't want to allow too much time to elapse between January 2, 2018, the date we will announce our intention to put the question of secession to a vote of the people of our three states, and the date of the vote. But we have allowed sufficient time for the U.S. Congress to call for a convention at the eleventh hour. If Congress acts before February 6, we will cancel the referendum on secession. If they call our bluff, however, we have to be ready to act with dispatch.

"As to your concern about only having three states and Texas being dominant, if we secede and the CRT is established, I will propose that Texas be divided into five states plus Austin, which will become the District of the Republic. When Texas joined the U.S. by treaty in 1845, it retained the right to subdivide into five states, but obviously never did so."

"So the proposed CRT would be comprised of seven states," commented Ding. "Have you got names and boundaries in mind for the new states?"

"Yes, but we'll leave it to the outgoing Texas legislature to debate and finalize the details. If the decision were left to me, the proposed states would be Houstonia, Victoria, Comancharia, Madisonia, and Trinity. Houstonia, obviously named in honor of Sam Houston, would border the Gulf Coast. Victoria, named for Guadalupe Victoria, the first president of Mexico after winning its independence from Spain, would extend from the Hill Country through south Texas to the Rio Grande River. Commancharia, named after the Comanche Indians who were an important part of the state's early history, would be the biggest new state in geographic size, covering west Texas and the Panhandle. The Father of the Constitution should have had a state named for him long ago. To rectify this, the new state in the Piney Woods of northeast Texas would be named Madisonia. Trinity would be in north central Texas encompassing the Dallas Fort Worth area, through which flows the Trinity River, the longest river entirely within Texas. As I said, Austin would be the District of the Republic, or DR, and the current state capitol would become the CRT capitol."

"Do you anticipate any other states seceding and joining the CRT?" asked Jake.

"No, and we don't want other states to secede. Three states that will become seven are sufficient to make our point to the federal government. After we secede, there will be thirty-three states with petitions before the U.S. Congress calling for a constitutional convention. That is more than two-thirds of the forty-seven states remaining in the Union, so Congress still will be pressured to fulfill its constitutional obligation. Belle, Travis, and I have been informed by our counterparts in at least thirty other states that they will express sympathy with the CRT, recommend that the U.S. negotiate in good faith with it, and loudly condemn any military action the U.S. government may consider."

"Once the CRT is created, are there any terms under which you could see it voluntarily rejoining the Union?" asked Ding.

"Until now, we have simply insisted that a convention be called where amendments would be considered and those approved submitted to the states for ratification. While I am confident most if not all the seven amendments the Madison Committee has recommended would be adopted in convention, there is no guarantee that three-fourths of the states will ratify all or any of them. Once Oklahoma, Louisiana, and Texas secede and form the CRT, however, the price of poker goes up. I would support reunification only if the seven Second Bill of Rights amendments were adopted by the U.S."

"Back to my earlier question," asked Ding, "how will the CRT deal with entitlements and other programs its citizens currently receive from the federal government? And how will military and other federal government installations be treated?'

"The U.S. permits dual citizenship. Therefore, all CRT citizens will be citizens of two countries. Any CRT citizen may choose to renounce his or her U.S. citizenship, which some may do to escape U.S. taxes. Most people, I expect, will maintain dual citizenship. In that case, they will pay both U.S. and CRT taxes, but CRT taxes may be credited against U.S. tax liability, so there would be no double taxation. To the extent they have paid into the U.S. Social Security system, CRT citizens will be eligible under U.S. law for an annuity when they reach retirement age, irrespective of citizenship or country of residence. CRT employers would continue to withhold income and FICA taxes from dual citizenship employees and remit payroll taxes to the IRS. The problem is Medicare, because, unlike Social Security, it covers only eligible persons residing in the U.S. The CRT would endeavor to negotiate with the U.S. to grant an exemption for CRT residents on Medicare."

"What if the U.S. government plays hardball and refuses to pay Medicare benefits to CRT retirees?" asked Jake.

"The CRT will have leverage in that regard. I believe the CRT should offer to repay over a period of fifty years a pro rata share of the U.S. public debt at the time of secession. The specific terms would have to be negotiated, but if the U.S. refused to cooperate on Medicare and other issues, the CRT would refuse to assume any U.S. debt and stop remitting Medicare taxes to the IRS. At first, the U.S. may resist dealing with the CRT, but in time I predict it will accept the new reality and recognize that collaboration would be mutually beneficial. The CRT should be a closer friend, ally, and trading partner of the U.S. than is Canada. How soon a cordial relationship could be established would be up to the U.S., but it would be in our mutual interest to do so with all due celerity."

"What will be the disposition of all the military and other federal facilities in the CRT?" asked Ding. "The U.S. will resist ceding them to the CRT, but if the CRT does not have sovereign power over everything within its borders, it has not won true independence."

"This would be a matter of negotiation and linked to the assumption of debt issue. My view regarding military bases is that the status quo ante secession should prevail for a period of two years. During that time, the two countries would negotiate a long-term arrangement. It might be mutually beneficial to have the U.S. maintain a lasting military presence on CRT soil as it does in many NATO countries. The key would be that the U.S. would remain at the pleasure of the CRT. If and when the U.S. departs, the CRT would pay some reasonable compensation for the bases."

"If the CRT is going to assume a portion of the U.S. debt and possibly pay for U.S. military and other installations, where will it get the money?" asked Ding.

"The CRT's population of about 33 million equals 11 percent of the current U.S. population. For the sake of our discussion, the pro rata share of publicly held U.S. debt plus capitalized interest assumed by the CRT will be $2 trillion. Assuming a 50-year amortization, it would cost $40 billion per year to retire the debt. The CRT's annual GDP is about $1.8 trillion, which incidentally ranks as the ninth largest economy in the world. For planning purposes, assume a 10 percent CRT personal income tax rate and a 17 percent corporate tax rate, which net of credits and exemptions will bring in annual tax revenue of around $180 billion. This will fund CRT government expenditures and cover the U.S. debt retirement. The plan is to adopt pro-growth policies and regulations that will promote strong GDP growth. The faster the CRT economy grows, the more tax revenue will flow into the government's coffers making it easier to retire the debt obligation."

"It appears the 'Three Secessketeers' have given a great deal of thought to the nuts and bolts of setting up a government," remarked Jake. "What are your thoughts on currency and a banking system?"

"Both will be immediate priorities for the new republic, and at my request, Abby Abbeville has been developing a monetary framework. Most business and investment transactions are settled through banks via check, credit card, wire transfer, or electronically, and that will continue. To facilitate the transition, we will continue to use the dollar, but within a few months, we plan for the CRT to introduce its own currency, the 'alamo.' Abby's idea is to peg the alamo initially at parity with the dollar, but its value thereafter will be tied to a weighted basket of commodities including oil, corn, soybeans, wheat, cotton, gold, silver, copper, aluminum, and perhaps a few others. We rejected solely linking the alamo to gold, because of its intrinsic volatility, and the fact that we don't possess any gold reserves. We believe it is imperative to establish the CRT's currency as a stable store of value and fixing its price in terms of a commodity standard will achieve that objective. The government, not a central bank, will determine the money supply, which will be based on lagging GDP growth plus no more than 1 or 2 percent per year in anticipation of improved productivity."

"The alamo is a great name for the CRT's currency," said Ding. "You, Belle, and Travis seem to have considered all the critical issues for establishing a republic. I imagine there aren't too many experienced hands at this sort of thing."

"We are relying on our most trusted advisors and key players in our respective legislatures. I am trying to stay ahead of the secession train as it gathers steam. My biggest immediate concern is the potential for a terrorist attack somewhere along the border. Intelligence reports I receive from the Rangers and Department of Public Safety make it clear something is afoot, but we can't nail down any specifics, and Homeland Security in Washington thinks we are overreacting. If an attack occurs in the next month or two, there will be a lot more people in Texas willing to secede, because they will largely blame, fairly or unfairly, the federal government for not providing sufficient resources to secure the border despite our incessant requests for more help."

"Is there anything more I can do to help you out, Reb?" asked Jake.

"As a matter of fact, there is, Jake. One of many reasons the South lost the War of Secession was its failure to obtain diplomatic recognition from any important country. The CRT must do everything possible to secure international recognition from countries other than enemies or pariah states like Iran, North Korea, or Venezuela who would recognize the CRT just to spite the U.S. We don't want to claim legitimacy as a sovereign country based on the imprimatur of such regimes. I know you have maintained your contacts with important players in Brazil over the years. If the secession referendum passes on February 6, I would like you to go to Brazil and lobby the government to recognize the CRT as soon as possible after secession is formally declared in March.

"The CRT's paramount foreign policy objective will be to establish an alliance and permanent friendship with Brazil that encompasses free trade and all other matters of mutual interest. For reasons I can't fathom, U.S. foreign policy toward Brazil has always been marked by benign neglect and mild condescension. Understandably, Brazil has quietly resented this treatment, which we should be able to exploit to the CRT's advantage. The largest and most resource rich country in the southern hemisphere, Brazil has a booming economy, and it is a democracy whose culture and values are compatible with ours. I also hope at least one significant European country will have the backbone to defy the U.S. and grant the CRT recognition. If we have success wooing Brazil, we may be able to win over one or two countries in the EEC."

"I'll be happy to undertake that assignment when the time is ripe," replied Jake. "The finance minister is a friend of long standing, and I know several senior people in the foreign ministry."

"Probably the best bet for gaining recognition by a major European country is France," opined Ding. "She has a proud history of pursuing an independent foreign policy without any fear of irritating the United States. My biggest concern, however, is how Mexico will react to the CRT. With a shared border of over twelve hundred miles, quickly establishing friendly diplomatic relations with our neighbor to the south is imperative."

"I could not agree more, Ding," replied Reb. "I expect Mexico will do nothing until it sees what the U.S. government does in response to secession. It won't want to antagonize the U.S., but if Brazil and France, or another European country, recognize the CRT, that will give Mexico cover to accept a diplomatic overture from the new republic on its northern border. I would like to move quickly to normalize relations with Mexico and reach an accommodation on the question of legal and illegal immigration. I'm not sure the public will agree, but I have reluctantly concluded that unless we legalize marijuana and cocaine, the Mexican drug traffickers will continue to tear down Mexico's civil society through bribery and murder. Having a failed state on the CRT's southern border and the inevitable spillover of drug crime on our side of the border will lead to disaster. Illicit drugs should be legalized under strict government control and regulation, as well as effective education and rehabilitation programs. This will be unpopular with many people, and I sympathize with that viewpoint, but legalization with strict regulation is the only practicable way to eliminate the enormous profits, which fuel the power of the drug lords, and to diminish their active cooperation with various international terrorist groups."

"Legalization of drugs will be a tough sell in Texas, Reb," commented Jake, as Ding nodded in agreement. "Of course, a lot depends on the trust and confidence the voters have in the CRT's leaders, especially its president. I trust you will be the first CRT president. I can't think of anyone else better qualified for such a thankless job."

"I appreciate your endorsement, Jake. I am willing to be a candidate for the office of CRT president in the planned March 2018 transition election, but if I were to win, I would only serve until the first regular full-term election in November 2019. Belle and Travis have been badgering me to run, and I agreed to do so, provided she runs as my vice president and then for a full four-year term as president in 2019. She has consented to do this."

"Well, Reb, I'm relieved to know you will run to be the CRT's first president," said Ding. "The long odds against the success of this enterprise would be nearly hopeless if you are not the CRT's first chief magistrate. We haven't yet addressed the elephant in the room, however, which is how President Bucknell and the U.S. government will react to three states seceding from the Union. Will the government mobilize troops, move them into the seceded states, and arrest the ringleaders? Or will there only be a lot of saber rattling and intimidation followed by serious negotiations if the CRT refuses to capitulate? You came within an eyelash of winning the presidency last year. Assuming you had won that election, what would you do if you were confronting this situation?"

"Had I won the presidency, I would vigorously oppose secession. Unlike Bucknell, however, I would challenge the American people to write their senators and representatives to demand a constitutional convention. Bucknell can't support a convention even if he wanted to, because, as you have told me, that was his quid pro quo with Lashette LaRue in return for the votes he needed in the House to win the presidency. That was not a corrupt bargain, but it may turn out to be the most calamitous political bargain in the country's history. Because of his backroom deal with Lashette, he has painted himself into a corner without any good option for resolving the secession crisis other than to resort to threats, which I doubt will work."

"So what do you think he will do if Texas, Louisiana, and Oklahoma secede?" asked Ding.

"There is no way to predict the future in such a tumultuous situation. Some trivial or unforeseen event could set in motion a chain reaction that spirals out of control. No one foresaw or could have imagined the four-year nightmare of bloodshed that followed the firing on Fort Sumter in 1861. Notwithstanding that sanguinary experience, there no doubt will be armchair generals across the political spectrum demanding that Bucknell follow Lincoln's precedent of restoring the Union by military force, if necessary. I don't know how Bucknell will react under enormous pressure, but I'm wagering he will not resort to coercion. In the age of the Internet, Twitter, Facebook, and YouTube, any military move against the CRT and its people will spread instantly around the globe and besmirch the U.S.' image.

"I'm confident CRT citizens in large numbers will take to the streets peacefully to defy any aggressive action by the U.S. Moreover, I don't believe American soldiers will fire on or take other hostile action against unarmed protesters. The CRT won't take up arms against the U.S. It would be suicidal, and we want no armed conflict. We will lay out in a bill of particulars that the U.S. government has broken with the Constitution, which justifies secession and the formation of the CRT. I believe people around the world will rally to our cause."

"Pray that you are right," said Ding, "but if Bucknell lets secession stand, many people in both parties will accuse him of losing Oklahoma, Louisiana, and Texas. He might be impeached, would certainly be a one- term president, and his name in history would go down in infamy. Facing such a bleak legacy, he could decide he has nothing to lose by drawing the sword against the CRT and compelling reunification."

"Ding, I believe we are in the right, and there is no other option available to us to return to our constitutional principles, and secure liberty's blessings for future generations. In the end, we may lose and the CRT's leaders might pay a heavy price for what will be seen as folly. Not to be melodramatic, but Belle, Travis, and I have pledged our lives, our fortunes, and our sacred honor to this endeavor. Congress has forced the issue by its audacious, brazen refusal to fulfill its constitutional duty to call a convention. But this is only the latest and perhaps most egregious usurpation of power by the federal government over many years. If we don't take a stand now with dramatic action, America may never have another chance to restore limited constitutional government, individual liberty, and fiscal solvency."

"Look, Reb, I am with you on this and also ready to pledge my own life, fortune, and honor to the cause, but is the time ripe? Perhaps we should ratchet up public pressure on Congress and give it a bit more time to take appropriate action on the state applications for a convention. Once you play the secession card, you can't renege. You will have crossed the Rubicon."

"The people and the states have already waited too long to take action to rein in out-of-control government. Each new expansion of federal power is rationalized as being just or necessary and usually is popular with a large cohort of voters. Over the years, the federal government has kept chipping away at the Constitution until it has amassed vast, virtually unlimited powers that never were intended. It has gone on so long that when an objection is raised over an incremental expansion of government power, it is ignored or dismissed, because this is the way government has done business for seventy-five years; ergo, it must be okay. Nearly a year has passed since the requisite number of states petitioned Congress to call a convention. That it has refused to do so is incontrovertible evidence that the federal government has placed itself above the law of the land. This justifies secession."

"The American people," remarked Jake, "have ignored at their peril Thomas Jefferson's admonition: 'The price of freedom is eternal vigilance.'"

"Amen to that," replied Reb. "Government in a free society, over the long run, reflects the character of the people. Each citizen in a free society not only must maintain constant vigilance over government, but more importantly over his or her personal character, ensuring it manifests self-reliance, self-discipline, self-accountability, and moral health. These are essential character traits of a people who cherish individual liberty. If free people of able body and sound mind gradually exchange their independence for dependence on government, vigilance will wane, and freedom inexorably will be ceded to government."

Ding said, "I admire your courage, Reb, in leading this crusade to reaffirm liberty. I don't have that kind of courage. Please look out for yourself. You will be savaged by your enemies, and I fear for your safety."

"Ding, when you are certain the course you have set is right and your cause is freedom, it is not difficult to muster the courage to go forward. We have an inescapable obligation to all past and future American generations to ensure liberty's incandescence remains ever bright and never dims. I think Supreme Court Justice Louis Brandeis captured it best when he wrote, 'Those who won our independence…believed liberty to be the secret of happiness and courage to be the secret of liberty.'"

44

As Ding and Jake departed the Marcoy Foundation following their chat with Reb, they walked together in silent contemplation along the broad sidewalk of Flora Street, which bisects and runs the length of the Dallas Arts District. Jake broke their silence. "Reb McCoy has been my friend for over a quarter century. I liked him the moment I met him. He is engaging, sincere, honest, and fun to be around. He possesses charisma and humility, two qualities rarely found in one person. I would trust him with my life, my wife, my bank account. But it wasn't till today that I understood what Duane Darby meant when he once told me he would follow Reb McCoy through the gates of hell."

"Yeah, I know," responded Ding, "Duane credits Reb not only with saving his life in Vietnam, but also motivating him to enroll in college, take responsibility for his future, and not allow his bitter resentment of racism to define his character. There's no question that Reb is a terrific guy, but what intangible, esoteric quality elevates some men and women to greatness? While I fully agree with the decision for Texas, Louisiana, and Oklahoma to secede from the U.S. and establish the Constitutional Republic of Texas, I admit I don't have the courage to conceive or lead such a daring course of action. Like you, I've always known Reb to be a man of honor, integrity, and outstanding intellect, but today I had an epiphany that our friend has the essence of true greatness."

"I'm sure there are other qualities essential to greatness," remarked Jake, "but courage has to be common to every great person. It takes tremendous moral and possibly physical courage to attempt to upend the entrenched old order. Greatness also requires the vision to imagine a better future, the leadership to persuade others to embrace that vision, the commitment not to give in to fierce perhaps belligerent opposition, and absolute certainty the cause is just and worth the sacrifice required to achieve victory. And, of course, every great person must be blessed with good timing and good fortune."

"I agree, Jake. I doubt any so-called great man in history lacked any of those qualities, especially courage. One of my favorite nineteenth century intellectuals is Horace Mann, the father of universal public education in America. He was the first president of Antioch College in Ohio. In his last commencement address, delivered to the class of 1859 two months before his death, Mann said, 'Be ashamed to die until you have won some victory for humanity.' Another favorite quote attributed to Mann is, 'If any man seeks for greatness, let him forget greatness and ask for truth, and he will find both.' I believe Reb McCoy's life journey reflects both these ideas. Reb has never sought greatness, but he has sought out the truth about the state of liberty, limited government, and fiscal solvency in America. In so doing, he has spoken truth to power and to the people ever since he entered politics four years ago, and this has revealed his capacity for greatness. He certainly is trying to preserve and reaffirm liberty in America, which would be a victory for future generations."

"Can't say as I have ever heard of Mr. Mann," responded Jake, "but believe it or not, I loved studying Shakespeare in college. One of my favorite plays is his comedy, *Twelfth Night,* or *What You Will.* I have never forgotten the famous line, 'Be not afraid of greatness: some men are born great, some achieve greatness and some have greatness thrust upon them.' I believe greatness is about to be thrust on Reb. I only hope history remembers him so."

"There's no way to predict how history will be written, Jake, and I'm sure that is the furthest thing from our friend's mind. Usually the winners write the first draft of history, and future historians generally look with favor on the winners. There are exceptions, of course. History views the little Corsican who rose to be Emperor of France, Napoleon Bonaparte, as a great man. He possessed all the great man attributes you mentioned except I believe his cause was not just. He sought personal glory and to advance the grandeur of France through domination of much of Europe. He had spectacular success, but in the end he overreached and lost it all. And yet, he is regarded as one of the greatest figures in history. Thankfully, Reb McCoy is no Bonaparte, but two traits they have in common are ambition and the decisive courage to seize the moment. Reb probably would agree with Napoleon's observation that 'Glory is fleeting, but obscurity is forever.'"

45

During evening prime time on December 6, 2017, President Bucknell held a rare press conference in the White House. His stated purpose was to announce a couple of new administration proposals to boost the economy, but he knew most of the questions would be about secession. Demonstrations were occurring across the country demanding a convention or secession, and this topic was consuming TV pundits, talk radio programs, and editorial pages in heated debate. The president's primary reason for enduring the unscripted, often impertinent questions of the White House press corps was to deflate the secession balloon. After reading his prepared remarks, the president, appearing confident and in command, invited questions from the assembled journalists. The first two reporters he recognized he knew would ask questions related to foreign policy or the economy, which would allow him to boast about all his administration's initiatives and accomplishments. The third correspondent, however, asked the question on everyone's mind.

"Mr. President, there is increasing talk of two or three states seceding from the United States. One of the reasons cited to justify such action is Congress's refusal to call a constitutional convention as requested nearly a year ago by thirty-six state legislatures. Do you support a convention, and if so, have you indicated this to the leaders of the Senate and the House? Also, if any state were to secede, what would you do in response?"

"To your second question," answered the president, "I won't comment on a hypothetical, actually unthinkable situation. As far as a constitutional convention is concerned, that is a matter exclusively within the purview of the Congress. The Constitution does not grant any authority in this regard to the Executive Branch. Therefore, I defer to the judgment of Congress on this matter and suggest you talk to the Speaker of the House and the Senate majority leader."

'Sir, if I may follow up, do you believe secession is unconstitutional?"

"The American Civil War settled that question. The United States is indissoluble. Moreover, the Supreme Court in a case decided a few years after the Civil War ruled that a state may not secede from the Union without the approval of the other states."

"But, sir," shouted a backbench reporter, "the Constitution neither approves nor prohibits secession. Doesn't the Tenth Amendment reserve all rights not specifically granted to the federal government to the states or the people? Do the states enjoy any independent sovereignty?"

"As I already stated, secession is impermissible. This was decided one hundred fifty years ago following the bloodiest war in American history and subsequently ratified by the Supreme Court. Regarding sovereignty, states are not sovereign or independent in the manner of a nation. They are political and geographic subdivisions of the United States, and under our federal system, they have jurisdiction over all matters not delegated to the federal government."

"Does that mean Mr. President," shouted out another reporter, "that if a state were to secede, you would go to war to compel its return to the Union?"

"Look, as I said at beginning of this line of questioning, I am not going to comment on a hypothetical circumstance. I believe any talk of secession is inappropriate, and frankly a waste of time. It would be more productive to direct our energies toward finding bipartisan solutions to America's longstanding economic challenges including the debt, deficit spending, and unemployment."

The next questioner Bucknell called on stood and asked, "Mr. President, if the federal government refuses to comply with the Constitution, what recourse do the states and the people have to redress their legitimate grievances? If Congress continues to ignore the states' petitions for a constitutional convention and neither the president nor the Supreme Court can compel the Congress to do its duty under the Constitution, what can the states do to assert their rights?"

The president responded, "The Congress is still deliberating the convention question. The Senate and the House have passed separate resolutions regarding a convention, but the differences have to be reconciled into one resolution to be voted on by both chambers. The legislative process often is painfully slow, but that is the nature of democracy. I would counsel patience while Congress works its will. Ultimately, if Congress does not respond to the will of the people, the voters in each state can register their displeasure at the ballot box in November 2018. Thank you."

With that, the president departed the podium and the press conference was concluded. The president failed to achieve his objective of tamping down all the secession talk and probably added fuel to the fire. He was unequivocally clear, however, that secession was illegal. Left unsaid is what action the federal government would take if one or more states seceded.

Ironically, the effort by pro-secession demonstrators to pressure Congress to call a convention was having the opposite effect. The demonstrations actually hardened the views of anti-secession congresspersons who feared a convention would spin out-of-control and lead to amendments even more threatening to their power than the detested Second Bill of Rights. These congresspersons persuaded themselves they were safeguarding the Constitution by refusing to accede to a convention.

The day after the president's press conference, a network news reporter interviewed Belle Chevalier in Baton Rouge. "Governor Chevalier, recently there have been several unsubstantiated stories that Louisiana may consider seceding from the United States. Is there any truth to those reports? If so, after hearing President Bucknell's remarks last night, do you have any second thoughts about pursuing secession?"

"In the event the federal government usurps power and rights that belong to the states and to the people, I believe secession might be an appropriate course of action. Such action by a state should be a last resort after reason, persuasion, and all legal options have failed. As to your second question, I believe the president is incorrect as to the right of states to secede."

"What would be the justification for secession?" the reporter then asked.

"There are several, but one is the refusal by Congress to call a constitutional convention under Article V. A second justification is the unsustainable, ever-increasing national debt and irresponsible federal budget deficits, which will lead to financial calamity if not brought under control soon. Any ten-year-old can understand this, yet for years successive congresses and administrations of both parties have done nothing substantive to address this issue other than engage in empty talk and finger pointing. This is scandalous, a profile in political cowardice. We are condemning Americans who come after us to involuntary financial servitude. Consequently, the federal government is derelict in its solemn obligation as set forth in the Constitution's Preamble to secure liberty's blessings for future generations of Americans. The citizens of some states refuse to bequeath such a bleak future to their children and grandchildren."

"Are other states considering secession?"

"I'll let other states speak for themselves, but I will say that Louisiana is not the only state contemplating that course of action."

"When do you expect to make a decision about secession?"

"It's not up to me; it's up to the people to decide in a referendum. Congress has had nearly a year to call a constitutional convention. If it does not act on the state petitions by the end of the year, I believe a vote on secession could occur early next year."

Belle's blunt remarks, delivered in her soft, charming voice with its heavy southern accent, created a sensation in the media and ratcheted up the tension in Washington and around the country.

In Oklahoma City, Gov. Maxwell was asked if there was any truth to rumors that the Sooner State might join Louisiana and Texas in seceding from the United States. Travis said, "I have nothing to add to what Governor Chevalier said in her recent remarks."

The reporter then asked, "Is December 31, 2017 a drop dead date for Congress to call a constitutional convention?"

Maxwell responded, "I don't issue ultimatums, especially to the U.S. Congress. But, in my opinion it is long past time for Congress to honor the thirty-six state petitions for a convention. Patience may be a virtue, but if not ultimately rewarded, it is tantamount to submission."

When a reporter caught up with Reb and asked him to comment on Belle and Travis's statements, he said he supported what they had said and had nothing to add. The reporter then asked Reb if Texas was about to join

Oklahoma and Louisiana in leaving the Union. Reb followed President Bucknell's example by declining to answer a hypothetical question.

As Christmas approached, there was a diminution in the wild rhetoric by both pro- and anti-secessionists across the media and the blogosphere. The outdoor rallies for a constitutional convention tapered off because of the holiday season and the early arrival of winter weather, but increasingly people were appearing at these events carrying signs saying, "Death to Traitors," and "Secession is Treason."

For the first time since childhood after he lost his parents, Reb was finding it hard to sleep. Normally, he fell instantly asleep any time and place he could steal away fifteen or twenty minutes for a nap. Lately, he would go to bed, but be unable to sleep as his mind churned over all the plans and details if Texas were to declare secession. He also tried to envision the federal government's response to secession and how best to counter those actions. As he lay in bed wide awake beside his softly sleeping wife, doubts and second thoughts crept into his mind about the fateful road down which he might soon be leading the people of Texas.

> Who am I to lead the break up of the United States of America? My entire life I have defined myself as an American patriot. My parents and grandmother raised me to love and honor the flag and the freedom it represents. I am steeped in America's history and admire the many great men and women who built and when necessary defended this marvelous country over the past two-and-a-half centuries. Ronald Reagan always referred to America as a "shining city on a hill," a beacon of liberty for oppressed people from around the world, a place where a good, hardworking immigrant seeking opportunity could make for himself or herself a new and better life.
>
> Who am I to second guess the god-like Abraham Lincoln, the nation's savior, emancipator, and martyr? Have I the right to persuade and lead the good citizens of Texas out of their beloved country into a "more perfect" republic, and a new experiment in liberty? Would it not be better to

work within the system to bring about needed change rather than promote secession? As I have accused Lincoln, perhaps I also am guilty of casuistry, and am merely rationalizing and justifying secession by engaging in sophistry. And what if secession leads to the use of armed force against the Texas people I am entrusted to govern and keep out of harm's way?

No, I am right in what I am about to do. The federal government has exceeded its constitutional powers at the expense of the rights of states and the people. Over time, the separation of powers among the legislative, executive, and judicial branches has been blurred or erased. Each branch of government is invested in expanding and protecting federal power, and no branch is dedicated first and foremost to limited constitutional government. If the states and the people don't take a principled stand now, limited government, individual liberty, and financial stability may be forever lost. Are we a constitutional federal republic or a nation state where the majority of the moment makes the rules? The states are not seceding from the Union; the federal government has seceded from the Constitution. Is my first allegiance to the federal government, the Union, or the Constitution? I place my allegiance to the Constitution above all.

Remember secession is not the end but the means to an end. Ratification of the Second Bill of Rights is the objective, because that offers the last best hope for turning America back from the financial abyss and restoring limited government and individual liberty. So, why not wait another three, six, or twelve months? Perhaps given more time, Congress will call a convention, but only a naïve, diffident fool would count on that. Secession, however, might concentrate the mind of Congress. The energy around secession has attained critical mass, which will rapidly dissipate if no man on horseback emerges to channel that energy to achieve a greater objective. History often is commingled with myth, but even if distorted, it can record only what was, never what might have been. For better or worse, history is written by decisive men of action and reaction. The moment to act is now or never. Time is fast running out for the country to halt its march of folly.

In the midst of his insomnia induced silent soliloquy, Reb would cast his adoring eyes on Marlenna, eternally grateful she was his lover, best friend, and life partner. For all the happiness she had brought to his life, he now felt deep remorse for the worry, stress, and tension his action was going to cause her. The intellectual debate with himself always concluded that secession must go forward, but his heart was against it because of the emotional toll his decision would take on his daughter, grandchildren, and Marlenna.

When finally Reb would drift off to sleep long past midnight, he often was visited by a strange and haunting dream. Sometimes he would awaken during this dream and realize tears were running down his cheeks. Instinctively, he would gently touch Marlenna without awakening her to assure himself she was still at his side.

The dream's details might vary, but the setting always appeared to be New Year's Eve on Copacabana Beach in Rio de Janeiro, located astride the Tropic of Capricorn and one of the world's most spectacularly beautiful cities. During the years they lived in Brazil, he and Marlenna twice happily rang in the New Year there with Jake Fillmore and his first wife Roxanne. A million people, engaged in uninhibited revelry, nearly all dressed in white, were laughing, hugging, and kissing, illuminated by fires all along the beautiful white sand beach. They danced to loud, happy, melodic music with a bossa nova beat, exuding palpable optimism about the good fortune the New Year surely would bring. At midnight, the music stopped and an armada of small wooden boats and rafts sans people would be set ablaze and pushed out into the Atlantic, some sort of offering to a pagan god. He, Marlenna, Jake, and Roxanne took in this spectacular tableau, either among the throng on the beach or from the seclusion of their hotel suite's balcony.

In his recurring dream of the past two months, he is enigmatically aboard one of the floating pyres drifting out to sea. Unlike the other makeshift boats around him, however, his appears to be a white ceramic vessel with a palm frond arising from its deck, perhaps cut from one of Rio's countless palm trees, he thought. Why does he not jump off the boat and swim to shore? Off in the distance, a couple miles as a seagull might fly, he can clearly see the hundred-thirty-foot statue of Christ the Redeemer, brightly lit against the night sky and looking down upon Rio from atop Corcavado mountain rising twenty-three hundred feet above sea level. In the dream, his attention is focused on his beautiful Marlenna, looking angelic in her white strapless summer dress standing barefoot on the beach surrounded by many people, all strangers except for Jake. He anxiously calls out her name, but she only walks as far as the breaking surf, hand outstretched to him, with tears streaming down her cheeks. As the tide carries him further away from his beloved Marlenna, the dream he cannot fathom always ends leaving him to wonder what will come next.

46

Declaration of Secession
Austin, Texas

As expected, Congress recessed for the Christmas and New Year holidays without passing a resolution calling for a constitutional convention. By then the "Three Secess-keteers" were already drafting a declaration of secession to be announced publicly on the first business day of 2018. Reb took the lead in drafting the declaration. Belle, Travis, and Reb agreed to make no further public comment on secession until they jointly promulgated the declaration.

By mid-December, Reb had sent a draft declaration to Belle and Travis for comment. They held a lengthy secure teleconference the week before Christmas to exchange editorial suggestions and agree on final wording. Once it was formally presented to the public, the Oklahoma, Louisiana, and Texas state legislatures would be asked to approve a proposal from the three governors calling for a referendum on the declaration of secession to be held in each state on Tuesday, February 6, 2018. All three legislatures were certain to vote overwhelmingly in favor of the referendum.

In Austin at 3:00 p.m. on Tuesday, January 2, 2018, Govs. Chevalier, Maxwell, and McCoy appeared before a gaggle of print and television reporters who were alerted a few hours earlier that the three governors would make a joint public announcement. There was no press release prior to the event, nor were there any back channel leaks to favored reporters, so the journalists were left to speculate as to what would be announced. The consensus among the reporters was that the governors would demand that Congress call a constitutional convention and if it did not do so by some deadline, they would threaten secession. They were as unprepared and shocked as were the federal government and American people when Reb McCoy strode to the podium and began to speak.

"Ladies and gentlemen, thank you for arranging to be here on short notice. I trust you and your families all had a wonderful holiday. Governor Chevalier, Governor Maxwell, and I wish to make the following joint declaration:

"January 2, 2018

"A Declaration of the Causes, which Impel the Sovereign States of Oklahoma, Louisiana, and Texas to Secede from the Federal Union of the United States in order to Establish the Constitutional Republic of Texas."

The grizzled, ever cynical reporters who were sure they had seen and heard it all, either gasped audibly or went slack-jawed. Did McCoy really just say what they heard him say? TV producers watching from their studios in New York, Los Angeles, and elsewhere, shouted f-word expletives and ordered that regular programming be pre-empted to carry McCoy's historic and shocking announcement. Reb continued reading.

"We the people of the sovereign states of Oklahoma, Louisiana, and Texas, subject to an affirmative vote exceeding 60 percent of all votes cast in each state on the sixth day of February 2018, declare that our consent to be governed by the United States of America is revoked and our federation with that Union is terminated. Pursuant to this Declaration of Secession, the people of the sovereign states of Oklahoma, Louisiana, and Texas, by virtue of our natural right of self-determination, hereby establish, ratify, and form the Constitutional Republic of Texas.

"In choosing to dissolve our connection and common bond with that Union of which we have so long been a part, it is altogether just, fitting, and proper that we should declare the causes that impel us to separate and establish a new democratic constitutional republic based on the principles of limited government and federalism, and centered on securing the blessings of individual liberty to ourselves and our posterity.

"The legislative and the executive branches of the United States government, often with the acquiescence and forbearance of the judicial branch, have over many years gradually and inexorably usurped the powers and rights reserved to the people or the sovereign states by expanding the federal government's powers far beyond those enumerated, implied, or intended by the Constitution of 1787 as amended. Among the United States government's recent and more egregious unconstitutional usurpations of power are the following:

- Refusal of Congress to honor the applications by the legislatures of thirty-six sovereign states, two more than the minimum required by Article V of the Constitution, to call a constitutional convention to consider amendments.

- Failure of Congress and the Executive to reduce the federal government's deficits and national debt to prudent levels, thereby imperiling the financial stability and security of the United States and abandoning the solemn obligation to secure the blessings of liberty to posterity, as stipulated in the Preamble to the Constitution.

- Trampling of the rights of sovereign states and disdaining the principle of federalism by, inter alia, enacting legislation mandating that the sovereign states provide eligible citizens a Medicaid entitlement and comply with various environmental regulations without appropriating the necessary funding, thereby compelling the states to raise the necessary revenue.

- Expanding the meaning of the "general welfare clause" in Article I, Section 8, of the Constitution beyond any reasonable standard by regularly and frequently appropriating federal funds for parochial expenditures in states and congressional districts that have no impact on the general welfare of the nation.

- Infringing individual liberty without constitutional authority by expanding the scope of the "commerce clause" in Article I, Section 8, of the Constitution to require citizens to purchase a product or service, e.g., health insurance.

- Abdication by Congress of material legislative powers vested exclusively in it by Article I, Section 1, of the Constitution, to the Executive, thereby subjecting the people to regulation without representation.

- Awarding particular corporations, industries, and professions favored treatment, including special subsidies, tax breaks, and regulatory exemptions, thereby distorting the free market and perpetuating the corrupting influence of crony capitalism in setting public policy.

- Allocating inadequate resources to secure, protect, and defend the country's sovereign international borders against illegal immigration, crime, and terrorism.

- Enacting legislation with a cavalier disregard for its constitutionality, particularly with respect to the Ninth and Tenth Amendments, thereby expanding the federal government's powers far beyond those specifically enumerated in the Constitution.

"We the people of the sovereign states of Oklahoma, Louisiana, and Texas grant all due honor and respect to the United States, but fidelity to the Constitution stands paramount to preservation of the Union. As set forth in the foregoing bill of particulars, the federal government of the

United States is guilty of manifest and unjust usurpations of power and effectively has seceded from the Constitution. Therefore, without malice but with deepest regret, we have reluctantly resolved to undertake this separation for the purpose of establishing a constitutional republic dedicated to limited government, federalism, individual liberty, and fiscal solvency.

"While of necessity we sever our political bonds with the United States, our bonds of deep affection shall never be severed, nor shall our shared often glorious history ever be forgotten or dishonored. We depart in peace and friendship, and fervently trust to divine Providence that as separate, free, and sovereign republics, we will forge an alliance of mutual interests based on mutual respect and affection.

"This Declaration of Secession is hereby adopted by more than a 60 percent affirmative vote of the people in Oklahoma, Louisiana, and Texas on the sixth day of February in the year of our Lord 2018."

On finishing his reading of the Declaration of Secession, Reb said that Govs. Chevalier, Maxwell, and he would take a few questions. Immediately, there was bedlam as nearly fifty reporters in unison shouted out questions. Reb acknowledged a veteran TV journalist in the front row who asked, "Governor McCoy, isn't secession illegal, and by making this declaration today, are you triggering a civil war as occurred in 1861 when eleven southern states including Texas and Louisiana seceded?"

Reb calmly responded, "The Constitution does not prohibit nor even mention secession. The Tenth Amendment of the Bill of Rights explicitly states that powers not granted to the United States government by the Constitution, nor prohibited by it to the states, are reserved to the states respectively, or to the people. Therefore, secession is an implicit power reserved to the people of the respective states."

"As to the possibility of inciting a second civil war," continued Reb, "this is not 'déjà vu all over again,' as Yogi Berra might say. We don't live in the nineteenth century; we live in the twenty-first century. Should the people of Oklahoma, Louisiana, and Texas vote to secede and establish the

Constitutional Republic of Texas, it will be done in peace and with regret, not with the rancor and belligerence that characterized the secession of 1860 and 1861. There will be no equivalent of Fort Sumter, which touched off a long, bloody war in 1861. We are not seceding to preserve the inhuman, indefensible, undemocratic institution of slavery. We are departing the Union, because the U.S. government has seceded from the Constitution. If the people of our three sovereign states vote to secede from the United States, they will be exercising their natural right of self-determination. This was an argument the Founding Fathers cited in the Declaration of Independence to justify separation from Great Britain. Over the past century, Presidents Woodrow Wilson during World War I and Franklin Roosevelt during World War II championed the right of all peoples to self-determination."

Another reporter shouted, "By this declaration, aren't you and your states entering into a rebellion against the United States, and isn't that treason?"

"We are seceding, not rebelling," replied Reb. "This is a crucial distinction. Words have meaning. We have no intention or desire, much less the capacity, to overthrow the United States government. That would be rebellion and treason. We will be seceding, withdrawing from the Union to go our separate way in peace and to establish a constitutional republic deriving its just powers from the consent of the governed. We harbor no malice or ill will toward the United States."

The next questioner stated that while the Constitution said nothing on the matter of secession, the Supreme Court ruled it illegal in a case shortly after the Civil War.

"You are referring to the 1869 *Texas v. White* case in which the Court, as you noted, ruled the Union is indissoluble, thus secession is illegal. Not surprisingly, considering the consequence of the last secession, no state since then has challenged that Court ruling. The Constitution in Article III, Section 2, states that the Supreme Court's judicial power shall extend to all cases in law arising under the Constitution. But the Constitution does not address secession; therefore, the Court exceeded its inherent power by declaring secession illegal. The larger issue, however, is what recourse is available to the sovereign states and the people to redress unconstitutional usurpations of power by the federal government? In a federal republic, if the federal government cannot or will not restrain itself from exceeding its constitutional mandate, the last bulwark against tyranny resides with the sovereign states and their ultimate defense is secession."

A reporter asked Gov. Chevalier why Louisiana and Oklahoma would want to join in a union with Texas, which, because of its size, would dominate the other two states.

"Governor Maxwell and I were concerned about that, which is why Texas has agreed to split itself into five states, each with its own particular interests. Therefore, the Constitutional Republic of Texas will be comprised of seven states with its capital in Austin."

The next question, directed to Gov. Maxwell asked if a constitution had been drafted for the new republic.

Travis said, "Yes, it is the Constitution of the United States, except that all references to slavery in the original will be deleted. In addition, a constitutional convention will consider the seven amendments of the Second Bill of Rights, which we anticipate will be adopted. Those amendments, we believe, will help to ensure the new Republic is one of limited government, individual liberty, and financial responsibility."

47

WORLD TURNED UPSIDE DOWN...UNITED STATES TO BREAK APART! So blared the Drudge Report Internet headline, moments after Reb McCoy read the Declaration of Secession. The hysterical headline emblazoned across the width of the front page of the January 3 edition of *The New York Times* read: SECESSION DECLARATION COULD MEAN CIVIL WAR. Beneath the lead headline, the main story title was "OK, LA, TX in Rebellion." Despite Reb's explanation the day before, editors and journalists stubbornly insisted on treating secession and rebellion as synonymous terms. The *Times* story went on at length about whether secession was treason, explaining how Abraham Lincoln responded to secession in 1861, and implying that was the precedent President Bucknell should follow in 2018. Only in the last few paragraphs of a lengthy, agitated story did the *Times* get around to summarizing why the governors of Texas, Louisiana, and Oklahoma felt compelled to recommend to the citizens of their respective states that they secede from the United States.

While most major newspapers were both aghast and opposed to secession, many papers in the South, Midwest,

and Southwest expressed admiration for the fortitude displayed by the three governors, and several actually editorialized that secession was justified. The January 3 headline in *The Dallas Morning News* read: BLOW STRUCK FOR LIBERTY & STATES RIGHTS: OKLATEX STAND UP FOR CONSTITUTION AND DECLARE SECESSION.

The unexpected and fascinating political aspect of the secession crisis was not that it divided the country along party lines, as did most contentious issues but that it resulted in intra-party splits. Chevalier, Maxwell, and McCoy received vituperative condemnation as well as effusive praise from both ends of the political spectrum. Many Democrats and liberals alleged that secession was a naked attempt to coerce government into rolling back all the wonderful social and entitlement programs that progressives had struggled for many years to get enacted into law. Others on the left in effect said good-bye and good riddance. A number of Republicans and conservatives, especially military hawks, railed that a break up of the U.S. would do irreparable harm to the country's vital national interests by making it appear weak and inviting disrespect from its enemies. Many on the right, however, particularly those who believe in limited government, federalism, and a strict interpretation of the Constitution, supported secession as a means of compelling the federal government to reform its ways.

As always in the face of shock and uncertainty, the global financial markets plummeted. It's one thing for unrest or war to break out in the Middle East or the Korean peninsula, but the threat of the world's superpower, the United States, becoming destabilized and breaking up terrorized investors around the world. The bellwether Dow Jones Industrial Average of thirty major U.S. stocks went into freefall at the opening bell on January 3, dropping 10 percent in ten minutes triggering an automatic half-hour halt in trading. When trading resumed, the market plunged another 20 percent triggering a two-hour trading halt.

For Love & Liberty

From his Michigan home, legendary investor Gordon Midaston, the eighty-five-year-old "Sage of Saginaw" and reputedly the third richest man in the world, appeared on all the network and cable channel afternoon news and business programs. Exuding confidence, he calmly advised investors not to panic, and certainly not to sell off their stocks and mutual funds. His sixty years of investing experience told him markets always overreact to unsettling news and long-term investors should ride out the storm. Midaston pointed out that even if Texas, Louisiana, and Oklahoma seceded, it was unlikely to cause a serious disruption to the global economy. In fact, the threat or fact of secession might be beneficial if it bestirs the U.S. government to take long overdue measures to control its spending and borrowing. As soon as the stock market reopened, he was planning to buy up shares in great companies that were suddenly great bargains because of the market melt down. Midaston had enormous credibility with investors and almost single-handedly restored a semblance of order and sanity to the financial markets when they resumed trading the next day.

The president's press secretary released a brief statement ominously warning the citizens of Texas, Louisiana, and Oklahoma against secession. If they did secede, they would bear responsibility for the consequences that would ensue. No further elaboration was offered. The White House was trying to appear stern and resolute against secession without committing itself to any course of action. Clearly, Bucknell was buying time to see how this played out with the public, and whether any of the three states failed to get a 60 percent vote for secession in which event the issue would die. The president's political operatives would do everything they could between now and February 6 to influence the outcome of the vote.

Twenty-two governors, however, within twenty-four hours of Reb's public reading of the proposed Declaration of Secession, offered loud and vigorous support for it. They all hailed the courage of Govs. Chevalier,

Maxwell, and McCoy for standing up to federal government tyranny and voiced their hope that this action would shock the Congress into respecting the call for a constitutional convention, as well as addressing the other issues cited in the Declaration's bill of particulars. The supportive governors also warned the federal government not to take any coercive measures against the seceding states. If it did, other states might secede and join the Constitutional Republic of Texas.

Georgia Governor Lillian Duzmore, Reb's running mate in 2016, was particularly outspoken in her support for Oklahoma, Louisiana, and Texas. When she was asked why she did not propose secession for Georgia, she replied that, "a massive breakup and Balkanization of the U.S. is not the objective. The primary objectives are to restore limited government, federalism, and fiscal sanity. The secession of three contiguous states like Texas, Louisiana, and Oklahoma is sufficient to send a clear, unambiguous message to the federal government to heed the rights of the sovereign states and the people, and obey the Constitution."

Several polls conducted over three days following Reb's announcement revealed that the nation as a whole opposed secession 51 percent to 49 percent, but that result was within the margin of error, meaning the population was evenly split over the issue. Likely voters in Oklahoma and Louisiana supported secession by well over 60 percent. In Texas, 56 percent of voters were in favor of separation, 11 percent were undecided. Reb's personal approval rating in Texas topped 60 percent, but nationally, his popularity had plummeted to 40 percent, 12 points lower than his vote count in the 2016 presidential election a little over a year before.

Reb had always figured that secession would be decided by the voters of Texas. He had reassembled the team that was with him for his gubernatorial and presidential campaigns. Substantial funds were left over from both those campaigns, which would be used to finance an intense one-month blitz in

Texas to secure a 60 percent majority vote on February 6. The president would be equally committed to defeating the referendum. One advantage Reb had was that Bucknell's approval among Texas voters hovered around 45 percent. Moreover, the president's campaign against secession would have to rely on surrogates, because if he campaigned personally and lost, it would not only weaken him politically, but limit his options for dealing with the crisis post secession. By campaigning in person, Bucknell would be giving de facto presidential approval and recognition of the outcome. This was a risk he dared not take, lest the secession referendum obtained a 60 percent vote majority.

Reb, Jake, and Hopalong Cassidy quickly outlined a comprehensive, aggressive strategy for a virtually nonstop campaign over the five weeks until February 6. A series of educational public service ads were quickly put together explaining all aspects of secession, why it was necessary, and how the Constitutional Republic of Texas would secure liberty's blessings for all its citizens, now and in the future. Tally Ho conducted daily tracking polls to help shape the message and target districts where support was soft. Sen. Ding Bell and almost the entire Texas congressional delegation were enlisted in the campaign, along with most of the Texas state legislators, who favored secession by an overwhelming margin. Of course, the lead figure in the campaign would be Reb who crisscrossed the state giving speeches and interviews. He put in twelve- to fourteen-hour days every day except Sundays. Occasionally Marlenna would join him for a day or two, but most of the time he traveled alone with his security detail.

A few days into the campaign, Reb sat down for a nationally televised interview with the feisty Dillon O'Rooster, host of *The No Blarney Zone*, cable TV's most watched prime time news program. Excerpts from this interview would be used in Hoppy's TV commercials. Some of the interview questions allowed Reb to reprise answers and arguments he had made previously in other venues, but new ground was covered as well.

O'Rooster's first question was, "How does it feel to be called a traitor to your country, Governor?"

Reb replied, "Like anyone else, I don't like being labeled a traitor, but it would be far worse if it were true. From my perspective, what the people of Oklahoma, Louisiana, and Texas are on the threshold of doing is every bit as patriotic as what our Founding Fathers did in 1776."

"There are folks who say you are leading the secessionist cause, because you feel you were cheated out of the presidency. What say you?"

"That is preposterous. When the election finally was decided in the House of Representatives and President Bucknell won fair and square, I was comfortable with the result. I am not a career politician who has lusted to be president. Due to my prominence in leading the fight for a constitutional convention and the Second Bill of Rights, I felt obligated to take that message to the American people, which is why I ran for president. Even though I lost, I achieved my primary objective, which was to get at least thirty-four states to petition Congress for a constitutional convention. Unfortunately, Congress has shown its high-handed contempt for the states by not fulfilling its constitutional duty. Congress lit the fuse of secession."

"Many pundits and former government officials say you are a revolutionary. Is that how you would describe yourself? I mean, you don't look like a wild-eyed, fanatical revolutionary."

Laughing, Reb replied, "I am hardly a revolutionary. My wife and daughter, as well as anyone else who truly knows me, I am sure would be overcome by convulsive laughter at the thought of me being considered a revolutionary. No one will ever confuse me with Che Guevara. A revolutionary wants to overthrow the existing regime, expunge the former ruling class, and impose radical change on society through violent means. In the context of secession, a constitutional convention, and the Second Bill of Rights, I would label myself a conservator."

"You mean conservative?" interrupted O'Rooster.

"No, I mean conservator. The dictionary defines a conservator as one who conserves, preserves, or protects from injury, violation, or infraction. From the time I became a member of the Madison Committee and later went into politics, I have tried to be a faithful conservator of the Constitution."

"Some of your critics, Governor, and there are many, say this secession business is an effort to impose the conservative agenda on America, and defeat progressivism and all it represents. True?"

"No, that is absolutely false. First, if Texas, Oklahoma, and Louisiana secede and join together in a new republic, how can that threaten the liberal agenda in the forty-seven states that remain in the Union? In all probability, U.S. progressives will be relatively stronger post-secession. Second, while I am personally conservative on most political issues, I have no objection to any political philosophy, left, right, or center as long as it is pursued and implemented within the framework of the Constitution and will not bankrupt the country."

Continuing in this vein, O'Rooster said, "Progressives say the Constitution is a relic of the eighteenth century and if followed literally in every respect is too inflexible to meet the needs of modern society. They also say it is too hard to amend the Constitution, so it must be interpreted broadly, or liberally, to remain relevant. How do you respond?"

"I reject that logic. The Constitution is a solemn compact with the sovereign states and the American people. It embodies our fundamental founding principles of limited government, individual liberty, and federalism, which transcend any political philosophy or agenda. If the Constitution is outdated in some respects, then amend it. The fact that amending it is difficult is no justification for stretching the meaning of its language to expand the federal government's powers beyond those specifically delegated to it by the sovereign states."

O'Rooster again interrupted Reb saying, "Come on, Governor. As brilliant as the Founding Fathers were, they could not have imagined the high tech, highly diversified, and complex society we live in today. Everything has changed over the last two hundred or more years. How could a governing document written back then fit the needs of today's society? You know amending the Constitution is extremely difficult. On balance, it's probably a good thing that over the years smart politicians and judges have been able to find clever ways to reinterpret its language and meaning to keep it relevant in a modern, ever-changing America."

"I agree a lot has changed since 1787," replied Reb, "but truth and fundamental principles are constant. In the governance of a free people by their elected representatives, it is wise and prudent to make it difficult to change the supreme law of the land. The people of the sovereign states created the Constitution and delegated specific and limited powers to the federal government. We are supposed to be governed by law, not men. Of course, men and women make the laws, but those entrusted with the power and honor to govern the rest of us must enact laws that are faithful to the Constitution. Otherwise, the law is whatever a transient majority of elected representatives arbitrarily say it is. My ancestor and namesake Edmund Burke, a renowned eighteenth century British politician and philosopher, once observed of human laws, "Where mystery begins, justice ends." If the Constitution is construed as a "living" or "evolving" document, it becomes "mysterious" and susceptible to capricious interpretation by the ruling majority of the moment. In such a circumstance, no citizen can be certain what the law of the land will be from one regime to the next, which means there can be no standard of justice. Without justice, the people must pray for benevolent rulers, but more likely they will descend into tyranny."

"You make some excellent points, Governor, but I still think there has to be room for flexibility because of the difficulty and time required to go through the amendment process."

"Well, Dillon, should we apply your theory of constitutional flexibility to all contracts?" asked Reb rhetorically. "Assume your boss walked into your office tomorrow and announced that instead of you doing five programs a week, per the contract you negotiated in good faith, he has decided unilaterally to cut you back to four shows a week so he can groom your future replacement. And since you have 20 percent less work now, he is also cutting your compensation commensurately. Now, this all sounds reasonable to me, but you might have a different view as you have not agreed to these changes, neither of which is provided for in your contract. Obviously, you would file a breach of contract lawsuit and no doubt win your case in court. Too many elected politicians in Washington have too often disregarded America's ultimate contract, the Constitution, in similar fashion. It's long past time for the government to be called to account for its usurpations of power and profligate spending."

"Well, you're absolutely right that a contract is based on mutual trust and its terms should be meticulously honored by all who are parties to it. And there is no doubt that the Constitution is the mother of all contracts. Tell me, Governor, what specifically has the U.S. government done that is so egregious that secession is justified?"

Reb considered O'Rooster's question a moment and then said, "Our great ship of state, the U.S. Constitution, is foundering. Once upon a time, it was a sleek, fast vessel whose crew adhered to the limited powers for which it was designed. Over the past three quarters of a century, its crew steadily, inexorably expanded its powers far beyond its design limits. Consequently, our once sleek ship of state has been haphazardly converted into a top-heavy leviathan offering something for everybody. It sails in a stormy sea of red ink, and its rusting hull has been breached below the water line. The ship of state now lists heavily to port, is dead in the water, and no longer seaworthy. It is in grave danger of being capsized by a tsunami of debt. Future generations of Americans will inherit a sunken wreck and the enormous financial obligations run up by our generation.

"At least thirty-six states," continued Reb, "believe the federal government's disastrous course can be changed only by adopting amendments to the Constitution known as the Second Bill of Rights. To that end, these states petitioned Congress to call a convention, but Congress has violated its constitutional duty by failing to honor these petitions. It's bad enough that Congress places itself above the law by exempting its members and staff from many statutes it imposes on the American people. Now, Congress has flagrantly placed itself above the Constitution. I believe we have no option but to mutiny by seceding.

"I brought with me," Reb went on, "a pertinent quotation from Thomas Jefferson's correspondence recently brought to my attention that I would like to share with your viewers. He wrote, 'We must not let our rulers lead us with perpetual debt. We must make our election between economy and liberty or profusion and servitude.' Mr. Jefferson's wise admonition frames the choice the American people face today. The feckless federal government obstinately steers the ship of state on a course of profusion that inevitably will see it and the American people sink into the bottomless depths of financial servitude. On February 6, the people of Texas, Oklahoma, and Louisiana, I believe, will choose economy and liberty, not only for themselves, but for posterity."

O'Rooster next asked, "How sure are you that 60 percent of Texas voters will support the Declaration of Secession? The polls I've seen suggest that if the referendum was held today, it would fall short of the supermajority required to pass. And you know the president and his people are going to fight hard to persuade, scare, and intimidate Texans to vote no on secession."

"Any effort to win a Texas election by trying to scare or intimidate the voters will backfire. Texans fought for and won their independence from Mexico. In one of the most famous battles in history, the defenders of the Alamo, outnumbered ten to one, were defeated by the Mexican Army, but they fought to the last man and did not surrender. A sovereign nation before joining the United States in 1845, Texas is the only state to enter the Union by treaty. Texas's rich history of revolution and independence, the cowboy, and the oil wildcatter have indelibly marked its culture of rugged individualism, self-reliance, and competitive free spirit. This history and ethos make Texas fertile soil for limited government, individual liberty, and fiscal responsibility. Once Texas voters hear all the arguments pro and con, I am confident at least 60 percent will vote for the Declaration of Secession."

"Governor, how did this marvelous country, its people, and elected politicians end up in the terrible predicament we now face where many serious, thoughtful, people such as yourself have concluded there is no alternative but to break up the Union?"

Reb responded, "To recite the long history that has brought us to this pass would take more time than we have even to summarize. The proximate causes of the secession crisis are the imminent fiscal calamity the country faces, but the government does nothing to avert, and the impasse over a constitutional convention. The root cause of our discontent, however, is the century-old philosophical schism over how the government of a modern democracy should be organized. One faction avidly embraces progressive democracy centered on a national government of virtually unlimited powers and majority rule. The other faction fervently believes in the Founding Fathers' concept of a constitutional republic of limited powers based on federalism and centered on individual liberty.

"I suppose either theory of freedom and self-governance is legitimate, but in the long run they are incompatible. The people must choose one or the other; they cannot coexist. I believe a constitutional republic is ideal, because power is diffused; government expansion is restrained; and individual liberty is maximized. In a progressive national democracy, power is concentrated, government tends to expand without restraint, and social justice and equality are esteemed more highly than individual liberty."

"Governor, you make a compelling case for secession and no doubt a lot of Americans are persuaded by your arguments or at least sympathetic to your cause. You come across as a sincere person whose motivations are honorable. There also are many folks who disagree with you, respectfully or otherwise. A substantial number, I believe, would say this is all just political jockeying for power, and even if the federal government has overstepped its bounds, secession is a remedy too extreme. Many viewers have emailed me with the identical sentiment, 'My country, right or wrong.'"

"With all due respect to those viewers," replied Reb, "it is not only silly, but also dangerous for any American citizen to have that attitude toward his or her country. It is not patriotic to support one's country or government when it is in the wrong. The highest form of patriotism, I believe, is fidelity to the Constitution. Defend or amend it, but don't abuse or offend it. If our elected officials obeyed this maxim, our country could rarely ever go seriously wrong."

O'Rooster then said, "Governor, have you and Govs. Chevalier and Maxwell considered the possibility that secession may lead to civil war? If that occurred, would you not be personally responsible for any bloodshed?"

Reb replied, "The Declaration of Secession states that Oklahoma, Louisiana, and Texas will depart the Union in peace and friendship. This is the twenty-first, not the nineteenth century. I can't imagine the United States, the foremost champion of freedom and self-determination in the world, would consider using military force to reverse secession. The Soviet Union broke up peacefully. Czechoslovakia peacefully separated into the Czech

Republic and Slovakia. Great Britain has acceded to the popular demand for greater autonomy in Scotland and Wales via devolution of government to their respective parliaments. The Constitutional Republic of Texas will not pose any threat to the United States. It will not engage in nor threaten any hostile action against the U.S. On the contrary, the new republic will offer its hand in friendship and seek promptly to establish a cordial and special relationship with the United States. The Constitutional Republic of Texas will neither initiate nor fight a war with the U.S. Therefore, I don't see how the new republic's leaders could be justly held responsible for one-sided hostilities commenced by the nation from which we will have peacefully separated."

"I hope you are correct, Governor, but if the United States declares Texas, Oklahoma, and Louisiana to be in rebellion, that would almost certainly impel President Bucknell to resort to force to restore the Union. In that event, are you still prepared to go through with secession?"

"The United States government's unconstitutional actions over many years have precipitated this crisis. If the United States reacts to secession by unleashing its peerless military might against the Constitutional Republic of Texas, the outcome is foretold. But such action will cost the United States dearly in ways that can't be foreseen and will stain indelibly its prestige and national honor. We may reap the whirlwind, but freedom is not free and has never been won by the timid or faint of heart. Our cause is noble and just, and posterity demands that we pursue it irrespective of the personal price some of us may be required to pay. We have no honorable alternative. Before drawing the sword, President Bucknell might do well to reflect on words penned by the seventeenth-century English poet, John Milton, in *Paradise Lost*: 'Who overcomes by force overcomes but half his foe.'"

48

Grant Serrano had been working under deep cover for two months, day and night, trying to run to ground the details on an expected terrorist attack on the United States that presumably was being planned in Mexico. Except for the constant danger of one's cover being blown, espionage was like standing in a room of funhouse mirrors at a carnival. Every image is distorted and in constant motion making it difficult if not impossible to discern reality. One never knew for sure if any piece of intelligence was accurate, and the accumulated pieces rarely fit neatly into a completed puzzle. Grant was under intense pressure from his boss, the director of the CIA's Special Operations Group, to uncover the plot ASAP, because an attack appeared imminent.

Serrano was one of the CIA's very best and most versatile Cobra agents, but he and the shadowy figures he associated with were stymied. He had concluded that Hezbollah operatives were working with either the Zeta or Gulf cartel of Mexican drug smugglers. He also had confirmed that Hezbollah had smuggled Katyusha rockets into Mexico, probably via Venezuela, which had a cozy relationship with Hezbollah's Iranian sponsors. This type of rocket was used by Hezbollah to attack Israel from Lebanon. An anonymous tip led Serrano to a cache of these weapons in a warehouse outside Nuevo Laredo, Mexico, just across the Rio Grande River from Laredo, Texas. There were five BM 21 and six BM27 model rockets. The former has a range of fifteen miles and a forty-five-pound warhead; the latter has a thirty-mile range and a two-hundred-twenty-pound warhead. The Mexican drug gangs were armed to the teeth, but this was the first evidence they now had Katyusha rockets.

Contacts and informers convinced Serrano a major attack was in the works and probably would be attempted soon, although the target or targets were unknown. The motive was unclear, other than to terrorize the U.S. Under orders from his superior, Serrano was not permitted to discuss his activities with the Mexican authorities, because the CIA had come to assume any and all Mexican officials might be compromised. Moreover, there would be diplomatic hell to pay if the Mexican government discovered the CIA was running a covert operation inside Mexico.

The drug cartels gave the authorities in a region where the cartels held sway the choice of either cooperating and being well compensated, or being eliminated with extreme prejudice. Unsurprisingly, given those options, most opted for cooperation and compensation. Just to make sure everyone got the message, the cartels regularly assassinated senior law enforcement or military officials who gave any indication they might oppose the drug traffickers. Serrano understood his orders, but that did not diminish his exasperation in being denied potentially reliable sources of information that might fill in the missing pieces.

While Serrano was trying to thwart a terrorist attack on the U.S., President Bucknell was desperately trying to thwart secession. He directed his vice president, Lola Lovett, to meet secretly with Gov. McCoy to determine if he could be persuaded to back away from or at least postpone the February 6 referendum on secession to allow more time for Congress to deliberate the constitutional convention issue. Reb agreed to meet Lola who had spent the two days before their January 16 tête-à-tête campaigning against the referendum in Houston, San Antonio, and Austin. Reb told only Belle, Travis, and Marlenna about the meeting.

Lola sashayed into Reb's office in the Governor's Mansion wearing an elegant, tailored charcoal suit that fit snugly her still fine figure, and flashing a warm, pearly white smile. Reb greeted her with a handshake and a kiss on the cheek, saying, "Madam Vice President, welcome to Austin."

"Reb, please dispense with the formality. We shared a lovely teenage summer romance some fifty years ago, so we will always be on first name terms."

"That's good to know, Lola. Could either of us back then have dreamt our life journeys would take us down the paths we each have followed?"

"Not a chance," replied Lola. "Springfield, Ohio, was so innocent and so long ago, but a wonderful place to grow up and have my first crush. That's a lovely memory I'll treasure forever, Reb. We both have had great life adventures since departing Springfield to conquer the world."

"Yeah, my only complaint about Springfield was the unpleasantness during my campaign stop there in 2016."

"That was absolutely ghastly, my dear Reb. Thank God, you recovered fully. But you really can't blame poor Springfield that a professional assassin decided to attempt his awful crime there. Reb, I know your time is valuable, so I'll get down to business. I am the president's personal emissary sent to ask you to turn back from the fateful step of secession. If you agree to this request, the president will work behind the scenes with congressional leaders in an effort to break the logjam holding back passage of a resolution to call a constitutional convention. He also will publicly announce his full support for a convention."

"Lola, this offer is too little too late. The time to get Congress to act has passed. Ding Bell informs me that Speaker LaRue will not allow a convention resolution to come to the House floor for a vote. And he thinks the votes aren't there any longer to pass a resolution in the Senate. The old bulls of both parties are circling the wagons to protect their power and privileges at any cost. I fully appreciate the president wants to avert secession, but the fast-moving current of history has swept past the point of no return. Unless the referendum fails on February 6 in any of the three states planning to depart the Union, secession and the Constitutional Republic of Texas will be a fact."

"What would you do if you were president now, Reb? Would you be advocating or supporting secession?"

"No, I would argue against secession. Had fate made me president, I would have fought for a constitutional convention from my first day in office. That and the Second Bill of Rights was the centerpiece of my campaign. As president, I would emulate Teddy Roosevelt by assertively using the bully pulpit, perhaps the presidency's greatest inherent power. And I would lobby members of Congress shamelessly employing every legal and ethical blandishment, threat, or legerdemain I thought might win the necessary votes. Unfortunately, President Bucknell has not done any of this. According to my reliable sources, he pledged to Lashette that he would not support a convention, which in retrospect was a terribly high political price to pay for her support in rounding up the twenty-six state congressional delegations he needed to win the presidency."

Offering no reaction to his answer to her question, Lola said, "If I fail in my mission, Reb, the United States government will seek to obtain a court injunction to block the secession referendum."

"We've anticipated that, Lola. The federal courts have no jurisdiction over state elections. In any event, the referendum technically will not authorize secession. If at least 60 percent of the voters in each state approve it, the respective state legislatures will formally vote to authorize the declaration."

"While it is not unanimous," said Lola, "the National Security Council has advised the president that secession will jeopardize national security and must not be permitted."

"You can't be serious, Lola. If Oklahoma, Louisiana, and Texas secede and establish the Constitutional Republic of Texas, the United States militarily still will be the most powerful nation on earth. Its population and land mass, respectively, will rank third and fourth in the world as they do today. The U.S. economy may slip into second place behind China, but that will happen in a few years anyway. Actually, by peacefully acceding to secession, the U.S. image around the world will be burnished to a high gloss. Conversely, if the U.S. resists secession by force, its world image and credibility will be irreparably tarnished, and I believe history will be unkind to the Bucknell administration. There is no parallel here with the Civil War. No matter how you try to spin it, the federal government has provoked secession by its usurpation of power and abrogation of the Constitution."

"If Texas, Oklahoma, and Louisiana go through with secession," continued Lola, "there are many leaders in both parties who are urging the president to declare a state of rebellion and deploy the army to restore the Union. If he resists taking a strong stand against secession, he may face impeachment."

"Well, if he is convicted of impeachment, Lola, you will be president. Would you use force to deny the citizens of three sovereign states their right to self-determination?"

Ignoring the question, Lola said, "I'm confident the president will not be impeached, and certain that the Senate would never convict him."

"Even contemplating the use of the U.S. Army against unarmed, peaceful civilians is reprehensible," interjected Reb. "A number of other states sympathetic to our cause will denounce any use of force, and a few may secede as well. I've also heard that several high-ranking generals will resign before carrying out such an order. And many soldiers in the ranks would defy an order to fire on citizens demonstrating in the streets for their independence. Such a spectacle would be broadcast on television and the Internet around the world. This would be an unmitigated disaster for the United States, which would be perceived as just another ruthless, authoritarian regime. You people in Washington have taken leave of your senses. Give me the names of some of the key people gung ho for using force to subdue secession."

"There are too many to mention, but one of the most vociferous is Congressman Strank," replied Lola.

"Does that partisan hack have no sense of shame or honor? If you wanted to assign blame to one individual for precipitating the secession crisis, Portnoy Strank might be an excellent candidate. He and Lashette are blocking a constitutional convention. And the idea that Strank is eager to let loose the military on former Americans is beyond irony. This is a guy who fled to Canada during Vietnam to evade the draft and returned, only after Jimmy Carter granted him and his fellow travelers a general amnesty. He has vociferously opposed every use of the American military since he entered public life thirty years ago. But now he is eager to send in the army to put down secession by force. He's beneath contempt."

"That may well be true, Reb, but the president must protect the rights of those citizens in Oklahoma, Louisiana, and Texas who are and want to continue to be American citizens, not citizens of the Constitutional Republic of Texas."

"Lola, the United States recognizes dual citizenship. All citizens of the CRT will also be American citizens unless they choose to renounce their U.S. citizenship. And any CRT resident who wants no part of being a CRT citizen will be free to relocate to the U.S., or remain in the CRT as an expatriate. Employers of CRT citizens who wish to retain their U.S. citizenship will continue to withhold U.S. income and FICA taxes from their pay and remit those funds to the U.S. Treasury."

"If secession takes place, several congressmen will introduce a bill to strip CRT citizens of their U.S. citizenship. In the heated emotion of the moment that bill likely will pass and the president probably will sign it into law."

"That would be like cutting off your nose to spite your face, Lola. It also contradicts the president's concern about protecting the rights of Americans residing in the CRT. If such a law is enacted, the U.S. will forfeit a great deal of tax revenue. Following secession, Chevalier, Maxwell, and I, in the spirit of comity and fair play, plan to propose to the U.S. government that the CRT assume a negotiated share of the U.S. debt to be repaid over fifty years. Should the U.S. revoke American citizenship from those who wish to maintain dual citizenship, and otherwise treat the CRT in a dismissive or belligerent manner, there will be no assumption of debt."

"Well, Reb, I've exhausted all my arguments to dissuade you from pursuing secession. It seems to me it would have been prudent and wise had you, Belle, and Travis allowed more time for Congress to debate and ultimately come to the realization that it must accept a constitutional convention. Secession is a blind leap into the unknown that could spiral out of control with disastrous consequences. I implore you to reconsider."

"Lola, it may already be too late for America's future. We can't wait any longer. Look, history has proven time and again that old, entrenched, and powerful institutions are incapable of reforming from within. Half a millennium ago, in 1517, an obscure German priest, Martin Luther, nailed his *95 Theses* to a church door, which challenged the Catholic Church to end its many abuses, including the sale of indulgences, simony, and the rampant corruption of the Church hierarchy. Several Renaissance popes were so depraved, it would be more apt to describe them as Vicars of Satan, not Vicars of Christ. The Church first ignored and later excommunicated Luther, which unleashed the Protestant Reformation, forever changing Christianity and the history of Western Civilization. The Reformation ultimately had a salutary effect on the Roman Catholic Church, as it found renewal and revitalization through its own Counter Reformation that purged the Church of its corrupt, sinful ways and introduced a number of long overdue reforms."

Leaning forward in her chair, Lola bemusedly asked, "Pray tell, what on earth do the trials and tribulations of the sixteenth-century Catholic Church have to do with what we have been discussing?"

"I'll tell you. Our two-hundred-thirty-year-old republic is long overdue for its own reformation. The federal government over the past seventy-five years has repeatedly engaged in unconstitutional actions and usurpations that have diminished individual liberty, obliterated states' rights, and bankrupted the country. Over the past decade, presidents and congresses of both parties periodically have piously warned about the dire consequences of the country's ever increasing debt, but the only actions taken have driven the debt even higher. Like the Catholic Church before it, the U.S. government cannot or will not reform itself from within, absent outside intervention.

"Whether they are priests or politicians, powerful men and women in great institutions are often afflicted with pride, hubris, and the delusion of infallibility. These afflictions typically lead to self-righteous arrogance, inflexibility, intransigence, and corruption or abandonment of fundamental principles. Such weaknesses are pandemic in human nature and exacerbated in humans who possess the power to govern others. The Founding Fathers recognized this unalterable fact and endeavored to design a government that would check and balance man's inherent weaknesses. They did a splendid job, but just as the advance of technology is never ending, so does the politician ceaselessly conjure ways to escape the constitutional boundaries meant to restrain him from his worst albeit natural impulses.

"We don't have *95 Theses*, but we have the seven amendments of the Second Bill of Rights, which if adopted, we believe, would herd politicians and government back within their proper limits. Luther and his fellow Protestants 'seceded' from the Catholic Church, which was the catalyst that enabled the Church to undergo its revival. The impending secession of Oklahoma, Louisiana, and Texas is perhaps the last chance to catalyze a rebirth of freedom and recommitment to the Constitution by the U.S. government."

"You may be correct in your assessment, Reb, that the United States government is inherently incapable of reforming itself. Ultimately, reform must emanate from the people, because, in large measure, I believe government reflects the people's will. Therefore, the people, or at least a majority of them, get the government they want and deserve. Every two years, they have the opportunity to send a clear message through the political candidates they elect to represent them as to the direction they want government to go. Secession is not, in my view, a legitimate part of our democratic process and must be resisted by the federal government."

"The people of thirty-six states," responded Reb, "through their respective state legislators sent an unambiguous message to Congress that they want a constitutional convention. But if the people's elected representatives to Congress violate or disregard their solemn oath to uphold the Constitution, and treat the sovereign states as 'political or geographic subdivisions,' as the president described them in a recent press conference, the people are left with only two options. They can either meekly accept their diminished liberty, or stand up for their natural right of self-determination and secede from the Union."

"Reb, we obviously can't find any common ground. I told the president I did not think there was much chance you would step back after announcing the Declaration of Secession on January 2. Nonetheless, he felt it was imperative to make the effort. I deeply regret my mission has failed."

"Lola, I am grateful you took the time to travel to Austin to meet with me. Regrettably we must agree to disagree. Earlier you asked what I would do if I were president instead of Bucknell. At the risk of being presumptuous, I would like to tell you what I would do if I were vice president. For what it's worth, I would counsel the president to denounce secession, but to demonstrate he understands and has empathy for the legitimate grievances that have impelled three states to take this drastic action. I would also advise him to extend the hand of friendship and cooperation to the new republic and reject the use of force to restore the Union. Finally, I would recommend he devote the remainder of his presidency to leading a reformation of the U.S. government. If a true reformation occurred that included ratification of the Second Bill of Rights, I expect at some future date, the seceded states would seek to rejoin the Union."

"And if the president rejected his vice president's advice and counsel on how to deal with secession and reform the government, what would you do?"

"Because there is no rational or acceptable policy alternative that I could support, I would resign my office and return to private life."

49

A Pundit's Perspective
January 2018

A fortnight before the February 6 referendum, Tally Ho's polling showed that 58 percent of likely Texas voters favored secession. Voters in Oklahoma and Louisiana favored secession by 64 percent and 68 percent, respectively. If the referendum didn't top 60 percent approval in Texas, the secession movement would collapse, and Congress almost certainly would use that as an excuse to kill off once and for all any idea of a constitutional convention and with it the Second Bill of Rights. Like a condemned man who knows he will be hanged in a fortnight, the specter of losing focused everyone's attention on the campaign. During the run up to the referendum, Reb and all his fellow "Secessketeers" redoubled their efforts, putting in eighteen- and twenty-hour days. The referendum might lose, but not for any lack of effort.

On January 21, Walter Rothmann's syndicated column appeared in Sunday newspapers across the country. Over breakfast, as she often did, Marlenna read the column aloud while Reb savored his favorite meal of the day: orange juice, cereal and fresh blueberries, yogurt, and hot tea.

Rothmann wrote:

"G.K. Chesterton, the figurative and literal giant of 20th century English letters, thinker extraordinaire, and master of the epigram, once said, 'It is terrible to contemplate how few politicians are hanged.' For many years the politicians entrusted with directing the affairs of American government have brought the nation to the brink of ruin by stubbornly pursuing policies that ultimately could have no other outcome, yet no one assumes responsibility or is held accountable, much less hanged.

"A democratic republic rests on the rule of law and a broad consensus of the governed, especially the minority who must trust that their rights will be protected and believe their opinion will be given respectful consideration. This requires elected officials who view themselves as humble servants representing the people. Instead we are misgoverned by politicians representing special interests and who assume the mantle of arrogant masters, which might be tolerable if they governed with wisdom and courage. What our masters have wrought, however, is imminent financial collapse, high-handed disregard for the Constitution, and diminished opportunities for pursuing happiness by future American generations.

"We have a federal government that acknowledges virtually no constraints on its power or profligacy. For a year, the Congress has refused to call a constitutional convention as it is required to do having received applications from thirty-six state legislatures to do so. Apparently, Congress's contempt for the rights of states has gone too far. For only the second time in the Republic's history, three states are likely to secede from the Union.

"Why Speaker of the House Lashette LaRue has stood fast against a convention, in flagrant defiance of Article V of the Constitution, is an unfathomable mystery. LaRue is a woman of considerable personal charm and skill, but her highly regarded political acumen has deserted her on this issue. The Speaker's uncompromising stand is America's great misfortune, because the nation now faces the apocalypse of secession.

"If secession should come to pass, we all must hope it has a more felicitous denouement than the last time it was tried in the winter of 1860-1861. Civil war is the most uncivil of all human conflicts and must be avoided, no matter the cost. This time around, the secessionists have much the better argument and may justly claim the moral high ground. That is not to say secession is justified, legal, or wise, but the federal government's usurpations, incompetence, and insane prodigality have led the governors of three states, with the sympathy of numerous others, to advocate more in desperation than exaltation approval of a declaration of secession.

"In this hour of existential crisis, the United States looks to its president to lead wisely and navigate safely the rapids of secession. Instead, President Bucknell has little to say and is usually nowhere to be found. Perhaps the press should look under his desk where he may be cowering hoping to ride out the storm. While he has no constitutional authority to direct Congress to honor the Constitution and call a convention, he could publicly demand that it act and privately meet with key congressional leaders to persuade them to carry out their sworn duty. Of course, this the president should have done months ago, and now it may be too late to avert secession. In the absence of presidential leadership, the din of discordant voices, many irrational, few sober and sensible, creates a cacophony in which both witless and intelligent commentary are treated with equal seriousness.

"In the center of this maelstrom is the unlikely man who many credit or blame for the secession crisis. He is Rogers Edmund Burke, aptly known to all as Reb McCoy, Governor of Texas, and putative first president of the Constitutional Republic of Texas, if the February 6 secession referendum passes in Oklahoma, Louisiana, and Texas. Judging from his life history up until six months ago, there was no inkling that McCoy would lead a rebellion. He is quick to admonish that he is advocating secession not rebellion. He has no desire to overthrow the U.S. government and replace it with another. He and his fellow governors, Belle Chevalier of Louisiana and Travis Maxwell of Oklahoma, understand secession is a radical if not rebellious act, but they argue the federal government leaves them no alternative if they are to have any chance of securing liberty's blessings for future generations of

Louisianans, Oklahomans, and Texans. They hope secession will shock the U.S. government and its elected officials into stepping back from the abyss into which they are leading the nation.

"The question remains why is McCoy risking everything over secession? By reputation a man of unimpeachable character, he is a quintessential American, whom many now label a traitor to his country for inciting insurrection. How can a highly decorated veteran who saw combat in Vietnam and was awarded the nation's second highest medal for valor be a traitor? This must be the ultimate oxymoron: traitorous hero or heroic traitor.

"An articulate, highly intelligent, self-made man, who has never craved the limelight, McCoy nearly won the presidency a little over a year ago and was one of the most respected and admired figures in America. Now, his advocacy of secession has brought calumny upon his once good name. This is not what your typical sixty-something former corporate CEO, mega-millionaire philanthropist, and doting grandfather, who smilingly affirms he has been happily married more than forty years to an indisputably beautiful woman, does during retirement.

"Why would he, Chevalier, Maxwell, and many others possibly risk their lives, fortunes, and honor for the quixotic adventure of secession? With calm conviction, McCoy replies that the great cause of reaffirming the Constitution and its promise of limited government and individual liberty for us and our posterity transcends the life, fortune, and even honor of any one individual. As he said repeatedly in stump speeches all across America during the last presidential campaign: 'Each generation is called to honor liberty by securing its blessings to posterity. Will our generation answer the call?'

"Responding to a columnist's questions in his elegant office in the Texas Governor's Mansion, which soon may be the official residence of the president of the Constitutional Republic of Texas, McCoy exudes a humble self-confidence and appears at peace with himself. Despite his lifelong nickname, by which he is known to everyone, he admits there is no clue in his résumé that he is a radical, much less an anti-establishment revolutionary. With sang-froid, he laughs off the charge that he is a traitor to his country. On the contrary, given his certitude that America's experiment in democracy is staring into a cataclysmic abyss, he would be a traitor not to employ his powers of persuasion to build broad support for dramatic, perhaps radical action to wrench the country back from that abyss.

"The proximate cause of secession is Congress's failure to call a constitutional convention. That is a flagrant violation of the Constitution, but the convention is merely a means to achieve the ultimate goal of restoring limited government, individual liberty, federalism, and fiscal responsibility, as well as securing the blessings of liberty to America's posterity. A constitutional convention would debate, and McCoy believes approve, the so-called Second Bill of Rights, which would stand an excellent chance of being ratified by three-quarters of the states and made part of the Constitution. Without a convention, there can be no amendments, and therefore no chance to return America to its constitutional principles and save it from financial collapse. Congress and the federal government are congenitally unable to reform themselves. History demonstrates that neither monarchs nor elected satraps voluntarily surrender power.

"An admirer of the aforementioned G.K. Chesterton, McCoy cites one of Chesterton's maxims, 'Self-denial is the test and definition of self-government.' The federal government utterly fails this test. Over many years, it has steadily usurped powers at the expense of the states and the people. Money is spent with reckless abandon, resulting in chronic budget deficits and crushing debt that will impose financial servitude and a diminished standard of living on all future generations, who having no vote are rarely represented by today's myopic politicians.

"In any responsible democratic society, McCoy notes, the current generation is bound by honor, duty, and fiduciary responsibility to ensure the next generation's freedom and chance for happiness is unimpaired by imprudent decisions of its forebears. This is the solemn, inviolable social contract that binds all past, current, and future generations.

"McCoy remonstrates against the gradual erosion of individual liberty in exchange for ever greater dependence on government, which inevitably steals away one's dignity and self-respect. Dependency ultimately vitiates the admirable human virtues of self-reliance and self-accountability, which are indispensable to freedom. Moreover, dependency on the State results in massive entitlement programs that bankrupt the nation. He also rues the emasculation of the states, and the concomitant extinction of federalism, which was the foundation upon which the Republic was established. The original sovereign states created the Constitution and the federal government, delegating to it limited and specific powers. Tension between the states and the federal government were inevitable, but the Civil War and subsequent Reconstruction Era altered forever the relative balance between the states and the federal government.

"The overwhelming military defeat and occupation of the Confederacy restored the Union, transforming the United States from a plural to a singular noun, and effectively made the states subservient to the federal government, which was now preeminent both in perception and reality. As the U.S. emerged as the military and economic colossus of the world during the twentieth century, the federal government's power grew exponentially. The Depression brought the first significant and permanent intrusion of the federal government into many areas of business, commerce, and the lives of individual citizens, theretofore unimaginable. Some Depression era New Deal programs were needed, worthwhile, and within the spirit of the Constitution; others were not. The next great leap forward in expansive government arrived with the Great Society programs of the 1960s. As time passed, earlier programs grew to unsustainable levels, others outlived their purpose, but were never reformed or abolished, and new programs were added regularly without Congress or the president bothering to justify their constitutionality or explaining how they would be funded in the future.

"The states, rather than being an independent and sovereign check on the central government, as the Framers intended, became its supplicants, competing with other special interests for money and favor. With federalism extinguished, the Supreme Court was the last check against an overreaching federal government. As McCoy points out, however, the Court generally defers to the federal government by upholding its usurpations of power. Consequently, the deck is stacked in favor of those who would continually find ever more ways to aggrandize power to the federal government, irrespective of the Constitution's plain exposition and the Framers' intent.

"The last best hope to curb unrestrained government and restore the nation's fiscal affairs to sanity and order was for thirty-four state legislatures to apply to Congress to call a constitutional convention. Despite thirty-six states having done so, Congress has ignored their applications. From McCoy's perspective, the only option left to get Congress to act is secession. He claims at least twenty other governors support what he, Chevalier, and Maxwell are doing. When asked, in light of the macho bellicosity recently emanating from Washington's anti-secessionist war hawks, if he has considered the possibility the federal government might use force to quell secession, he replies such action would be unthinkable, unconscionable, and immoral. Many of his fellow governors and leaders of civilized nations around the world, he believes, would agree. He remarks that Thomas Jefferson held the right of self-determination to be more important than the Union, and adds that fidelity to the Constitution also is paramount to the Union, Abraham Lincoln notwithstanding.

"In any event, McCoy's perhaps forlorn hope is that secession will compel the Congress to call a convention. But how can the adoption of seven constitutional amendments reverse the government's course and solve the nation's grave problems? Isn't the real issue changing government policy? McCoy quickly responds that the Second Bill of Rights will change the culture and weaken the cult of government, which in turn will leave future Congresses and presidents no option but to reform government and adopt fiscally sensible policies."

Marlenna paused, but continued reading to herself.

"Is that where his column ends?" Reb asked.

"No, he goes on to summarize the proposed amendments, which you obviously already know." She began reading aloud again.

"If these seven amendments were ratified, they would radically alter the way the federal government has operated within the memory of virtually every American alive today. From McCoy's perspective, these amendments are not revolutionary, but in keeping with the letter of the Constitution and the intent of its Framers. As he contends, there can be no guaranty of individual liberty without clearly delineated and observed boundaries on the power, reach, and scope of the federal government. He believes the Second Bill of Rights would go a long way toward restoring the Republic to its original and proper balance. Unfortunately, Congress will not permit the convention, which is prerequisite to considering these amendments. If the Constitutional Republic of Texas is established, however, McCoy is confident the Second Bill of Rights will be adopted, along with the Constitution as its supreme law of the land.

"An intrepid man of resolute conviction, one can imagine Gov. Reb McCoy as a Founding Father had he lived in the time of the American Revolution. G.K. Chesterton might have had a man like McCoy in mind when he said, 'He is a very shallow critic who cannot see an eternal rebel in the heart of a conservative.' Wherever one stands on the issue of secession, I assert that McCoy and his fellow 'Secessketeers' revere the Constitution and are patriots for all seasons."

Marlenna put down the paper. "Well, hotshot, you obviously left a positive impression on Mr. Rothmann."

"Clearly, he is an astute judge of character," Reb deadpanned.

"He should have interviewed me to get another, more objective opinion," riposted Marlenna. "Now, let's talk about last night. I don't know if you remember, but I had trouble sleeping in the middle of the night. You seemed to be sleeping soundly until suddenly you became very agitated, called out my name, and awoke with tears running down your cheek. I reached out to comfort you, after which you turned on your side and went back to sleep. Do you remember what you were dreaming?"

"I don't recollect waking up, but for the past couple months I've had the same dream two or three nights a week, and it always ends at the same point." Reb then related the details of the dream for Marlenna, after which he said, "Weird, isn't it? I can't decipher it, but you can't imagine how relieved I am when I awaken and reach out to find you still by my side. I doubt I could live without you, Marlenna. I love you with every breath I draw, and every beat of my heart."

Marlenna held his hand and kissed it. "Back at you, cowboy. You are and always will be my knight in shining armor and the love of my life."

She hid her concern about her husband's disturbing dream, hoping it was not some premonition, although like Reb, she could not analyze what it meant, if anything.

50

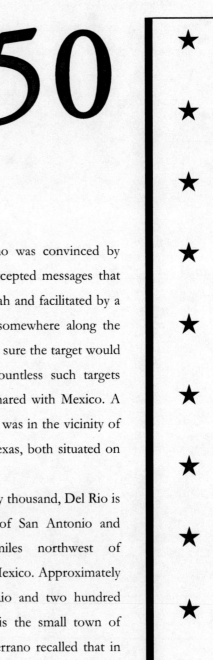

Rio Grande River
January 2018

By mid-January, 2018, Grant Serrano was convinced by human intelligence sources and intercepted messages that an attack probably involving Hezbollah and facilitated by a Mexican drug cartel was imminent somewhere along the Texas border. He also was reasonably sure the target would be infrastructure, but there were countless such targets scattered the length of the border shared with Mexico. A preponderance of the message traffic was in the vicinity of the towns of Del Rio and Zapata, Texas, both situated on the Rio Grande River.

With a population a bit over thirty thousand, Del Rio is one hundred sixty-five miles west of San Antonio and about three hundred twenty miles northwest of Brownsville, Texas and the Gulf of Mexico. Approximately two hundred miles south of Del Rio and two hundred thirty miles south of San Antonio is the small town of Zapata, population five thousand. Serrano recalled that in June 2010, a primitive plot to use dynamite to blow up the Falcon Dam, thirty miles south of Zapata was foiled by

U.S. law enforcement officials. The plot received scant national press attention and was quickly forgotten. Serrano also was aware that Del Rio and Ciudad Acuna, a city of two hundred thousand people on the Mexico side of the river, were twelve miles southwest of the Amistad Dam. Analyzing the incomplete information available to him, he concluded that one or both dams might be the intended targets of the anticipated attack. Unlike the 2010 incident, the presumptive attackers not only were more sophisticated, but also armed with Katyusha rockets.

Grant urgently requested UAV or Unmanned Aerial Vehicle reconnaissance flights over a stretch of the Rio Grande running thirty miles north of the Amistad Dam to Roma, Texas, ten miles south of the Falcon Dam. If either dam was the intended target, he deduced the attack probably would be launched at night from a distance within the range of the Katyusha rockets. Spotters having a direct line of sight to the targets and equipped with night vision goggles and cell phones would inform the launch locations where rockets landed so any necessary adjustments to range, elevation, and coordinates could be made to zero in on the intended targets. Perhaps the UAV's aerial photography would reveal an arms cache or likely terrorist base near either dam, although Serrano knew this was a long shot, because the bad guys likely were hiding in plain sight in safe houses in the nearby border towns and would move into position only when they were ready to launch their rockets.

Constructed pursuant to the 1944 Water Treaty between the U.S. and Mexico, the two dams are jointly supervised by the International Boundary and Water Commission. Falcon Dam, built in the 1950s, and Amistad Dam, constructed in the early 1960s, offer imposing targets. Their purpose is to provide flood control, conservation, recreation, and hydroelectric power to both sides of the border. Both are earth fill embankment gravity dams. Falcon is one hundred fifty feet high and five miles long; Amistad is two hundred fifty-four feet high and over six miles long. The dams impound the Rio Grande and create huge upstream reservoirs. The Falcon's reservoir holds about 1.3 billion gallons of water, and the Amistad's, which extends seventy-five miles upstream, contains 1.8 billion gallons of water. The dams release water downstream through their spillways. Falcon has six gates; Amistad has sixteen.

If either dam's spillway was breached, or the reservoir water crested its earth embankment and overflowed the dam, the entire structure would quickly fail, releasing a torrent of water downstream. In such an event, the Rio Grande would overflow its banks, flooding low-lying areas, causing great economic loss and untold deaths. Because of unusually high rainfall in late 2017, and milder than normal temperatures in Colorado and New Mexico, the dams' reservoirs were nearly filled to their maximum safe level. A direct rocket hit on a spillway would be catastrophic. Three or four rockets hitting the same general location on an earthen embankment would probably create a channel through which water would escape. Once an earthen dam overspills, it quickly erodes and washes away the base of the dam, causing the embankment to collapse under the enormous water pressure.

Serrano had done a remarkable job with little time and less support to ascertain the outlines of a likely attack, but he was unable to avert it. In the early morning hours of January 24, less than two weeks before the referendum on secession, a barrage of ten rockets was fired on the Falcon Dam. Simultaneously, about two hundred miles north, another fifteen rockets were launched against Amistad Dam. At Falcon Dam, three rockets landed harmlessly in the reservoir, but seven hit the dam, with two direct hits on the spillway. At Amistad Dam, six rockets overshot the dam, landing in the reservoir, but nine hit its earth embankment, gouging out two craters that allowed the reservoir to overspill the dam wall. Both dams were fatally breached and the pent-up reservoirs ejected a surging wall of water into the river, sweeping everything in its path downstream.

Within minutes, downtown Roma, Texas, population ten thousand and located ten miles south of the Falcon Reservoir, was flooded. Even harder hit was the city across the border, Ciudad Miguel Aleman. About the time Roma was inundated, the water from the Amistad Reservoir rushed past Del Rio. Damage there was not as great, because most of Del Rio is some distance from the river bank, but Ciudad Acuna in Mexico was not so fortunate. By the time reported deaths were confirmed and those missing were accounted for, over four hundred Americans and more than a thousand Mexicans tragically had lost their lives. Flooding occurred many miles south of the dams, resulting in total property losses in excess of $2 billion in Texas, and at least half that amount in Mexico. This was the first major terrorist attack on U.S. soil since 9/11, sixteen years earlier.

The attacks were a shock to most Americans and Mexicans, but Reb was only surprised by their audacity. He immediately asked the U.S. government to declare a state of emergency, which it promptly did, and within hours he traveled to Roma and then Del Rio to comfort victims and oversee initial recovery efforts. While he did not betray it to the public, he was livid that his repeated entreaties for additional security along the border had gone unheeded by Homeland Security. Of course, even if more resources had been in place, there was no certainty the attack could have been prevented, but now no one would ever know.

In the first several days following the attack, Mexicans, Texans and all Americans moved from a state of shock and horror to sympathy and support, which occurs after every major disaster, to anger at the unidentified attackers. No group came forward to take credit for the attack, although the rival Zeta and Gulf drug cartels blamed each other. The Mexican authorities rounded up and arrested half a dozen suspects within days of the attack. Two died under mysterious circumstances in prison. No incriminating evidence was found to implicate the other suspects, and it appeared no one would be brought to justice for the terrible crime. Within a week after the event, many Texans began redirecting their anger against the federal government for failing to take more aggressive measures to secure the border. Reb did not exploit this anger, but the terrorist attack shifted most undecided and not a few anti-secession voters into the pro-secession column.

Belle, Travis, and Reb waited a week to decide whether to postpone the referendum, but with secession gaining dramatically in public opinion polls, they decided to move forward as scheduled. A number of the relatives of victims came out publicly in favor of secession, saying that the U.S. government had failed its foremost obligation to safeguard its international borders and the country's sovereignty. Much of this sentiment was emotionally driven in the immediate aftermath of the attack, but it resonated with many people. Of course, President Bucknell in an Oval Office address to rally the nation two days after the attack, pleaded with the country to come together in support of "our fellow Americans in Texas and neighbors in Mexico, who were the victims of this dastardly, unprovoked attack." In Texas, Oklahoma, and Louisiana, the president's summons generally fell on deaf ears.

Before the attack on the dams, the polls in Texas ranged from 59 to 61 percent approval of secession, which made the referendum's outcome too close to call. A week after the attack, Tally Ho's polling showed that those in favor of secession had jumped to 64 percent with only 5 percent undecided.

Within minutes after the polls closed on Tuesday, February 6, the major television networks, based on exit polling, declared that the secession referendum had carried in all three states by comfortable margins. The final vote was 67-33 in Oklahoma, 65-35 in Louisiana, and 63-37 in Texas.

Remarkably, over 70 percent of the voting-age population in each state turned out to vote. In recent presidential elections, voter turnout averaged only 55 percent.

For Reb, it was a bittersweet outcome. He was heartsick that secession had come to pass, but he also was certain there was no other alternative given the events of the past year and a half. To paraphrase Churchill's famous remark about the deficiencies of democracy as a form of government, Reb thought secession was the worst available option except for all the others. He would not gloat. There would be no celebratory victory speech. Reb also knew that the final vote was closer than it appeared to be. Prior to the terrorist attack two weeks before the referendum, the vote was too close to call. Had the attack not occurred when it did, the referendum might have lost in Texas, which would have ended any idea of secession. Reb regretted that the outcome possibly turned on the timing of a deadly terrorist attack, but there was nothing he could do about that. He knew the hinge of history often turned on unforeseen, uncontrollable, at times seemingly unrelated events, and that virtually nothing is inevitable, although it often appears to be when viewed through the narrow, blurred lens of future historians. Despite the old adage, hindsight is not reliably 20/20.

A day after the referendum, Reb, Belle, and Travis held a press conference in Austin to explain what the next steps would be. Reb made an opening statement before the three governors took questions from the horde of reporters, perhaps a third representing foreign news agencies.

In his prepared remarks, Reb said:

> "Within the coming week, I expect the legislatures in Louisiana, Oklahoma, and Texas will adopt officially the Declaration of Secession referendum approved by the people yesterday. The legislatures also will call for a convention to adopt a constitution for the Constitutional Republic of Texas. It is anticipated that the U.S. Constitution, including amendments and a few modifications, will become the CRT's supreme law of the

land. The seven amendments known popularly as the Second Bill of Rights are expected to be ratified, as well.

"The Texas Legislature will vote to subdivide Texas into five states, expected to be named Houstonia, Madisonia, Comancheria, Victoria, and Trinity. With Louisiana and Oklahoma, the CRT will consist of seven states. The Constitution will be modified so that there will be three senators from each CRT state. Each two-year election cycle, one senate seat from each state will be up for election. The CRT House of Representatives will consist of one hundred sixty-seven congressmen, an apportionment ratio of approximately one congressman per two hundred thousand of population. This is far lower than the U.S. House apportionment ratio of one congressman per seven hundred thousand citizens.

"The declaration of independence and establishment of the Constitutional Republic of Texas are expected to be announced on March 2, the anniversary of Texas's declaration of independence from Mexico in 1836. Elections will be held March 6 for representatives and senators of the first CRT Congress who will assume office immediately. On that same date, a transitional president and vice president will be elected to a term expiring December 31, 2019. In November 2019, a president and vice president will be elected to serve a full four-year term. Elections for the House and one third of the Senate will be held biennially in odd numbered years."

The ensuing questions from the press were mostly banal or had been answered on several previous occasions in other venues. The one revelation made during the Q & A period was that McCoy and Chevalier, respectively, would stand for election as the CRT's transitional president and vice president. Reb, Belle, and Travis held forth for an hour, patiently and candidly answering the questions put to them. They were relieved when it ended, because they had an enormous amount of work to do and precious little time to complete it.

51

February 2018

President Bucknell now faced the most serious domestic political crisis any president had confronted since Abraham Lincoln became president in 1861. Bucknell was relying on the National Security Council for advice on handling secession, even though the NSC normally concerns itself with national security threats and foreign policy. Among its statutory members and regular attendees are the vice president; the secretaries of state, defense, and treasury; and the assistant to the president for national security affairs. The NSC's military and intelligence advisors are, respectively, the chairman of the Joint Chiefs of Staff, and the director of national intelligence, or DNI. The CIA director also attends all NSC meetings.

The NSC was divided in its counsel to the president. The secretary of state, DNI, and CIA director argued strongly that dissolution of the Union would result in grave and lasting harm to U.S. national security interests and must be not be permitted. Friends and allies would be less likely to accept U.S. leadership on global issues if the country fragmented; rivals and enemies would view the

U.S. as a paper tiger unworthy of fear or respect and would quickly challenge the country's interests around the world.

The secretary of defense and the chairman of the Joint Chiefs believed the only way to stop or reverse secession, now that the referendum had passed, would be to use military force, which they opposed. They saw no military threat whatsoever from a fledgling Constitutional Republic of Texas, and were not confident either generals or troops would obey an order to employ force against peaceful civilians demonstrating for their independence. Moreover, they said the country was divided on secession and overwhelmingly opposed military action against the breakaway states. Vice President Lola Lovett supported this viewpoint and added that allowing secession to occur and establishing friendly diplomatic relations with the CRT would benefit the U.S.' global prestige by demonstrating to the world we practice what we preach to all other nations about respect for the right of self-determination.

The president listened in silence to the conflicting advice of his NSC team, but Lola could tell from his facial expression and body language he was most displeased there was no consensus on how to deal with secession. This meant he would have to decide which course of action to pursue and risk causing a rift at the highest levels of his administration that would inevitably be revealed to the public. There was no third option evident to him, nor could he discern a compromise that would split the difference between the two options before him, like he could and happily did on almost any other political issue.

After hearing from each of his NSC advisors, the president, momentarily succumbing to self-pity and driven to exasperation, cursed McCoy and said sotto voce so that only Lola could hear, "Will no one rid me of this turbulent secessionist?" This was a paraphrase of the perhaps apocryphal remark England's King Henry II made in the year 1170 about his priest Thomas

Beckett, the Archbishop of Canterbury, who defied Henry's attempts to bring the Church and its clerics under royal control. Several of Henry's knights overheard their king and took his rhetorical wish to be their command by proceeding to murder Beckett in Canterbury Cathedral. Lola was relieved no one else heard Bucknell's remark, although she knew he did not mean it in a literal sense. The NSC meeting adjourned when the president rose and strode out of the room.

Later that day, Lola met privately with Bucknell to reiterate her belief that the U.S. should denounce secession, but acknowledge the reality that this is the will of a large majority of Texans, Oklahomans, and Louisianans. Therefore, with profound regret, the U.S. accepts their wish to go their separate way, but the door will always remain open should one day the breakaway states decide to return to the Union. Reconciliation not recrimination or intimidation is the best policy. The CRT should be a closer ally of the U.S. than Canada or any other country on the planet. The president thanked Lola for her candid counsel and said he would take it under advisement.

On Monday, February 12, during prime time, the president delivered a televised speech to the nation that was particularly addressed to the citizens of the seceding states. After invoking Abraham Lincoln's name, he said:

> "Our great nation is indissoluble and separation is not only illegal but unacceptable. We must rededicate ourselves to overcoming and reconciling our differences so that the country can be reunited. Once this is achieved, the seceding states must return to the Union without any penalty or prejudice."

Acknowledging the legitimate grievances many states have with the federal government, he pledged to do all within his power to persuade Congress to call a constitutional convention. He made it clear, however, that

> "The United States cannot permit the permanent separation of any state from the whole without the approval of all the other states. To permit unilateral secession would

be to abandon the bedrock principle of democracy, majority rule."

The president did not say what would be the consequences if the seceded states were not restored to the Union, nor did he set a deadline by when that must happen. The speech also lacked specifics on how to bring about reconciliation and offered no commitment to address the seceded states' grievances other than to make a good faith effort to call a convention. Described by one commentator as the "velvet fist in an iron glove" speech, it displeased just about everybody.

Three evenings later on February 15, Reb delivered a response to the president's speech that was broadcast by all the major networks. Among other things, he reminded the citizens of the CRT and the U.S.:

> "The original sovereign states established the Constitution and the federal government, not the other way round. Therefore, the people of individual sovereign states have an inherent right to sever without malice the bonds of Union for severe and chronic usurpations of power by the federal government the states created.
>
> "America's Founding Fathers established a federal democratic republic whereby the sovereign states delegated specific and limited powers to the central government. But the federal government's unchecked expansion, relegation of the sovereign states to the status of de facto subordinate departments, and profligate spending as if resources are unlimited, has diminished individual liberty, eroded federalism, and driven the country to the brink of fiscal catastrophe. Consequently, this generation of Americans will be the first in the nation's history to fail to secure the blessings of liberty to posterity, which is a central purpose for which the Constitution was drafted.
>
> "There can be no freedom without boundaries. This applies to individual citizens, as well as to government. The federal government has obliterated the boundaries placed upon it by the Constitution while recklessly incurring enormous debt and entitlement obligations, which cannot be honored and will be an unjust burden on future generations to pay. For decades, the politicians elected to Congress to represent the people, collectively, have abandoned foresight,

judgment, and common sense in favor of rationalization, dissembling, and political expediency.

"In light of these and other facts, the people of the sovereign states of Oklahoma, Louisiana, and Texas have reluctantly but decisively exercised their free will and natural right of self-determination to separate from the United States of America, in order to pursue life, liberty, and happiness as free citizens of the Constitutional Republic of Texas. Our shared history, common culture, and many mutual interests we trust will impel our two independent republics to forge an enduring special relationship as close allies and partners. We take our leave with deep affection and abiding friendship for the United States and her great people."

Following the referendum vote, except for his response to Bucknell's address, Reb devoted his time, attention, and energy to the myriad details of organizing a new government. He met almost daily in person or by video conference with Belle and Travis to determine the structure of the new government and identify people to fill key positions. They resolved to create only essential departments and agencies in the executive branch of the CRT. They had no inclination to replicate the monstrous organization chart of the U.S. government.

Ding Bell would be appointed secretary of state and lead the effort to win recognition of the CRT by major nations. To this end, Jake Fillmore had already been dispatched to Brazil with a package of proposals intended to win Brazil's recognition and close partnership with the fledgling CRT. Jake was paranoid he would not be permitted to depart the country if he flew out of Dallas or Houston to São Paulo. The U.S. immigration authorities still controlled the airports and might be alerted to bar the departure or return of anyone closely connected with the secessionist cause. A lover of intrigue, especially when it involved him, Jake arranged for a yacht-owning friend to sail him from Corpus Christi down the Gulf Intracoastal Waterway and up the Rio Grande to Matamoros, where he entered Mexico. From there, he flew to Mexico City and caught a flight to Brazil. He would return home via the same route without mishap. Reb was amused when he learned of Jake's itinerary and only hoped he was as creative and successful in persuading Brazil to recognize the CRT.

The post of treasury secretary would be filled by Abby Abbeville who would be responsible for creating the CRT's monetary currency, the alamo, and drafting income tax legislation. Belle, Travis, and Reb had tentatively approved Abby's recommendation of two personal income tax rates, a base rate of 5 percent and a 10 percent marginal rate on taxable incomes above $200,000, with deductions allowed only for dependents, charitable contributions, and mortgage interest on loans up to one million dollars in principal value. Up to 20 percent of an individual's gross income contributed to a qualified retirement plan would be exempt from taxes until distributed post-retirement.

The corporate tax rate would be set at 17 percent with no special exemptions for favored industries except a credit for bona fide research and development expense. Unlike the U.S., however, corporate income earned abroad would not be taxed by the CRT when repatriated. The simplified tax system would raise adequate income for the new government and make the CRT an attractive and competitive place to conduct business.

Other key cabinet positions that had to be filled were attorney general and secretary of public safety and security. There would be no defense department, because the CRT had no desire or plan to be a military power. The National Guard units in the three states would be consolidated under one adjutant general who would report to the CRT president. The three governors also agreed that the Texas Railroad Commission would be renamed the CRT Oil & Gas Commission with authority to regulate that industry and further its development. It would be an independent commission whose commissioners would be appointed to staggered six-year terms by the president with the advice and consent of the Senate.

Belle and Travis bought into Reb's novel idea of establishing a Department of Individual Opportunity and Dignity, DIOD, in lieu of an education and welfare department. The concept was to assist disadvantaged and unemployed citizens not only with a temporary unemployment or welfare check, but also with vocational training and education so they can become self-reliant citizens. Reb's Texas Opportunity for Disadvantaged Youth program would be folded into DIOD. Reb thought the CRT should experiment with new, perhaps radical ideas for lifting people up, so they can realize their innate potential, and eradicating the culture of victimization. Spending a limited amount of taxpayer money to turn disadvantaged people into productive citizens with the skills to obtain a good job and the means to pursue happiness should be a primary purpose of a free society.

Like any business, DIOD would be held accountable against objective criteria relevant to its mission, and its charter would sunset after five years unless renewed by the CRT Congress. Thus, if this turned out to be an impractical or lousy idea, the taxpayers would not continue throwing money at it forever. This is the philosophy Reb wanted applied to the entire CRT government. If Congress established the DIOD, and Reb was elected the CRT's first president, he planned to nominate his good friend and close confidante, Duane Darby, to be the first secretary of the Department of Individual Opportunity and Dignity.

Reb already had Judge Wyatt Solomon vetting candidates for the CRT Supreme Court. Although he was resisting on account of his advanced age, Reb also was pressuring Wyatt to accept nomination to serve as the CRT's first chief justice.

While Belle, Travis, Reb and their staffs were methodically working through the daunting task of setting up a new government, similar initiatives were underway in what would soon be the five new states carved out of Texas. The CRT constitutional convention was already in session. The convention delegates were not expected to require extensive time to debate and deliberate, because the U.S. Constitution plus the Second Bill of Rights, with only a few modifications, were expected to be quickly approved and submitted to the CRT states for ratification.

৵—ঌ

On February 20, Grant Serrano received orders to depart immediately for Tampico, Mexico, a major port on the Gulf of Mexico, about five hundred miles south of Houston, and two hundred fifty miles south of Matamoros. He was instructed to stay at a particular hotel popular with tourists and businessmen where he would meet his contact. Although his outward demeanor registered no sign of surprise, Grant was stunned when the director of SOG appeared at his table at the hotel's outdoor café during breakfast on the twenty-second. He invited Grant to go tarpon fishing that afternoon. Once they were several miles off shore, the SOG director cut the engines, played out a couple fishing lines, and got down to business.

"Grant, I am here on direct orders from the NCS director," which Serrano knew to be the head of the CIA's National Clandestine Service. "You have been selected for a most sensitive and obviously top-secret mission of vital importance to the national security of the United States. The American government at the highest levels believes secession will do grave, irrevocable, perhaps catastrophic harm to vital U.S. security interests. America's prestige around the world will be shattered and her enemies will be emboldened. Military action to coerce restoration of the Union apparently has been ruled out by the national command authority, because, in the eyes of the world, such aggression would place the U.S. on the same moral plane as Libya, Iran, or Syria."

Grant wasn't quite as certain as the higher ups in Washington that secession would be a national security disaster, but that was above his pay grade to decide. In a tone of profound regret, he said, "Had I been able to track down the bastards who blew up the dams before they did it, perhaps the secession referendum would have lost in Texas, not to mention a lot of innocent lives would have been spared. That was the biggest blown mission of my career."

"Grant, I know close only counts in horseshoes and hand grenades, but with all the constraints we placed on you and the short time you had, no one else could have done any better."

"So how is the government going to deal with secession, and where do I fit in?"

"NCS has concluded that the secessionist government must be destabilized in a variety of covert ways that can't be traced to the Company. Your assignment is to arrange to have the expected head of the new government and foremost leader of the secession movement eliminated. The hit will have to look like a disgruntled, mentally unstable Mexican did it, so you have to recruit a patsy and have him eliminated before he is apprehended and interrogated."

"Wait a minute," interrupted Grant, "you want me to take out the governor of Texas? I've never been directed to hit an American before. The last attempt on his life didn't work out too well, and the hit man got hit."

"The Company had nothing to do with that botched attempt during the 2016 election campaign. That was a private hit job using a hired killer. As for never hitting an American, having orchestrated the secession of three states, the governor is viewed as a traitor to his former country."

"Why am I tasked with this unenviable assignment?"

"You are one of our top Cobra assets," replied the SOG director. "Your cover has never been blown, even when you were imprisoned in Turkey some years ago, and this type job is your specialty. Also, you are wired into the Mexican underworld and can recruit a set-up guy to take the fall."

"But I always work alone or with another Cobra operative. I can't rely on a patsy. And how will I get enough advance notice of the target's itinerary so the hit can be planned and executed?"

"I'll take care of tracking the target's movements. We have access to his itinerary on a real time basis. You need a patsy, because we have to be sure the investigators and the public believe some obscure illegal immigrant or drug dealer is the assassin and worked alone. There can be no link or trail back to the American government and definitely not to the Company."

Grant's boss continued, "The FBI and the Company bamboozled the Warren Commission and most of the American public into believing Oswald acted alone in killing JFK, but he was the fall guy. Most of the books that try to prove there was a conspiracy to kill Kennedy are ignored or debunked as written by crackpots. I don't know if the truth about the Kennedy assassination will ever come to light, nor do I know all the details of what actually happened in Dallas in November of '63, but I'm certain Oswald didn't act alone. I'm not sure he was the hit man or even fired a weapon. By now, the truth of that conspiracy has been taken to the graves of the conspirators, and the carefully crafted cover-up is official history. This assignment must achieve a similar result."

Serrano was uncomfortable with the idea of taking out any American, particularly one as prominent as the governor of Texas. Involving a fall guy magnified the complexity of the assignment. He was proud of his service to his country. While he thought the CIA occasionally made mistakes and displayed questionable judgment, he never doubted that his superiors in the chain of command were honorable, patriotic individuals who were dedicated to protecting America's national interests in a world far more dangerous than the average American could ever imagine. He also took on faith that any order he was given to take out a target was authorized at the highest level of the national chain of command. But he had never before been ordered to carry out such an assignment on American soil.

While Grant was lost in his thoughts, his boss was struggling to reel in a five-foot, probably hundred-twenty-five-pound tarpon, which was putting up a hard fight with its spectacular twisting leaps out of the shimmering dark blue water. When the exhausted but still thrashing fish finally was reeled in, the SOG director asked Serrano to pop a scale for a souvenir, and then cut the line to release it back to the sea.

Once this was done, Serrano took the helm, powered up the engines, and headed back to the marina. On reaching cruising speed, he turned to the SOG director and asked, "Does this order come from the highest authority?"

"Grant, the NCS director personally tasked me with this assignment and directed that you carry it out. I've known him a long time, and he does not undertake any sensitive mission without proper orders and authorization. As always, you know the Cobra ground rules: in the unlikely event you are apprehended before or after this mission, the Company will disavow any knowledge of you and will be unable to assist you."

"Yeah, I know the ground rules. How soon do you expect the job to be accomplished?"

"You've got less than a month. No later than the Ides of March."

52

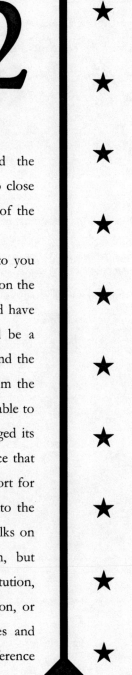

In late February, President Bucknell summoned the Speaker of the House to the Oval Office for an up close and personal chat in which the president did most of the talking.

"Lashette, I must renege on my pledge made to you after the 2016 election to remain neutral or negative on the issue of calling a constitutional convention. I should have made this decision six months ago. Secession will be a disaster for our country, as well as my presidency and the Democratic Party. The only chance I have to reclaim the moral high ground from the seceding states is to be able to tell the country that Congress has belatedly discharged its constitutional duty and called for a convention. Once that is accomplished, I may be able to build public support for taking action to compel the seceding states back into the fold. I fully understand why you and many other folks on the Hill are viscerally opposed to a convention, but preservation of the Union, as well as the Constitution, trumps any fears about an out-of-control convention, or Congress losing some of its cherished prerogatives and powers. I want you to break the logjam in the Conference

Committee and have a resolution calling for a convention to be voted on favorably in the House. I'm confident the Senate will follow suit."

"Mr. President, I am not opposed to a convention per se, but I am adamantly opposed to the so-called Second Bill of Rights, the seven amendments the states would likely adopt. I view them as a coup d'etat by the states to emasculate the power of the federal government. These amendments, if ratified, would drive a stake through the heart of progressivism and everything the Democratic Party has stood for over the better part of a century. In a few years, I think the seceding states will have a change of heart and seek re-admittance to the Union."

"Me thinks thee doth protest too much, Lashette. The problem with progressivism in practice is that it accepts no limits on the scope and intrusiveness of government, or the resources that should be spent on all its programs. McCoy is correct when he says the country is headed for a fiscal calamity and that we are betraying our commitment to future generations by condemning them to financial servitude. The federal government has no fiscal discipline. The smallest, most insignificant government program has a vocal constituency that will howl at the moon over how cruel and inhuman it would be just to curb the rate of growth, much less cut or eliminate that precious program. The Second Bill of Rights would force Congress and the president to make hard choices. Our party should stand proudly for its progressive ideals and also for fiscal solvency. Nearly half the country supports secession and over half the governors including several Democrats sympathize with the secessionist cause. We need to turn sentiment against secession. As president, I will not stand idly by while the country breaks apart. Can I count on you to get a convention resolution passed by the first of March?"

"I will try, Mr. President, but I doubt I can get Portnoy Strank to reverse his position, and he controls enough votes in the Conference Committee to block a resolution."

Pounding his fist on his desk, the president angrily bellowed, "To hell with Strank! I won't let that fatuous, insipid fool hold the fate of the country hostage. He is proof certain that there are more horses' asses in the world than there are horses. Remove him from the Conference Committee, Lashette, and replace him with your boy toy Hedenjoy, or somebody else who will vote out a convention resolution."

Lashette was aware of the president's reputation for finding out all he could about the personal lives and foibles of his political allies and enemies, but she was surprised he was informed about her torrid, although obviously no longer discreet, affair with the playboy Congressman Hedenjoy. Lashette would not give the president the satisfaction of reacting to or even acknowledging his gauche remark.

"I won't humiliate Strank by removing him from the Conference Committee, but I believe I can persuade the Senate leadership to agree to expand the committee by two new members from each chamber who will favor a convention. This will achieve your objective, but I can't guarantee it will be done by March 1.

Even if Lashette came through for the president by March 1, it would not shake the resolve of Oklahoma, Louisiana, and Texas to proceed with secession and establish the Constitutional Republic of Texas. On March 2, speaking on behalf of the citizens of all three states, Reb formally declared secession and independence in the tiny hamlet of Washington-on-the-Brazos, about seventy-five miles east of Austin, and the site where Texas declared its independence from Mexico on the same date in1836.

Four days later, turning out in huge numbers, voters went to the polls for the first time as citizens of the new republic to elect a transitional government until regular elections were held in November 2019. Although he spent no time campaigning for the CRT presidency, Reb was concerned about appearing unopposed on the ballot, fearing it would evoke images of a third world dictatorship where the strongman pretends to be popularly elected by over 90 percent of the vote. He prevailed upon lifelong Democrat Nick Lockhart, a popular two-term Texas governor who had been a successful investment banker prior to entering politics. Nick was a Democrat only because he was raised during a time when, as Jake liked to remind him, "Texas Republicans were about as rare as a virgin in a whorehouse, and a whole lot less popular." Lockhart supported secession and immediately understood the importance of Reb not running unopposed. Out of a sense of duty, he agreed for the first time in his life to take on a challenge he had no chance of winning. Even so, to Reb and Nick's relief, the final vote was respectable, all things considered. Reb won the CRT presidency by a vote of 62 percent to 38 percent. Belle was elected vice president.

On March 7, President Bucknell reiterated the U.S. government's position that it does not recognize secession, which is illegal. He went on to say that the previous day the Senate and the House passed a joint resolution calling for a constitutional convention to be held in Philadelphia commencing in August. As this was the main point of contention in the declaration of secession, he strongly encouraged Oklahoma, Louisiana, and Texas to return to the Union and participate in the upcoming convention. Failure to do so would result in severe sanctions against the rebelling states. Bucknell refused to refer to the former U.S. states as the Constitutional Republic of Texas.

President McCoy released a statement the next day saying he was pleased that Congress had finally called a constitutional convention, which would provide the people of the United States an excellent opportunity to return to the founding principles of limited government, individual liberty, and fiscal solvency. "The people of the Constitutional Republic of Texas wish our U.S.

friends and neighbors well in their great endeavor, because a troubled world needs a strong, free America." He did not respond to Bucknell's threat of severe sanctions if the seceded states did not rejoin the Union, which they would not do.

A day later, Bucknell announced that the state of readiness at all U.S. military facilities in Oklahoma, Louisiana, and Texas would be elevated from DEFCON 5 to DEFCON 3. An acronym for the defense readiness condition of the armed forces, DEFCON 1 means war is imminent; DEFCON 5 is the normal peacetime alert posture. Since the alert system had been established in 1959, the U.S. military's force readiness level had been elevated to DEFCON 3 or higher only three times. During the 1962 Cuban missile crisis, the armed forces went DEFCON 3, except for the Air Force's Strategic Air Command, which went DEFCON 2. This is the only time SAC's nuclear bombers and land-based missiles ever were ordered to such a high readiness level. The military also went to DEFCON 3 during the Arab-Israeli or Yom Kippur War in 1973, and again after the 9/11 terrorist attack in 2001.

Within the borders of the CRT, the United States military had an extensive presence with no fewer than ten air force bases, three naval air stations, ten army forts, fifteen army camps, and several other facilities. Bucknell justified his provocative action, saying he had a duty to safeguard the nation's military facilities and personnel, which might be the target of sabotage or attack by the rebelling states. He knew this was absurd, as there was not the slightest threat to any of these military facilities.

The U.S. president also announced he was imposing a naval quarantine effective immediately on the Gulf Coast at the mouth of the Mississippi River, the Sabine Pass, and Galveston Bay. Most of the CRT's seaborne imports and exports transited these bodies of water to and from the Gulf of Mexico. If the U.S. Navy interfered with the free passage of inbound and outbound shipping, the CRT's economy would soon be crippled. A naval quarantine is tantamount to a blockade, but under international law, a blockade is an act of war against another country. The U.S.' official position was that the seceded states were in rebellion and remained part of the United States. A naval blockade would undermine that assertion, hence the quarantine. This was a real threat to the CRT's sovereignty, although initially it was intended to intimidate and not actually disrupt the free passage of vessels to and from CRT ports.

Former U.S. Senator Ding Bell, now the CRT's secretary of state, denounced the naval quarantine, saying it was "provocative and unworthy of a great country that proclaims itself an exemplar of freedom the world should emulate. The Constitutional Republic of Texas is a free, sovereign nation that has the right to freedom of the seas and wishes to have friendly, peaceful relations with the United States."

Bucknell's hard-line posture did not please some key figures in his administration. Two four-star general officers, one army and one air force, abruptly retired rather than support the president's policy, which they feared was intended to provoke war, thereby giving the U.S. an excuse to invade and quickly occupy the CRT. A day after the quarantine announcement, Vice President Lola Lovett shocked the administration, the country, and the world by resigning her office, effective immediately. In a brief statement, she said she could not in good conscience support the administration's policy for dealing with the seceded states, and was returning to private life. The unprecedented resignation of a vice president over a major policy difference with the president was a public relations disaster for Bucknell, but he refused to alter his policy or soften his rhetoric toward the CRT.

Lola sent Reb a handwritten note telling him that after reflecting on their recent meeting in Austin, she realized she agreed with what he told her he would do were he in her position. She pleaded with the president to adopt a conciliatory posture towards the CRT, but in the end he accepted the counsel of other advisors. Reb was grateful for Lola's principled stand and her gracious note.

Further pressure was brought to bear on Bucknell when thirty governors sent him a public letter protesting in strong language the U.S. government's unfriendly, hostile, and provocative policy toward the CRT. Bucknell's popularity cratered. Within the United States, his approval rating was lower than McCoy's, which was shocking. If this trend continued, he might not be able to secure his party's nomination to a second term. In fact, if Lola Lovett, a hugely popular figure in the Democratic Party, decided to challenge him, she likely could defeat him in the 2020 presidential primaries.

The CRT desperately needed its diplomatic initiatives to bear fruit. The stakes were enormous. If two or three major, democratic countries recognized the CRT as a sovereign nation, the United States' position that secession was an internal matter would be nearly impossible to sustain, especially given America's power and image in the world. Reb was anxious for good news on this front. He knew U.S. diplomats were calling in all their chits and aggressively using both carrots and sticks to pressure its allies' foreign ministers and heads of state around the world not to recognize the CRT.

As usual, except for Canada and Mexico, U.S. diplomacy basically ignored the countries in its own hemisphere. The U.S. government's long history of benign neglect toward Brazil provided Jake Fillmore the opening he needed to get a sympathetic hearing from senior officials he met with in Brasilia, the federal capital of Brazil.

Until 1960, Brazil's capital had been Rio de Janeiro. In the mid-1950s, the Brazilian government commissioned world renowned architect Oscar Niemeyer to plan, design, and build an entire city on an uninhabited plateau in Central-West Brazil to be the country's new federal capital. More than fifty years later, although somewhat rundown, the architecture is still stunning and futuristic. The Ministry of External Relations is located in Itamaraty Palace, one of Niemeyer's most dramatic buildings. The palace is columned on all sides and appears to be floating on an enormous ornamental pool featuring islands of tropical plants of the Amazon, and a sculpture carved from a four-ton block of Carrara marble. Visitors access the building via a long pedestrian bridge spanning the pool. Inside is housed one of the largest public art collections in Brazil. The massive main hall is free of interior columns, and the second level offices are reached via a spiral staircase nearly eight feet wide that has no banister. This is where Jake spent much of his days while in Brazil for a week. At night, he would wine and dine senior officials at posh restaurants.

By the time Jake departed for home, he had an agreement that Brazil would recognize the Constitutional Republic of Texas no later than mid-March. As soon as the two countries exchanged ambassadors, they agreed to enter into fast-track trade talks aimed at negotiating a free trade treaty, something the U.S. had never been willing to do. One of Brazil's primary national objectives was to become an influential player on the world stage consistent with its rapidly developing economy. Recognizing and partnering with the CRT furthered this objective and simultaneously provided payback to the United States for never having accorded Brazil the respect and attention that were its due.

Reb was elated with Jake's success and promptly contacted Brazil's president to open direct communication between the two leaders and start the process of building a close personal relationship. In the meantime, Belle Chevalier had well-placed friends in the French government lobbying for France to recognize the CRT. As soon as the French learned Brazil was going forward with recognition, they also decided to grant recognition by April.

In February, before the new republic was formally established, a Chinese envoy called on Reb to say his government proposed to grant the CRT recognition immediately and negotiate a trade agreement. As a permanent member of the United Nations Security Council, China also would be pleased to nominate the CRT for UN membership. Not wanting an authoritarian rival of the U.S. to be the first nation to recognize the CRT, Reb tactfully told the envoy it was premature to commence such discussions, but he would be eager to do so sometime in April after the transition government was elected and had taken office.

Ding Bell's overture to Mexico initially was rebuffed. The Mexican government was reluctant to discuss the exchange of ambassadors out of respect for the U.S. Ding persisted pointing out the obvious fact that, because they shared a two-thousand-kilometer border, the CRT and Mexico must establish close diplomatic ties and negotiate mutually beneficial treaties on a range of issues. The two countries also urgently needed to move forward to rebuild the Falcon and Amistad Dams. Ding's arguments were given serious consideration by his Mexican counterpart, and he was confident that by May or June, Mexico would join Brazil, France, and China in recognizing the CRT. Reb believed this would lead many other countries to follow suit, which would likely checkmate the U.S., making its contention that the CRT was not an independent, sovereign nation untenable.

While all the chess moves between the U.S. and the CRT were being played out, Grant Serrano was moving hastily to complete his plan to carry out his mission. A long-time, high-level source within one of the major Mexican drug cartels recruited a hit man who would fill the role of patsy nicely. The loco yet extremely shrewd head of the cartel, a man addicted to violence, had expressed casual interest in taking down McCoy, because he feared he might legalize narcotics in the CRT, taking away a lucrative cartel market. McCoy also was perceived as being much tougher than the U.S. authorities in securing the border and controlling illegal immigration, especially in the wake of the attack on the dams. In the warped world in which the ruthless cartel boss lived, preemptively murdering all perceived enemies was the key to one's own survival, and it had the added advantage of striking fear in the hearts of ambitious underlings.

When Serrano's source proposed eliminating McCoy to the drug cartel honcho, he laughed uproariously and thought it a splendid idea. The source recommended Miguel Murtry, a twenty-three-year-old cartel enforcer nicknamed El Diablo. As Serrano knew, Murtry was a cold-blooded murderer whose soul had died years before, but who went on existing for the sole purpose of killing, and he was very good at his chosen profession.

The product of an American father and Mexican mother, Murtry possessed the good looks that often come from mixed parentage. Before fate and tragedy altered his life forever, Miguel apparently was a normal, happy kid growing up in a middle class section of Laredo, Texas. His older brother got involved with a drug gang that operated across the border in Nuevo Laredo. At some point, his brother's gang had a territorial dispute with a rival gang. The fight escalated and one night, when Miguel was fourteen, several members of the rival gang invaded his home and murdered his parents, brother, and sister, presumably to send a message and settle a score. Miguel escaped his family's fate by hiding under his bed. The shattering experience left him orphaned, desolate, and impoverished.

After grieving for six months, he concluded there was no God and, therefore, no morality except what one imposed on others by brute force. He dropped out of school, joined his late brother's gang, and before he turned sixteen, had committed the first of many murders.

Murtry's drug gang was absorbed by the large cartel he now worked for as an enforcer. Because he was an American, and appeared more Anglo than

Hispanic, Miguel was particularly valuable, because he could move back and forth across the border without difficulty. An expert marksman who knew how to handle a variety of weapons, Serrano knew he was a good choice for the mission. Also, because of the countless capital crimes El Diablo had committed without ever being brought to justice, Grant felt little remorse about his patsy's ultimate fate. Serrano was pleasantly surprised that Murtry took instruction well and did not drink or use drugs. This meant he would be reliable. He apparently had no friends outside the drug cartel, which was also good.

Serrano knew the CRT president did not have the protective security bubble that is afforded the U.S. president or even a U.S. presidential candidate. The Texas Rangers were excellent at their job, but did not have at their disposal the enormous resources available to the U.S. Secret Service. In fact, the CRT president's protective detail was essentially the same as it had been when he was governor of Texas. Moreover, McCoy frequently complained to the head of his security detail that he was too closely covered, which isolated him from the public. Reluctantly, the security chief from time to time would encourage his people to back off a bit and not smother Lone Star, the radio call sign that had stayed with Reb since his presidential run in 2016.

Taking all this knowledge into account, Grant concluded the kill shot would have to be taken from a distance of fifty to a hundred yards, the closest practical distance the shooter could get to his target without detection. He decided the widely available Remington 700 rifle, popular with hunters and police, was the weapon best suited for the assignment. At a firing range in Mexico, El Diablo proved he could handle the weapon expertly. Because it would be foolish to try crossing the border with the rifle, at the appropriate time and place, an identical weapon would be made available in Texas.

The issue yet to be decided was where and when to carry out the mission. On Friday, March 9, the SOG director communicated to Serrano the CRT president's schedule and itinerary for the coming week. Grant thought to himself that the guys at Langley, CIA headquarters in Virginia, were super efficient. Evidently, they had already hacked into the CRT president's inner-office computer system to gain real time access to his itinerary. Through a process of elimination, he settled on the date and place that offered the best opportunity to accomplish the mission, eliminate the patsy afterward, and make his escape leaving behind no fingerprints. Grant ordered El Diablo to meet him in Dallas on March 10.

53

The Ides of March

An early spring brought Dallas beautiful, sunny days in March of 2018. Temperatures were in the high seventies to low eighties, and blossoms suddenly appeared everywhere, signifying nature's season of rebirth and hope. This time of year lifted Reb's spirits and always called to mind Myrlie's favorite apolitical quote attributed to their common ancestor, Edmund Burke, to wit: "Beauty is the promise of happiness." And, Reb thought to himself, spring is the promise of beauty.

On Wednesday, March 14, Reb and Marlenna arrived in Dallas to spend a rare evening and sleep over in their Highland Park residence. They both missed being away from their lovely home where they relaxed and felt, if only briefly, like normal, private citizens. Marlenna prepared them a light dinner accompanied by wine and music. In a mellow, romantic mood, they snuggled together on the family room sofa following dinner and listened to Frank Sinatra, Tony Bennett, and Andy Williams's interpretations of "Days of Wine and Roses." Marlenna loved Henry

Mancini's mesmerizing melody, while Reb was especially taken by Johnny Mercer's wistful lyrics.

> The days of wine and roses
> Laugh and run away,
> Like a child at play,
> Through the meadowland toward a closing door,
> A door marked nevermore
> That wasn't there before.
>
> The lonely night discloses,
> Just a passing breeze,
> Filled with memories,
> Of the golden smile
> That introduced me to
> The days of wine and roses and you.

After debating which artist did the best rendition of this classic song, they retired to their bedroom, with Reb still humming the tune until they reached their bed, whereupon they made unhurried but passionate love. She still excited him no less than when they were young.

"Pretty, it was your golden smile and bewitching beauty that introduced me to a lifetime filled with days of wine and roses. I treasure every moment we have shared together."

Marlenna noticed a tear running down her husband's cheek and asked, "Honey, what's wrong? Why are you crying?"

"I don't know. Perhaps because of all the happiness you've brought to my life. Or perhaps because, at my age, I worry each time we make love may be the last."

Holding his face in her hands, she said, "Oh, baby, don't be silly. We are both blessed with great health and will have many more days and nights like this."

Soon they drifted off to sleep.

Easter would come early, on April 1, and the McCoys looked forward to a week's vacation in Galveston commencing March 25. Ravenna, Jeff, and the grandchildren would join them over Easter weekend. The Gulf would still be too cold for a swim, but the sun's warmth would be perfect for enjoying the beach. On a lovely March 15, however, Reb would host the fifth anniversary celebration of the Madison Committee at the Rosewood Mansion on Turtle Creek, where it first met on March 16, 2013. Due to Reb's prior commitments in Austin on the actual anniversary date, the celebration had to be advanced a day.

While the Madison Committee met, Marlenna enjoyed having lunch and catching up with her SMU sorority sisters in another private dining room of the hotel. Amazingly, twelve of them had been getting together bimonthly to play bridge and have dinner ever since the first reunion of their college graduating class. Since her husband's entry into politics nearly five years ago, Marlenna had been unable to attend most of the bridge parties, but this was a perfect opportunity for the lifelong friends to spend a couple of hours together. As soon as the Madison Committee meeting ended, Marlenna and Reb would depart for Love Field to fly back to Austin.

In addition to its original members, attending the Madison Committee meeting were the CRT vice president, the Oklahoma governor, and Jake Fillmore. They convened for a luncheon and conversation in the FDR Suite on the second floor. Reb reluctantly had come to accept that everyone outside his immediate family, even long-time friends, now addressed him formally as Mr. President, and treated him with great deference out of respect for him and his high office. Indeed, except for Wyatt Solomon, chief justice of the CRT Supreme Court, and Travis Maxwell, governor of Oklahoma, everyone at the celebration now worked for him. Although not everyone would comply, he said at the outset that he preferred to be addressed as Reb at this private social gathering of friends and peers.

Once the group was seated for lunch, Secretary of State Ding Bell offered a prayer, after which he proposed a toast, "To the Constitutional Republic of Texas."

In unison and with enthusiasm, everyone responded, "Hear, Hear."

Wyatt then offered a toast to James Madison, which received a similar response from the group.

From the head of the table, Reb added, "And may each generation of our great Republic honor its sacred trust to secure the blessings of liberty to posterity."

Again, all responded, "Hear, Hear."

In a reflective mood, Reb said, "Who among us five years ago could have imagined that Ding Bell's innocent idea of forming the Madison Committee would turn the world upside down? Originally, we were merely six citizens deeply concerned about the direction and future of America, but it turned out millions of Americans shared our concerns. We were the catalyst that touched off a veritable revolution. I occasionally wonder if Mr. Madison would approve of what his namesake committee hath wrought."

Wyatt opined, "It's no more than conjecture, but I believe he would be pleased with the Second Bill of Rights, disappointed that the Union has broken apart, but astonished that it lasted as long as it did. Neither Madison nor any other Founding Father could have imagined a United States of such enormous size and diversity, or a federal government no longer bound by the limited powers delegated to it by the Constitution. He would probably be amazed the United States had not long ago split into four or five countries, given the polarization inherent in modern U.S. politics. There was polarization in Madison's time, but the issues were relatively few compared to today. The reason we have more issues to disagree about is because politicians have taken it upon themselves to immerse government in matters that the Founders never intended."

"I'm inclined to agree with you, Wyatt," replied Reb. "None of us wanted to lead three states out of the Union. Unfortunately, the U.S. government was in dire need of renovation and repair, but the people's elected representatives could not bring themselves to face that reality. We did what we had to do. As practiced by professional politicians, ideologies like conservatism, liberalism, and progressivism have evolved into quasi-religions. The Constitution represents an obstacle these competing ideologies must overcome to realize their respective agendas. The Constitution is all that separates liberty from the tyranny of ideology, but only if we never forget that the Constitution transcends and must take precedence over ideology. Embracing a political ideology is fine as long as it's pursued within the constitutional framework. Edmund Burke once remarked, 'Nothing is so fatal to religion as indifference.' The same may be said of the Constitution."

"Based on my personal experience," chimed in the irrepressible Jake, "I compare the separation of the CRT from the United States to a once contented marriage that falls apart after many years. The husband gets addicted to gambling, and, while he has occasional streaks of good luck, over time he's a big loser. Before long, there are two mortgages in default on the house, the retirement savings are gone, and the creditors are at the door. He won't or can't quit, so his wife, who has a good job, finally divorces him to restore financial order to her life and provide for their college age children. She still loves the big dope, but he's not the responsible guy she married and he's taking her and the kids down with him. Like the gambler husband, the U.S. federal government is an out-of-control, reckless spender. And like the long-suffering wife, the citizens of the CRT reluctantly divorced the United States and its federal government in hopes of restoring limited government, financial solvency, and a future for their children and grandchildren."

"That's an interesting analogy, Jake," responded Reb. "Another pertinent Edmund Burke quote is, 'Frugality is founded on the principle that all riches have limits.' Our illustrious Secretary of the Treasury Abby Abbeville is working hard to make frugality a cornerstone of the CRT government. Abby, please tell us about your plans for the CRT's currency, which, as you all know, will be called the alamo."

"Thank you, Mr. President, I mean Reb," responded Abby. "We will not have a central bank, nor will the CRT government be able to print money at will. The CRT Constitution, like the U.S. Constitution, vests in Congress the power to coin money and regulate its value. We propose that the alamo's value be fixed against a commodity exchange standard. Foreign governments, businesses, and individuals will be able to settle international business and currency transactions with the CRT Treasury in alamos or a fixed basket of commodities. As a practical matter, no foreign debtor or creditor will elect to make or receive payments in commodities, but the commodity standard will determine the rate for converting foreign currencies into the alamo and vice versa. Annually the CRT Congress, based on the president's recommendation, will approve any increase in the money supply based on the change in prior year's GDP and the upcoming year's anticipated productivity.

"Our objective," continued Abby, "is to make the alamo a store of value that does not depreciate significantly like the U.S. dollar has done for many years. Over the twenty years from 1995 to 2015, the U.S. dollar's purchasing power declined 68 percent. What you could buy for a dollar in 1995 costs $1.68 in 2015. A democratic government that believes in private property rights should safeguard the value of its currency. The CRT will not have a federal reserve bank with the independent power to print money at will, nor will the CRT government live wildly beyond its means relying on huge debt to finance its programs. The commodity exchange standard will stabilize the CRT's currency and inspire confidence in the alamo."

Chief Justice Solomon commented, "In 1792, the U.S. Congress established the dollar's value in terms of a specific quantity of pure silver.

They also mandated the death penalty for anyone who debased the dollar by diluting its silver content. Now, that's taking the value of the nation's currency seriously."

Vice President Chevalier added, "I've always been amazed at how the American people accept with little objection the steady depreciation of their hard-earned dollars. If we redefined a pound as being equal to five instead of sixteen ounces, and still called it a pound, would anyone agree to that? Or if the hour was gradually expanded over twenty years from sixty to a hundred minutes, and you were still paid by the hour, would you accept that? People would rightly call any devaluation of an hour or a pound as property theft. Yet Americans have come to accept the steady devaluation of their currency."

"You frame the issue in terms we can all relate to, Belle," remarked Reb. "Few people have raised a ruckus about the devaluation of the U.S. dollar, because it occurs gradually, plus most folks in the workforce receive wage increases annually that compensate for inflation. But retirees and others on fixed incomes, as well as investors who hold bonds, experience serious losses of purchasing power over time. Abby's plan for the alamo, which has broad support in the CRT Congress, will mitigate this problem for our citizens. We intend to establish the alamo's initial exchange rate at parity with the dollar, but before long I expect it will appreciate against the dollar, because the latter currency will continue to depreciate.

"Duane, how is the new Department of Individual Opportunity and Dignity coming together?"

Duane Darby, the first secretary of DIOD answered, "We're still in the planning and organizing stage until the new Congress appropriates funds and confirms personnel for key positions, but I am excited by the challenge. This is an audacious experiment, but if it works, it will have an enormous and positive impact on the lives of many people who live outside the mainstream of our economy. Based on the success already achieved with the Texas

Opportunity for Disadvantaged Youth, I'm confident DIOD will do something similar for adults who are chronically unemployed, need to develop new skills, and have lost their dignity, self-confidence, and self-respect. Collectively, these folks have enormous potential and represent a tremendous untapped resource for society.

"Our goal is to offer disadvantaged, down-on-their-luck people the opportunity to have a realistic chance of being able to pursue their individual happiness, not simply abandon them to welfare. Another profound quote attributed to Edmund Burke you once shared with me, Reb, and I've never forgotten is, 'Education is the cheap defense of nations.' Through education, training, and retraining, plus the support of the private sector, DIOD can have a huge impact on the CRT's economic growth and well-being of its citizens."

Reb thanked Duane and said, "As you all know Jake, Ding, and Belle have had remarkable success in getting early recognition of the CRT by Brazil, France, and in the near future, Mexico. Also, China is eager to recognize the CRT and make us a member of the UN, which I view as a mixed blessing. These phenomenal foreign policy achievements, along with the strong support of many U.S. governors, the recent resignations in protest of the U.S. vice president and two senior U.S. generals, have prompted the Bucknell Administration to reassess its hard line attitude toward the CRT. Another contributing factor is President Bucknell's plummeting popularity over the way he has dealt with the CRT. While I find it amusing, I'm sure the U.S. president and his advisors don't find any humor in the fact that I have a higher favorability rating in the U.S. than does Bucknell. All this prompted the U.S. government two days ago to initiate secret, back channel discussions about reaching a détente. Belle, Ding, and I are very encouraged by this development, and I am pleased to inform you that Pip Pippin has agreed to be my personal envoy to negotiate a rapprochement with the U.S. Pip, please share with us the framework of an agreement that you and your counterpart have already discussed."

"Certainly, Mr. President," replied Pip. "We have requested the U.S., in an immediate good faith gesture, to return the military units based in the CRT to their normal peacetime readiness status and to lift the naval quarantine. They have agreed to do so. We will also seek diplomatic recognition, a free trade treaty, a long-term agreement on military bases within the CRT's borders, and a guarantee those CRT citizens who wish to retain U.S. citizenship will be permitted to do so. What the U.S. wants from the CRT, which could be a deal breaker, is reunification of the CRT with the U.S., perhaps not as states, but in the form of a political union similar to the relationship between Scotland and Great Britain. The CRT would remain a political entity with certain powers and its own legislature, but not an independent, sovereign nation."

Reb interrupted. "I'm not prepared to agree to this proposal, although we might consider it in the future. My counteroffer will be that five years from now, the CRT will hold a referendum in which its citizens can vote on whether or not they want to rejoin the Union as states or in some other political affiliation perhaps along the lines Pip just discussed. The U.S. Congress has just called a constitutional convention. We must wait and see if the Second Bill of Rights is ratified as part of the U.S. Constitution, and if the U.S. government seriously addresses all the issues that caused the people of Oklahoma, Louisiana, and Texas to secede. I think it will take five years to determine if reform takes root in the U.S. By then, sufficient time will have passed for the CRT's citizens to reassess fairly their situation and decide if reunion or continuing independence is in their best interests.

"It will also be imperative that should the CRT vote to reunite with the U.S., all treaties the CRT enters into between now and then will be honored by the U.S. within the CRT's borders. We will be unable to negotiate treaties with other nations unless they can be assured the CRT will abide by them irrespective of its political arrangements with the U.S. I am encouraged by this initiative of the U.S. government and am confident Pip will represent us well in negotiations."

Pushing his now clean dessert plate off to the side, Ding wiped his mouth and said, "Through luck, skill, and divine Providence, we have made astounding progress in just one week. Bucknell hit some terribly off-key notes that caused me a great deal of consternation, but he is a man open to reason and willing to change his mind when the facts confronting him change. This is all going to come out all right."

Reb concluded the meeting saying, "I am guardedly optimistic that in due time both the CRT and the United States, if not reunited, will enjoy cordial relations. I am also hopeful that limited government and fiscal solvency will be restored, and that individual liberty will be strengthened in both countries. If it were left up to me, the permanent and paramount mission of the Constitutional Republic of Texas would be to secure the blessings of liberty to posterity. If every generation of citizens and politicians undertakes to fulfill that mission, liberty will endure forever."

Belle indicated she wished to speak. "Mr. President, if each generation is blessed with leaders who exhibit the courage, vision, integrity, and commitment to liberty that you embody, liberty certainly will be eternal. It is an honor and privilege to serve you and the Republic."

Everyone stood, turned to face Reb and applauded. Reb's cheeks flushed momentarily. After a moment he stood and said, "Thank you. I am deeply touched and forever grateful for your friendship and support. I am also genuinely humbled, because I recognize that whatever good we have achieved required the personal commitment of many thousands of liberty loving people, few of whom will ever be known to history. We stand on their broad shoulders, as well as the broad shoulders of all those who came before us who were willing to risk and if need be sacrifice their lives to secure and defend liberty."

54

As soon as the door to the FDR suite swung open, President McCoy's personal security guard alerted the first lady's security detail that the president was heading for the lobby and would be ready to depart for the airport in five minutes. The vice president, chief justice, secretary of state and others who attended the Madison Committee meeting bade Reb farewell and departed the Rosewood Mansion from its underground garage. Only Jake, whose car was valet parked outside the hotel entrance, accompanied Reb to the lobby. Marlenna soon joined them there, smiling and looking radiant. She reached for her husband's hand, and they shared a quick kiss.

Hotel staff gathered around gawking and offering polite applause, a few mustering the courage to ask for Reb's autograph, which he was only too pleased to provide. A member of the housekeeping staff diffidently approached the first lady and presented her with a lovely bouquet of tulips and roses in shades of red, pink, and fuchsia. Tulips were Reb's favorite flower, while Marlenna was partial to roses. Marlenna graciously expressed her appreciation with a warm thank you and a captivating smile that could warm the hardest heart. Jake escorted the first couple out the lobby entrance and down the red carpeted steps covered by a canopied awning.

From a fourth floor office of the eight-story building across the street, El Diablo had been intently observing the presidential limousine, a black, armored Cadillac Escalade, since it pulled up to the Rosewood Mansion's entrance fifteen minutes earlier. This meant his target was about to appear. Fortuitously for Grant Serrano, the office El Diablo occupied had been vacant for two months until a few days earlier when a CIA front company leased it for six months, paying the rent in advance. The lower portion of the window, from which El Diablo watched the hotel entrance, opened inward about six inches to permit ventilation. He had removed the struts that limited the window's aperture, so that it could be dropped open completely offering an unobstructed line of fire.

The president's security detail had not swept the office building prior to McCoy's unannounced visit to the Rosewood Mansion. A list of the tenants had been provided beforehand and none attracted suspicion. The highest level security procedures were not considered necessary, because Reb's meeting with the Madison Committee was not on the president's public calendar, and he would be out in the open just briefly on arrival and departure.

Marlenna emerged from under the awning and was escorted around the rear of the SUV and helped into the left rear seat. The president exchanged a laugh and a few final words with Jake, then turned to walk to the limo's right rear door being held open by his personal security guard.

El Diablo peered through the scope of his silenced Remington 700 rifle, took aim at the president's left temple, and squeezed the trigger. An instant later, the president collapsed against the SUV's rear fender. Because there was no sound from the rifle, at first the bodyguard thought the president had stumbled or suddenly become ill. A split second later, he saw a fast spreading stain of dark crimson on the left side of president's head behind his ear that had already reached his shirt collar and suit jacket.

"Lone Star down, Lone Star down!" shouted the bodyguard. Marlenna instinctively reached out to her stricken husband trying to pull him into the SUV while kneeling on the back seat. A moment later, the limo screeched out of the parking area heading for the nearest hospital. Marlenna cradled her husband's head in her lap, oblivious to the blood now staining her dark beige skirt, and caressed his cheek. She pleaded, "Reb, darling. Hang on, honey. We'll be at the hospital soon."

Reb opened his eyes. Struggling for breath, his voice low and raspy, he said, "Marlenna, pretty, are you okay?"

"Yes, darling I'm okay. I'm here with you. Don't speak."

"I love you, baby," were the last words he spoke.

"I'll never stop loving you, my darling Reb."

He closed his eyes. As his life slipped away, the recurrent dream on the beach in Rio momentarily filled his fast fading mind, only now it seemed less vivid. He caught a glimpse of Jake, but mostly he saw his beloved Marlenna. What was she saying to him? Why was she crying? Why could he not comfort her? Now, all he could see was a soft, intense light coming toward him, suffusing him in its warmth, beckoning him to follow, its power irresistible. Without effort, he took in a last deep breath, everything went dark. His earthly journey had ended.

Marlenna knew the love of her life was gone. Incongruously, his countenance appeared completely serene. She leaned forward and gently kissed his lips, then buried her face in his chest and sobbed uncontrollably.

When the news of President McCoy's assassination broke, a pall fell upon the republic. After the initial shock, most citizens mourned his loss as if he were a close family member. Their new republic's first president was extremely popular. His death only increased the people's affection and esteem. The funeral and burial would be held Monday, March 19. President Chevalier offered to handle the arrangements, but Marlenna, despite her all-consuming grief, insisted on planning the funeral herself with the support and guidance of Bishop Sean O'Faherty, head of the Catholic Diocese of Dallas. The bishop was Marlenna and Reb's family priest and close friend of many years. There would be no lying in state in Austin. The funeral service and Requiem Mass would be held in the Dallas Arts District at the nineteenth-century High Victorian Gothic Cathedral Shrine of the Virgin of Guadalupe, where Reb and Marlenna had been married and attended Mass regularly ever since.

Burial would be in Lee Park, a quiet residential area a couple blocks from the Rosewood Mansion on Turtle Creek and not far from the McCoys' home. Ironically, five years earlier in Lee Park, Ding Bell had urged Reb to run for governor of Texas after a meeting of the Madison Committee. The park was open to the public, making it easy for people to visit and pay their respects. There would be no statue or grand mausoleum or eternal flame. Reb would not have approved of an ostentatious memorial, and Marlenna would not permit one, despite pressure to do so. There would be an inscribed granite marker laid upon her husband's grave and for the remainder of her life, she would have fresh roses and tulips, always in shades of pink, red, and fuchsia, placed there twice a week.

By midnight of the day of the assassination, El Diablo was hiding out in a "safe" house three blocks from where he shot the president dead. As soon as he had taken out his target, Miguel Murtry quickly exited the building unobserved via its stairway and made his way unnoticed to a residential street time had passed by. The surrounding blocks were filled with recently built, upscale homes and condos, but this particular street had not yet been gentrified and featured 1940s era and earlier middle class homes. Serrano had rented one of these houses and directed El Diablo to go there and lie low until Grant told him it was safe to leave Dallas.

The second part of Serrano's plan was to have Murtry eliminated in a way that would bring the case to a close and not implicate the CIA. Because the rifle that killed the president was silenced, the Texas Rangers and Dallas police needed some time to pin down the shooter's location. They quickly deduced that the office building across from the hotel was the probable location from which the shot was fired. Within fifteen minutes of the shooting, the building had been secured, no one in or out, but that allowed Murtry ample time to make his escape. When the police reached the fourth floor office Murtry had used as his sniper's nest, all they found was the weapon. There were fingerprints on it, but they did not match any prints on file with the FBI or Interpol, because Murtry did not have a police record. All his prior hits had been committed in Mexico, but he had never been identified as a suspect in any of those unsolved cases. A subsequent investigation into the firm that rented the office space a few days before would reveal it to be fraudulent.

Without a physical description or any other clue who they were trying to apprehend, law enforcement feared that the shooter might be able to get away with his crime. Serrano's SOG director had provided him with the name of a CIA agent working undercover as a detective on the Dallas police force, who had been directed to take instructions from Serrano when contacted by him. The agent-cop volunteered to join the manhunt for the assassin. Serrano contacted him with an "anonymous tip" that a suspicious individual, a stranger to the neighborhood, had just been seen furtively entering a house that had recently been rented. Serrano told the agent-cop that this was the shooter, and he must not be taken into custody alive. Along with two other officers, the agent-cop headed for the "safe" house.

Serrano had repeatedly told Murtry not to be taken alive, because he would be subjected to unbearable torture. This was untrue, but Murtry was impressionable and disposed to believe the worst about the police. He knew how the Mexican police treated drug gang members and cop killers, and assumed the same or worse was true of Texas cops. When the Dallas police, led by the agent-cop, burst into the "safe" house, Murtry began shooting with his 9mm Glock handgun. The agent-cop returned fire and shot El Diablo through the heart, for which he was later awarded a medal for bravery in the line of duty. No one else was hurt.

The dead suspect's fingerprints matched those found on the rifle at the scene of the crime and the newspapers trumpeted that the case was solved. El Diablo was carrying a Texas driver's license, which revealed his identity, but there were no further leads or motive for his crime. The Texas Rangers and Dallas police officials did not believe the shooter had acted alone in planning and carrying out the assassination. The whole operation seemed too neat and tidy, no loose ends. How did Murtry know the president's schedule, which had not been made public? How did he arrange to rent expensive office space? And why did he not flee the area, when he had the chance, before the police locked down the surrounding neighborhood and began a house-to-house search? Had he done so, it is almost certain he would have escaped without ever being detected. Was he set up to be killed in a shootout with the police? Unfortunately, investigators only had strong suspicions. There were no facts or solid leads. The case was at a dead end, and in time would be considered closed.

A month later, the Company transferred Grant Serrano to Pakistan to help fight the endless war on terror against the Taliban and al Qaeda. In an eerie coda to the case that would never come to light, Grant traveled to Dallas at the end of March, shortly before departing for his new assignment.

He had been reading all he could about Reb McCoy's life and was struck by the terrible tragedy the slain CRT president and his assassin, El Diablo, had in common. Both were orphaned as children, but their respective life trajectories following that common experience could not have been more dissimilar.

Serrano now knew there had been no national security justification for McCoy's assassination. The United States and the CRT had agreed to coexist peacefully and were in treaty talks that might someday lead to restoration of the Union. Serrano had been the willing instrument in carrying out a horrific, inexcusable crime. He became consumed by guilt and remorse. Although raised a Catholic, he had not been to church in years, yet the purpose of his Dallas visit was to go to the Cathedral Shrine of the Virgin of Guadalupe to confess his mortal sin.

Occasionally, Bishop O'Faherty took confession and as it happened the Saturday Grant Serrano appeared, the bishop was on the other side of the wooden screen in the confessional. The penitent stepped inside, closed the door, and knelt. After saying, "Forgive me, Father, for I have sinned," Grant confessed that he had planned and was responsible for the assassination of President McCoy.

Bishop O'Faherty could not believe his ears and let out an audible grunt of shock and anger. His instinct was to smash through the screen that separated him from the penitent and choke the life out of him, but he immediately regained his composure. "Why would you do such a thing, my son?"

"Father, I believed I was acting on the lawful orders of my superiors in the Company, and that my mission was vital to the national interests of the United States. I now realize that that was wrong."

A lover of espionage novels, Bishop O'Faherty surmised his penitent was speaking of the CIA. "My son, do you feel contrition?"

Grant acknowledged that he did and with help from the bishop stumbled through the prayer of contrition. The bishop then gave him penance of saying the Lord's Prayer every night for two weeks before retiring. Grant agreed to do so whereupon the bishop gave him sacramental absolution and asked that God have mercy on his soul. With that, Serrano departed the cathedral as unobtrusively as he had arrived.

The Seal of Confession is absolute, and a priest may never under any circumstances divulge the sins of a penitent to anyone, not even another priest. In the Church's two-thousand-year history, there is no record of any priest, not even one who was immoral or defrocked, ever violating the Seal of Confession. The bishop certainly was not going to be the first to do so, and in any case, he had no clue to the identity of the man who had just made this startling confession.

When Serrano arrived in Pakistan, he began volunteering for missions that were almost suicidal, as if he had a death wish. The risks he took were insane. Sooner or later, his luck would run out. Finally it did, on the Ides of October, seven months to the day after the McCoy assassination. Failing to return from a dangerous assignment, he was reported missing in action. In actuality, he had been betrayed, ambushed by Taliban fighters, and buried in an unmarked grave halfway around the world from the site of the crime his conscience would not let him forget.

In the future, several books would be written postulating various conspiracy theories behind the McCoy assassination, but they were no more than conjecture and none ever came close to the truth. How much of history has been buried in an unmarked graveyard of the past and will never be known; and how much of what we believe to be history is merely myth or outright fiction? The truth often is elusive and known only to God, or perhaps a priest confessor.

During the first two days following Reb's death, Marlenna willed herself to endure her overwhelming grief and plan the funeral. She wanted to curl up in bed and never again see the light of day, but she refused to succumb to the pain that consumed her soul. On Sunday, March 18, however, after returning home from a private Mass with Bishop O'Faherty, she surrendered to her shattered heart and collapsed into tears. Ravenna spent Sunday night with her mother and gave her a mild sedative that allowed her to sleep for the first time since Reb's death. By Monday, the day of the funeral, Marlenna had recovered her composure. If one could look past her beauty and charm, they would discover a woman possessed of quiet courage and an indomitable will.

The splendor of the great cathedral, filled to overflowing, and the pageantry and ritual found only in a Catholic Church made the funeral service and Requiem Mass especially moving. Sunlight filtered and refracted through a hundred-and-one stained glass windows illuminated the nave of the church, leaving the transept and chancel in the shadows.

The dead president's closed casket, draped in the Lone Star Flag of the Constitutional Republic of Texas, was carried down the center aisle to the front of the church by Texas Ranger pallbearers and placed in front of the altar. Marlenna walked slowly behind the casket to her front row pew, hand in hand with her two grandchildren, followed by her daughter and son-in-law. Wearing a black dress, high heels, and a round, wide-brimmed black hat with a low crown, one of the most recognizable women in the world appeared elegant, touchingly vulnerable, and breathtakingly beautiful in mourning. Her mind briefly floated back to her blissfully happy wedding day many years before, when she walked with her father down this same aisle to be united in marriage with the handsome young man standing at the altar awaiting her arrival with great anticipation and the unmistakable look of unconditional love and adoration.

An estimated three thousand people were crammed into the pews, and thousands more were turned away for lack of space. Among the foreign dignitaries in attendance were the presidents of Brazil, France, and Mexico. The United States secretary of state was on hand, which was de facto recognition of the Constitutional Republic of Texas. Former Vice President Lola Lovett was there. Eighteen state governors, including Lillian Gish Duzmore, were in attendance to pay their last respects to the man they admired for inducing liberty's reaffirmation, first in the Constitutional Republic of Texas, and thereafter the United States of America.

President Belle Chevalier and Reb's daughter delivered warm, touching eulogies, and Bishop O'Faherty offered a homily that at times was funny, poignant, and uplifting. There was laughter, there were tears, and there was much reverence. A tall man of enormous girth, a bellowing laugh, and with a twinkle in his eye, the bishop was an engaging man filled with bonhomie and loquacity. His extemporaneous homily for Reb was deeply sincere and personal.

"I have been blessed to have known Reb and Marlenna McCoy for over forty years. They are among my dearest friends. As a young neophyte, I married them in this cathedral over forty-two years ago. At that happy event, there were perhaps ninety guests on the bride's side of the aisle, and fewer than ten on the groom's side, one of whom was the best man, Duane Darby, who is here today on this sad occasion. I presided when Reb was initiated into the Catholic faith. It was my privilege to preside at their daughter Ravenna's baptism and first communion. I also baptized their son Kyle McCoy, and conducted his funeral Mass after he tragically passed away many years ago when he was only five years old. Later I officiated at the marriage of Ravenna and Jeff, and attended the baptism and first communion of Reb and Marlenna's beautiful grandchildren, Kyle and Deanna. As a man now past seventy and obviously a wee bit overweight, never did I imagine that I would preside over a funeral Mass for my friend and parishioner Reb McCoy.

"We've heard wonderful eulogies for Reb from President Chevalier and Ravenna. He was a man worthy of our honor, respect, love, and admiration. He was a sinner like us all, but his virtues far outweighed his shortcomings. When I recall Reb's many endearing qualities, the descriptive words that come to mind are equanimity, integrity, humility, kindness, generosity, gratitude, and courage. I wish it could be truly said that I possess all these wonderful virtues. And his word was his bond."

The closest O'Faherty came to commenting on secular matters was when he said, "A man of strong convictions, Reb so cherished liberty, a natural right granted by God to all mankind, that he willingly pledged his life, his fortune, and his sacred honor to preserve, protect, and defend it, not for himself, but for all generations to come. His courageous stand may have cost him his life.

"Reb lived life to the fullest and he loved with a deep passion. On several occasions over the years, he told me that he felt cursed when he was orphaned as a young lad and lucky when he returned home whole from Vietnam. But the first time in his life he not only felt, but also was certain he was blessed was when his beloved and beautiful Marlenna agreed to marry him. Theirs was a storybook marriage and love affair that was real and not a fairy tale. Marlenna returned her husband's undying love and devotion in full measure."

By now, there were few dry eyes in the congregation and even the bishop had to pause, take in a deep breath, and concentrate to keep his own emotions in check. He concluded his homily saying, "Nothing we can say here today will provide comfort to Reb's grieving widow, or child, or grandchildren, or dear friends. Nor can we comprehend the evil that possessed the tortured soul of the sinner who struck him down. We are left only to place our trust and faith in God and His divine Providence. But as long as we gathered here shall live, Reb McCoy will live on in our hearts, and our fond memories of him will give us endless joy and pleasure. We are all blessed to have had our lives enriched for having known Reb McCoy. He was a good and decent man, a wonderful husband and father, and a true Christian. We now commend God's humble servant, Rogers Edmund Burke McCoy, to the care of his Lord and Savior, Jesus Christ. We pray that he may be granted eternal rest and everlasting peace. Amen."

Marlenna had selected the music for the Mass, which included Mozart's "Requiem in D Minor" and her husband's favorite hymn, "Rain Down," which was based on the 33rd Psalm. It was in a key suited to his voice, and he particularly loved the refrain:

> Rain down, Rain down,
> Rain down your love on your people.
>
> Rain down, Rain down.
> Rain down your love God of life.

At the conclusion of the Mass, the forty-nine-bell carillon atop the cathedral's two-hundred-twenty-four-foot bell tower mournfully tolled once for each year of the deceased's life. The hearse bearing the casket, followed by a procession of limousines, wended its way the three miles to Lee Park, Reb's final resting place. Marlenna refused having a horse-drawn caisson followed by a rider-less horse with boots reversed in the stirrups, the ancient symbol for a fallen leader, considering it too grandiose. Tens of thousands lined the cortege's route in respectful silence.

At the burial site up the hill from the equestrian statue of Confederate Gen. Robert E. Lee, Bishop O'Faherty presided over the interment. He read Reb's favorite Bible passage from Proverbs 14, verse 13: "Even in laughter the heart is sad, and the end of joy is grief."

In closing, the Bishop remarked, "With Reb's passing, we who knew and loved him are left with a profound sadness and grief as great as the joy and laughter he gave to us in life." Following a 21-gun salute, taps were played, the furled flag from the coffin was presented to Marlenna, and finally her beloved husband, life partner, and soul mate was laid to rest.

A few days later, the widow Marlenna returned with her daughter, son-in-law, and grandchildren for the placement of the gray, polished granite grave marker.

Beneath the cross was inscribed:

ROGERS EDMUND BURKE MCCOY
1950-2018

FATHER OF THE SECOND BILL OF RIGHTS

DEFENDER OF THE CONSTITUTION

CHAMPION OF LIBERTY

"EACH GENERATION IS CALLED TO HONOR LIBERTY
BY SECURING ITS BLESSINGS TO POSTERITY."

Stooping down on bended knee, Marlenna laid upon the marker a spray of red tulips and deep pink roses, as well as a single palm frond. Touching her hand to her lips, she gently pressed her fingertips on his name, then stood, turned, and silently walked away.

Stephen M. Grimble was born in Dallas, Texas, spent many years in Delaware and Brazil, and currently resides in Albuquerque, New Mexico. A retired corporate and university executive, and Vietnam veteran, he is the author of *Setting the Record Straight: Baseball's Greatest Batters*. *For Love & Liberty* is his first novel.